With Paulus at Stalingrad

With Paulus at Stalingrad

Wilhelm Adam and
Otto Rühle

Translated by
Tony Le Tissier

Pen & Sword
MILITARY

First German edition published by
Verlag der Nation 1965 as *Der schwere Entschluss*
This translation first published in Great Britain in 2015 by
PEN AND SWORD MILITARY
an imprint of
Pen and Sword Books Ltd
47 Church Street, Barnsley
South Yorkshire S70 2AS

Translation copyright (c) Tony Le Tissier 2015
Photographs by courtesy of the Taylor Library.

ISBN 978 1 47383 386 9

The right of Tony Le Tissier to be identified as
Author of this Work has been asserted by him in accordance
with the Copyright, Designs and Patents Act 1988.

Printed and bound in England by
CPI Group (UK) Ltd, Croydon, CR0 4YY

Typeset in Times by CHIC GRAPHICS

Pen & Sword Books Ltd incorporates the imprints of
Archaeology, Atlas, Aviation, Battleground, Discovery,
Family History, History, Maritime, Military, Naval, Politics,
Railways, Select, Social History, Transport, True Crime,
Claymore Press, Frontline Books, Leo Cooper, Praetorian Press,
Remember When, Seaforth Publishing and Wharncliffe.

For a complete list of Pen and Sword titles please contact
Pen and Sword Books Limited
47 Church Street, Barnsley, South Yorkshire, S70 2AS, England
E-mail: enquiries@pen-and-sword.co.uk
Website: www.pen-and-sword.co.uk

Contents

Translator's Note

This is the story of the battle of Stalingrad in 1941–2 as related by Colonel Wilhelm Adam, the senior ADC to General Paulus, commander of the German 6th Army, giving an intimate insight into events at the army's headquarters and the author's excursions and adventures that won him the Knight's Cross, an unusually high award for a person of his rank.

The story continues with an account of his captivity from the end of January 1942 to September 1948, during which he was allowed, as the only colonel, to remain with Paulus and other generals. He used some of his time to study with the aid of the well furnished libraries provided, and eventually became a convinced Communist and member of the pro-Soviet National Committee 'Freies Deutschland' and the League of German Officers, both organised by German expatriates and prisoners of war, despite meeting considerable hostility from his more conventional fellow prisoners.

Upon repatriation in 1948 he decided to work at promoting Communism in the Soviet Zone in Germany and eventually became director of the academy for officers of the East German National People's Army in Dresden, and had the honour of leading the May Day parade in East Berlin in 1956 before retiring two years later. Only then did he start work on this book. Adam's work is noticeable for the complete lack of any criticism or adverse comment about the Soviets. Paulus was eventually repatriated in 1953 and retired to Dresden, where Adam assisted him in his work until Paulus's death in February 1957.

Although he mentions his wife and daughter, whom he also sees on the two occasions when he manages to obtain leave, Adam makes no mention of them after his repatriation, which prompts the idea that they might well have declined to join him in East Germany.

Introduction

The former Field Marshal Friedrich Paulus himself intended writing a book about the battle on the Volga, but death tore him away from his work before the intent could be realised. This made me feel even more called upon and duty bound to write about the decisive years of my life, in which my fate was so closely bound up with that of the Field Marshal, for the general public. Various responsible tasks with Socialist reconstruction in the German Democratic Republic left me no time for writing history; they demanded involvement in making history. Only in 1958, as I came to the end of my 65th year and left the National People's Army, could I begin writing the account. It took years of demanding work, which had to be broken off several times because of my unstable health, before the manuscript was complete in its first draft. It is due to the services of my friend Professor Dr Otto Rühle, whose close working association assisted in the publication of this book. For over a year he dedicated the material to the intensive scientific and literary work that gave the book its final form. I thank him especially for the completion of the last part of the report, which involved an extensive study of the sources. All in all, I consider myself lucky to have found a co-editor in Otto Rühle, who – also a participant in the battle on the Volga – found the wish to survive, just as I did, through similar experiences, conflicts, problems and perceptions. With his thoroughness, sincerity and energy, he has contributed considerably to the success of this book, which ran to five editions within a year and sold 95,000 copies in all.

Wilhelm Adam, November 1965

Maps

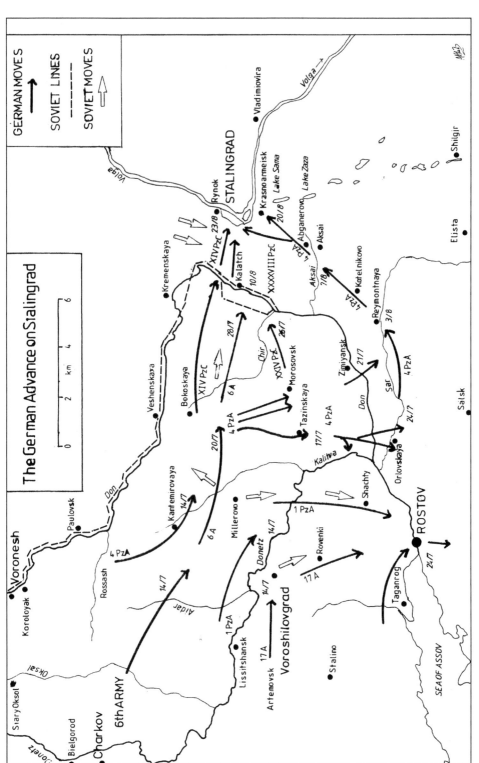

Map 1. The German Advance on Stalingrad.

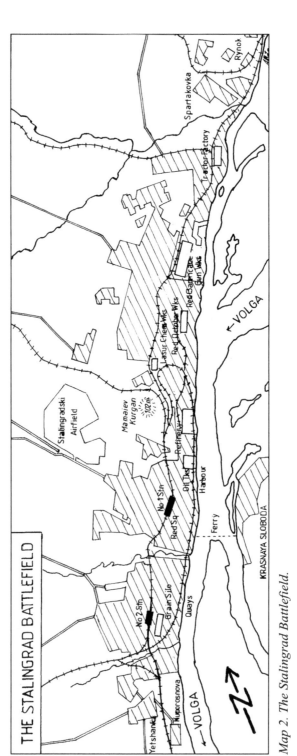

Map 2. *The Stalingrad Battlefield.*

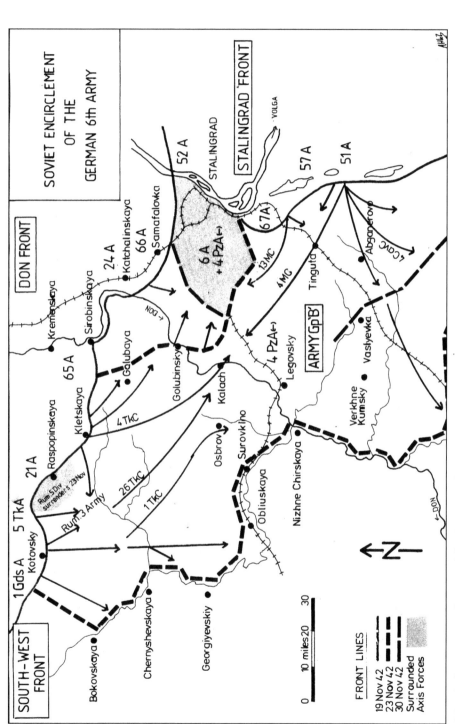

Map 3. Soviet Encirclement of the German 6th Army.

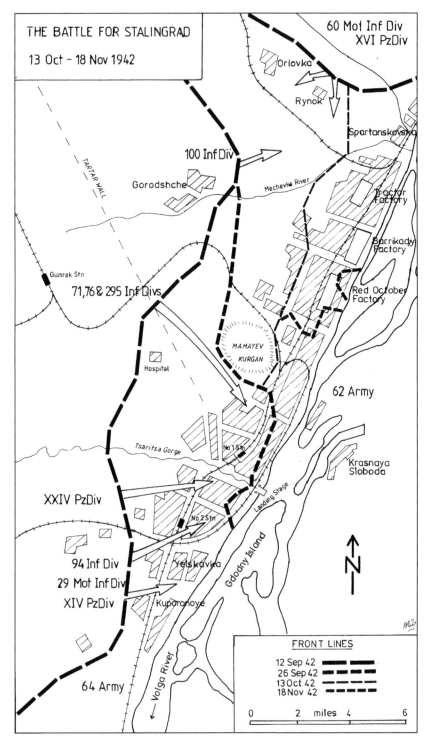

Map 4. The Battle for Stalingrad, 13 October–18 November 1942.

Chapter 1

Marching to the Volga

The death of the Field Marshal
Poltava, 14th January 1942. The officers of the 6th Army's headquarters were sitting in their mess chatting. Lunch was already over and we were waiting for the commander-in-chief, Field Marshal von Reichenau. This was nothing unusual. Reichenau was not so strictly punctual with off-duty matters. He thought nothing of appearing in a tracksuit. We knew that he had made his usual cross-country run with his adjutant, the young cavalry lieutenant Kettler, which was why he had not noticed the time.

As we knew Reichenau's habits, we were not concerned about his late arrival. But something unusual happened. He made his way uncertainly to the table as if he was having trouble standing upright. While he usually ate with pleasure and a good appetite, today he hesitated over his dish while groaning faintly. Colonel Heim, the 6th Army's chief of staff, noticed this. He looked at Reichenau concernedly. 'Don't you feel well, Field Marshal?'

'Don't worry, Heim, it will soon be over. Don't let me hold you back from your work.'

At this juncture I was asked by an orderly to go to the anteroom, where the army's court martial adviser, Colonel Judge Dr Neumann, was awaiting me.

'Can you please inform the Field Marshal that I need some urgent signatures from him? The post has to go to the Army High Command today.'

When I conveyed this wish to Reichenau, he said that the court martial adviser would have to wait a few minutes.

Outside I talked briefly with Dr Neumann and one of our orderly officers. Then the door opened and Reichenau appeared. He signed the files laid out for him. One of the orderlies stood ready to help him into his greatcoat, but this did not happen. The Field Marshal suddenly collapsed. We were able to catch the heavy man as he fell.

The shock hit me several minutes later as I stood in front of the chief of staff. 'Colonel, the Field Marshal . . .' Shocked, everyone ran into the anteroom. The once so strong and active Field Marshal hung slackly between two orderly officers, his eyes staring into nothingness. He appeared to have lost consciousness.

The 9th Army's senior doctor, Dr Flade, had gone off to Dresden on duty two days earlier. I therefore called the senior doctor at the hospital in Poltava. We took the Field Marshal to his residence in a car.

The hastily summoned doctor identified a stroke, with a loss of consciousness. He shook his head thoughtfully. Reichenau's right arm was drooping, as was the right side of his face.

Colonel Heim immediately informed the Army High Command and Führer Headquarters. Reichenau was commander-in-chief of Army Group 'South' as well of the 6th Army. Both were now without a commander. This was particularly awkward as Soviet units were successfully attacking our army front at two points.

Once Staff Surgeon Dr Flade had been ordered back by telegraph, Heim proposed to the Army High Command that Reichenau's home doctor in Leipzig, Professor Dr Hochrein, who was at this time on the Northern Front, be flown to Poltava. The Army High Command agreed. On the 16th January Professor Dr Hochrein and Dr Flade landed in the same aircraft at the airport.

Reichenau's condition had deteriorated considerably before the doctors arrived. The diagnosis was deeply located bleeding of the brain. There appeared to be a slight improvement on the evening of the 16th January. The assembled doctors wanted to make use of this improvement to convey the patient to Professor Hochrein's clinic in Leipzig, especially if this difficult illness could perhaps still be helped.

Two aircraft took off at 0730 hours on the 17th January 1942. The Field Marshal had not survived, having died shortly before. Dr Flade took the dead man with him in the first machine; Professor Hochrein was in the second.

Lemburg, where they were to refuel, came into sight at about 1130 hours. The machine with the corpse started to land, but apparently touched down too late. It careered into the hangar and was totally destroyed. The corpse of the dead man was so cut up that it had to be bound together with bandages. Dr Flade broke his leg. In a letter of the 11th February 1942 written to General Paulus about the accident a short time later, he said: 'My aircraft pilot thought that he could land in Lemburg and continued flying on to there, where the accident occurred at 1130 hours while attempting to land . . . it was a wonder we were not all killed, especially when one saw the machine afterwards.'

Hitler ordered a state funeral for Field Marshal Reichenau. The 6th Army was represented at the funeral by Major-General von Schuler, Reichenau's aide-de-camp for many years. The hard fighting at the time did not allow a single section leader of our staff to attend.

Paulus, the new commander of the 6th Army

Field Marshal Bock was tasked with the command of Army Group 'South', taking over the command on the 20th January 1942. That same day Lieutenant-General Paulus, the newly named commander-in-chief of the 6th Army, arrived at Poltava.

Both men had difficult tasks ahead of them. Northeast of Charkov, near Voltshansk, units of the Red Army had driven the 294th Infantry Division out of its positions. The Soviet offensive either side of Isium at the junction of the 17th and 6th Armies had made a deep breach in our positions. Charkov, Poltava and Dnepropetrovsk were threatened, and there were no reserves available. Infantry and artillery battalions were withdrawn from those divisions not attacked and deployed to the right flank of the armies with a front facing south. A security division taken from the army's rear areas was hastily extracted to prevent a further advance by the Soviet spearheads, and emergency battalions were formed from the army's supply units for the immediate protection of the threatened towns.

The army's situation was far from rosy when I collected Paulus from the airport. He stood tall and thin in front of me. He received my report with some reserve at first. Then a smile went over his gaunt face: 'Also from Hesse?'

'Yes, General,' I replied,

'Well then, we shall soon get to know each other, Adam.' Then he greeted an old acquaintance who had accompanied me to the airport, our Mess Officer, Captain Dormeier.

His first question came when we were sitting in the car: 'What does it look like at the front? I have read yesterday evening's report from the army. Have things changed meanwhile?'

'We are concerned whether the thin defensive front that we have formed by throwing units together can withstand the growing pressure from the Red Army. The chief of staff is very pleased that you have now arrived.'

Paulus immediately drove to see Colonel Heim, the 6th Army's chief of staff, who, together with the other officers of the staff, had prepared a briefing for the new commander-in-chief. The situation map was brought up to date, together with the losses of the past few days. The Ia (Operations) and Ic (Enemy reconnaissance and defence) reported on their own fighting strengths, combat experience and intelligence. They explained the composition of the Soviet troops and the most recent reconnaissance results. Colonel Heim suggested that the combat teams of the various regiments and divisions be brought together under a new command. The choice went to General of Artillery Heitz, commander of the VIIIth Corps. Paulus knew him as a tough soldier, and so it fell to him. In fact Heitz quickly turned the combat teams into a combined force. He gave them strong support with a strict organisation of the artillery and enforced the construction of defensive positions. The 113th Infantry Division was given to the VIIIth Corps and deployed with its front facing the breakthrough point south of Charkov. The danger seemed checked.

During these days I discovered once more how carefully Paulus worked. The liberal attitude of the dead Reichenau was alien to him. Every sentence that he spoke or wrote was carefully weighed, expressing every thought clearly so that there could be no misunderstanding. If Reichenau was a decisive and responsible commander-in-chief, who specifically expressed himself with a strong inflexible will and determination, Paulus was exactly the opposite. Already as a young officer he had been called 'Cunctator', the waverer. His knife-sharp brain and his invincible logic impressed all his colleagues. I had hardly ever experienced him underestimating the enemy or overestimating his own strength and capabilities. His decisions came only after long, sober consideration after lengthy, detailed discussions with his staff officers, and were carefully structured to cover all contingencies.

To his subordinates, Paulus was a benevolent and always correct superior. I experienced this for the first time when I drove him to the subordinate corps and divisions. On the afternoon of the 28th February the chief of staff informed me that I was to escort Paulus to the front on the 1st March. Using this opportunity, he showed me a list of promotions that had come by post from the Personnel Office. I looked at it briefly. One name was underlined. The chief of staff shook my hand. I had been promoted to colonel with effect from the 1st March 1942. 'I am telling you now so that you can tell the commander-in-chief early before he leaves. You can be proud of having been promoted from major to colonel in one year.' And I was proud of it.

I quickly made up my situation map. The chief of staff advised me on the route to take. We would be away for three or four days.

By jeep to the subordinate corps
Next morning we drove off in a cross-country jeep to visit all the units at the breakout position east of Poltava, escorted by several motorcyclists. It was a clear ice-cold day. Even our fur coats offered scanty protection from the raw east wind. Frequent snow barriers blocked the route. Columns of soldiers from the rear services and local civilians could only clear these great obstacles for a short time. Walls of snow four metres high on both sides of the road reduced our view to the road. In only a few places was there an open view of the wide Ukrainian landscape, which spread out before our eyes like a desert of snow, its crystals sparkling like diamonds in the sun. Trees and bushes were only to be seen alongside streams and in the villages between the low, white-washed buildings covered with straw or shingles. Fat cranes puffed themselves up on the naked asters.

Paulus was communicative all along the way. He spoke of his concerns and expectations. 'When I took over command of the 6th Army six weeks ago,' he began, after a general discussion of the day's events, 'I was a bit concerned about how my relationship with the commanding generals would work out, they all being older than me and senior in rank.'

'I had similar thoughts myself then,' I said, 'but then, from what I heard from the corps' adjutants, I now have the impression that you command great respect from all of them.'

'Certainly, Adam. I also believe that I have found the right tone. I will use this trip to make closer contact with them. The task of a commander is to establish a real confidence with his subordinates, in which mutual understanding is the most important factor. That eases the command considerably. Have you already met the generals personally?'

'Colonel Heim introduced me to the commanding generals in the first few days, but I do not know all the divisional commanders. Until now I could only form a picture of them from the comments in their personal files.'

'Use these few days. We will find out much about them. I would appreciate it if you would write down the impressions you have gained about the commanders upon our return.'

'I will see, General, if I can speak with some of the regimental commanders. I will obtain opinions of them all, but I would like to make my own judgements.'

'That is right and necessary. I presume that some heavy fighting lies ahead of us this year. I can look at your proposals when we start losing commanders. An error in filling a command post always has unfortunate consequences for the troops. So look at all of them carefully!'

We were driving down a hill. The vehicle began to slide and spun around several times on its own axis, until the driver corrected it. This brought our conversation to a halt, our attention being drawn to the mirror-like road.

We first visited the divisional commander, Lieutenant-General Gabke, who commanded the units in the westerly bulge. After a short orientation on the situation and the deployment of the troops, Paulus visited the artillery positions. They were located on open ground, being neither dug in nor camouflaged, so easily discernible to the enemy. This was quite irresponsible.

Paulus talked with the gunners and the gun commanders. 'Is the gun in order? Have you enough ammunition?'

'Yes, General!' replied a gun commander.

'Where are your gun carriages and horses?'

'The horses are over there in the stables, the gun carriages right next to them.' The gunner pointed towards the settlement only a few hundred metres away.

The commander-in-chief turned back to the gun commander: 'Do you consider this position suitable? Why are the guns not camouflaged?' Close by were some large haystacks. 'Why not use those haystacks?'

The battery commander came running, fearing a ticking-off. But Paulus was no wild general who only gave reprimands, but, as in this case, set the soldiers light-heartedly to work. 'I have spoken with your gunners about the positions the guns are in. They stand there as if on a presentation plate. Should the enemy resume his attack, your battery would be wiped out in a matter of minutes. Change position this evening and use the haystacks for camouflage!'

He had spoken quietly in a convincing and comradely manner. The battery commander stood before him with his right hand to his hat. 'Certainly, General!' He was so astonished, he could not say anything else.

'Fine, just get everything in order.' And with these words General Paulus left the baffled officer.

Has Timoshenko lost steam?
We sat back in the jeep and froze miserably, despite our fur coats. The next conference was to be at the headquarters of the VIIIth Corps in a village south of Charkov. Paulus said not a word, being engaged with his thoughts. Suddenly he looked up. 'I do not understand why Timoshenko has not pursued his attack. The defensive positions we have just seen would not have stood up to an earnest attack.'

'I had noticed it while we were at the artillery position. I only exchanged a few words with the observer, who had made a place for his periscope in the straw. He volunteered that Russians were as cold as we were and would certainly not continue the fighting. They were sitting in their settlements like us.'

'That is certainly so. At the moment it is more or less a fight for the villages. But we must not overlook the fact that the Russians are significantly better equipped for the winter than we are, and that they can resume unexpectedly. In any case our headquarters in Poltava are as threatened as ever.'

'I think, General, that Timoshenko has run out of steam, or he would have used the situation to his advantage.'

'I don't share your opinion, Adam. The Russians operate systematically, not taking risks lightly. I think we will discuss this question in detail this evening. Let us hear first how General Heitz, who has been here longer, assesses the situation.'

Heitz was already waiting for us. He was quite small, his movements concise. His jutting chin gave his small face a brutal appearance.

It was interesting for me to see how Paulus led the situation briefing. He seemed to be content with a superficial description. As a trained staff officer, he wanted to gain an exact picture of the situation, asking about the sources of information on the Soviet Army. He sharply distinguished between the essential and the inessential, considering again and again the various aspects of the enemy and demanding appropriate decisions.

General Heitz hinted specially at the strong Soviet tank units and then summarised: 'Should the enemy hit us with a clenched fist here, Charkov could not be held and the 6th Army would be threatened in the rear. We lack large calibre anti-tank weapons. I request that some batteries of 88mm Flak be allocated to me. This would enable us to defeat an enemy tank attack.'

Paulus was fully conscious of the danger threatening at Charkov. Naturally he had to first check which Flak batteries could be made available. Turning to General Heitz, he said: 'I will speak to the chief of staff about Charkov immediately. Hopefully, we will be able to help you.'

Our orderlies awaited us in Charkov, where we occupied quarters on a small housing estate. The two rooms and little kitchen were comfortably equipped and, following our drive in the icy cold, were comfortably warm. We had our dinner together in Paulus's house. He was living immediately nearby. There were potato pancakes and bean coffee.

We sat together for a long time after supper. The commander-in-chief took up the conversation from that afternoon. 'I have already told you, Adam, that I don't share your opinion on the restricted operational ability of the Red Army. The Russians not only stopped our tanks in front of Moscow but, as you know, went into a counterattack on the 5th December 1941 with the Kalinin Front, threw our troops back a long way and inflicted severe casualties on us. I experienced the first part of this at the Army High Command.'

'I have gone over this again thoroughly, General. In fact the Reds showed at Moscow what a great potential they still had. They soon spotted our weak points, broke through our positions and thrust deep into the interior. General Schubert, whose adjutant I was until November of last year, has written to me about it. His XXIIIrd Corps was surrounded near Rshev for several days and it was only by calling for a last effort that he was able to prevent himself from being surrounded. Many places that we took with heavy losses have been lost, such as Toropez, for example.'

'Yes, Adam, the situation became very serious at Rshev, we lost so much valuable material. The Russian attack on the central front brought the Army High Command great difficulties. One hardly knew how the gaping holes could be closed. You will understand why our army's situation gives me great concern. Timoshenko's army that broke through near Isium threatens our deep flank south of Charkov. The forces confronting Timoshenko's army are in no position to withstand another attack. Also northeast of Charkov, near Voltshansk, the danger cannot be excluded. New forces are still not available, so that under these circumstances we would be obliged to hold our positions with the units already deployed and, moreover, eliminating the enemy breaches as quickly as possible. If this does not happen, we remain in an especially dangerous position.'

The map lay in front of us. The latest situation reports had been entered on it. Paulus spoke by telephone with the chief of staff about General Heitz's request for 88mm Flak units to be deployed in an anti-tank role south of Charkov. The chief of staff briefed the commander-in-chief on the situation on the remainder of the army front. I listened with only half an ear. Our talk had brought me back on an even keel. My thoughts went over the events of the day once more. I had come across depressed spirits among several front-line officers. There was no longer the noticeable verve, the victorious assurance of the first years of the war among many soldiers. Hitler and the Army High Command said knowingly or unknowingly that the Red Army was beaten when they addressed the world. But a defeated army cannot go on attacking various positions ceaselessly in the middle of winter. But why these doubts? Once the winter is over, everything will look different. I tried to persuade myself so. Nevertheless it took a long time before I fell asleep that night.

The next day we visited the headquarters of the XVIIth Corps and the XXXXth Panzer Corps located at Charkov. I met the commanding general of the Panzer Corps, General of Tank Troops Stumme, for the first time. He was known jokingly in the army as 'the Bullet Blitz'. This name was well chosen for this small, plump, fast-acting general. His panzer division had forced back the enemy that had broken into our positions northeast of Charkov.

Here too, Paulus impressed me in his talks with the two commanding generals and their chiefs of staff. He did not use his commanding position to dominate but rather tried to convince his subordinates with the correctness of his opinion. His skill did not fail to impress the older generals. I observed with satisfaction that they had a profound respect for their commander-in-chief.

A horrible experience in Belgorod

On the third day we drove into Belgorod to see the XXIXth Corps. I was pleased to see the chief of staff again, Colonel von Bechtolsheim. I had worked for several months with him on the staff of the XXIIIrd Corps. Paulus too knew him well. During the Polish and French campaigns he had been the 6th Army's Ia (Operations).

We were already approaching the town when Paulus pointed to the right and said: 'Look, this is where the road that is so important for supplying the troops in the Belgorod area was almost broken by the Red Army attack. You know that the 294th Infantry Division only offered a weak resistance, partly fleeing to where this flat ground starts. The old situation could only be restored with the help of our tanks.'

Soon we were in Belgorod. There suddenly in the middle of the town was a horrible sight. I was startled. A gallows had been erected on a big square. Several civilians were hanging from it. Paulus turned white. A strong inner anger came from the eyes of this normally calm person. He said scornfully: 'What is this criminal exhibition? I cancelled Reichenau's order immediately after taking over my post!'

I remembered Reichenau's order quite clearly. It was in November 1941. I had been posted to the staff of the 6th Army and was travelling to my new post. What kind of spirit ruled here became immediately clear to me. At the steps to the entrance of headquarters hung a large notice, entitled 'Behaviour of the Troops in the East' and signed 'Reichenau, Field Marshal'. It was monstrous what was demanded here of members of the army. This was an order that included a demand for the murder of the Russian civilian population, women and children. It had nothing to do with what I understood about the conduct of warfare. Reichenau's order was even worse than the 'Commissar Order', by which the political commissars of the Soviet Army were not to be dealt with as soldiers or as prisoners of war, but rather they were to be sorted out and basically eliminated immediately. What had happened to the Hague Convention? On taking over the 6th Army, Paulus had withdrawn Reichenau's order, but these gallows were still standing in Belgorod.

The commanding general, General of Infantry von Obstfelder, and Colonel von Bechtolsheim were waiting for us at the entrance to the headquarters. Paulus turned to Obstfelder: 'Why were the civilians hanged?'

Obstfelder looked at my superior. 'The town commandant arrested them as hostages for several soldiers that had been found dead in the town. They were then hanged on the main street as a shocking example.'

Paulus stood before these officers bent slightly forward. There was a nervous twitch on his face. Then he spoke. 'And with that you believe that you can stop partisan activity? I am of the opinion that with such methods exactly the opposite is achieved. Reichenau's order on the behaviour of our troops in the East has been withdrawn by me. Take care, therefore, that this atrocity is immediately removed from the square.'

That was Paulus. Acts of revenge and cruelty contradicted his conception of soldierly behaviour. He had withdrawn Reichenau's barbaric order. That was already something, but it was not enough. He was inwardly shocked. He had ordered the removal of the gallows, but the town commandant of Belgorod, who had allowed the hostages to be murdered, got off unpunished. I too did not react to this inconsequence.

On the fourth day we turned back to Poltava.

A depressed atmosphere back home
I had had no leave for two years. After an examination by the army's internist, our Medical Doctor-General, Professor Dr Haubenreifer, I finally

applied for my overdue leave. Despite the tense situation, my application was approved by Paulus. I could leave everything to my deputy, who was informed on all matters. I wanted to go before Easter.

Paulus had been permitted by the commander of the army group to attend the baptism of his twin's grandson in Berlin. We travelled back home together. We went by Field Marshal von Bock's special train from Poltava to Kiev, taking Paulus's personal car on an open goods wagon. Paulus wanted to drive from Kiev to Berlin in his car.

One of our vehicle maintenance companies in Kiev had orders to put a vehicle at our disposal as far as the Reich border. Accompanying me was a young orderly officer from our staff. Shortly after our arrival in Kiev we set off on our journey. All seemed set fair for the trip, but that evening a strong snowstorm began and we could hardly see the road. We decided to overnight in Shitomir and continue in daylight. But this time I was plagued with bad luck. While tanking up, the vehicle slipped into a pit and the exhaust pipe snapped off right next to the engine. I drove it to the workshop next morning. I had to use all my powers of persuasion to get the damage repaired straight away. It was almost midday when we set off again. We had tanked up and the reserve fuel tank was full. That must have been our lucky break. The vehicle ran well, the snowstorm had abated. In spirit I saw myself in Krakau already, where the planned leave train would take me on to Frankfurt am Main. In a cheerful leave atmosphere, I chatted with the driver, a young soldier and auto-mechanic by trade.

'Have you been a soldier for long?' I asked him.

'Since the beginning of the war, Colonel.'

'How long have you been with the vehicle maintenance company?'

'After my training I was posted to the company as a mechanic, took part in the Western Campaign and then came here.'

'How do you find Kiev? Yesterday afternoon I only saw a little of the city, but I got a good impression of it.'

'Yes, Colonel, Kiev is a fine city. We have good accommodation and a proper repair shop. If only it was not so insecure.'

'What do you mean by that?'

'It is not advisable to go out alone in the evenings. Since we have been here there have already been a whole number of soldiers and officers that have vanished without trace. Not from our unit, we were taught and warned right from the beginning. If we go to the cinema or Soldiers' Home in the evening, there is always a big gang of us and we take our weapons along with us.'

'No, no, it can't be so bad.'

'Colonel, I am not exaggerating. There must be partisans organising the attacks even in the city. We would rather be in a smaller place in which one knows all the civilians. It would be even better if the war ended soon.'

'You have a longing for the West?'

'It was better in every respect there. It was a fine time for us.'

'And now you are fed up with the war?'

'Quite frankly yes, Colonel. You should hear how our old hands complain. According to the accounts from those on leave, many German soldiers must have bitten the dust in front of Moscow. My friend brought a newspaper of a small country town from home. Whole pages were filled with death notices.'

We drove over a freshly gravelled road. Stones as big as one's fist hit the underside of the vehicle. The driver slowed down. We resumed speed after several hundred metres. As we were approaching Rovno, the officer sitting behind me tapped me on the shoulder. 'Colonel, I think there is something wrong with the vehicle. We are leaving a trail. Either the tank or the radiator is leaking.'

We stopped. A stone had made a small hole in the tank. Petrol was leaking out of it. By topping up from the spare tank we were able to reach a petrol station in Rovno. There was no workshop available. The driver blocked the hole with oakum and refilled the tank. We reached Przemsyl with the last drops of petrol and drove on to an army workshop. The duty mechanic said that the repair would take at least two days, so I decided to continue my journey by train next morning. The following day I was in Frankfurt am Main, the journey having gone without incident. Several hours later I took my wife from the station in Münzenberg to a small town near Bad Nauheim.

The next morning I sought out an old acquaintance, the master joiner Hartmann, who was especially well informed on politics and history. I sat next to him in his small workshop. Without interrupting his work, he conversed with me for hours. We talked about the war.

'The mood of the inhabitants of our small town is divided. Those who have relatives in the West and in the northern countries are, as before, on to a good thing. They can hardly understand how these soldiers can send them food, materials, underwear, clothing. Now women, who under normal circumstances can hardly afford stockings, are going about in fur coats. They don't have to depend on the lives of their husbands and sons, so let the war continue well.

'It is different for those whose families are in the east. They live in constant fear. Any day the postman can bring a letter with the note: 'Fallen on the field of honour.' One has to understand how to read between the lines of the army reports. We have been thrown back a long way. Streams of German blood apparently flow in front of Moscow. Look in this newspaper!'

Truly what the young driver had told me was not exaggerated. Whole pages of death notices!

'Goebbels cannot hide this defeat from the people. The reports of the people on leave and the wounded about the retreat from Moscow reveal their lies. I can only tell you that the mood is rapidly sinking. Ever more of our citizens see the end of the war getting nearer. Even among the Party members there are already some no longer talking about final victory. I don't believe that we can defeat the Russian colossus. Hitler has presumed to demand the whole of Europe. This can't lead to any good end.'

I sat on the bench and listened to the master joiner. He put down his plane from time to time to tap his pipe, to strop his file, or to relight his pipe with a wood splinter when it had already gone out.

Old Hartmann was strongly religious. He regularly went to church and the Bible always lay near him in the workshop. 'The Communists don't want to have anything to do with religions,' he said, 'which is why I am against Communism. I am really no friend of the Russians, but I am also no National Socialist. What one hears from the men on leave is shocking. Innocent people are murdered, civilians hanged. That I do not understand. And what is being done with the Jews is a disgrace. Why should they be weeded out? They too are people and do their duty like us. No, this is leading to no good ending. And the two-front war. That we cannot maintain, as the First World War showed. Russia has vast areas and a big human reservoir at its disposal.'

'We will soon make it!' With these words I parted from my old acquaintance. But what I had heard from him gave fresh impetus to the doubts I had discussed with General Paulus a few weeks before, and robbed me of my sleep. Did other people at home think like the joiner? I listened around, spoke to farmers, small tradesmen, workers and teachers. Most treated me with caution, avoiding my questions. For them I was a high-ranking officer. This immediately made them suspicious and this did not help me share my thoughts. My wife also told me that people lived in constant fear of the Gestapo. A thoughtless word could lead to arrest and a concentration camp. Mistrust was distorting communal life.

I experienced the same depressing atmosphere in a short visit to my brother in Eichen. Several of my young relatives had already fallen, farmers' sons who were supposed to take over the home farm. Earlier I had always liked going to my home village to see relatives and friends. This time I had to make condolence visits. Almost everywhere the women met me with crying faces.

A call on General Keitel while on leave
Upon my return from Eichen I found in Münzenberg a telegram from the city commandant in Frankfurt. 'On the orders of the 6th Army, break off your leave and report to the Army Personnel Office in Berlin next day.'

This was an unpleasant surprise. My wife was quite upset. She had so much enjoyed my leave. What plans we had made! Now everything had come to nothing. My bag was quickly packed. I found the parting very difficult. I caught a night train to Berlin in Bad Nauheim. Immediately upon arrival in the morning I reported to the Personnel Office. I was expected and immediately sent on by the duty officer in the courier train to Lötzen. I had hardly time to say 'Hullo' on the telephone to my brother-in-law, Lieutenant-Colonel Dr Wagner, a departmental chief in the Wehrmacht High Command.

Upon my arrival at Lötzen the haste was explained to me. Here I learnt at last why my leave had had to be curtailed: a flight to Poltava, where the head of the Army Personnel Office, General Keitel, had arranged a conference with the army adjutants of Army Group 'South'.

I spent the night in Field Marshal von Brauchitsch's special train, which was camouflaged in a wood near Lötzen. It consisted of several sleeping cars, a restaurant car and a saloon wagon set out with tables and chairs. The commander of this special train had assigned me a sleeping compartment and an orderly.

As I climbed out of the vehicle at Lötzen airfield, the special aircraft that was to fly General Keitel to Poltava was already waiting. He himself came shortly afterwards, accompanied by several heads of departments from the Army Personnel Office.

I looked upon the flight with mixed feelings. A strong wind had blown up and my stomach had already gone on strike. We took our seats. The machine started up and soon the Lötzener Lake lay before us. Already just a few hundred metres up, the aircraft was being strongly shaken by the storm. I had never been airsick before, but this time I was severely tested. My knees were still weak when we made an interim landing at Shitomir. Understandably, I had no wish to leave the machine. The flight on was pleasanter, but nevertheless I was pleased when I had firm ground beneath me once more at Poltava.

The conference began the next day at the army group headquarters. In addition to Keitel and the departmental heads of the Army Personnel Office, taking part were the 1st Adjutant of Army Group 'South', Colonel von Wechmar, and the 1st Adjutants of the 2nd, 6th, 11th and 17th Armies, as well as those of the 1st and 4th Panzer Armies.

We were instructed to check over the staff of the commanding positions, to report those not fully qualified to the Personnel Office and to propose alternative employment for them. If possible, those affected would be replaced by other officers from the army group.

Our 6th Army had proposed suitable lieutenants as battalion commanders, and young but proven majors as regimental commanders. After four weeks they would be confirmed in their appointments, and promoted to the next highest rank after a further two months. This proposal was approved. The Personnel Office recommended that the adjutants should deal in the same way with the loss of commanders as the 6th Army. I emphasized that from previous promotions not only the appointment of company and battalion commanders of the same rank should be encouraged, but also the ambitions of these officers.

General Keitel then told us that before the beginning of an offensive, a leader reserve of officers of various ranks should be formed.

By evening the conference came to an end. Subsequently I reported immediately to the chief of staff and General Paulus on the outcome.

The following day saw me back at work. Leave was out of the question.

A sergeant turns back a Soviet prisoner
A further crisis soon occurred at the breakthrough point south of Charkov. The Red Army sought once more to breach our front. Their advance was checked only with difficulty by the commitment of 88mm Flak units and a newly arrived division. The Soviets were able to take a number of prisoners from the 44th Division from Vienna. Among them was a sergeant platoon commander in an infantry regiment, whose name I have forgotten. To our astonishment the division reported several days later that the captured sergeant had returned to his unit. The Ic of this division added in his report that upon his return the soldier related that he had been well treated by the Red Army soldiers and officers. This was in contrast to our own propaganda news, and the Ic had recorded the matter in harsh terms. I was against this when he introduced the case at the next conference with the chief of staff. He had already ordered the sergeant to army headquarters escorted by an officer, as he thought that there was something strange about the case. In the interrogation by a staff officer from the Ic department, the sergeant claimed that he had been able to escape. Nevertheless, he had been correctly handled as a prisoner, not only by the front-line troops, but also by the higher ranking staff who had questioned him; he had been given food, drink and cigarettes. There was no mention of mishandling or a shot in the neck.

This all seemed unbelievable. The Ic was of the opinion that the sergeant had been sent back with the task of undermining the morale of his unit. Even if that was not the case, his retention would remain a danger to the troops' fighting morale. He therefore suggested that the sergeant should be transferred to a replacement unit with specific instructions not to be sent to the Eastern Front. This proposal was approved.

These measures could not prevent the matter being widely discussed within the division. Most took the view that the prisoner had been sent back for a definite reason, which is why he had been so well handled. Only a few believed his report. What really happened is still unknown.

This case also gave rise to discussion among the officers of the staff. Throughout, I took it as possible that this did not involve desertion, but I took to Paulus my thoughts on the sergeant's transfer to the replacement troops. 'By doing this are we not organising a negative discussion in the regiment, or in the division? The sergeant had a good report from his company commander as an exemplary, dutiful, committed soldier who always led well. He had never been punished before, and enjoyed the respect of both his superiors and his inferiors. I believe that as soon as this unpleasant discussion is over, the subject will be avoided. Some of the soldiers will begin to doubt the veracity of our propaganda.'

Thoughtfully the army commander explained: 'Let us accept for once that the returned man had no special mission. Even then his remaining with the troops brings a certain danger that he will have to speak and answer questions. So let the matter lie, and use the enemy propaganda. That is why I agree with our counter-espionage section's proposal.'

I also spoke to the officer who had conducted the interrogation and expressed my fears to him.

He laughed. 'We recognised this danger too, which is why the section was informed as follows: *The examination by the army staff has proved that what the sergeant said was not the truth. He had been tasked by the Russians to persuade his comrades to desert.*'

I was speechless. 'Is that really true?' I asked him.

'Naturally not literally,' replied the officer, 'but I am of the opinion that in this way the discussion among the troops will be diminished.'

I was concerned about how this would all end. Doubtless there was some contradiction between our official propaganda and the truth. We all continually taught our soldiers that the Russians let no prisoners survive. It was declared and then spread. The sergeant spoke of German soldiers who had been prisoners since 1941, and said that they were well. What should one believe? The sergeant named the soldiers and their units that he had seen over there and spoken with. This information could be checked. A lie was easy to prove. But what were the Reds aiming at by sending back a platoon leader? What was his real task?

That is how it goes when one's thoughts rumble on. There was another incident in our headquarters. Colonel von Bechtolsheim, the XXIXth Corps' chief of staff, was transferred as chief of staff to the 1st Army in France. His successor, Colonel Kinzel, formerly of the Foreign Armies East section at Army High Command, reported to Paulus and joined us for lunch. During the conversation Paulus announced his astonishment that the Army High Command, especially Hitler, had the impression that the Red Army had been destroyed.

'The activity of the Red Army since January, especially in front of Moscow and here with us, proves that this is debatable. What do you think, Kinzel?'

'Hitler's revised thesis on the destruction of the Red Army was never acknowledged by my section. In my reports I have always indicated what lies before us, numerous confirmed reports from the Soviet Union that it is only just beginning to reveal its full military strength. They have established numerous new armies, their armaments industry is running and at even higher capacity. But Hitler does not want to know that, for it does not fit into his wishful dreams. He brushes our reports off the table with his hand.'

Truly these were no grounds for comfort. What unforeseeable consequences would there be if the commander-in-chief set out on such a false appreciation of the enemy? But why do the generals at Army High Command and the Wehrmacht, why does the General Staff allow such false reports to circulate? It is absolute nonsense building the strategic and tactical direction of the war on such propaganda. Could such criminal recklessness really be possible?

The question would not leave me alone. How bitterly I came to learn the truth, which had not occurred to me in my deepest dreams until now. Above all I believed in Paulus. He would surely not let such an irresponsible underestimation of the enemy lull him into insecurity. He would follow his clear, sharp intellect. He had already displayed this in the few weeks since he took over command of the 6th Army.

Rising doubts about one's superiors or comrades of equal rank seemed impossible to me and quite dangerous. I had already once known an officer whose straightforwardness had attracted me – the army's new chief engineer, Colonel Selle – but we knew too little about each other, apart from that he was a holder of the golden badge of the Nazi Party. Despite several critical remarks that he had made, I took him as an unconditional follower of Hitler. Only during the course of time did I discover that Selle himself had many doubts and had had many serious disappointments with the way that Hitler was conducting the war. We became good friends.

Propaganda Leader Fritzsche
The big summer offensive of 1941 lay before us. Major Menzel was sent as a liaison officer to the staff of the 6th Army from the Army High Command. Through his decisive reserve, he soon made quick contact with the headquarters and enjoyed general trust. Shortly before the operations began, we had another surprise. One of the senior men in the Propaganda Ministry, Herr Fritzsche, was posted to our staff as a war correspondent. He reported to Paulus in the uniform of a specialist with the rank of captain.

After our usual lunchtime walk I sat next to Colonel Voelter, our 1st staff officer, and during our conversation I asked him the question: 'Why have they sent us one of Goebbels' closest staff?'

'At the Army High Command and Wehrmacht High Command they are apparently expecting a change in the way the war is going. Our defeat at Moscow has strongly shaken confidence among the troops and back at home in a victorious end of the war coming soon. The atmosphere has not only sunk in our army's sector. The High Command want to revive it with special reports of victory on the Eastern Front. With the destruction of the Russian troops that broke through south of Charkov, and especially with this year's summer offensive, we will provide material for new reports of victory. Goebbels' fellow worker, Fritzsche, is tasked with writing special reports. As soon as he arrived he wanted to know the names of the soldiers and young officers that distinguished themselves in the defensive fighting, but you know that yourself,' ended the officer's explanation.

'As long as I am able, Voelter, I will come often to you.'

'That's fine. I am looking in the morning and evening reports for material that can be properly used for the press and radio.'

'The first results of your work are already ready. In the Kiev '*Soldiers' Newspaper*' is one of your ever-repeated front-line experiences. It actually talks of making something out of everyday heroism. And what soldier would not be proud to see his name appear in the Front newspaper? I am keen to know whether the war correspondent will be as active when the battle really begins.'

'I have already asked the question. We shall see. One must incidentally accept that it will play a little to one side. As at present we have nothing more important to do, we shall send him to the divisions, where he will immediately be able to hear the sounds of battle.'

Hitler's attack aims for 1942
'Do you know, Voelter, I don't envy you the double work-load you have on your back, preparing the destruction of the enemy who have broken through our positions south of Charkov, and with it the planning of the summer offensive. That is no piece of cake. The army group adjutant told me that several newly formed divisions are already on their way from France.'

'Hopefully we will not be obliged to deploy these divisions south and north of Charkov as fire brigades. There have been indications of enemy activity at both those breaches. The commanding generals are very concerned and are urgently asking for reinforcements, as they are expecting a resumption of the enemy offensive.'

Order no. 41 from the Wehrmacht High Command on the 5th April 1942 laid down the goals for Army Group 'South' for the 1942 summer offensive. The whole operation would begin with an attack out of the area south of Orel towards Voronesh, to which the 2nd Army, the 4th Panzer Army and the 2nd Hungarian Army were allocated. Our 6th Army had the task of breaking through from the Charkov area to the east and, in combination with the motorised units of the 4th Panzer Army thrusting towards the Donau, of destroying the enemy forces. Afterwards, in the third phase of the summer offensive, the 6th Army and the 4th Panzer Army would unite in the Stalingrad area with the forces thrusting eastwards from Taganrog–Artiomovsk (Artemovsk). The city on the Volga would be reached and this important armaments and vehicle centre isolated.

To finish the operation, a crossing over to the Caucasus was envisaged. It was clear that Hitler was going for the important oilfields that would be decisive in the pursuit of war.

Spring attack on Charkov
At the beginning of May some of the infantry divisions expected from France arrived in the Charkov area, including also the 305th, the Bodensee Division, to whose motorised ambulance company belonged my later but then unknown friend and co-writer, Otto Ruhle.

Our preparations for setting off on the summer campaign of 1942 were in full swing. The 6th Army would be pitched against a strong, new, probing enemy advance. The Soviet units started off from the Isium bulge and near Voltshansk in a renewed attack on the 12th May with strong forces, including numerous tanks. The situation was menacing. The attackers were able to break through the defensive ring in several places. The 454th Security Division was unable to hold fast. What Paulus had feared as early as the 1st March now occurred, and the division gave way. Also the VIIIth Corps had to withdraw about 10 kilometres when a Hungarian security brigade under Major-General Abt proved not strong enough against the storming enemy. Soviet tanks stood only 20 kilometres from Charkov. The 3rd and 23rd Panzer Divisions mounted a counterattack but this bogged down.

Hardly less serious was the situation at Voltshansk, northeast of Charkov. It literally needed the 6th Army's last reserves to bring the enemy to a halt. But then came the change. On the 17th May Army Group 'Kleist', with the IIIrd Panzer Corps under General von Mackensen, attacked from the south towards the Isium bulge. Simultaneously the 6th Army conducted a main attack from the north, and in the bitter fighting it became possible to surround the attacking Soviet units. Two exciting weeks ensued. We did not get out of our boots day or night, and our uniforms were soaked with sweat.

The spring battle for Charkov ended on the 29th May, the dangerous breach at Isium having been removed. Paulus received the Knight's Cross. Army headquarters moved from Poltava to Charkov.

Fritzsche gets a reprimand
Specialist Fritzsche had been waiting impatiently for the beginning of the operation at Charkov. His pen then sent to the waiting homeland brilliant, enthusiastic accounts of the battles, giving a dubious and frightening new impetus. The cruel Russian winter, and the defeats at Moscow and in the Crimea paled into insignificance. Herr Fritzsche believed that it was

especially good to write an article in the Kiev '*Soldiers' Newspaper*' in which he praised Paulus's promotion to General of Panzer Troops as that of a great commander. His circumspection and unerring leadership had to be thanked for the victory achieved in the first rank. I recalled that we on the army staff had read this article with pleasure and pride. The Specialist rose in our esteem, but Reichs Propaganda Minister Goebbels reacted otherwise. On the day on which this article appeared in the Kiev '*Soldiers' Newspaper*' this fellow worker in the army headquarters was sitting next to us at supper when he was called to the telephone. He returned with his head hanging down. What had happened?

Goebbels had reproached him because he had praised Paulus as a field commander. This attribute only applied to the Führer and Reichs Chancellor of the Great German Reich. Fritzsche stayed on with the 6th Army for several more months. I never heard of him making another error.

Paulus was angry when he heard of this matter. 'What do these people have to worry about? As if this was the main question! The fact that we have to deal with this mess because the High Command has underestimated the enemy does not interest them.'

'I find it especially remarkable, General, that the failure of the army and army group commanders should be taken into account. General Guderian, for example, was dismissed after the defeat at Moscow and sent home. Victory is the main obligation of the Führer's commanders.'

'My dear Adam, hopefully you will not express such heretical thoughts in Herr Fritzsche's presence! I would be sorry if you got into trouble.'

'I will be careful, General.'

Schmidt, the 6th Army's new chief of staff
At the beginning of May 1942 the headquarters of the 6th Army changed location. Heim, the former chief of staff promoted to major-general a few days previously, was released upon request to Field Marshal von Bock's Army Group 'South'. Bock believed that some difficult situations would not have arisen in the spring of 1942 had Heim not pessimistically condemned the enemy breakthrough at Voltshansk. Paulus informed me that he was not convinced about this condemnation, but he did nothing to prevent Heim's release. I found this surprising myself. I prized Major-General Heim as an able officer. All the section leaders in the army headquarters liked working with him and regretted his departure.

Heim took over the 14th Panzer Division. His successor on the staff was Colonel Artur Schmidt. Was such a change good in the middle of preparations for an attack shortly before the beginning of the summer offensive? Even Paulus was unhappy about it, as was the Quartermaster-General responsible for the whole supply situation. Colonel Pampel was replaced by Colonel Finckh. Schmidt and Finckh had only a short time in which to work with the trains of thought of their predecessors. Schmidt achieved this very quickly. This shopkeeper's son from Hamburg was clever, agile and of good intellectual ability, with a hardness that frequently turned to stubbornness. He differed from the former chief of staff essentially on one point. Heim understood the need to have a good rapport with all the headquarters establishments, never leaving them in the lurch. Schmidt in contrast was intolerant and overbearing, cold and inconsiderate. Mostly he pushed his will through, seldom letting another opinion count. Conflict repeatedly arose between him and the heads of departments, especially with the G1, the Quartermaster-in-Chief and sometimes also with the Chief Engineer. This was not helpful in the final preparations for the summer offensive. Several of our staff officers applied for transfers. Paulus was above the antipathy directed against the new chief of staff, using every opportunity to smooth the way, but he did not earnestly consider an alteration in the attitude of the chief of staff.

I was sorry that the well trained staff officer Schmidt had so little contact within the army. Even his attitude towards Paulus was not what it should have been. Schmidt tried to keep the commander-in-chief on a leading rein. This was also known by the commanding generals, so that Schmidt met with strong reserve.

The army needs replacements
The 6th Army had suffered considerable numbers of casualties in the fighting at Charkov. About 20,000 men had been lost, killed or injured. My task was to close the gap by the accelerated bringing forward of reserves. All the divisions had to be brought up to full fighting strength before the imminent summer offensive.

Our requisitions went to the regional army commands back home. Only a few days later we were informed that the first troop transport was on its way. Replacements arrived daily at Charkov, where they were assigned to the divisions.

The last division to have been raised in France was also among them, as well as the staff of the LIst Corps under General von Seydlitz-Kurzbach. The divisional commander reported to Paulus at his headquarters in Charkov, the adjutants handing me their lists of officer appointments.

Among the divisional commanders were two men well known to our commander-in-chief: Lieutenant-General Jaenecke, commander of the 389th Infantry Division, and Lieutenant-General von Gablenz, commander of the 384th Infantry Division. Paulus discussed matters with them for a considerable length of time. He was interested in the front-line training status, the battle-worthiness and combat experience of the regimental commanders. I was present when Lieutenant-General Jaenecke reported. What he had to say was not welcome. His division consisted almost completely of soldiers with no or little experience of the East, and this also applied to the infantry regimental commanders. They were elderly officers who in the past had been employed in reserve roles such as office duty. They had then been sent on a short course at the French training grounds at Mourmelon and afterwards appointed as commanders.

'They are not naturally commanders, as they lack the experience as well as the basic training in the command of troops. Two of them, from what I have seen, are not even physically up to the coming demands,' said General Jaenecke. 'I would be grateful if you could place two battle-experienced battalion commanders at my disposal. The Personnel Office, on the contrary, want me to give reasons for releasing these two regimental commanders.'

'That is not necessary, General,' I interposed. 'We have orders to test all the commanders again before the beginning of the offensive and, where necessary, to make transfers.'

The change took place next day, both old officers being transferred to the reserve.

Could this problem not have been resolved more quickly and simply? It was considerably more difficult to fill gaps during the fighting. This above all applied to the replacement of men who had fallen in battle. The winter and spring battles in the East had demanded a high toll in blood. I think that the Wehrmacht's losses in the winter of 1941/2 amounted to half a million men. The replacement question was already very urgent by the beginning of the 1942 offensive. It was worrying when one looked at the widespread goals that the High Command had in mind.

Conference with Hitler in Poltava
On the 1st June 1942 there was a big Führer conference at Army Group 'South' headquarters in Poltava. Hitler appeared escorted by Field Marshal Keitel, the chief of the Operations Section, Lieutenant-General Heusinger, the Quartermaster-General, General Wagner, and several adjutants. Ordered to the conference room were Field Marshal von Bock, commander of Army Group 'South', Lieutenant-General von Greiffenberg, later to be chief of staff to Army Group 'A', Colonel-General von Kleist, commander of the 1st Panzer Army, Colonel-General Ruoff, commander of the 17th Army, Colonel-General Freiherr von Weichs, commander of the 2nd Army, General of Panzer Troops Paulus, commander of the 6th Army, General of Panzer Troops von Mackensen, commander of the IIIrd Panzer Corps and, from the Luftwaffe, Colonel-General von Richthofen, commander of Air Fleet 4. The conference concerned the planned offensive in the southern sector. Hitler showed the attack goals that had been decided at the conference on the 5th April. He was betting with high stakes, and he himself said: 'If we don't take Maikop and Grsony, I must put an end to the war.'

The Red Army was to be bottled up and destroyed in a vast surrounding operation in southern Russia west of the Don. The approaches to the Volga and the Caucasus with its ground oil resources would thus be cut off and the Soviet Union dealt a heavy blow.

Paulus briefed our headquarters on the forthcoming operations. On the German side, and our Allies, more than one and a half million soldiers, more than a thousand tanks, thousands of aircraft and several thousand guns of all calibres would participate. The 6th Army had to take on the flank protection of the tanks attacking towards Stalingrad. Our commander-in-chief was confident. We all went back to work with renewed vigour.

Although the previous undertaking, Operation Fridericus I, had smoothed out the Isium bulge, some other things still had to be done to arrange a better starting position for the 6th Army. Thus an attack was made on Voltshansk on the 13th June as Operation Wilhelm, and another attack was carried out towards Kupiansk on the 22nd June as Operation Fridericus II, in cooperation with the IIIrd Panzer Corps, which remained attached to the 6th Army. The tanks raced forward as the infantry and artillery assumed their attack positions. Following a short but massive bombardment from hundreds of guns, our troops advanced in a pincer movement. Within a few days the encircled units had been defeated and more than 20,000 prisoners marched into the rear area past the German troops in their new attack positions.

Major Reichel shot down with the operation plans
On the 19th June I was sitting in the room with Colonel Voelter after a busy day. He had already sent off several messages to the corps for the further direction of the army group. Then the telephone rang. Voelter was urgently wanted by the 1st Staff Officer. 'Put him through!'

I could not make sense of the long conversation, but I noticed Voelter's face getting darker. He banged down the telephone angrily. 'That's all we need! The 1st Staff Officer of the 23rd Panzer Division, Major Reichel, has been shot down in a Fieseler 'Stork'. He had with him orders and maps for the first phase of our offensive.'

I was so perplexed, I could find nothing sensible to say. I had hardly said a few words when Voelter hastily interrupted. Major Reichel had wanted to return to this division from a conference at the XXXXth Panzer Corps in Charkov in a Fieseler 'Stork'. He had yet to arrive when night fell. The senior duty officer then called the corps staff on the assumption that Reichel had been delayed, but that was not the case. The Panzer corps immediately conducted a search for the missing officer. Then the news came from a division that the enemy had shot down a Fieseler 'Stork' between the lines that afternoon. Infantry scouts soon found the aircraft about four kilometres from their front line. The aircraft had been forced to land by a shot in the fuel tank. The bodies of Major Reichel and the pilot were buried.

There was no trace of either orders or maps. This was disastrous, as his papers also contained the orders and tasks for the planned operation for our left-hand neighbours, the 2nd Army and the 4th Panzer Army.

Hitler became personally involved. The commanding general, General of Panzer Troops Stumme, his chief of staff, Colonel Franz, and the commander of the 23rd Panzer Division, Lieutenant-General von Boineburg, were stripped of their commands and brought before a court martial. General Paulus and Field Marshal von Bock immediately interposed for all three, for they had no direct involvement, but this influenced neither Hitler nor Göring, the chairman of the War Council. Stumme was given five years and Franz three years imprisonment; only Boineburg was released.

The 'Reichel Case' was the catalyst for Hitler's subsequent order that in future no commander of a neighbouring formation should be informed about their neighbour's orders. This order had to be so strictly adhered to that it made the coordinated direction of an attack very difficult.

Colonel of Panzer Troops von Schweppenburg was appointed as the new commander of the XXXXth Panzer Corps. Even if he had the necessary experience and ability, this change shortly before the beginning of the new offensive was detrimental in other respects. Every new commander needs a certain amount of time until he has the reins firmly in his hands and confidence in the units under his command. Paulus and Bock were even more concerned, as the XXXXth Panzer Corps was to open the way to the big Don Bend and prevent the enemy escaping over the river. Both commanders were also uncomfortable with the court martial sentences as, in their opinion, Reichel had merely behaved carelessly.

So the 'Reichel Case' and the way it was handled weighed heavily as a handicap to the forthcoming offensive. We discussed it a lot at army headquarters.

'Can we pursue our Operation Blue 1 in the planned form and to the fixed dates?' I asked Voelter. 'The Russians are not stupid. They will try everything to ruin it.'

'Of course we will have to deal with unpleasant surprises, but what can we do? We cannot alter the plan, which would mean putting back the operation a few weeks. We are coming to winter and will perhaps experience one even worse than last year before Moscow. These matters must be considered by the Army High Command and the army groups.'

A few days later Paulus informed us that the army group was against any alteration of the plan; in fact, it was demanding that the date of the operation be brought forward.

Propaganda Chief Fritzsche was not idle in this matter. The success of the 6th Army in the battle at Charkov, the elimination of the breaches and the subsequent actions to improve the starting positions dominated the reports in the press and on the radio. The German forces achieved new feats and new victories. The defeats of the winter were over, with the strength of the Red Army coming to an end. Their attacks at Isium and Voltshansk were a last effort. They lay under the fire of our glorious weapons and were smashed by our brave soldiers in counterattacks.

So proud were we of our successes in these last three weeks that most of us artificially exaggerated them, so much so that the reporting went too far. It clearly bore the stamp of the propagandist, contradicting military thoughts and feelings. We now knew well how hard the fighting was and how many losses it was costing our side. With this conclusion, we gave up this unpleasant matter.

The propaganda had another side to it. Daily the officers hammered home to the soldiers that becoming prisoners of war meant a shot in the back of the neck, so they were to sell their lives as expensively as possible. This assertion did not lack results. I too essentially believed in it, recalling the sergeant of the 44th Infantry Division who had reported the good handling of German prisoners of war.

But who knew on what grounds he was spreading such news? Why should I worry my head about a situation in which I would never find myself? Now the decisive attack was about to begin and we should be concentrating on that.

Field Marshal von Bock has to go

The 6th Army was part of Army Group 'South', which came under the Army High Command. After Hitler had dismissed Field Marshal von Brauchitsch in December 1941, he himself took over the command of the Wehrmacht and also of the Army. Among the higher staffs there was a general impression that Hitler treated most generals with a certain mistrust. It was also said that Goebbels, Göring and Himmler were especially anxious to keep his doubts alive.

Certainly Hitler's boundless personal striving for power and his permanent anxiety thrust aside or at least narrowed down any confidence so that he treated the generals of the old school with distrust. That is how Field Marshal von Bock also came under suspicion. If one takes him correctly, he had, like the other generals, given Hitler loyal service. In the Polish campaign he had commanded the northern army group as a colonel-general. In the Western campaign nine months later von Bock had commanded Army Group 'B', which invaded the neutral countries of Holland and Belgium. After the end of the Western campaign he was promoted to field marshal. But his command of the operations of Army Group 'Centre' went less smoothly against Russia in 1941. Despite the commitment of the 'last battalions', he was unable to take Moscow. Then on the 2nd December 1941 he declared in an order: 'The enemy defence is on the verge of a crisis.' In fact, this did not apply to the enemy but to his own attacking armies. When the Red Army went over into a counteroffensive on the 5th December 1941, the German troops suffered extraordinarily high casualties and were driven back several hundred kilometres. Bock had then reported sick. Hitler named Field Marshal von Kruge as commander of Army Group 'Centre'. Several weeks later, following Reichenau's death, Bock took over command of Army Group 'South'. It did not go much better for him than it had at Moscow. He was unable to prevent the Soviets making breaches on either side of Isium. His appearance, already sunken since the defeat at Moscow, no longer lit up Hitler's eyes.

The experience of the winter of 1941/2 enabled the field marshal to take a more realistic view of the assessment of the enemy. His evaluations were more cautious. Like Paulus, he was not of the opinion that the Red Army had been beaten. So he reckoned in the spring of 1942 that it would try to recover Charkov any day. The earnest differences of opinion between Bock and Hitler were further complicated by the termination plan for doing away with the summer offensive threatening either side of Charkov. While the field marshal wanted to iron out the Isium bulge in the area southwest of the Donetz, Hitler demanded an attack from the north by the 6th Army. While Bock wanted to attack the enemy breaking through northwest of Charkov using the favourable weather, Hitler made the beginning of this attack dependent upon the recapture of the Kerch Peninsula. These differences were also known to our army staff. I heard about them from Voelter.

An opportunity for getting rid of the out-of-favour field marshal soon arose. On the 7th July Army Group 'South' was split into Army Groups 'A' and 'B'. The command of Army Group 'A' was taken by Field Marshal List, that of Army Group 'B' by Colonel-General von Weichs. Field Marshal von Bock received no new command and was retired.

The summer offensive begins

At the end of June 1942 Army Group 'South', consisting of the 17th Army, the 1st Panzer Army, the 6th Army, the 4th Panzer Army, the 2nd Army, the 2nd Hungarian Army and an Italian corps, was ready to attack along a front of 8,000 kilometres and 'D'-Day was fixed. The army's headquarters were established in a former students' hostel on the northern edge of Charkov. Paulus wanted to conduct the breach of the Red Army from this handsome building. The army's signals regiment had orders to follow the progress of the XXXXth Tank Corps.

Grouped into Army Group 'Weichs', the 2nd Army, 4th Panzer Army and the 2nd Hungarian Army went into the attack on Voronesh on the 18th June, the XXXXth Tank Corps thrusting forward simultaneously.

Unexpected and fierce enemy resistance was encountered between Voltshansk and Neshogel, where numerous tanks had been dug in to support the bitterly fighting troops. This resistance temporarily delayed the advance of the XXXXth Tank Corps and gained the enemy several valuable hours which he used for redeployment. The 6th Army's 1st Infantry Division attacked on the 1st July after a short but heavy artillery preparation, and on the 3rd July the units of the Red Army were evicted from their bitterly defended positions at Oskol.

Our divisions thrust eastwards in a forced march of 30 to 40 kilometres per day, but the expected success did not materialise. In the first few days we came to realise that we had been fighting against numerically weak but well armed rearguards, their determined defence leading to high losses among our forces. Most of the Soviet troops were able to escape from the threatening destruction.

Already by the second day of the attack the 6th Army headquarters had moved up behind the Soviet troops' former positions. Every evening we waited tensely for the Army Report, which the Ic took from the radio and presented to the commander-in-chief. We were not a little astonished when we heard of our great victory. It was later announced that Army Group 'South' had decisively defeated the opposing enemy army.

The staff of the 6th Army regarded this opening success in a much more sober manner. 'Victory' would have entailed hundreds of thousands of prisoners on this vast front and a battlefield covered in dead and wounded. The reality was completely different. Only at Oskol were several thousand prisoners of war brought in. As a rule, reports of numbers of prisoners taken from the divisions were not a source of conversation. Only a few Red Army dead and wounded were found on the battlefield. The enemy were also able to take their heavy weapons and vehicles with them.

The XXXXth Panzer Corps was unable to prevent the weakened enemy from retreating along the Don. The enemy had reached the Don near Korotoiak, and two days later were west of Novaya Kalitva; they were already east of Kantenmirovka. The corps' three divisions were widely spread out from each other, their movement hampered by lack of fuel, so that the enemy was able to escape again and again through the wide gaps and avoid encirclement.

After one of the very hot days of summer I was walking with General Paulus to and fro near the headquarters, enjoying the cool evening air. The commander-in-chief began the conversation: 'You will have already noticed that the set goal of destroying the enemy has not been achieved. Our attack was just a thrust into empty space. I presume that the most difficult task still lies ahead of us. Also the XXXXth Panzer Corps will hardly be in a position to overtake and surround the enemy in the future. That task can only be achieved if the 4th Panzer Army thrusts into the Don Bend and cooperates with the XXXXth Panzer Corps. But it is still tied up near Voronesh. Despite the most strenuous commitment of Army Group 'Weichs', it has not yet been able to occupy the rest of the town and disrupt the railway line to Stalingrad. Indeed, the chief of staff tells me that Hitler has now decided to draw away the 4th Panzer Army to the southeast. Hopefully he will do this soon.'

Meanwhile the army headquarters were trying to get a quick connection between the infantry divisions and the tank corps. The offensive continued without a break. The weakened enemy remained in flight, and not giving them any time to rest was the task that Paulus had given to the infantry corps. Army headquarters was frequently moved, following immediately behind the divisions so as to keep up pressure on the speed of attack. The army's signals regiment received orders most days to advance the army's main signal cables several dozen kilometres to maintain direct contact. There was also radio connection with the XXXXth Panzer Corps.

Paulus drove daily to the divisions, encouraging the troops to force the pace. They had to get the last out of themselves. They were fighting and marching constantly, and their rest periods at night were only short.

We had already left the Donetz and Oskol behind us. Before us lay the extensive Don Steppe. The July sun burned mercilessly out of an azure blue sky on the dust-covered marching columns. There were no proper roads here, no trees or bushes to give shade, no springs to quench the burning thirst. Wherever the eye looked, one saw only steppe grass and wormwood with legions of ground squirrels in between.

And yet this landscape, so monotonous, had its charm and attractions. I have seldom experienced such beautiful sunsets as we did here. The whole steppe seemed to glow. The air was filled with aromatic scents. There was life in the tall grass; crickets chirped, mice whistled, birds sang their evening songs. Then the night covered everything in deep silence. Only some rifle shots from the night guards broke the silence.

This area was very scantily settled. Villages were almost only to be found in a few stream valleys running from north to south, visible from a distance along low depressions in the ground. They were just about empty. The population had gone off with their herds of cattle as the troops of the Red Army withdrew. The buildings, where they had not been damaged or destroyed by our artillery and our tanks, were in good condition, clean and cared for.

We set up our headquarters in such a village on the wide Don Steppe. The command section worked in a building complex belonging to the school, whose entrances had been blocked by barricades as usual.

Deeper into the big Don Bend
The chief of staff of the 4th Panzer Army landed here in a Fieseler 'Stork'

on the 9th July. Its staff had orders to take over command of the XXXXth Panzer Corps, which was involved in the hard fighting that had developed near Kantenmirovka. The chief of staff formed the advance party. He reported that upon the instructions of the High Command, the 4th Panzer Army was already on the march to the southeast, which entailed crossing the 6th Army's line of attack. If we were not careful, both armies could get mixed up together, which was why it needed the understanding of our staff. This was soon achieved, and the chief of staff of the Panzer army was able to continue his flight to the XXXXth Panzer Corps. This was able to break the Soviet resistance near Kantenmirovka. On the 11th July it reached the Chir near Bokovskaya. On the same day the XXXXth Panzer Corps left the command of the 6th Army and came under the 4th Panzer Army.

On the 13th July the whole 4th Panzer Army received orders to turn south from the Chir to block the retreat to the east of the enemy weakened by the 17th Army and 1st Panzer Army, to form bridgeheads on the left bank of the Don and, finally, to take Rostov, together with the 1st Panzer Army.

I was already with Paulus for the briefing. He had heard of these measures shortly before. Excitedly he paced to and fro in the low room. 'The advantage that the XXXXth Panzer Corps has achieved has gone. We are still several days' march from the Chir. In this situation turning the panzer corps to the south means that the terrain has to be fought for all over again.'

'We are expected to carry a load that previously four armies would have been allocated, General!'

'Unfortunately that is so. The 6th Army alone is obliged to conduct the attack on the big Don Bend and at the same time to take over the protection of the northern flank which will become longer day by day.'

'I have heard from Voelter that the 2nd Hungarian Army will take on part of the task,' I replied.

'Correct, Adam. But until now the majority of the Hungarians are in the area south of Voronesh, where they fought in Army Group 'Weichs'. It will take a while for the Hungarian divisions to leave their positions and be able to replace our divisions on the Don.'

'Are we really going to conduct the attack on Stalingrad without tanks, General?'

'According to a previous briefing by the army group we will get a panzer corps again, apparently the XIVth. Hopefully, straight away.'

Even a great optimist could not have been confident in the 6th Army's prospects.

On the 20th July we crossed the Upper Chir near Bokovskaya, the place that nine days previously had been occupied by the XXXXth Panzer Corps. Two assault groups were formed for the further thrust into the Don Bend, the northern one from the XIVth Panzer Corps (which had been attached to us in the interim), together with the VIIIth Corps, and the southernmost by the LIst Corps. The divisions intended to protect the northern flank were placed under the XVIIth Corps.

The spearhead of the 6th Army was now the XIVth Panzer Corps. On the 23rd July its divisions forced their way into the big Don Bend south of Kremenskaya. Within a short time the Don was reached near Sirotinskaya. But yet again this was a blow into empty space. The enemy had escaped over the Don.

Replacements and supplies give concern

Although we had sustained no unusually high casualties since the beginning of the offensive, the fighting strength of the infantry was greatly reduced. On average the infantry companies had a fighting strength of only sixty men. Many of our men were ill as a result of uninterrupted marches that demanded all their strength to extremes. With this came circulatory problems, stomach and bowel sicknesses, caused by the unaccustomed steppe climate with its constant big swings in temperature. By day the quicksilver columns of the thermometers rose to 40 degrees, falling at night to 10 degrees. There was no protective cover for most. Erecting tents for the short rests at night was not worthwhile, but the casualties from the difficult conditions considerably exceeded the fighting casualties.

Understandably my concerns as the Army's 1st Adjutant increased. Who would bring up the replacements to close the gaps? I telephoned the adjutant of the army group. Some weak marching companies were established from soldiers who had been released from the field hospitals as recovered and fit for the front. But what were a few hundred replacements when we needed several thousand?

I briefed General Paulus on the personnel situation at the evening conference. 'According to army group the army should receive some marching companies in the next few days. Further replacements are temporarily not available. We have now advanced fighting for about 400 kilometres. Several companies have lost a third of their original fighting strength. Will the army be relieved by a second batch, or will army group send us fresh divisions from the reserve?'

Paulus's mouth formed a bitter smile. 'If the offensive reaches a certain sector, the pace of the second batch of the reserve will speed up. That is what we learnt as tactical instructors at the War School, did we not? I too know nothing else. But I must tell you that neither the one nor the other is available. In the Führer Headquarters one believes it possible to throw proven basic rules of strategy and tactics to the winds. The Highest Command lets itself all too often be led by political and defence economic goals, and then believes them capable of achievement by our undoubtedly excellent and experienced troops. But everything has its limits. Our army is overstretched, fought out and seriously weakened should it come to decisive fighting. At the beginning of the attacks the army group had two German infantry divisions in reserve. The Allies following us up should be relieving our divisions on the northern flank, but their fighting strength is only half that of our own, nor are they suitable for the attack. We will have to carry the burden of the fighting for the Volga city on our own.'

'How will this continue, then? Our panzer corps on the Don is already 150 kilometres ahead of the infantry divisions. That is why we have to strike for the bridges as soon as possible. Apart from that, the front that we have to secure to the north will become even longer. There are not half a dozen divisions remaining for a further attack.'

'Tomorrow the XXIVth Panzer Corps, which previously belonged to the 4th Panzer Army, joins us. It will reinforce the right-hand attacking group of the LIst Corps. But what is that? To fill a hole one digs up another spot.'

Paulus's critical intellect as a general staff officer could not escape from Hitler's weaknesses, mediocrity and fantasies in the conduct of warfare. This gave him concerns that nagged at him. But he was an outright soldier, believing in his knowledge and trust in his divisions, hoping to be able to compensate for the failures and faulty planning of the High Command.

I went back to my tent to work on some recommendations for the Knight's Cross and the German Cross in Gold. But I could not get the conversation with Paulus out of my head. If he could only keep his health, for he did not look well. He stood pensively in front of the map, which was made of strong paper and hung next to his desk. I thought about it.

The Red Army was making its way even further eastwards. We were becoming further and further distant from our supply bases, ever more unfavourably for the fighting requirements of our divisions. There were no proper roads and only one single-track railway. Resupply was becoming increasingly difficult. A strong cloudburst, such as we experienced more than once since the attack began, was sufficient to leave the heavily laden trucks stuck in the mud.

The army's transport ability hardly sufficed to bring up the required items such as ammunition, fuel, food, etc., over these wide expanses to the fighting troops. If the fuel supplies failed, the attack could often be delayed for days. The chief of staff raged, but the senior quartermaster responsible was powerless. The fuel convoys we had ordered were repeatedly diverted south to Army Group 'A', shortly before reaching their intended destination. Protests by the senior quartermaster, even by the army's commander-in-chief, were not taken into consideration.

I was summoned by Paulus. His quarters consisted of a porch, a large room and a smaller room. He worked in the larger room. A simple right-angled table served as his desk. There was a chair on one of the long sides. A blackboard had been set up behind Paulus's working space and on it was pinned the situation map. The commander-in-chief's personal orderly officer was responsible for keeping the map up to date. Paulus was standing in front of the map when I entered the room. 'The army group's chief of staff, General of Infantry von Sodenstern, rang me a few minutes ago. Colonel-General von Weichs will be taking off in about half an hour. He will be visiting us. The chief of staff has already ordered a cross to be marked out on our landing field. You will collect the Colonel-General in my car from there. Drive off straight away and check that all is in order at the landing field. My driver is on his way to your tent.'

The auxiliary landing strip, in the area best protected on the steppe, was not far from the village in which the army headquarters were located. On the edge of it stood a *Ju 52*, some courier machines and some 'Storks' that were used by headquarters. I waited with the commander of our air staff near the edge of the landing strip, which was marked out with white cloths. The machine soon appeared, flying very low. It crossed the air strip and came in to land. Out stepped a large, gaunt general wearing horn-rimmed glasses, who looked more of a scholar than an officer. I reported myself as the 6th Army's 1st Adjutant. Although we had never met each other before, he greeted me like an old acquaintance, nodded at the others standing around and climbed into the waiting vehicle.

At headquarters he had a long conversation with Paulus and Schmidt. Later I heard from our army commander-in-chief that it was about the difficult situation that the 6th Army was in, since the withdrawal of the 4th Panzer Army. The colonel-general showed understanding and said that he would provide any possible support from his side. Paulus said: 'Of course he cannot give us new divisions. He will, however, take care to ensure that our units that are deployed on the Don to protect our northern flank are replaced by the following Allied armies as soon as possible. The headquarters of the XVIIth Corps are to remain there.'

'Then we will be lacking a corps headquarters. The VIIIth Corps headquarters cannot possibly command all the infantry divisions of our northern group,' I ventured to say.

'The withdrawing headquarters will be replaced by XIth Corps headquarters. The commanding general is General of Infantry Strecker,' Paulus added. 'I know Strecker very well, he previously had the 79th Infantry Division that supported us near Charkov. He is a man that we can leave things to.'

The disastrous Order no. 45
The tasks of Army Groups 'A' and 'B' were set out in Order no. 45. Upon what assumptions were the Army High Command and Wehrmacht Headquarters operating? In the first section of the order it said: 'Only the weakest enemy forces of Timoshenko's army have been tasked with

completing the encirclement and reaching the southern bank of the Don.' This was obviously a completely false interpretation of the results of the summer offensive. Few prisoners taken, almost empty battlefields, and only a few dead – these were the actual facts that Order no. 45's assessment clearly contradicted.

Then the goals of the further operations were set out. Army Group 'A' was to go with part of its forces into the western Caucasus and thrust along the Black Sea coast, take the Maikop and Grosny oilfields, block the pass routes over the central Caucasus and finally advance to Baku. The Order went on: 'To Army Group 'B', as already ordered, falls the task, after building up the Don defences in the thrust on Stalingrad, of defeating the enemy forces being built up there, of occupying the city itself and of blocking the peninsula between the Don and the Volga. . . . In connection with this, fast units are to be deployed along the Volga with the task of thrusting towards Astrakhan and similarly blocking the main arm of the Volga there.'

While Order no. 41 had foreseen that the forces of both army groups would reach Stalingrad and then conduct the further operation, Order no. 45 demanded the simultaneous fulfilment of all these tasks: that is, the extension of the front from 800 kilometres at the beginning of the summer offensive to 4,100 kilometres at the completion of the planned operation. This inevitably meant that the striking forces of both army groups would be split, although our already recorded losses had in no way been sufficiently replaced to meet such an extensive task.

This instruction altered nothing of the 6th Army's task, after the withdrawal of the 4th Panzer Army, of occupying the big Don Bend to the south, which was our next goal.

Scientific work in a steppe village
Yet again we had moved our headquarters forward. While my section followed with the vehicles, I myself was flown ahead in a Fieseler 'Stork'. We soon reached our destination. Below us lay one of the usual spread-out steppe villages of small, single-storey wooden houses with flowery front gardens and fenced-in yards along a wide, dusty main street. At the landing ground I was awaited by the army headquarters commandant. He gave me some brief information about the village and drew my attention to a low, sturdy brick building, which stood out. He wanted me to follow him there. 'Do you want me to accommodate my section here?'

He shook his head. 'No, I want to show you something. Let's go in.' Through the open door I saw a laboratory. On the tables stood tripods, bottles and beakers, test tubes and microscopes. In a white glass cupboard lay pincers, syringes and scalpels. My further glance around fell on glass containers that apparently contained chemicals, and various bottles filled with liquids. Finally I discovered a swarm of white mice and guinea-pigs. How did this laboratory come to be in this steppe village? What role did it play? Our commandant did not know either.

On the way to the headquarters accommodation we met the 1st general staff officer. I told him of our discovery. He too could make no sense out of it, and wanted to task the chief interpreter to solve the mystery. The latter discovered from an old man that the inhabitants of this village were involved in the forefront of cattle breeding. The state had built the laboratory for them. It was directed by a veterinary surgeon who, together with her female assistants, had taken the cattle to safety away from the village when the German troops approached. In the days to follow I went past this small veterinary-medical research laboratory several times. Always one of the old remaining villagers was around. Apparently a kind of guard had been organised, a sign of the value the farmers placed on this establishment.

But we now had time to think about how Communism apparently had a good side to it! The next days gave us a Communist surprise of another kind.

A bad atmosphere at Kamenski
On the 25th July several staff officers were sitting down after eating together. The chief of staff had already gone off to his quarters. Then a signaller appeared with a radio message, which the Ia officer took. This produced a 'Donnerwetter' from between his teeth, before he jumped up and hurried after the chief of staff. What was up?

The XIVth Panzer Corps had come up against strong enemy units in a further thrust towards the Don southwest of Kamenski. A bitter battle had been raging for hours, but the enemy was not giving way. That evening the XXIVth Panzer Corps, which had recently joined the army, reported the same. It was supposed to support our LIst Corps blocking the way to the Lower Chir. In doing so it had come up against a strong enemy defensive front near Nishne-Chirskaya. The infantry divisions reported enemy resistance west of the Liska Stream. Once the various reports had been entered on the situation map, it was obvious that the Red Army west of Kalatch had established itself in a wide bridgehead stretching from Kamenski to the mouth of the Chir.

Our corps had tried to break through the Soviet defensive front on the move and to throw the Red Army back over the Don. But they were biting on granite. And not only that. The Soviet divisions identified weak positions on our side and went into a counterattack on the 31st July, throwing back our already badly decimated divisions over the Liska Stream.

For several days there had been a bad atmosphere in the 6th Army. The enemy, moreover, was able to get some large units across the Don to the south near Kremenskaya and place them in the rear of the XIVth Panzer Corps, which had to turn several regiments to the north to counter this move.

The XIVth Panzer Corps now stood widely dispersed along the Don north of Kamenski. Those infantry divisions of the 6th Army west of Kletskaya, which had been relieved by the slowly following Italian 8th Army, could now be released. The VIIIth Corps closed the Soviet bridgehead from the northwest with its divisions, having contact with the LIst Corps on its right wing. The southern end of the Lower Chir was blocked by the XXIVth Panzer Corps. In this setting the 6th Army repulsed the enemy attacks and simultaneously prepared to smash the Soviet bastion.

By the end of July and the beginning of August the Italian 8th Army was so far advanced that it could relieve the 6th Army's divisions deployed west of Kletskaya to protect the northern flank. Some of the XIVth Panzer Corps' regiments deployed in a security role were relieved by infantry divisions from the XIth Corps. These drove the enemy back and formed a defensive position.

High-ranking visitors
While preparations for the attack were being made, the 6th Army headquarters received various high-ranking visitors at its location in the steppe village. The most interesting one for me was an encounter with the Wehrmacht's communications general, Fellgiebel. I got to know him through our army's chief of signals, Colonel Arnold. That evening the three of us walked to and fro along the village street. The general started speaking about the war situation. His appraisal was somewhat sceptical, almost pessimistic. We too had many concerns, but they mainly arose out of our own situation, from this or that episode in our army's area, perhaps too about the Eastern Front. Fellgiebel, though, had doubts about the whole war. 'In the West our troops stand widely separated from the North Cape to the Pyrenees. Rommel is fighting in North Africa. In Yugoslavia and Greece our divisions are conducting an exhausting little war against partisans. And what happened last year in front of Moscow you know for yourselves. Hopefully all goes well for your army. I can understand Paulus's concern about the long-stretched northern flank. If only we had not undertaken this offensive.'

Several times I cast a glance at Arnold. Like him, I closely followed the words of the signals general, who continued in the same quiet voice: 'Germany now has a two-front war. We three were there already in 1914 to 1918 and know from our own experience how we were bled dry then. Have the circumstances improved since 1918? I would strongly doubt it.'

I listened attentively. There was a hardly concealed mistrust in the war planning of the High Command, a criticism of Hitler, disbelief in final victory. Could Fellgiebel be disagreeing with Hitler's conduct of the war? He was speaking against the two-front war. What alternative could there be? The general turned towards me: 'How high have the losses been up to now?'

'The losses from enemy action have been within reasonable boundaries. In contrast, the numbers of sick have been very high, because of the climatic conditions with which we are so unfamiliar. The fighting strengths of the infantry companies are frequently reduced to a third or less, and the hardest fighting is yet to come.'

With 'That is no happy prospect', the general ended the discussion.

It was a lovely summer evening. In the distance a sheet of lightning flashed against the darkening sky. I breathed in the refreshing evening air. Suddenly I shivered. I then realised that I was still wearing a thin summer jacket. I quickly went to my tent. My batman had already laid out my bed and blacked-out the small window. I switched on the electric light, powered by a generator, and sat down at my desk. But I was not thinking of working. The general's words were more powerful. They sank in, forcing my thoughts along their track. Actually, Fellgiebel had only said what anyone would have said after sober reflection.

General Fellgiebel flew off again the next day. None of us suspected that he would have a role to play in the conspiracy against Hitler on the 20th June 1944. Perhaps he had been looking for fellow conspirators among our staff and found no resonance. But we still had to go through much horror and bitterness in order to get correctly to the bottom of the military situation, not to mention the human and political crimes of this war. At that time our heads were filled with the preparations for the attack on the Soviet bridgehead west of Kalatch. General Paulus had hardly any time free to devote to his friend Fellgiebel. If he was not absolutely committed at army headquarters, he was driving out to the divisions and regiments. He was trying to build up a personal picture of the situation and the mood of the soldiers at the front in order to improve their lives as much as possible. He mainly returned apparently silent. He was very depressed with the growing losses of troops that were already occurring even before the decisive battle.

The forthcoming operation, the endangered northern flank of the 6th Army, and the sinking fighting strength of the companies were the main themes for his discussions with Major-General Schmundt, Hitler's chief adjutant, who landed in his Fieseler 'Stork' on our provisional landing ground. Paulus and Schmidt included me in the discussions at times. I reported plainly about the worsening personnel situation. Schmundt should also have an immediate impression of the front-line sectors that the 6th Army was preparing with the greatest concern. Therefore Paulus drove with the chief adjutant to the divisions on the northern bank of the Don, east of Kletskaya. Here it had not been possible to throw the enemy back across the Don. Our divisions had only occupied an observation position there in order to conserve their strength.

At the headquarters of Infantry Regiment 767, 376th Infantry Division, the commander, Colonel Steidle, described the situation. On its left wing the regiment had contact with the Italian 8th Army, which had just occupied its positions. Steidle was one of our best commanders, personally brave, circumspect and esteemed by his soldiers. Paulus had known him since the First World War, and was aware that the colonel also had no inhibitions in dealing with his superiors. Steidle was also not embarrassed, despite the presence of the adjutant from Führer Headquarters, to criticise the dangerous situation on the northern flank into which the 6th Army would be manoeuvred. The division's losses in the last days had increased once more. Most companies now had only twenty-five to thirty-five men carrying arms. Paulus told me later that Steidle had forcefully demanded reinforcements.

While Major-General Schmundt was still with us, the Luftwaffe reported that the enemy were bringing reinforcements across the Don near Kalatch, especially tanks. This was yet another argument to demonstrate to Hitler's adjutant the necessity of bringing forward reinforcements as soon as possible. Laden with the burning demands of the 6th Army, Schmundt flew on to the army group and from there back to Führer Headquarters. Paulus brought him personally to our air strip and, while saying farewell, again asked him to obtain an effective securing of the northern flank from the Army High Command.

Another prominent visitor at this time was General Oschner, chief of the smokescreen troops. A smokescreen mortar brigade was to be attached to the army for the attack on Stalingrad. These mortars had seldom been used by the Army High Command. I had got to know them for the first time in the attack on Velikiye Luki. Their rounds raced with long fire trails and unbearable howling through the air. Even our infantry, who had been told about them shortly before by the mortar company commander, anxiously ducked their heads as the rocket-like rounds flew over their positions. The effect on the surprised enemy's morale was enormous. Even after the town had been taken, many of the Soviet soldiers remained as if paralysed.

General Oschner was only with us for a short while, one or two days. He discussed the tactical use of these weapons with the chief of staff. Upon his leaving, Paulus said to him: 'Hopefully this does not turn out to be an empty promise. You have seen how relentless the fighting has become here. The enemy no longer gives way under our pressure. He defends himself obstinately and hits back whenever he can. We definitely need the horrors of your mortar brigade.'

Oschner departed with the words: 'You can be assured that I will not leave you in the dirt.'

That was generally how we dealt with our visitors. Each time it cost us considerable time and strength to inform the generals. The superior establishments had now material and knowledge enough to confirm our alarming reports. Our 1st general staff officer, Colonel Voelter, said:

'Schmundt was apparently impressed when we returned from the drive to the front. What he had seen with his own eyes and heard on the spot had shocked him somewhat. Hopefully he will not hold back the truth from the Führer, so that at last the talk about the destruction of the Red Army will end and the enemy will be taken seriously.'

'As I see it,' I said, 'above all General Fellgiebel saw it clearly. In the discussion that Arnold and I had with him, he pointed out the whole situation on the war fronts more earnestly and soberly than I could have done myself until now. How General Oschner is involved, I do not know, as I only exchanged a few words with him. One can only wish that at last the truth will reach the High Command.'

The armies of the Allies
As already mentioned, the 6th Army was to screen the northern flank of the Panzer armies thrusting forward to the Volga. Order no. 41 of the 23rd June 1942 gave it the new task of taking Stalingrad in cooperation with the 4th Panzer Army. As flank protection in the area from Kletskaya to north of Korotoiak, the Allied armies were deployed in order from the west: the Hungarian 2nd Army, the Italian 8th Army and the Rumanian 3rd Army.

What did we want from the Allied armies? We knew that they had been formed into independent army formations shortly before the 1942 summer offensive had begun. Only a small part of the newly formed armies in the rear area of Army Group 'South' (with effect from the 7th July 1942 Army Group 'B') had combat experience. Equipment and weapons were in short supply. In view of this, the Rumanians and Hungarians were advised completely, the Italians partly, to turn to the German armaments industry.

How does it help if, when push comes to shove, the northern flank has the strongest anti-tank weapons and the Allied armies are totally lacking in heavy tank-busting weapons and heavy artillery? For example, the Rumanian tank division was equipped only with captured light Czech and French tanks. In comparison to the German divisions, the fighting strength of our Allies amounted to only 50 or 60 per cent. Clearly, in view of their insufficient armament and equipment, these armies could never withstand an attack by an enemy equipped with T-34 tanks.

But this applied not only to their weapons; it applied even more to the soldiers using them. Rumanian divisions since 1941 had proved successful in the aggressive fighting in the southern sector. The soldiers were brave, disciplined and unassuming, being mostly farmers. As long as they were still fighting near their home boundaries, the war had had some sense for them. Then one or another had been tempted by the soil in Bessarabia, or in the territory between the Dnestr and the Bug, which Hitler had promised to Marshal Antonescu as 'Transnistrien'. Perhaps one could be a free farmer there. This was not possible in the old Rumania of the great landowners.

But what was the Rumanian farmer-soldier doing between the Don and the Volga? Then there were the unbelievable conditions in the Rumanian army, such as corporal punishment. My friend Otto Ruhle told me that he himself had once seen a Rumanian soldier beaten and mistreated by an officer. Such things did not raise the fighting morale of the Rumanians, and this showed particularly when the going was hard.

General Paulus regarded the Rumanians highly, and also had confidence in the Hungarians. But he had fought against the Italians in the First World War, and knew them too from an inspection that he had carried out as senior quartermaster of the army headquarters in North Africa. He took it as being especially necessary to place them within the strong corsets of German divisions. The fighting morale of the Italians was certainly influenced by their living even further away from the Soviet Union than the Rumanians and Hungarians. If it was 1,500 kilometres from Bucharest to the Volga, and 1,900 from Budapest, the Romans and Milanese were fighting almost 3,000 kilometres from their homeland. Fighting for what? For Greater Germany? It was quite understandable that they should have little liking for it.

The ways and means adopted by the German High Command to deal with the weaknesses of their Allies only strengthened their mistrust. As already said, our Allies were almost totally dependent upon Germany for their heavy weapons and a large part of their equipment. In fact, they received little enough. Therefore it was firmly stated in Order no. 41: 'For occupying the more and more extending Don Front in the course of this operation, the Allies' units will be in the first line to be called upon, with the stipulation that German troops are to be inserted as strong supports between the Orel and the Don as well as the Stalingrad isthmus, the rest of the individual German divisions remaining available as front attack reserves.'

All this contributed to the Allies slowly taking up their sectors. The Hungarian 2nd Army, which had carried out the attack on Voronesh, took over the securing of Donau as far as Novaya Kalitva in conjunction with the German 2nd Army.

At the end of July and the beginning of August the Italian 8th Army replaced those infantry divisions of the 6th Army in the area from Bogutshar to Kletskaya that were urgently needed for the attack on the Kalatch bridgehead. The German XVIIIth Corps came under the Italian 8th Army.

The Rumanian 3rd Army was now on its way, the Italian troops temporarily having to take over the area allocated to them. Widely separated from each other, the inadequately armed and ill-equipped Allies now stood on the Don. There were insufficient forces to construct a continuous position. This was no defensive front, rather only a thin security line. This could not remain concealed from the very active enemy. No wonder that the army headquarters looked anxiously to the north. 'Should the Russians take advantage of the weakness in our deep flank, we will be in a more than unpleasant situation, Adam. Look at how the front runs! It is like a clenched fist.'

'Really devilishly unpleasant, General. The enemy only now needs to apply the scalpel to the wrist and the fist is off.'

'Let's hope that Schmundt is presenting a true picture of the situation at Führer Headquarters. We told him clearly enough. Let us hope further that our Allies get the heavy weapons they lack.'

The coming weeks would bring us the most bitter disappointment for all our hopes.

The battle at Kalatch
For days the Luftwaffe had been reporting that the Russians were reinforcing their bridgehead west of Kalatch. The effects were next detected by the LIst Corps. Its regiments got a bloody nose when they attacked the Soviet bridgehead east of Surovkino. Meanwhile, however, some of our divisions had been replaced by the Italian 8th Army and moved into their temporary areas. Infantry divisions took over the northern bank of the Don from Ostrovski to Kletskaya in the sector occupied by the XIVth Panzer Corps, enabling the panzers to move into the attack north of Kamenski.

During the first days of August the 76th and 295th Infantry Divisions, which had come under the 17th Army until then, were brought forward to reinforce the 6th Army's right flank. On the 6th August the preparations for the big blow against the Soviet bastion were completed. Our units had taken up their launching positions and were supplied with sufficient ammunition and fuel. According to the reports, lying before us on the enemy side were twelve rifle divisions and five tank brigades. Their line of retreat across the Don had to be blocked. They were to be surrounded and destroyed. The operational plan allocated both panzer corps the task of erecting a barrier on the Don. The XIVth Panzer Corps had to thrust forward from the Kamenski area to the Don, the XXIVth Panzer Corps from the Nishne-Chirskaya area to the Don.

Early on the 7th August the earth groaned under the weight of the tanks rattling forward. The morning silence was suddenly broken by the exploding of shells and torn by the whipping of the belts of machine-gun fire. Our tanks were able to break through the Soviet defensive positions. The spearheads of the two attacking corps met within a few hours. Then, however, the real fighting began. Our attacking infantry divisions struck a skilful and bitterly resilient enemy, who had immediately recognised the threatening danger from the German tanks and, fighting with their backs to the Don, counterattacked the panzer corps. The latter fired whatever was in their gun barrels. Nevertheless, elements of the Red Army were able to cross over to the east bank of the Don. After four days of hard fighting, the battle was over. A great German victory was proclaimed with blasts of fanfares. It did not mention that we had had to pay a high cost in men and materiel. Certainly the enemy losses were still larger, but left on the Kalatch battlefield were numerous burnt-out or shot-up German tanks, and this was especially bad news for us, for our homeland was more than 2,000 kilometres away, making it difficult to bring up replacements. Above all, the Red Army won valuable time for the construction of a new defensive front between the Volga and the Don on the approach to Stalingrad. It was able to stop the 4th Panzer Army, which had already come out of the Zimlianskaya area through the Kalmuck Steppe to Stalingrad-South on the 1st August. In order to improve its penetrating strength, the 6th Army had to give up the 24th Panzer Division and the 297th Infantry Division to the 4th Panzer Army on the instructions of the Army High Command. Both these divisions crossed the Don on a military bridge near Potemkinskaya.

To make best use of the success achieved at Kalatch the 6th Army should have immediately continued the attack over the Don. But it was not in a position to do so. Again valuable time was lost. The units had to be reorganised, the lost weapons and equipment replaced, ammunition and fuel replenished.

Growing losses and sinking morale

I saw the casualty reports that had been prepared in writing by the divisions. I went myself to those that had suffered the most. Among them was the 376th Infantry Division, commanded by Lieutenant-General Edler von Daniels. At the conclusion of the fighting it stood together with the 384th and 44th Infantry Divisions in the Don Bend east of Kletskaya. The three divisions had had the task of throwing the Red Army back over the river. This goal was achieved, but subsequently several Soviet units were able to cross back over the Don at various points and establish bridgeheads.

In this fighting too our troops had to suffer a heavy toll. Consequently many companies of the 376th Infantry Division had a fighting strength of only twenty-five men. Things were a little better in the 44th and 384th Infantry Divisions, but companies with fighting strengths of between thirty-five and forty men gave no cause for optimism.

As the 6th Army approached the Volga, the streams flowed with German blood. The cheap successes of the Western Campaign were long since past. Gone too was the carefree military atmosphere of the summer of 1941, and the months of May and June 1942. In my journeys in my cross-country jeep I kept coming across stragglers looking for their units after some hard fighting. I especially remember two soldiers who had taken part in the battle near Kalatch. They belonged to a division that I was looking for. I took them with me. Still full of fresh impressions of the battle they had experienced, the corporal sitting behind me recounted: 'I had never smoked so much since I had been in the East. Ivan gave us such a blistering that one could lose one's hearing and eyesight. Fortunately we had dug ourselves in deeply or nothing would have remained of us. All watch out for the Russian artillery, which operates en masse. Their hits detonated only a hair's breadth from our position. One could only pull in one's head and stick it in the dirt. Many of us were wiped out. We cursed the '*Stalin Organs*' most of all. Where they landed it was too late for most to make their wills.'

His comrade, who, I learnt in the course of the conversation, had been deprived of his *Arbitur* (school certificate) by being called up, added: 'And how their infantry attacked! Their "*Urrah!*" would soon have driven me mad. Only their guts and indifference to death brings them on. Is it really only the commissars that make them do it, standing behind them with a pistol? I have the hollow feeling that there are things about the Russians that we know nothing about.'

The corporal went one step further than his comrade. He turned directly to me: 'Three weeks ago our company commander told us that the Red Army was completely wiped out, that soon we would be able to relax in Stalingrad. That doesn't seem to be happening. On the 31st July they annoyed us more than a bit. Only at the last minute were our artillery and anti-tank guns able to stop the Russian counterattack.'

'Will this not end soon, Colonel, sir?' asked the young soldier. It was noticeable that the course of the war was important to him. Perhaps only six months ago he had been singing at school 'Today Germany belongs to us, tomorrow the whole world.' This exuberance had flown away for the moment.

Both of them awaited a response from me. I turned round to them: 'I am no prophet, therefore cannot prophesy, but the war will not come to an end so soon. You have yourselves sensed that the Russians are now hitting back. Now we first have to take Stalingrad, and then we will be able to see further ahead. How is the mood in your company?'

'What can one say, Colonel, sir?' said the corporal. 'You will not be angry with me if I speak openly? The war has already gone on too long, our older ones are longing to get back home. The letters coming from there are discouraging too. The wife of a farmer who had had a lot of trouble with a prisoner of war wrote that she no longer knew what to do to get the work done properly. In the towns, especially among the workers' families, food is getting ever shorter. The women no longer know what to do to fill the hungry stomachs of their children. That depresses the spirits. The high losses are also not without effect. When we marched across the battlefield on the 11th August and saw the many dead and wounded, my mate said so that everyone could hear him: "We will all perish on this damned, uncomfortable steppe." He is a good and brave soldier. He got the Iron Cross First Class already last autumn.'

I was thinking over what I had just heard when the vehicle stopped. We had reached the divisional headquarters. With a 'Thank you' and a smart salute, the two soldiers excused themselves.

So that was how it was in their company. The older ones longed for home and the younger ones had already had enough. Was it the same in the other companies?

Once I had obtained a personal picture of the fighting strengths of the divisions, I reported to the chief of staff. Major-General Schmidt was not surprised. He knew how hard the fighting had been in the last days. He gave his opinion: 'The question of replacements is a burning one. Take all possible steps immediately with the subordinate commands! But report to General Paulus first. He has been going round the divisions all day and can surely give you further instructions.'

Paulus received me with the words: 'Now, Adam, how is it with the divisions?'

'I now have an apparently clear idea. It is pleasing that many of those taken to be missing have found their way back to their units. Also a number of the lightly wounded have been sent back to their units after brief treatment by the first aid posts. But what significance does this have when the fighting strength of the companies is down to about thirty or forty men. We have paid a high price for our success. The hard fighting and the heavy losses are getting on the soldiers' nerves. There is widespread depression. I share Major-General Schmidt's view that the subordinate commands must receive replacements as soon as possible.'

'I agree with your assessment and proposed measures completely. All the commanders that I have spoken to in the last few days regard replacements as the most important issue. The Russian bridgehead near Kalatch was a hard nut for us to crack. Our divisions must be filled immediately. Use the teleprinter and state the demands!'

While I was talking to Paulus, my deputy had been putting together the replacement requests, but the teleprinter to the Commands back home had been removed. That night I spoke by telephone with the adjutant of Army Group 'B', who promised his support.

The next day the deputy Commands at Kassel, Wiesbaden, Hannover, Vienna and Berlin gave almost the same replies. Trained replacements were unavailable; recovered wounded declared fit for service by the doctors would be despatched as soon as possible.

Paulus was as surprised by this reply as I was. We knew that Germany had no great manpower reserves after the third year of the war, but in the end the 6th Army should have sufficient forces to engage in the main operational goal of 1942.

We could expect only a few marching companies from Army Group 'B'. We were grateful for this in view of the impending attack across the Don.

Every additional soldier added to the weight, especially if he had combat experience. But we needed more than a few marching companies. The big city on the Volga had to be taken. Street and house-to-house fighting awaited us, which we knew from previous experience demanded heavy casualties. Were our already badly decimated divisions in a position to cope?

Paulus looked at me: 'What do you propose?'

'Permit me, General, to fly to Führer Headquarters at Vinniza. I consider it necessary to report personally to the head of the organisational section about the 6th Army's personnel situation.'

'Agreed, fly there very early in the morning. You can then be back before dark.'

'I will use the opportunity to speak to the Personnel Office about officer replacements.'

Returning to my tent, I packed my papers for the talks in Vinniza. Equipped with the latest lists of fighting strengths and officers' posts, I went early next day, shortly after sunrise, to the western exit of Ossinovka village where we had established our headquarters. Under the cover of some trees and bushes, camouflaged from the air, stood the army staff's courier aircraft. One of them would take me to Charkov. It was already ready to leave. I had hardly climbed aboard when the engine started up. A few minutes later the machine was racing down the steppe track and rose from the ground. We flew at a low height. The rising sun was still low in the eastern sky, shedding its light on the endless steppe. The drops of dew on the arid grass glittered like pearls and diamonds. It was a wonderful sight. But there was something rather sinister about it. The wonderful flying weather was not quite without its dangers. It offered enemy fighters several advantages, with clear sight and the sun behind. Things could go badly for us in an attack. The pilot could not fail to notice my careful look to the East. But he grinned: 'Don't worry, Colonel. When our fighters are in the air no Russian '*Yak*' dare be around. Do you see those sparkling points over towards the sun? They are ours. They will dive down on the enemy like birds of prey should he dare appear.'

We flew over the route that the army had taken in the last few weeks, but in the opposite direction. Only seldom was a village to be seen. For long stretches we flew over the main road on which convoys laden with supplies were streaming eastwards. The escort teams waved at us. Here and there in the seemingly unending steppe appeared destroyed tanks, guns or abandoned trucks. The trench systems that only shortly before had been occupied by Germans and Russians were clearly seen. Often my eyes fell on the corpse of a fallen Red Army soldier or a horse with its legs grotesquely raised up. Down below thousands of German soldiers and officers had breathed their last, and their loss was the reason for my flight to Vinniza. While their stiff bodies were buried by comrades in foreign soil, no one found the time to care for the dead Soviet soldiers in the same way.

After making an elegant curve, the pilot set the machine down on the runway. Slowly it rolled up to a *Ju 52* standing nearby with its engines running. It was the courier machine to Vinniza. Our army headquarters had radioed through from the steppe village to the airport at Charkov. They were waiting for me. I was aboard within two minutes. Several couriers had already taken their seats. The engines roared and the machine started off. It quickly gained height. The flight to the west offered a richly varied picture. The fruitful fields of the Ukraine stretched to the horizon, criss-crossed by strips of woodland, rivers and streams. The network of settlements was considerably thicker here than in the first stage of my journey. Long, stretched-out villages alternated with smaller and larger towns. Our pilot wanted to maintain a height of about a thousand metres, so we could easily see the transport columns rolling eastwards along the many roads. More conspicuous were the trains steaming towards Charkov, carrying supplies, ammunition, fuel, weapons and equipment. Charkov was the supply centre for Army Group 'B'.

Disappointment at Vinniza
After just two hours we landed without incident at Vinniza. A car took me to the Personnel Office, which was in the town. There I had a long conversation with General von Burgsdorf. The advance to the Don had taken a heavy toll of young infantry officers. But army group was unable to fill the gaps. 'I understand your concern,' said von Burgsdorf, 'but at the moment we can hardly help at all. The other units of Army Groups 'A' and 'B' also have large requirements. We need several hundred company and battalion commanders alone. Training courses have been under way for several weeks, but apparently will not end until December. Until then I can assure you that we have a full understanding of the 6th Army's situation, but currently it would only be possible to support you at best in individual cases.'

'That is poor consolation, General.'

'Consider again what you can do yourselves within the army! Check what suitable NCOs you have to put forward for commissioning! Perhaps other possibilities will offer themselves to compensate for the lack of officers in the infantry. I am thinking of certain young army officials in the rear services. Incidentally, what does it look like with the youngsters in the artillery and the signals detachment?'

'At the moment I have no sufficient overview. But a short while ago the commander of the army's signals regiment was complaining to me about his potential officers having no chance of promotion. Once I am back I will have all the signals and artillery units report their potential officer candidates, but not many will stand out.'

Once I had spoken to the section commanders for panzer and engineer officers, I went to see the head of the organisational section, Colonel Müller-Hillebrand. This section was also in the town, not far from the Personnel Office. Hopefully I would have a bit more luck here. I entered the building with these thoughts. Like everywhere in the Führer Headquarters, all passers-by were carefully checked. The duty officer read my pass through at least twice, checking the seal and signature, looking from me to the photograph. Then I was reported to the section leader. 'You are coming to me about replacement questions. I know your urgent requirements.' Müller-Hillebrand greeted me with these words.

I said that he had presumed correctly and placed the latest documents that I had brought with me before him. I described our predicament in detail. 'Before flying here, I contacted the Deputy Commands. All replied that worthwhile replacements are not available at the moment. I want to say frankly that we at 6th Army Headquarters have the impression that the homeland departments are underestimating the difficulty of the task facing us. How can we take a big city of about 300 square kilometres with companies of a fighting strength of thirty to forty men? After our last experience in the big Don Bend we can expect the enemy to defend every house, every stone.'

While I was speaking the chief of the organisational department was leafing through my papers. I looked at him expectantly.

'We know how it looks to you, and you can be assured that I would very much like to help you. Unfortunately it is really just as the Deputy Commands at home have said. The newly called-up replacements will not complete their training until the end of December. Reinforcing the infantry regiments is not possible before January 1943.'

I looked at Müller-Hillebrand in shock. The offensive on Stalingrad was due to begin now, not in January 1943. What would then happen if our units were not even up to half strength? The colonel noticed what was going on inside my head: 'Tell your commander-in-chief that I will do everything I can to help him. In the coming months we can use some soldiers that have been released as healed from the field hospitals. I will ensure that the marching companies assembled from them will go primarily to the 6th Army. I very much regret that I have not the slightest chance of doing more.'

I said farewell. In the whole of the war I had never been so downhearted as now, when I had to take the flight back to headquarters.

I got to the courier machine to Charkov just in time. It was filled to almost the last seat with couriers, specialists, Wehrmacht officials and commanders of units returning from leave or training courses. A seat had been reserved for me immediately behind the pilot's cabin. A lively conversation was going on around me but I hardly heard it. It did not suit me being the deeply defeated person that I had become after the experiences of this day.

Had the Army High Command and Army General Staff really believed that we could advance more than 600 kilometres without suffering considerable losses? Army Group 'B' had not been able to bottle up and destroy the mass of Soviet troops at all. The enemy had been able to withdraw over the Don and would doubtless give us plenty to do in the forthcoming fighting for the big city on the Volga.

What kind of war planning was this that set powerful strategic goals but forgot to prepare the timely commitment of men, weapons and equipment? At every war school it was taught that breaking through a well constructed enemy defensive position demanded considerable casualties from the attacker if it were to succeed. Already in the First World War the Russians had shown themselves masters of defence. Had they forgotten this at Army High Command? Had not immediate measures been introduced when the first heavy casualty reports from our attacking army were presented? Had we not early enough briefed Hitler's chief adjutant, Major-General Schmundt, and Generals Fellgiebel and Oschner on the worsening fighting strengths, advised them urgently enough of the threatening situation that must inevitably arise if there were no reinforcements?

We had received nothing but words, and nothing was done. More than ever the thought tormented me that the enemy was underestimated by the High Command in an irresponsible way. What would happen if further casualties were incurred in the forthcoming fighting. Were there any divisions on our 1,000-kilometre front that could be drawn upon without the front being torn apart?

I had still found no solution when the machine landed at Charkov airfield, where there was lively activity, with connecting flights standing ready to fly off in various directions. A pilot from our staff was waiting for me. We immediately took off and were in Ossinovka by evening.

I went straight to General Paulus from the landing ground. His face was strained and fatigued. His formerly erect figure was bent forward. I could see how heavily the burden of responsibility lay on him. 'Now Adam, what did you achieve at Führer Headquarters?'

Without using a lot of words I reported on the depressing outcome of my flight. I forced myself to control my own anger and disappointment.

'So it seems I have to take Stalingrad with fought-out divisions', said Paulus bitterly, as I completed my report.

'Müller-Hillebrand assured me that the forthcoming march battalions will be allocated in preference to our army. Of course that is far too few. One has to accept, however, that the Army High Command is concerned with the timely relief of our exhausted divisions if sufficient replacements are unavailable.'

I myself did not believe in that possibility, but wanted to say something that would not further weigh down the threatening situation. But Paulus did not let it pass. 'No, Adam, that is illusory. Where would those divisions come from? We have already talked often about the question of reserves. Hitler does not want to know about it. Carelessness and superficiality already seem to have made their mark on the planning of this offensive. We can therefore make no reproaches. We have done everything within our capabilities. From the first day of the offensive we have been reporting truthfully. You know that I have never underestimated the enemy. And I have not held back my warnings from Schmundt, Fellgiebel and others.'

'That I can confirm to the best of my knowledge and conscience, General.'

'The fighting at Kalatch showed us that the enemy is no longer prepared to give up ground without a fight. Our soldiers are exhausted from the physical and mental stresses of the last days and weeks, and technical equipment and weapons have been lost in considerable numbers. Now exhausted troops that have not had a day off for seven weeks have to start a new attack.'

'I know all this myself, General; I painted our picture at Vinniza in the blackest colours.'

Paulus reflected, then went on: 'General Blumentritt, my successor as 1st Senior Quartermaster in the Army General Staff, is on an inspection journey to the Eastern Front. He has also reported to me. I will describe everything to him. If there is any way, he will certainly help us.'

Once I had left Paulus, I quickly sought out the chief of staff, who was already expecting me. I knew that Schmidt would not give in so quickly. Once he had heard my brief report, he blustered: 'Our infantry have marched fighting over 500 kilometres. What that means, the gentlemen in the Army High Command seem to have forgotten. Nevertheless, everything too tightly drawn tears apart the bow. Despite everything, Adam, we are not going to hang our heads. I trust our brave soldiers. Of course they complain, but when the order to attack comes, they march. I am convinced that we will attain our goal.'

'Do you think, General, that the forthcoming battle will result in fewer losses?'

'No way. For the crossing of the Don we have in any case allocated two divisions that are almost up to normal strength, the 76th and the 295th. I have given them the last of the march battalions. Their commanders are reliable. In addition, you will have heard from the commander-in-chief that General Blumentritt is visiting us. We will be speaking clearly to him once more.'

Thrust over the Don

General Blumentritt had arrived at army headquarters. The last preparations for the attack on Stalingrad across the Don were complete. The divisions were waiting in their ready positions. Paulus and Schmidt discussed the conduct of the attack with him once more. The commander-in-chief expressly stressed that success could only be assured if every threat to the 400-kilometre northern flank was eliminated. Blumentritt obtained a very instructive impression of our endangered situation from this meeting.

On the 19th August the 6th Army's orders to attack went out to the generals' commands. That afternoon I was at Major-General Schmidt's for a conference. In his office hung greatly enlarged aerial photographs of Stalingrad. For the first time I saw a clear representation of the city, which was marked only by a small cross on our maps. It extended for more than 60 kilometres in a 4–7-kilometre wide strip along the western bank of the Volga. I had not realised how big it was until now. The question immediately arose: 'Will we be able to take this vast city in the first attempt off the move? The enemy already know our intentions. While we were fighting for Kalatch the Russians had set out – as our airmen reported – several belts of fortifications with anti-tank ditches. While we were having to put our forces in order and regroup, he had gained another fourteen days. Despite reinforcement by the 24th Panzer Division and the 297th Infantry Division, the 4th Panzer Army had been unable to thrust across the Volga south of the city. Our current attack would in no way come as a surprise to the Russian High Command.'

'What you say is quite correct. If we can punch through with a clenched fist to the northern edge of Stalingrad, and the 4th Panzer Army simultaneously enters in the south in a further attack, then the enemy will have to fight on two sides about 60 kilometres apart. Whether they are in a position to do so, I have strong reservations. We have thought through all the variations. Ammunition and fuel is available in sufficient quantities. Without doubt the High Command of the Red Army has used these last four weeks or so to bring forward reinforcements, clear the factories, evacuate the civilian population and prepare the city for effective defence. That will bring us some hard fighting. But I am convinced that we will soon achieve it.'

Listening to Schmidt, it seemed possible that our headquarters had taken everything into account. We expected some hard fighting with apparently also heavy casualties. But at the end victory would be ours.

I left the conference with the army orders and went to my tent to study the documents in detail. In my mind I could still see the aerial photographs of the city on the Volga. Stalingrad was of great strategic significance. It was the connecting link between the Caucasus and Central Russia. Once we had the city in our hands, the enemy would be cut off from the cornfields of the Kuban and the oil wells between the Caspian and Black Seas. One of the Russians' most important traffic routes would be broken at its strongest junction. But what if we were unable to take the city in the first attack?

Chapter 2

The Shattered Attack
on the City

Ready positions on the west bank of the Don

Reconnaissance of the terrain had shown that the sector of the Don between Lutshenski and Ostrovski offered a ready starting point for the 6th Army's attack on Stalingrad. The western bank was wooded. Thick bushes and deep ravines in the steep bank running down to the Don offered wonderful camouflage, enabling the positioning of equipment and the construction of tank-carrying bridges right up to the river's edge without the enemy being able to see them. In addition to this, from the west bank we could see for kilometres over the flat eastern terrain.

Paulus described the plan of attack to the commanding generals at headquarters. He had the intention to use the LIst Corps, to which the 295th and 76th Infantry Divisions were attached (two divisions that had suffered few casualties so far), to form bridgeheads on either side of Vertiatshi east of the Don, and from these to thrust to the Volga north of Stalingrad with the XIVth Panzer Corps. After breaking through the enemy defensive line, the LIst Corps should protect the left flank and the VIIIth Corps the right flank of the tanks storming through to the Volga. The XIth Corps should remain to provide flank protection in the Don Bend between Melov and Kletskaya, while the XXIVth Panzer Corps, with only the 71st Infantry Division at its disposal after giving up both the 44th Panzer Division and the 297th Infantry Division, would form a bridgehead near Kalatch and attack eastwards from there.

The army's headquarters had been as busy as a beehive over the past ten days. Orderly officers came and went, messages were sorted and evaluated, commanding generals appeared for personal consultations, pilots reported on their observations, conferences took place continuously. Now there was an expectant hush. What would the next day bring?

This question was the centrepoint of our table talks on the 20th August. 'I can hardly think', said the 1st general staff officer, 'that the crossing will cost large casualties. The enemy position is easily visible from our side, our artillery has the ranges, the infantry and engineers have been carefully instructed. After a short artillery preparation the assault craft will cross the Don. By the time the Russians come to their senses on the other side, we will be on the opposite bank.'

'If everything goes smoothly, agreed,' I said. 'But if our artillery does not cut off all their machine-gun nests, then the crossing will be really expensive. Two days ago a divisional adjutant told me that he himself was on the river bank, and saw where the enemy had carefully camouflaged their nests. It was particularly difficult to pick out the nests lying immediately on the river bank.'

Schmidt said: 'Don't worry, gentlemen, it won't be easy, but we will soon do it.' Whereupon he left.

I had already long before sought out two old regimental comrades that were with the 76th Infantry Division. Who knew whether I would see them again after the forthcoming battle? I had therefore quickly asked permission from Major-General Schmidt to drive to the 76th. 'Of course you can go, Adam. Greet General Rodenburg for me. I wish him all the best. Arrange your journey so that you are back before nightfall!'

The time dragged. Within fifteen minutes I had driven off in a cross-country vehicle. Despite the heavily congested road, we made good progress. The black dust that the motorised vehicles were throwing up was very troublesome. In overtaking a convoy of trucks we plunged into a thick cloud of it. The driver tried to speed up, but soon the windscreen was covered in such thick dust that he had to stop. I climbed out to brush the dust off with a cloth. I had to laugh when I saw him through the now shiny glass: his face was as black as the ace of spades. The driver was no less amused and invited me to look in the mirror. I did not look any different! The dust had penetrated every crevice in the vehicle. Even the engine was covered with dust a centimetre thick.

Going forwards was almost impossible. We therefore turned off the road and drove across the steppe by compass. Several times streams obliged us to turn back onto the road to get across a bridge. Here chaos ruled an inconceivable throng. Dozens of ammunition trucks were trying to reach their artillery positions before nightfall. Jeeps and horse-drawn carts were rushing forward. In between motorcycles twisted their way through. Engines, horses and humans caused such a din that one could not understand a single word.

The 76th Infantry Division before the attack
I reached the headquarters of the 76th Infantry Division between 1500 and 1600 hours. It had been set up in a small wood immediately behind the regimental preparatory areas. In front of the tents on the edge of the wood stood the desk of the divisional commander. Major-General Rodenburg was

leaning over the maps on which the lines of attack and objectives were shown. Next to him stood his 1st general staff officer, Lieutenant-Colonel Breithaupt. I directed my driver to drive right up to the table, which caused the lieutenant-colonel to approach us angrily. Who was daring to bring a vehicle up so close? Then he recognised me, with pleasure. We had not seen each other since the autumn of 1936. At that time we were company commanders in the same battalion in Giessen and Worms. I had always got on very well with Breithaupt, a farmer's son from Thüringen.

Rodenburg greeted me: 'It is good that you visit us for once. We have already often spoken about you. If you had come here an hour earlier you would have met General Paulus. He chatted with us for a long time. Previously he had been to the 295th Infantry Division.'

'Was the commander-in-chief content?'

'We think so, yes,' answered Breithaupt. 'He had us report exactly how the attack would be conducted. Then he approved our orders. He had me escort him to an infantry regiment in the front line and finally visited an artillery observation post.'

'How do you rate our chances of success, General?'

'You know that I am an optimist. Without doubt our preparations could not have remained completely concealed from the enemy, but we will soon get it moving. Until now I have always been able to leave things to my Brandenburgers.'

Breithaupt added: 'Paulus spoke to the sappers up in front. Everything is ready. As soon as we have driven the enemy back from the river bank, the sappers will immediately begin constructing the bridge. Until the bridge is ready, the tank hunters and artillery will follow the infantry on ferries. Artillery observers are going forward with the first attacking wave. You can see that everything must go well for us. We will also be breaking strong resistance.'

'What is the atmosphere among the troops, Breithaupt?'

'Paulus asked us the same question. How can I answer. You should go to the regiment, Adam. They can tell you themselves. We are happy with our soldiers.'

It was really time to drive on to Abraham, if I wanted to be back at our headquarters before dark. I said goodbye to Rodenburg and Breithaupt. As I was climbing into the vehicle I was wondering whether everything would go as the two of them thought. Certainly Breithaupt was a competent chap. But the enemy knew what stood ahead of him. The Russians have certainly not become idle.

A messenger from one of the regiments that had been detached to the divisional headquarters accompanied me, a lively youngster with flashing eyes. I asked him: 'So how is it in your regiment?'

Willingly he replied: 'We hope that it will start soon and we can get to

Stalingrad at last. We have been tramping enough and are enjoying our longer rest period. We have had enough of the steppe. One does not find any proper accommodation at all. In France it was nicer and we would all like to go back.'

'Will you make it to Stalingrad?'

'Our regiment, Colonel, has not yet refused anything. With the last replacements many old soldiers returned to us. They complain, but if anything happens they are there. Most of them have been wounded several times so they are proper "front-line pigs" on whom our colonel can depend.'

'That is fine, then nothing can go bad for us.'

'There is the regimental headquarters, Colonel.' The soldier pointed to a still young wood in front of us.

Abraham was already waiting for me, Breithaupt having signalled our movements. We had not seen each other since the beginning of the war. Already in greeting each other I noticed that he had changed little. Or was he only giving that impression as he greeted me somewhat flippantly?

'Adam, I was already thinking that the army adjutant had forgotten his old comrade.'

'How can you say something like that? You know what has been going on with us these last few weeks. Only today, before the attack begins, has there been a bit of peace. And I immediately used this opportunity to visit my old friends. Are you content now?'

'It was not meant seriously, old chap. I am delighted that we can see each other again at long last. How lovely it would be if we only had one of the bottles of beer that we emptied so many times together in Trier. But in this dried-up steppe there is never enough drinking water.'

We slipped through the light wood towards the Don. There was not a soldier to be seen. Only painted signs showed that dozens of units had been here. Telephone cables hung from the boughs of the trees. Mortars were hidden in the bushes. Once we had crossed the wood on a beaten path we came to a wooden shield fastened to a tree. 'Regimental Commanders' Command Post' was written on it, with an arrow pointing to the Don. We now came to the edge of a deep cleft.

'It leads directly to the river,' explained Abraham. 'That is an eroded valley, a so-called *balka*.'

'I have heard of them. Today is the first time I have seen what such a gorge looks like. It is astonishing what work the water has done. One could accommodate a whole company in it.'

'And more! In this *balka* at least two companies have had ample room. There are at least half a dozen such gullies in my position alone.'

An observation post lay before us in a thick clump of bushes. Beyond it the ground fell steeply to the river, on whose dark flood the evening sun was mirrored. Over the opposite bank my view went far across the steppe.

Behind there must be the big city on the Volga. I looked through the telescope. 'Is the east bank occupied at all?'

'Of course, but the Russians have camouflaged themselves so carefully that hardly anything of them is discernible. By day nothing moves on the bank. But they have their machine-gun nests there. We have tried offering them suitable targets, but they whistle at them. Not a shot is fired. Not even at night when it becomes livelier over there. We have identified some nests. I'll point the telescope for you. Do you see the nest in the cross-hairs?'

I looked through it. It took at least ten seconds for me to identify the machine-gun position. When I turned back to Abraham, his face seemed to have changed. The derisive expression on his face had disappeared. His lips were pressed together. His eyes looked at me earnestly, quite rigidly. 'If our heavy weapons don't completely smash the enemy positions, the river crossing will cost us a lot of men. We have discussed the coordination of artillery, mortars and sappers in detail. Nevertheless there remains a big question mark.'

'I would bring the infantry guns far enough forward for them to be able to destroy the newly advancing enemy in the direct line of fire.'

'That has happened, and you can see them for yourself. I am interested in something else,' said the regimental commander. 'How is it with replacements that are certainly so necessary before the forthcoming fighting?'

'That is a dark chapter. The newly conscripted recruits will not be trained until the end of December. We must just hope for good luck.'

Evening was approaching. It was high time that I was making my way back. But Abraham wanted to show me the artillery positions. One had to recognise that the regiment had not treated them lightly. The guns were well camouflaged and had a wide and free field of fire. Slit trenches for the crews, piles of ammunition, and immaculate positions – everything done exactly according to the fighting instructions. Abraham remarked that there was a certain fatigue and exhaustion detectable among the soldiers. There was also some complaining. But that was typical of soldiers, who always complain about something or other.

'And how is it with you personally, Abraham?'

'Nothing special. The regimental doctor wanted to put me in hospital a few days ago. Of course I refused. How would it look if the commander left his regiment in the muck shortly before an attack?'

'What is wrong then?'

'The doctor wanted to send me to a specialist because of my nerves. I can hardly sleep any more. I am as if shattered during the day, But now we have to get across the Don.'

'Let me know immediately if it gets worse. You will be no good to the troops if you collapse. And now, for tomorrow, all the best!'

It had already become late when I climbed back into my vehicle. 'Will we reach our headquarters before nightfall?'

'I don't think so, Colonel. The sun has already vanished and the night comes here very suddenly,' said my driver.

'We can at least reach the supply route before dusk. We must go to the west of this village to reach it,' I said, with a look at the map spread out on my knees.

Again we were smothered in a cloud of dust. Even in the half light of the departing day the journey was no easier than on the drive here in the afternoon. As we moved against the stream of traffic, coming towards us were trucks, field kitchens and horse-drawn carts that we had to avoid. So we crept forward, often having to stop, driving in the first and second gears.

I must have been quite a time lost in my thoughts when the driver's voice gave me a start: 'Colonel, I think we have lost our way. We should have been on the main road a long time ago.'

Damn it, yes. My luminous watch showed 1830 hours. It was already dark. The oncoming traffic had disappeared without my having noticed until now. Angry with myself, I had us stop. We were standing on a road that was overgrown with steppe grass. Heavily used stretches no longer had any grass. There was often black, powdery dust here in the daytime. So we must have got onto a little used road. What now? Turn around? Five minutes later we reached a crossroads. I looked with a pocket torch for our car's tracks. But it was a hopeless task, there were vehicle tracks everywhere. At that point some white flares went up not far from us. With the help of my compass I established that they had been fired to the east of us. That was where the front line must be. Apparently we had taken a route that ran parallel to the Don. I instructed the driver to keep going north. At some point or other we should come across the main road. It did not take long until a light blinked at us. We drove up to it. It came from a truck that had broken down. The two soldiers with it, who belonged to a 76th Infantry Division supply unit, told us that we were on the right route. We reached the main road after about 1,500 metres. We progressed only slowly. It was 2300 hours before we reached our headquarters in Ossinovka. They were already concerned about us as the 76th Infantry Division had reported our departure.

It was no longer possible to think about sleeping. I reported my impressions. Paulus too was happy to have returned from his journey. Our opinions were that all preparations had been made to ensure the success of the offensive.

The Don crossing is made

The clock showed 0200 hours. I lay awake on my camp bed. The light was switched off. The fresh night air came in through the open window. The moon touched the little room with its weak shine. Or was it the dawning day already? I looked at the clock: 0230 hours. Another 60 minutes. Unrest gripped me. I left my quarters and went to the 1st general staff officer. Several orderly officers of the Ia section had assembled here. Practically all of the headquarters staff were present. Once more the time was confirmed with the general staff. Then General Paulus also entered the room. It was time.

Punctually at the fixed time the thunder of the guns ripped through the quiet of the yielding night. It provided the horribly exciting overture for the thrust over the Don. Following a short bombardment, the assault and inflatable craft were put into the water with infantrymen and sappers.

Smoking a cigarette, Paulus sat at a map table, his face twitching. We were all tensed like this. What would the first reports bring?

The 1st general staff officer had gone directly to the telephone exchange. He was in constant contact with the LIst Corps, which was leading the attack. It seemed to us an eternity before he finally returned. The talking stopped and all eyes were directed expectantly at him. 'General, the first report from the LIst Corps. The 295th Infantry Division has reached the opposite bank and is advancing further. Few losses. Of the 76th Infantry Division only one regiment has crossed the Don. The attack by the second infantry regiment was repelled with heavy losses. Numerous inflatable craft and assault boats have been lost. The commanding general has gone to the 76th Infantry Division.'

'What has the corps done to help the regiment?' asked Paulus.

'The report was passed by an orderly officer. I know no details at the moment, but will go immediately to contact the corps' chief of staff.'

Silence reigned in the room. Apparently, what Abraham had told me the day before on the steep bank of the Don had come to pass. 'If our heavy weapons don't completely smash the enemy positions, the river crossing will cost us a lot of men.' Confirmation of this was brought by the 1st orderly officer, who had already entered. 'The 76th Infantry Division, via the LIst Corps, has just given the reason for the failure of its regiment advancing on the right. When the boats of the first wave were already two-thirds across the river, they were hit by murderous defensive fire coming from some excellently concealed machine guns and mortars. The regiment has suffered severe casualties. The boats have been sunk. Only a few soldiers were able to swim back. The corps ordered the 295th Infantry Division on the opposite bank from the right-hand sector of the 76th Infantry Division to relieve them by making a thrust in the enemy rear.'

Paulus agreed with the measures taken by the corps. He told the orderly officer: 'The corps is to report when the regiment's attack is resumed.'

The army staff officers went off to their offices. The news soon came through that the renewed attack by the infantry regiment had been successful. The enemy was being rolled back. Thus both divisions of the LIst Corps were able to form bridgeheads on the eastern bank of the Don, which quickly repulsed several hefty attacks by the enemy.

Meanwhile the sappers were working feverishly at constructing the bridges. To enable the XIVth Panzer Corps to take part in the attack on the Volga, bridges were being built near Peskovatka and Vertiatshi.

The 'Land Bridge' between the Don and the Volga
On the 23rd August the 16th Panzer Division, as well as the 3rd and 60th (Motorised) Infantry Divisions, went into the attack from the Don bridgehead. In the early hours of the morning they broke through the enemy defensive line and advanced over the range of heights north of Mal Rossoshka–G. 137–Konny Halt, reaching the Volga north of Stalingrad in the evening of the same day. This thrust formed a 60-kilometre long, 8-kilometre wide corridor. It went so quickly that the infantry divisions could not follow up fast enough and were unable to prevent the Soviet units closing up their defensive front *behind* the XIVth Panzer Corps. The panzer corps was cut off for days. With a massive counterattack, especially against its unprotected flanks, it was in serious trouble. It had to be supplied by aircraft and convoys of trucks. Loaded with wounded, the vehicles broke through the Soviet lines towards the Don under the protection of the tanks. At the bridgehead the wounded were handed over to the main dressing stations. Afterwards the most important supplies were loaded up and, under escort by the tanks, the trucks returned the same way to the corps. The latter was unable to take the northern part of the city by surprise. It stood for days, isolated from the army, engaged in heavy defensive fighting on all sides. Only after a week, following the introduction of further infantry divisions in the bridgehead, was it possible to break the enemy resistance with hard fighting, despite many casualties, and to establish a continuous connection with the panzer corps. The VIIIth Corps then took over the protection of the army's northern flank in the area between the Volga and the Don. The army order described this sector as the 'Land Bridge'.

The headquarters of the VIIIth Corps followed immediately behind its attacking divisions. The quartermaster department had also crossed the Don and lay in tents not far from the newly constructed bridge near Peskovatka. This bridge was attacked every night by Soviet aircraft. It was a disastrous position for the tents. At the end of August I received a telephone call from the adjutant of the VIIIth Corps. He reported: 'An hour ago a bomb hit the tent in which the quartermaster and the officers of his staff were holding a conference. The quartermaster and several officers are dead, all the others severely or lightly wounded. The corps urgently needs replacements, otherwise the supply system will be imperilled.'

Before informing Paulus and Schmidt about this by telephone, I asked our exchange to connect me with Army Group 'B'. Hardly had I informed the two generals when the telephone rang. It was the army group. The duty officer took the message and my urgent request for replacements. Already the next day the requested replacements appeared.

But it was not only about the replacement of the quartermaster department. The enemy was attacking the VIIIth Corps without pause on the 'Land Bridge'. We suffered heavy casualties in the fighting south of the Kotluban. The LIst Corps also reported increasing casualties. It had to cover the right flank of the XIVth Panzer Corps and attack the city on the Volga via Rossoshka and Gumrak. But it was only slowly gaining ground. Counterattacks by the Red Army from the Rossoshka valley forced the corps onto the defensive for several days. It was the same with the 71st Infantry Division, which had managed the crossing of the Don on the 25th August near Kalatch, but had then become stuck. Likewise, the 4th Panzer Army that was supposed to take the southern part of Stalingrad failed to achieve its goal.

General von Wietersheim is relieved

The enemy was fighting for every foot of ground. Almost unbelievably, we received a report from General von Wietersleben, commander of the XIVth Panzer Corps. As his corps was having to fight in isolation, we were only receiving scanty news. Now, however, he reported that the units of the Red Army repelling our attacks were being supported by the whole population of Stalingrad with the utmost determination; not only were the city's inhabitants constructing positions, barricades and trenches, but the factories and large buildings were being turned into fortresses. Many more civilians were armed. Workers dressed in overalls were lying dead on the battlefield, often still with a rifle or machine pistol in their stiff hands. Dead workers still sat in the driver's seats of shot-up tanks. We had not experienced anything like this before.

General von Wietersheim proposed to the commander-in-chief of the 6th Army that the positions on the Volga be given up again. He did not believe that this vast city could be taken. Paulus declined this proposal, which was in contradiction to the orders of Army Group 'B' and the Army High Command. It came to an earnest difference of opinion between the two generals. Paulus regarded any general who doubted in final success as unsuited to command in this serious situation. He proposed to the Army High Command the dismissal of General von Wietersheim and the appointment of Lieutenant-General Hube, commander of the 16th Panzer Division, as his successor. The proposal was immediately approved.

The very next day a letter arrived in a sealed envelope for General von Wietersheim from the Army High Command. I was given the task of flying in a Fiescler 'Stork' to the Panzer corps headquarters, and handing it over in return for a receipt.

Wietersheim was with his chief of staff in his command bus in the middle of the steppe. I stood opposite this general for the first time. He was tall and slim, withdrawn and very much in control. His hair was grey lined. Quietly and controlled, he took the letter from me, sat down in a far corner and opened it.

I sat down at the entrance next to the chief of staff. Before I left, Paulus had told me that Wietersheim and his chief of staff were of the same opinion. What must be going on in the general's head! We dared not look at him. Then he was walking back to us with a firm tread.

'Here, Adam, the receipt for the letter.' He noticed my embarrassment and added: 'It is not always pleasant being an adjutant.'

He seemed to have everything under control. There was no tremor in his voice. Turning to his chief of staff, he said: 'Call General Hube; he is to report to me today!'

I excused myself. As I was leaving the command vehicle, Wietersheim called after me: 'My greetings to General Paulus!' The Fieseler 'Stork' was only a few steps away. I climbed in. The pilot sitting in front of me switched the engine on. With increasing noise and speed, the propeller sent dust and grass whirling. After a short take-off run we left the ground and flew back to headquarters. The feelings and thoughts within me in conflict, I turned to Paulus's side. He had certainly handled things lightly when he proposed the dismissal. Wietersheim had doubts about success. Such an attitude seemed unbearable to Paulus, who was of the opinion that the two attacking armies would still take the city.

We were already over the Don. The machine prepared to land and rolled to the southern exit of Golubinskaya, the new headquarters location.

I reported back to Paulus, handing him Wietersheim's receipt and passing on the recipient's greetings. 'How did he take the news, Adam?'

'The general read the letter without saying a word. As if nothing had happened, he ordered his chief of staff to summon Hube to the headquarters. This stoic calmness greatly impressed me. What will happen to Wietersheim now, General?'

'He will surely get another appointment. In the end he is a capable general who lost his nerve here. I cannot give up the attack just because the first thrust of the panzer corps on the city was repelled. We will have no problems with Hube, he is a daredevil, the ideal tank commander. By the way, the corps is still in a dangerous situation. The LIst Corps that was supposed to relieve him has been repelled by a strong Russian defence and has been stuck for days. Tomorrow I am going with General von Seydlitz to the 295th Infantry Division. It would be good if you could be there. This division has had considerable casualties. We have to consider how to close the gaps.'

'Of course I will come with you, General.'

The attack remains stuck

The courier post was waiting for me in my office. It was quickly examined and distributed to the clerks. Afterwards I went to the 1st general staff officer to orientate myself on the latest developments. 'Since yesterday there have been unimportant alterations. In the north the enemy is attacking between the Volga and the Don again and again. The VIIIth Corps and the XIVth Panzer Corps have been conducting some heavy defensive fighting. The LIst Corps is stuck fast, as is the 71st Infantry Division. Air Fleet 4 has been bombing the city ceaselessly since the 23rd August. Stalingrad is just a single sheet of flames. The thick black clouds of smoke show that the oil tanks have been hit. The 4th Panzer Army has extended its main line of attack to the left, thus hitting the enemy lying before us in the flank. Hopefully this attack will bring relief.'

I compared my map with that at the headquarters and made the necessary corrections. Then I made my way back to my quarters. I had dispensed with my tent for days. The nights were already quite cool. I was living with my batman in the last but one house at the southern end of Golubinskaya. I slowly strolled along the street. It had become late. The almost full moon poured its milky light over the single-storey white chalked houses and the pretty front gardens of this clean Cossack village. Roughly in the centre of the village stood the school, a two-storey building in which the army's chief engineer had found accommodation, along with his staff. Here too the street forked at the foot of the hill, going up to the 'Don High Road', a main road running south parallel to the Don, past Kalatch to Chir station and from there further on to Nishne-Chirskaya, a Don Cossack town.

Golubinskaya lay in the middle between the Don bridge near Kalatch in the south and Peskovatka in the north. If we wanted to get to the divisions on the Volga front by car or motorcycle, we always had to go first along the Don High Road to one of the army's bridges.

There was especially lively traffic on this road after dark. The sounds of engines forced its way into the quiet of our headquarters. Once there was the most terrible din. A beam of light from a torch swept around. Apparently it was yet another breakdown, which was hardly pleasant at this time of night. But regularly at about 2200 hours the 'Duty Pilot', flying the 'Sewing Machine', would appear. From a low height the pilot of this small double-decker would simply drop his bombs over the side at identified targets. Only a short time ago a young officer of our staff had been killed while seeking shelter in a slit trench next to his quarters. Today too the machine flew according to plan. Presumably the pilot had seen the light on the main road from a distance. The bomb was already exploding.

An officer wearing a steel helmet came towards me. It was our duty officer, whose task was to control the night sentries at the road entrance in front of the commander-in-chief's quarters and the officers' mess. He came up to me and reported.

'Everything in order?' I asked.

'Yes, Colonel, no complaints. The 'Sewing Machine' has spared us this time. It would also help if our troops observed the blackout drill.'

'But there seems to have been an incident on the main road. Let's hope that nothing serious has occurred.'

'I will soon find out. The headquarters commandant is expecting a vehicle bringing the people on leave back from Chir station.'

'Send a motorcyclist from our driver pool! Perhaps a doctor is needed. Report back to me if it something special.'

'As ordered, Colonel!'

Next morning at about 0600 hours I drove in a jeep along the Don High Road to the bridge near Peskovatka, where the VIIIth Corps was located. For days units of the Red Army had been attacking its divisions. The losses in dead and wounded were mounting rapidly. The commanding general, General of Artillery Heitz, received me with the words: 'You must help us with reinforcements, and quickly. If the Russians keep going on like this, I cannot guarantee a successful defence, not even if we do everything to reduce casualties by improving our positions.'

'We are doing everything within our power, General. But there is nothing much we can do,' I told him and then reported on my visit to Vinniza.

'That is indeed a murky prospect. The only thing left is to comb through the staff and rear services.'

Paulus had tasked me to drive from Peskovatka to the 295th Infantry Division. He himself had flown there in a Fieseler 'Stork'. So I said goodbye to General Heitz and drove on towards Stalingrad.

After about half an hour I recognised the headquarters on the steppe. There were two Fieseler 'Storks' standing there and several cars. Paulus had already arrived. He was talking to the commander of the LIst Corps, General von Seydlitz, the divisional commander, Lieutenant-General Wuthmann, and an air force general whom I was meeting for the first time. He was Colonel-General von Richthofen, commander-in-chief of Air Fleet 4, whose bomber and fighter units were supporting the attack on the Volga city. Evidence of their work was the thick cloud of smoke that had hung over the horizon since the 23rd August. I saw them climbing up into the sky from the headquarters of the 295th Infantry Division for the first time. The city itself covered a shallow height. It was a simultaneous contrast between natural beauty and the destruction of war.

The whole landscape was bathed in sunlight on this beautiful late summer day. But from the west, flanked by fighters, came the squadrons of bombers to drop their loads on the city with ear-deafening noise and prominent new mushrooms of smoke. 'That's how it goes all day long,' commented an officer of the engineer staff. 'One cannot see much left of the city. One has to accept that the hail of bombs is extinguishing everything alive.'

Paulus too spent a few minutes looking at the horrible spectacle. Then he had the divisional commander report on the course of the attack so far. 'We have only advanced slowly forward in the last few days. The Russian is using every fold in the ground and not giving up a metre without a fight. Our losses increase with every step that we take forward towards the city. Our breakthrough strength is no longer sufficient.'

During this report from General Wuthmann I was standing a little to one side with one of the division's orderly officers, who complemented his commander's report: 'The heavy losses are depressing the morale of our soldiers. The men have become listless, not having reckoned on such tough resistance. They thought that they would be in the city within a few days and at last have a chance to rest. But now most think it very doubtful whether we will ever reach Stalingrad. We have to contest this frame of mind very strongly.'

The division had reached the Don with about 13,000 men. After just a few days of fighting it numbered barely half that. General von Seydlitz, who was known as a hard and courageous leader of troops, made no secret of his concern over the further course of the offensive.

That afternoon, while in conversation with General Heitz, the thought came to me to fly to Führer Headquarters again. It was obvious to me that there was no other way. Paulus was of the same point of view.

Once more at Führer Headquarters

Once I had explained my proposal to Major-General Schmidt, I reported by telephone to the Personnel Office in Vinniza that I would be visiting next day. The head of my office, Sergeant-Major Küpper, put together for me a summary of the fighting strengths of the divisions. He added a report on the artillery and signals units where there were potential officers. There were almost two hundred who could not be promoted for lack of permanent posts. I had proposed that eighty of them could be trained as infantry officers on a course behind the front. Paulus and Schmidt agreed. The request for permission to hold such a course, signed by the commander-in-chief, lay before me, together with the training programme prepared by the staff officer responsible for training.

By chance that same day my appointment arrived to attend the cure hospital at Falkenstein in the Taunus Mountains for the second half of September. Schmidt grumbled a bit when he read the letter: 'You could have chosen a more suitable time for your cure! Speak to the Personnel Office tomorrow about a deputy. He must be acquired as soon as possible to get acquainted with the job so that you can go in time.'

After supper I was asked by Paulus's son-in-law, Specialist Baron von Kutzschenbach, the staff interpreter, for a chat. We walked up and down the village street. 'My father-in-law is giving me concern,' he began. 'You know as well as I do that he and Schmidt are not in harmony. While it has not come to an open fight between them, it is only because my father-in-law always gives in. Schmidt's overbearing and dogmatic manners are repugnant to him. It oppresses him that there is no confidence between his chief of staff and the department heads. It leads to the generals complaining about the way Schmidt treats them. He feels hurt when Schmidt makes decisions without asking him. On the other hand, he refuses to separate himself from Schmidt.'

'Schmidt is without doubt an intelligent officer; I am astounded by his great working ability and his energy. At the same time I am incensed when I see how Schmidt tries to behave like a schoolmaster to the commander-in-chief and all of us. That he does not notice in his cleverness how detrimental his conduct is and how it affects the work is beyond my understanding. Paulus should finally bang his fist on the table and show his teeth. He knows that we would all support him.'

'You know that he would never do that. That is why we have to help him. It would be good if while you are in Vinniza you spoke to Colonel von Zielberg, who is responsible for the filling of the general staff posts. Perhaps he could look into it.'

'So you are proposing to go behind your father-in-law's back to do this? You should know that I am no friend of secretive behaviour.'

'If we spoke to him, he would forbid it. But in his interest, and that of the staff, something must be done. I live together with my father-in-law and know best how Schmidt's behaviour torments him. He often speaks to me about it and complains about him to me. This must end.'

Kutzschenbach was right. It was in the interest of the command of the army to obtain a change. Paulus tried to keep himself out of the conflict. Nevertheless all the officers on the staff, and all the commanding generals and divisional commanders, knew how much the commander-in-chief spiritually suffered under the unpleasant characteristics of the chief of staff.

With a promise to undertake an appropriate move in Vinniza, I parted from Paulus's son-in-law. But nevertheless I was not too happy about the business. Was it right to speak to Colonel von Zielberg without Paulus's knowledge? I went with these doubts to the 1st general staff officer and told him about my conversation with Kutzschenbach. 'There is no other way, we must help Paulus,' he said.

The next day I flew without incident to Vinniza. I had a circuitous programme to complete. Our proposal for setting up a training school for officers from the artillery and signals units was approved by the Personnel Office after some brief discussions with the responsible officers. This was the first success of my trip. Also the second matter, which concerned me personally, went better than I thought: finding a stand-in for me during my cure. The department head responsible immediately said: 'That fits nicely. A lieutenant-colonel from the Personnel Office has been tormenting us for a long time for a job at the front. He can stand in for you and when you return he can take over an infantry regiment in the 6th Army. As soon as he has handed over his work here, we will send him to you.'

With a hopeful heart I went next to Colonel von Zielberg. His words of greeting made my task easier. 'Now, Adam, what is Schmidt, the new chief of staff, up to? Does he get on with Paulus, or is he making a racket?'

'Firstly, Herr von Zielberg, I must stress that I have not come to you on Paulus's behalf. If I had told him that I was coming to speak to you about Schmidt, he would have forbidden me. The reason for my call is a conversation I had with Herr von Kutzschenbach, Paulus's son-in-law, who is employed on our staff as an interpreter. He was really anxious about Paulus.'

Once I had described Schmidt's unfriendly attitude towards Paulus, I went on: 'I am afraid that this disharmony between the chief of staff and the commander-in-chief disastrously restricts the command of the 6th Army. The High Command should consider whether a change of chief of staff is advisable. Naturally I cannot decide whether now is the right time for it. Of course one must talk to Paulus beforehand.'

Colonel von Zielberg shared my opinion. 'I doubted from the first whether this team would get on together. I will speak to the Chief of the General Staff, Colonel-General Halder, and submit an appropriate proposal to him.'

Then I drove on to Colonel Müller-Hillebrand. There was not much time left before my return flight. But my interlocutor knew the state of the 6th Army so that not many words were required. This time I came with a suggestion: 'There are many young soldiers in the rear services that I believe are suitable for the front. Would it not be expedient to relieve them with older soldiers who are no longer fit for the front? That way it might be possible to fill the worst gaps.'

'I don't know if one could get much out of it. As far as I know, the companies have already got auxiliary volunteers, prisoners of war, as drivers.'

'Yes, of course, but I was thinking also in the established columns, workshop companies and so on in the army's rear areas.'

'We will check that out, Adam.'

Müller-Hillebrand had fulfilled the promise that he had made during my visit in the middle of August. We had received a number of march battalions that were very welcome to us, even though they did not fulfil their task of filling up the divisions by a long way. Now the colonel promised to send us available march units as a priority. I knew that he could not do more. We shook hands in farewell. Then I took the flight back.

After my arrival in Golubinskaya, I reported first to Schmidt and then to Paulus. To both of them it was clear that we had to go ahead with the replacement situation. They were pleased with the permission given by the Personnel Office for the training of infantry officers. Quietly Paulus was hoping that the army would get some new divisions.

In stormy weather with the commander-in-chief

The next day I was summoned to Paulus at an unusual time. What did it mean? In the outer office I was greeted by his personal orderly officer, Lieutenant-Colonel Zimmermann. 'Stormy atmosphere, Colonel.'

The commander-in-chief asked me to take a chair opposite his desk. I detected that he was trying to control an increasing anger. 'Yesterday you spoke to Zielberg about Schmidt?'

'Yes, General.'

'Why did you do this without my knowledge?'

'Because you, General, had forbidden me to take this step. However, we could not watch you being mentally driven under by the self-serving gall of Schmidt.'

It seemed to me that the angry lines on Paulus's forehead had fled. He must have detected from my open reply that we meant well for him. 'Who do you mean by "we"?'

'We, that is the whole of the section leaders, at the head the 1st general staff officer, the army's chief engineer, the army's signals commander, Baron von Kutzschenbach and myself, General!'

'I presume that you were led by pure motives. Nevertheless you should have informed me beforehand, or at least immediately upon your return yesterday evening.'

'Please excuse me, General, for neglecting to do so. I wanted first to speak to your son-in-law and the section leaders over the way, so that we could strike together. We had in mind convincing you in a joint discussion that you should separate from Schmidt in the interest of the army command. Then I would report on the steps I had taken in Vinniza. Who could have known that you would learn of my talk with Zielberg so quickly.'

'Colonel-General Halder rang me ten minutes ago. He first asked about the situation. Then he asked me the direct question if I wanted a successor for Schmidt. He had heard from Blumentritt that the personal relationship between myself and Schmidt could not exactly be described as good. Then he mentioned you. You can understand how surprised I was. Of course I had turned down a change of chief of staff in our present situation.'

'That I understand, General. Nevertheless you should decide once the current operation is over.'

'One thing I always expect from you: in the future I should be informed of such plans in reasonable time. In general it is not your business but mine. I do not want Schmidt to learn anything about this matter. Hopefully we understand each other, Adam.'

With that, the 'Schmidt Case' was over. Unfortunately, one must say. If Paulus was no straightforward, eager, fulfilling 'Faust', Schmidt was more the army's disastrous 'Mephisto' who would reveal himself bitterly again.

'How is it going with your stand-in?', asked the commander-in-chief as I was just about to leave the room.

'It is going well. A lieutenant-colonel from the Personnel Office will stand in for me. When I return, he will take over a regiment.'

'Then Schmidt will be pleased. You know that he will not work with our 2nd Adjutant, Major von Lüttitz.'

An officer cadet school behind the front
Things progressed. The 4th Panzer Army had crossed the Kalatch–Stalingrad railway line near Bessargino and was threatening the enemy opposite the 6th Army in the rear. As a result of this, the Soviet units had to abandon the bitterly defended Rossoshka position and switch over to the inner defensive ring on the western edge of the city. Now the LIst Corps went into the attack. The inner wings of both armies met near Jablotchni on the 2nd September and pursued the offensive together, the foreseen pincer attack becoming a frontal attack. The course of the Zaritza stream formed the dividing line between both armies.

There was a lot of work for me over the next days. I wanted to extend the officer cadet course so that it could continue to run during my cure. First of all a suitable place had to be found. The commander of the army headquarters and the army's chief of signals, who had made repeated reconnaissances west of the Don, suggested Suvorovski, south of Nishne-Chirskaya. I drove there with the staff officer for training (Id). Huts and earthen bunkers on the edge of the village provided the accommodation. The terrain was also suitable. So the choice fell on Suvorovski.

The infantry divisions received orders to name experienced officers and NCOs as instructors. The young Captain Göbel from the 79th Infantry Division was nominated as the commander, and went to the training area with an advance element. The participants were to meet at the end of September and early October. The preparatory work had to be completed by that date. I could see for myself that the divisions had selected the best young officers and NCOs, who took on their task with great enthusiasm. Naturally all of them were happy to be out of the combat zone for several weeks, and to get some sleep again.

Meanwhile our divisions were fighting their way into Stalingrad step by step. The outermost western edge was reached on the 10th September. Only the stone skeletons of the chimneys remained of most of the little wooden houses extending out into the steppe. The adjacent several-storeyed brick buildings were burnt out and reduced to rubble. Our troops lay in the cellars. A casualty-expensive battle for the city now began: a battle against individual buildings, a battle between man and man.

The 'Commandant of Stalingrad'
It was at this time that a colonel reported to me. He said: 'The Army High Command has posted me to the 6th Army as Commandant of Stalingrad. Once I have reported to the commander-in-chief, I want to take up my appointment.' I found it hard to contain my laughter. 'Then you will have to be patient for some time. Our divisions are still fighting on the edge of the city.'

'That cannot last much longer,' he said.

'Have you no idea? The taking of a single building can take days. Our tanks broke through in a thrust to the Volga as long ago as the 23rd August. But we still have not been able to occupy the city. It took us fourteen days to reach the outskirts. Go and report to the army's chief of staff, Major-General Schmidt. He can tell you much better than I can what is happening.'

The colonel looked at me with a disappointed face. I called Schmidt and prepared him for his visitor. He laughed out loud. When I went on to tell him that the 'Commandant of Stalingrad' had brought a whole staff along with him, he became seriously angry. 'What will we do with these people? Commandant of a city that long since has not been taken, that is simply grotesque. I will suggest to Paulus that he send these gentlemen back to Army Group 'B'. Get into contact with the adjutant there and prepare him for it!'

My comrade at the army group agreed to Schmidt's proposal. We were all agreed that the keen old colonel would not be reprimanded. Why not, though, blame the Army High Command? Did they still believe that the Red Army was beaten and that the taking of this vast city was a piece of cake? How could such things happen when we were making daily situation and casualty reports?

'Registering Commandos' and 'Oil Brigades'
Another experience set me thinking. At about the same time several officers and soldiers reported to our headquarters. They called themselves 'Registering Commandos'. What was this then? The army's senior quartermaster could tell us. They were experts in metallurgy who had only been allocated to the army for accommodation and rations. They received their instructions directly from Führer Headquarters. They were to penetrate the city behind the fighting troops, secure all factory machinery, even half-made stuff and raw materials, especially non-ferrous metal, prevent their destruction and enable their immediate evacuation.

At the next meeting with the commander-in-chief, he cut through to the subject. 'So, Adam, what have you to say about our latest reinforcements?', he asked, smiling. 'These people won't be able to get their hands on much. The Luftwaffe has destroyed everything. Even the factories are now only heaps of rubble. Finally, who is going remove anything? Our soldiers have enough on their plate.'

'Are they really soldiers or simply civilians hastily dressed in uniforms, General?'

'Unfortunately I cannot answer that question. The main thing is that they do not disturb our operations.'

'Storage space they will certainly claim, General, or do they have a convoy of trucks at their disposal?'

'I don't know. By the way, according to Army Group 'A', which is thrusting on to the Caucasus, similar commandos are to take over the oilfields in Maikop and Grosny and later at Buku.'

Paulus had gone back across to Major-General Schmidt, but I could not get our latest conversation out of my head. I remembered a bit out of a speech or article by Goebbels: 'This is no war for throne and altar; it is a war for grain and bread . . . a war for raw materials, rubber, iron and ore.' Adolf Hitler had written something similar in *Mein Kampf* when he was looking to the east and spoke of ground policy in Russia. No doubt the 'Registering Commandos' and 'Oil Brigades' were to secure these war aims. I also recalled a talk I had had in the spring at Poltava with a talkative specialist who belonged to the 'Economic Staff East'. I had not thought much about what he had said at the time, as he talked about subsidiaries of the Mannesmann-Konzern in Kiev and Dnepropetrovsk, of a Siemens–Ukraine GmbH and a Friedrich Krupp AG, main office Ukraine. Finally I recalled an expression often heard among our staff that holders of the Knight's Cross would be given a farm in the eastern territories as a gift by Hitler at the end of the war.

Actually this dispelled everything very bad within us since the beginning of the Eastern campaign with the repeatedly hammered-in thesis that the fight against the Soviet Union was an indispensable preventative war to prevent the Bolshevists taking over Germany.

Something appeared to be wrong about the whole matter. But what? In any case, as I often said to myself, I am not responsible.

Mamai-Kurgan and Zaritza

The attack continued. On the 14th and 15th September our divisions were able to drive deeper into the city. Bloody fighting erupted at the central railway station and on the Mamai-Kurgan, Height 102. The railway station changed hands no fewer than five times on the 14th September. The Mamai-Kurgan offered a view over the whole city, including the harbours and the large industrial factories in the north: Red October, Barrikady and the Tractor Factory. Cut by deep gullies, the maze of buildings, streets and squares stretched for 60 kilometres, with the broad band of the Volga in the background. To the south the wooded Golodny Island rose above the stream. On the opposite bank one could make out the village of Krasnaya Sloboda, from which the Soviet troops fighting in the city received most of their supplies. It was quite understandable that the enemy would not give up their attempts to retake the commanding heights of Mamai-Kurgan, and they achieved it on the 16th September. Despite many expensive attempts during the next ten days, it was possible for us to reoccupy only half of the hill.

By the 27th September the 4th Panzer Army and the LIst Corps were able to take the southern part of the city bordered by the Zaritza, including the bank of the Volga. In comparison with this, the enemy dominated the centre and north of Stalingrad, despite the commitment of our last forces with ever-stronger positions. The most important part of the city, with its ferries to the Soviet maintenance and supply bases on the east bank of the Volga, remained in the hands of the defenders.

On the 12th September Colonel-General von Weichs, commander-in-chief of Army Group 'B', and General Paulus were summoned to a conference at Führer Headquarters in Vinniza. Paulus reported on the situation at the front, placing special emphasis on the army's northern flank. Hitler ignored this, sweeping everything aside to repeat his conviction that the Red Army was beaten, and that resistance at Stalingrad could only be expected locally. Apart from that, all measures had been taken to secure the northern flank. Then it was the 6th Army's turn, all its strength being concentrated on taking the city. Instead of Paulus's additional request for three battle-worthy divisions, only the XXXXVIIIth Panzer Corps was allocated to him from the 4th Panzer Army. Then the 4th Panzer Army was torn away from the front attacking Stalingrad and the 6th Army had to take over the operations for the whole extent of the city.

Shaking his head, General Paulus showed me the army group's orders. 'That is now called reinforcement. These divisions are as fought-out as ours. At the same time that I have to take over two further divisional sectors from the 4th Panzer Army, in reality I have only a badly weakened division more at my disposal.'

Gumrak main dressing station
My deputy from the Personnel Office had arrived. Once the business had been handed over at headquarters, we wanted to drive together to the various infantry divisions. This was on the day of my departure for the homeland, and we set off in the morning at about 0700 hours. Although it was already the middle of September, it was warm and windless. Uninterruptedly our bombers flew across the cloudless sky over the city escorted by nimble

fighters. Through binoculars we could see how the aircraft dropped their deadly freight from a great height. Meanwhile, the Stukas dived into the thick clouds of smoke that hung constantly over the burning city. Explosions ripped the air and brought new wounds to strike the city and its defenders.

'I did not realise how bitter the Russian resistance was. We were all of the opinion that the city would be taken within a few days,' said my companion, who was now seeing for the first time what was happening here.

'You are not the first representative of the Army High Command to say that to us. We keep repeating that the enemy has been wrongly assessed by the High Command, and that the situation can become even more costly for us.'

We had reached Gumrak. I knew that there must be a main dressing station here somewhere. While we were searching for it, we noticed that several artillery batteries had deployed hardly a thousand metres to the east of the place and were firing incessantly. The enemy was replying with heavy guns. The tall fountains of earth springing from the explosions were dangerously close. The exploding of the shells was so loud that one had to almost scream to make oneself heard.

There too was the main dressing station, a large building at the railway station indicated by the Red Cross flag. Wounded were constantly being brought in by ambulances, trucks and horse-drawn carts. Not all were lying on stretchers. For many there was only a woollen blanket beneath them, while others were simply laid on the bare floor of the truck. The surgeons and their assistants were working in a big room on two operating tables. Amputees were dealt with first, then air pipe injuries, then came the stomach and lung cases. Apparently one had to give preference to stomach injuries, but these operations lasted two or three hours here, so that the chances of survival were low. During this time a large number of amputees had been brought forward, for whom timely attention was less risky. We did not want to disturb them and satisfied ourselves with a quick look into the operating room. As we were standing at the door a medical orderly went past us. He was carrying a bucket filled with blood-soaked bandages, clothing and scraps of uniform, as well as a prominent, squashed object: it was a waxen, blue-black grained bone stump. It belonged to the young lad who lay anaesthetised on the table. The surgeon clamped the blood vessels on what was left of his thigh while a medical orderly made a dressing with gauze and bandages.

We had seen enough. Meanwhile the sergeant-major of the medical company had come up to us. He led us to the next room, where the badly wounded were waiting for transport to the army's rear area to await repatriation. They were lying on mattresses, heaps of steppe grass or the bare earth, a picture of misery. Strong young men shot into cripples. The sergeant-major indicated one soldier whose head was completely bandaged over, leaving only the tip of his nose and his mouth visible. 'A nineteen-year-old gymnast, blinded, but he doesn't know it. He asks everyone whether he will see again, and calls for his mother in his feverish dreams.'

There was another room there full of amputees. As everywhere, there were the smells of ether, pus and blood. But there were a number of iron bedsteads, giving the impression of a hospital. A young doctor was already making his rounds. Right next to the door lay a leg amputee, an infantryman who had had his leg smashed by a hand grenade in the street fighting. We went up to him. We had already handed out some of the cigarettes that we had brought with us. Once we had given him one, we got talking.

'All hell is let loose out there. I have never experienced anything like it in this war. And I have been in it since the beginning. These Ivans won't go back a step. The way into their positions goes only over corpses. But many of us bite the dust before that. Apparently there are no proper positions. Every ruin, every stone is defended by them. Death is waiting everywhere. Nothing is achieved by wild attacks, they just cost lives. We have to learn close-quarter fighting all over again.'

'Yes', said his neighbour, an NCO with the Iron Cross First Class, as we discovered during the course of our conversation, 'we can learn from the Reds. They are masters of house-to-house fighting, knowing how to use every heap of stones, every projection of a wall, and every cellar. I would never have believed it of them.'

An older soldier joined in the conversation: 'I can only agree with what these two have said, Colonel. It is laughable when the front newspaper keeps on writing that the Russians are at the end of their strength, no longer capable of resistance. The publisher should only come to us for three days and then he wouldn't talk such nonsense.'

'Until now we have always joked about the Russians,' interjected an NCO, 'but that was before. Many of us have forgotten how to laugh in Stalingrad. The worst is the fighting at night. If we can take a ruin or one side of a street by day, the enemy will certainly attack during the night. If we do not keep fully alert, he chases us out again. I am afraid that we will need months until the whole city is in our hands, if we can manage it at all.'

'Our company', the older one cut in, 'has had more casualties than I have experienced in any of my units during the whole war. When I was wounded we were down to twenty-one men, and they were tired and fought-out. We could hardly take another step forwards. In the end none survived.'

We looked around the room. All nodded at the words that had been spoken. This was more than instructive, especially for my deputy, who had come to Stalingrad with all the illusions of the Army High Command. The sergeant-major confirmed what we had heard. 'Colonel, they all say the same thing. It must be frightful up at the front. We see it in the many, many wounded that are delivered day and night. Our doctors perform miracles, finding no time for food and sleep. Just look at our head doctor. He can hardly stand on his feet.'

As we were leaving, we opened the door to the operating theatre again. The head doctor nodded to us tiredly, then bent back over the operating table to deprive the war of a victim – or at least to try to.

We climbed back into our vehicle without a word. I wanted to present my deputy to the nearby headquarters staff of the LIst Corps and then drive on to the VIIIth and XIth Corps. All were very busy. In the short encounters that we had, we met only earnest, worried faces. Even General von Seydlitz, known as an irrepressible daredevil, seemed to be weighed down by the heavy fighting. Colonel Claudius, his chief of staff, said to us adroitly, 'With such weakened divisions we cannot accomplish anything with this bitterly fighting enemy; we lack the strength to penetrate. On top of this, all the divisions report that a newly introduced enemy Guards division is engaged in the battle. Even sailors have been seen.'

'Has this report been passed on to the army?' I asked.

'Yes. I immediately informed the army's 1st general staff officer.'

Time was pressing and we had to go on. At the VIIIth Corps we met the adjutant, who gave us a brief orientation on the situation. Lastly we sought out General Strecker, the commanding general of the XIth Corps. It had become quieter in his sector over the last few days. Nevertheless, Strecker was unhappy about his left-hand neighbours, the Italians, whose weapons and equipment were totally inadequate under the given conditions.

By about 1800 hours we were back in Golubinskaya. I reported to Paulus and Schmidt that my deputy had taken over my duties. At the same time I reported my departure to the four-week cure at Falkenstein in the Taunus Mountains.

Talks on the train
For the third time in five weeks I flew on the courier aircraft via Charkov to Vinniza. But this time it was not to discuss reinforcements but for my return to Germany. I sighed with relief as I took my seat in the train to Berlin in Vinniza in accordance with my travel plan. Leaning right back in the comfortable cushions of the First Class carriage, I let the colourful autumnal landscape go past my eyes. Not once did the thought of partisans arise. I was looking ahead to the pleasure of seeing my wife and daughter again for four carefree weeks in my own homeland. In Berlin I had an immediate connection to Frankfurt am Main. In the carriage four young officers on leave had already taken seats, returning via Frankfurt to Paris. They were Berliners, cheerful lads, talking about theatres and cinemas, about girlfriends and friends, excursions and festivals. But nothing about the war.

Opposite me sat an older officer, a lieutenant-colonel. Like me, he smiled when one of the second lieutenants told an especially good story, and our eyes met several times. Then he spoke to me: 'Have you come from the east, Colonel?'

'Yes, from Stalingrad,' I replied gently, not to disturb the pleasure of the young people. But apparently not gently enough, for the talking among the young officers suddenly stopped. All sat up and looked at me expectantly. Even back home Stalingrad had become a talking point.

A blond infantry second lieutenant said: 'Paulus is certainly an outstanding army commander. He has already given the Russians a beating. Soon he will be chasing the last of them into the Volga.'

'Were you ever on the Eastern Front?' I asked him pointedly.

'No, Colonel, my unit is in France,' came the somewhat quieter reply.

With a few sentences I described to them the bloody fighting in the city on the Volga. The orderly atmosphere changed. 'I had really believed that the Russians were finished. That is what it says in every newspaper, as does every weekly cinema news bulletin and every radio report,' apologised the second lieutenant. One of the others said: 'Apparently we are getting a quite false representation of the fighting in the East. In Berlin I spoke with an acquaintance who told me about our advance into the Caucasus just like you, Colonel, told us about Stalingrad. I thought that he was way out and did not take his description seriously until now. Now I can see that he was not exaggerating.'

Quite contrary to my wishes, the war had extinguished the happy atmosphere. The talking now switched to remembrance of heavy fighting, fallen comrades, friends and relations. I was irritated with myself for I had not wanted this. Therefore I said: 'But that is enough, comrades. Let us return to more pleasant things! At last I am now too going on four weeks' leave. If that isn't grounds for happiness!'

Everyone tried to chase away their strained thoughts, but the unhappiness remained in our minds. With strong handshakes we said goodbye to each other at the main railway station at Frankfurt am Main. From there I had to travel on by a secondary line to Kronberg in the Taurus Mountains. I still had over two hours to wait. During this time I went to the railway station post office to telephone the officers' rest home at Falkenstein. A friendly voice told me that I would be met by a vehicle in Kronberg. After this telephone call, I strolled to the railway station exit. I knew Frankfurt very well from before: the beautiful old city with the Roman remains, Goethe's birthplace, the Paulskirche, the main business street and the university. Pulsating life then filled the trading metropolis. The people surged and pressed late into the night on the brightly lit Kaiserstrasse and the Zeil with their shops, hotels, restaurants, cafés and pleasure places.

This familiar picture had changed in all sorts of ways. The colourful streams of humanity had changed to field-grey uniforms. Especially conspicuous were the many amputees. I looked straight into a show window when a young second lieutenant hobbled past on two crutches. One could see that his movements were difficult. To my question he told me that he had only received his artificial limb that day. Frankfurt had become a centre for the fitting of such equipment. That is why one met so many war wounded here.

'Goethe-University' said a white enamel sign. A university institute was accommodated in the building. I recalled my own time as a student. Were the professors still alive and working who had heard my readings on mathematics in the 1920s? Schönfliess was the Rector then, and Eppstein. Twenty years had passed. I knew nothing about Stalingrad then.

It was time to return to the railway station. The train was already there, under steam ready to leave. I went through some of the carriages until I found an almost empty Second Class one. Only one young officer sat by the window. To my surprise, I knew him: he was the very same second lieutenant that I had spoken to on the Kaiserstrasse. I soon discovered that he belonged to Infantry Regiment 39 in Düsseldorf. We had even had a mutual friend in the regiment, Second Lieutenant Volz, who had fallen in the Western campaign.

I asked him where he was travelling to. 'Falkenstein,' he replied. 'I am on a cure there. May I assume, Colonel, that is where you are going too?'

'Correctly guessed, young friend.' The second lieutenant pulled himself up and gave his name, and I too presented myself.

'Now I know who you are, too, Colonel. You were a tactics teacher to Second Lieutenant Volz, who often spoke about you.'

'Hopefully not badly.'

'Absolutely not. He also talked about your son Heinz, who unfortunately also fell in France. I shared the same year of birth.'

I looked at him silently. He noticed that he had touched a sensitive spot and went straight on. 'The next station is Kronberg, Colonel, which is where we have to get off. From the station it takes another hour to Falkenstein.'

'We will be driven. I have ordered a vehicle from the chief doctor. Of course you'll come with me.'

The vehicle driver was already waiting for me on the station platform. We drove off once my luggage had been put in the boot. The contours of the dark Taunus Mountains rose sharply into the sky. Like a golden disk the sun was already apparently deep on the horizon. I took in the aromatic mountain air in deep breaths. Homeland air! How many times I had previously wandered here in happy company with a filled rucksack on my back. I especially liked the ridgeway from Bad Nauheim to Neuwied am Rhein along the *Limes*, the old Roman border wall, whose watchtowers and castles were still identifiable everywhere.

The cure at Falkenstein

At a fast pace we neared the Falkenstein cure place. The rest home was on the near edge of the town, closely nestled into the woods. The vehicle drove through a wide open gate to a large building with an entrance of broad steps. This was the administrative building. Left and right of it, and built in the same style, stood several other smaller buildings. The whole was framed with gardened spaces in which the autumn flowers were already blooming in lavish splendour.

'We are here,' declared my companion. 'If you permit, I will show you around tomorrow morning. But now we must go upstairs, where we are already awaited.'

On the steps stood an officer, a senior staff doctor, as I established when I got nearer. He was the official chief doctor. He came towards me and greeted me warmly, then we entered the building together. In the comfortably furnished vestibule a graceful sister took over. The doctor excused himself: 'Go to your room now, Colonel. Once you have freshened yourself up, the sister will take you to reception. Finally we shall meet up for supper in the dining room. I will use the opportunity to introduce you to our other guests.'

The sister asked me to follow her. We went down into the cellar. Before us lay a long illuminated corridor. 'What is this?' I asked.

The pretty girl looked at me with a smile: 'All our guest houses – perhaps you noticed outside that there are three on either side – are connected to the main building by this tunnel. There are various bathrooms and treatment rooms here. You can come here to the bathrooms in the morning in your pyjamas and dressing gown.'

'It really could not be more convenient.'

'A few more steps up and we will be there,' said the sister. Immediately afterwards I was standing in a large, bright room, well and tastefully set out. My luggage was already there. I stepped out onto the balcony through a half-opened door. Dusk had arrived. A light haze had sunk down over the wood. A heavenly peace reigned. I could hardly grasp that there could be so much beauty when 2,500 kilometres to the east of here hundreds of men were being torn and mutilated every second, where the groans of the wounded and the gasping of the dying were masked by the thunder of the guns and exploding bombs. I gently closed the door and went back into my room. The sister had left silently.

The next half hour sufficed for me to remove the dust of the journey and to complete the formalities of registering. The gong was already sounding for supper. All the guests had already assembled in the dining room when I entered with the doctor. At my request I was able to sit with the second lieutenant from Düsseldorf. Another table guest was Lieutenant Jacobi, a young Berliner. He too had lost a leg, but not his good humour.

I soon became fully accustomed to the routine. Every day we made a little walk in the woods or sat in the park in the mild autumnal sun. They could have been completely carefree days for me if the subject of Stalingrad had not existed.

Every day I waited tensely for the Wehrmacht Report. Every day the name of the city came up. But what I wanted to hear – that Stalingrad was entirely in our hands – did not come. As the longed-for report had still not arrived after two weeks, unrest grew in me. Astoundingly for me, almost all my fellow guests, even the village inhabitants, had great confidence in General Paulus. 'He will soon do it. Then hopefully the war will soon be over,' said an old farmer, with whom I often had a chat. But Paulus himself replied to my greetings card at the end of September: 'Everything still just as when you left.'

An experience in Frankfurt
On the day of my arrival in Falkenstein I was visited by my wife and daughter. Unfortunately there were drops of sorrow in the cup of joy at our reunion. My mother-in-law was dying. Completely paralysed, she lay in a sanatorium near Darmstadt. I was unable to see her again before she closed her eyes for the last time a few days later. Afterwards my wife and my daughter joined me for the rest of my cure at Falkenstein.

With them, and together with the two young officers, I went once to Frankfurt. Lieutenant Jacobi had suggested a visit to the cinema there. It could be that he wanted to take my thoughts off Stalingrad. In order to be able to move about more freely, we all went in civilian clothes. My wife had already brought everything necessary on her first visit.

The chief doctor had given us leave for the whole day. We went in a horse-drawn carriage to the station at Kronberg. 'Like a country party,' said my wife, smiling. 'Like almost ten years ago when we drove in a horse-drawn coach of the 3rd Cavalry Division from Weimar to Tiefurt, Belvedere, Bad Berka, or on the Ettersberg. How lovely it was then!'

We watched the workers in the fields from the moving train. The potato harvest was in full swing. We saw only women and children, at the most only one old man among them. But no, here were also some young men, French prisoners of war. The main burden of the work fell on the shoulders of the women. They took the hundredweight sacks to the wagons, drove the plough behind obstinate oxen and organised the prisoners, many of whom knew nothing about farming.

A leave train was arriving as we got off at the main railway station in Frankfurt. Excited women and children were clamouring at the barriers. The first soldiers, laden with bursting backpacks and other bits of luggage, were leaving the carriages. The officers were carrying heavy suitcases. It could only be a leave train from France or Belgium. What had the fathers, husbands and sons brought with them? The thoughts of presents only increased their joy at seeing each other again, which was manifested in happy calls, holding each other, and crying. Fourteen days' leave was a fourteen-day festival! It left no room to think that the lovely, rare things bought with worthless occupation money had been legally stolen from the French or Belgians.

A terrible contrast to this joyousness was offered by the farewell scenes on another platform. On the board on the controller's cabin were the names Frankfurt am Main–Dresden–Krakau: a train heading to the Eastern Front. Here too were soldiers with their wives or mothers in their arms, holding children by the hand. Silently they approached the barrier. Tears flowed from several white-faced women. Will he return? Are we looking at his dear face today for the last time? And what then? What has the war done for us?

Furtively I took a look at my wife. The tears were shimmering in the corner of her eyes too. I knew that she was thinking of our only son Heinz, who had fallen in France two years ago. In a few days' time she would be standing at this same station and watching the departing train carrying me off to the East. To what fate? She sighed: 'What sorrow and distress this unholy war has already brought us, and still no end in sight.'

We strolled along the Kaiserstrasse. Just as upon my arrival fourteen days previously, field grey dominated the human throng. But today I noticed that there were also considerable numbers of brown and black uniforms: officials, security service and SS people. 'Stones and walls also have ears here,' my wife whispered to me. 'A critical word spoken aloud can result in an immediate arrest. It is especially bad in Frankfurt. You have to be very careful here.'

'Is that why you have been so shy and taciturn?' I asked.

'You yourself have repeatedly warned me to be careful! Today thinking otherwise is no longer accepted!'

We had agreed with the two injured officers, who found walking on the pavement quite difficult, to have lunch in the Frankfurter Hof. It was already twelve o'clock when we entered. Previously one could hardly find a free place, but today only a few tables were occupied. Our companions were already waiting for us. We took our places. At the neighbouring table sat two men and two women, apparently two married couples, who I estimated must be in their late forties. I had hardly given them a thought when I heard the word Stalingrad. I understood bits of what they were saying: 'Our son wrote . . . officer . . . very heavy fighting . . . heavy losses, the Russians not giving away a metre of ground. The city a heap of rubble.' There were tears in the eyes of one woman, evidently the mother of the letter writer.

Her husband stroked her hand: 'Don't worry, mother, he is still alive.'

After lunch we made our way to the cinema. It was an insignificant film then running in the cinema at the Eschenheimer Tower. I have long since forgotten the title, as we were mainly interested in the newsreels. As we had plenty of time, we decided against taking a tram and went on foot. I looked concernedly at Lieutenant Jacobi, who was having difficulties with his artificial leg. But he laughed when I told him to go slower.

We were able to obtain five box seats. The afternoon show was already almost sold out, whilst there were hardly any visitors in the evenings. It seemed that no enemy aircraft dared fly to Frankfurt in the daytime.

The weekly news show began with pictures of the eastern war scene, also of Stalingrad burning. German troops stormed forward as if on exercise. Some, also as if on exercise, gave firing cover while others ran loose. Who on earth had filmed this? The spectators, among them many wounded soldiers, greeted this with laughter, whistles and calls of 'Swindle!' This was really a strong blow. The severity of the fighting was concealed, brushed aside. The swearing and complaining in the auditorium increased. Then something suddenly happened: somebody was pulled out of one of the rows and pushed through one of the exits on the side. The security service was at work. Various calls of protest were loud. Then a deathly silence reigned. Fear won over fact. Thoughtfully I left the cinema and the main film with my companions.

The days in Falkenstein passed in a flash. Swimming, woodland air, peace and the company of my dear ones gave me new strength and health. But the doctor was not content with the intermediate examinations and suggested extending the cure. I refused. Paulus had already written saying that my return was expected on the given date. So I had to keep to the four weeks. On the 16th October I stood with my wife and daughter, as well as my new-found friends, for the last few minutes on the platform in Frankfurt. I gave a final wave from the moving train. From Berlin I took the courier train to Vinniza and flew on from there on the courier aircraft to Golubinskaya.

Little success with great losses
My deputy collected me with the car from the airfield. On the way I noticed several changes that had occurred among the staff during my absence. My friend Voelter had been transferred as chief of staff to a corps outside our command. The senior quartermaster (OQu), the Ic and the army doctor had also been changed.

In contrast, there was nothing really new at the front in Stalingrad. Only in the north of the city had our divisions been able to push back the Red Army's advanced positions near Orlovka, take the Tractor Factory and push forward to the Volga. There had been some hard fighting around the Barricady and the Red October Factories. Our losses had mounted even further and could not nearly be made up by the few march battalions.

I reported back from my cure first to Major-General Schmidt. He gave an outward show of confidence. But when he showed me the run of the positions on the situation map, a certain disappointment came through from what he said. We had hardly moved forward in the city and there was no end to the punishing fighting in sight. The enemy was attacking our divisions almost ceaselessly between the Don and the Volga.

Next I went to see Paulus. My arrival was already known to him. His first question after receiving my report was: 'What have you to say about Halder's departure?'

I had heard nothing about it until then. Puzzled, I asked him: 'When was Colonel-General Halder dismissed, General?'

'On the 24th September. His successor is General of Infantry Zeitzler.'

Apparently this change among the generals had hit Paulus hard. He had worked with Halder, had been his deputy and prized him highly.

'Is it known why Halder was sacked, General?'

'Obviously not. But I recall that Halder repeated in my presence that Hitler was opposed to his own opinion. It may be that he was uncomfortable about this. But tell me now what happened to you during your four weeks in Germany and how your recovery went.'

We sat together for a long time. Paulus listened to my report without interrupting. I mentioned also what I had heard about him several times; that the commander-in-chief of the 6th Army would soon finish off the Russians, and then the war would come to an end.

Paulus smiled tiredly. 'That would be fine, Adam, but for the time being we are far from it. The Army High Command ignored our warnings about the north flank. That is why the situation has become even more serious. Several days ago I received alarming news from the 44th Infantry Division on the northern bank of the Don Bend of strong Soviet troop movements from east to west, and troops assembling along our front. The 376th Infantry Division reported similarly. The enemy appears to be ready to attack into our deep flank, and I have nothing with which to confront this deadly danger. Our divisions are bleeding in Stalingrad. The Army High Command has again authorised me to attack the city and to give me three new war-strength divisions. Unfortunately only five sapper battalions were allocated to us – as if they could take the city.'

The general spoke the last words bitterly. The nervous twitch in his face had become stronger. Lieutenant Zimmermann had told me shortly before I went in about Paulus's general state. An old intestinal pain had become noticeable again.

That was quite a series of bad tidings. I excused myself with mixed feelings. My leave deputy was already sitting waiting in the office. I wanted to resume my duties that evening.

The battlefield painter and the Stalingrad Shield
Everything was ready for the handover. The messages from the Army High Command had been clamped together in a folder. These interested me most of all. That is why I had asked the lieutenant colonel to tell me about them. I would go over them in detail in the next few days. My deputy took the folder: let us begin with the curious ones. Several weeks ago Führer Headquarters sent us a well known battlefield painter from Leipzig. He was to record the battle of Stalingrad in sketchbooks and on canvas. We sent him to General von Seydlitz, as he could best place him at focal points. The painter is to do preparatory work for a vast picture that he will paint in his Leipzig studio for Hitler.'

'Can we be responsible for the risks he will encounter at the front?'

'The painter, an old man, is wearing field-grey uniform. He should already be busy at work. Perhaps you will have the opportunity to discover for yourself on a trip to the LIst Corps,' replied the lieutenant-colonel.

'Right, carry on,' I urged him.

'When you gave me your impressions of the homeland on your return from the airfield, I was reminded of a recent decree from Führer Headquarters, by which we must constantly nominate soldiers, NCOs and young officers who display bravery in the battle for Stalingrad for the Knight's Cross or the German Cross in Gold and send their names to Hitler for confirmation. The first of these, a second lieutenant, returned four days ago. He told me that Hitler had received him very jovially. Finally he had given an account on the radio about his experiences at the front, which was extraordinarily highly honoured. The daily newspaper brought out his report with his picture. The propaganda at the front was not far behind. In the Kiev *'Soldiers' Newspaper'* appeared running descriptions of the battle from the pen of Specialist Fritzsche.'

'In any case there is some method in this. As long as we don't have Stalingrad, something has to replace it, even if it is only refined propaganda. My impression is that many people at the front and back home are no longer attracted to it. The number of people tired of the war is immense and grows daily. Certainly the final taking of the city will bring about a change of heart.'

'There is also a letter from the Army High Command along the same lines. On Hitler's suggestion, a Stalingrad shield is to be made, like the Crimean shield and the Narvik shield. The army has been tasked with producing the design for a memorial plaque by the 25th November.'

At this point the door opened and Paulus came in. We stood up. 'Sit down, gentlemen. I won't disturb you. As I was going past outside along the road I heard from Senior Sergeant-Major Küpper that you were still working. What is that letter you have in your hand?'

I passed him the letter about the Stalingrad shield. 'A sad chapter. We have hardly taken half the city and batter through the rest with our heads. With the present fighting state of the troops, it is hard to see us ever attaining the set goal. But they give hardly any thought to that at the High Command. Instead they bring up such trivial matters as a Stalingrad shield.'

After a short pause the general went on: 'It will interest you, Adam, that an artist from the Propaganda Company has already made a draft. You will have to work on the award proposals later.'

'I already have a horror of it, General. However, I am more impressed by how little progress we have made. When I flew off to my cure five weeks ago, I was hoping to see upon my return that the headquarters would no longer be here. On the contrary, everything remains as it was. I have not experienced anything like it in the three years of this war.'

The enemy has grown
'You know yourself that in most of our divisions the fighting strength of the regiments has sunk. But that is not the only reason. The ability of the Red Army soldiers to hold on has reached an extent in the last weeks that we had never expected. No soldier or officer speaks today of Ivan in disparaging terms, which used to be quite normal. The Red Army soldier is proving himself more from day to day as the master of close-quarter fighting, in house-fighting and in camouflage. Our artillery and air force virtually plough the enemy out of occupied ground before every attack, but as soon as our infantry leave cover they are hit by destructive defensive fire. Should we be successful in taking a place, the Russians immediately counterattack, throwing us back to the starting-point.'

Reflectively Paulus looked up and then continued: 'Moreover, the enemy leadership has become more single-minded. We have the impression that he will hold on to his positions on the west bank of the Volga at all costs. In some places the strips occupied by him are only 100 to 200 metres wide. If prisoner of war reports can be believed, the 62nd Army's headquarters are in the steep slopes of the west bank. Since the middle of September General Chuikov has been commander-in-chief of this army. Again and again he was able to bring new divisions forward over the Volga. His fighting strength grows, ours fades away. The five engineer battalions flown in by air suffered such severe losses in the northern part of the city that we had to withdraw them from battle.

'Certainly the enemy has enormous difficulties. Prisoners tell us that the 62nd Army is supplied at night over the Volga. As the army has hardly any vehicles or horses available on the west bank, weapons, ammunition and food have to be carried from the landing places to the positions. The troops have no rest day and night. The wounded and sick are taken across to the east bank in the unloaded boats. Until now it has not been possible for us to take the landing places or disrupt the water passage.'

'But these are the same people, General, that we were driving before us for months. How can one explain this bitter resistance?'

'I have already said that their command is assured of victory. General Chuikov seems to be a very energetic troop commander.'

The time had passed quickly. We escorted the commander-in-chief to the village street, which was already completely dark. With an orderly officer, who was waiting for him, Paulus went to the little house that he occupied. We, however, went back to work.

The lieutenant colonel picked up the file that he had prepared for the handover. 'I would like to mention another of the Army High Command's measures. You too described how in Berlin, similarly to Vinniza, wishful dreams have replaced reality.

'In the first days of October an engineer general reported to 6th Army headquarters with a fortress senior construction staff, two engineer regimental staffs, six engineer battalion staffs and a construction company. The Army High Command had instructed them to construct fortifications in Stalingrad. Our chief engineer, Colonel Stelle, blew his top when he heard. 'To build bunkers one needs cement, gravel and wood. It could be that one could get gravel out of the Volga or Don. Cement and wood must be transported for hundreds of kilometres. Even if that worked, we lack the necessary construction workforce. The close fighting in the city has also strongly involved the engineer battalions. Finally the Russians would not sit and do nothing while we built concrete fortifications.'

My deputy recounted further that Selle had proposed to the 6th Army's chief of staff that the engineers should be set to constructing rear positions. The Army High Command abruptly turned down these proposals. Naturally no building material for bunkers appeared. Now a new Führer Order demanded that these engineers should build heated bunkers for the tanks, which was equally unrealistic.

'I can vividly imagine how Selle reacted to such fantasy,' I said. 'All that you have just reported is, in view of our complicated situation, plainly depressing.'

The lieutenant colonel looked at me quizzically for a second. 'You know, Colonel, that I came from the Army High Command's Personnel Office. There I was several times astonished at the criticisms of the High Command uttered by the older commanders. During the five weeks that I have been standing in for you I have realised what damage nonsensical measures and orders from the Army High Command have done to the troops.'

'So it is', I replied, 'in this way that trust in the High Command has been put to a severe test. It would be good if the officers of the general staff responsible for such orders had worked for some months in an army headquarters. Perhaps they would then at last realise how dangerous it is if one starts off with false calculations in commanding troops. The gentlemen in Führer Headquarters have studied military history, operations results, strategy and tactics. Theoretically they are fully aware that a battle has never been won by underestimating the enemy and overestimating one's own forces, and that the troops have to pay with blood for the Command's mistakes. I must openly state that as a result of my experiences in the Eastern campaign, a considerable part of my once-high regard for the general staff has vanished. It would be good if after your return to the Personnel Office you could pass on your observations to a competent office. Or do you intend to take over one of our regiments?'

'This prospect remains as before. My role on the general staff has reinforced my decision. There is a regiment free in the 76th Infantry Division. Colonel Abraham is ill. General Rodenburg has asked for a replacement for him. Here is the letter.'

I read the piece of paper. 'The illness does not appear to be too serious. General Rodenburg has suggested he be given a command in the rear area for a few weeks. We will discuss that shortly, but before that, another question. How are things with our potential officer school in Suvorovski?'

'Unfortunately we were unable to start the course on the prescribed date. The fighting within the city forced us to delay its assembly. Captain Göbel was only able to start the instruction in the middle of this month.'

That did not please me at all, for we urgently needed young infantry officers. I could not reprimand my deputy, for he was not responsible for the delayed start. I decided to do everything I could to speed up the instruction. Then I had a thought: 'How would it be if Colonel Abraham was ordered to Suvorovski? He could recover there while at the same time advising Captain Göbel in the educating and training of the officer cadets. You yourself could take over Abraham's regiment.'

'I am agreeable to that, Colonel. Would Generals Paulus and Schmidt agree?'

'We will go to the conference together tomorrow morning and take the written application to the Army High Command for your transfer to the 76th Infantry Division with us. If all goes well, you could take over your duty in two days' time.'

Then I had to tell him another secret. In my last visit to the Personnel Office I had brought up the subject of my relief as adjutant. 'Should General Paulus be agreeable, Colonel Sommerfeld, in peacetime the adjutant of the IVth Corps in Dresden, would be my successor. I will speak to the commander-in-chief about it in the next few days. But now it is time we packed up for the day.'

Bad omens

At the beginning of November the commander of XIth Corps on the left wing of the army, General of Infantry Strecker, came to speak to Paulus personally. All the divisions on the northern front reported movements and concentrations of enemy troops in front of our left flank and the Rumanian 3rd Army, which had been inserted between the 6th Army and the Italian 8th Army on the 10th October. Strecker demanded urgent countermeasures as the 4th Panzer Army operating in the south had identified attack preparations by the enemy. At army headquarters and among the commanding generals there was no doubt about the enemy's intention to surround the 6th Army and the 4th Panzer Army.

The commander-in-chief of Army Group 'B', Field Marshal von Weichs, and his chief of staff, General of Infantry von Sodenstein, shared the fears of 6th Army Headquarters. But the Army High Command and Hitler could not accept this. The High Command simply did not take the 6th Army's reports seriously, doubting that the Red Army could even think of another counteroffensive. To counter the threatening encirclement, Paulus had proposed retaking an observation post behind the Don. Lacking any conscience or sense of responsibility for the lives of the hundreds of thousands of soldiers involved, the Army High Command rejected the request. I was present when the telephone call came. The chief of the army general staff, General of Infantry Zeitzler, was on the telephone in person and gave as an order Hitler's following remarks: 'The Red Army is defeated, it has no more worthwhile reserves, so is in no condition to engage in large attacks. Any assessment of the enemy must be taken from this basic point of view.'

Paulus was shattered by so false an appraisal. The crude reprimand injured him. 'The general staff must know what is about to happen,' he said strongly. 'Are there then only "yes-men" in Hitler's entourage approving every nonsense?' But then he fell quiet. The commander-in-chief of the 6th Army did not want to confine himself to an independent decision. Military obedience won over reason. An army reserve would be formed and placed ready behind the XIth Corps west of the Don southeast of Kletskaya. It was to consist of a mixed band of regimental strength, at whose core would be a tank-hunting unit of the 14th Panzer Division (divisional headquarters, a Panzer regiment, a tank-hunting unit, an artillery regiment and part of the signals unit).

Next day I was at a conference with General Paulus. Almost without looking at it, the commander-in-chief thanked me for my report. His eyes were fixed on the situation map lying before him on the table.

'May I ask, General, how the situation on our left flank has changed since yesterday?' I asked him.

'Much worse. The attitude of the Army High Command is simply incomprehensible to me. They imagine at headquarters, at a distance of more than 2,000 kilometres, that they can better assess the situation at the front than we can. That is absurd. Such a disregard of the enemy is unique.

If the Army High Command does not take measures to protect our flank soon, it could cost the whole of the 6th Army.'

'It is not just us signalling ever more clear indications of a counterattack. The 4th Panzer Army is seeing the same things on its front. That should alarm the people at Führer Headquarters. Why doesn't the army chief of the general staff come and see us himself? Here the threatening danger cannot be turned away with speeches.'

'I think so too, Adam, but this journey seems to put everyone off. Zeitzler would hardly dare to contradict Hitler. He delivered the proof of this yesterday. How can a chief of the general staff pass on such orders? And that was personal, too. Hitler booted Halder out of his company, the last general who at least had his own opinions on military matters. In relation to the political aim setting, there are no differences between Hitler and his generals. Apparently Hitler only wants collaborators like Keitel, who says yes to everything. The future will show whether Zeitzler went along with this illusionary strategy or whether he correctly assessed the strength and possibilities of the Red Army.'

After a few seconds he turned pensively: 'Let us hope that everything will go well for once!'

Winter preparations

By the beginning of October it was obvious to us at army headquarters that we would not be able to take Stalingrad with our badly hit divisions before winter set in. This brought some consequences. One of these was the redeployment of the army headquarters. Golubinskaya, on the west bank of the Don between the bridges at Kalatch and Peskovatka, had an unsuitable traffic situation. It also lacked a connection to the railway, and one could hardly speak of any sort of traffic system. After a reconnaissance sortie for a suitable headquarters, the choice fell on Nishne-Chirskaya. The railway from the west ended not far away, and direct roads led from here to the subordinate corps. All this spoke for Nishne-Chirskaya becoming the army's winter headquarters. In the first days of November the army's chief of signals reported that communications to the corps and army group had been established. The officers' mess and accommodation had been secured under the direction of the headquarters commandant, and I had checked out the prepared complex on the orders of the commander-in-chief. It was actually far better and more suitable than Golubinskaya. The little town at the mouth of the Chir on the Don gave a clean, cared-for impression. Whitewashed single or two-storey houses stood on the edge of wide streets. Gardens and yards completed the picture of the town. Almost all the houses were empty, as most of the inhabitants had left the place.

Although all preparations for the move had been made, the chief of staff hesitated to set a date. Schmidt feared that moving back the army headquarters from Golubinskaya to Nishne-Chirskaya would have an adverse effect on the morale of the hard-fighting troops in the front line. Therefore it was planned that the move would take place at short notice, the first to go to the winter headquarters being part of the command section and the army's signals regiment. The senior quartermaster's department would remain as before near Kalatch on the railway line to Stalingrad.

Looking after the problem child
After crossing the Don, the supply situation for the 6th Army tapered off considerably. Only one railway line was available for bringing forward fuel, ammunition and supplies. This came from the west via Morosovsk and the Don Bridge near Rytchkov to Stalingrad. However, the railway bridge had been blown, so that all the supplies had to be unloaded unto trucks at Chir station and driven just over the bridge near Verchne-Chirskaya, before being reloaded onto the railway wagons already waiting there. One can easily understand how complicated and time-consuming this was. Often the railway track was blocked by either empty wagons or hospital trains creating blockages, tearing the stream of vital supplies apart.

How would it be when winter came, if additional warm clothing, heating material and fodder for horses had to be delivered, if there were also deep snowdrifts and black ice? These questions brought up other anxious concerns.

In the middle of October the quartermaster-general of the army, Lieutenant-General Wagner, visited 6th Army Headquarters. He wanted to see for himself how the supplies were organised and how the whole supply system could be improved. But he too could not help. Our new 1st general staff officer, Colonel Elchlepp, told me afterwards that Wagner had talked about the conditions at Führer Headquarters. All the generals avoided contradicting Hitler. All feared the hysterical outbursts of this lofty dictator. Wagner himself had informed the Supreme Commander in the summer of 1942 about the lack of sources of fuel and requested the supply situation be brought into consideration in the planning of operations. Afterwards Hitler had let him go with the words: 'I had not expected another answer from my generals, thank you.'

We had already often heard such accounts. How did that help us? Not at all. The generals complained about Hitler, but they went on playing the game with him. With their tactical assistance that hysterical man could continue pursuing the war. The generals might be contemptuous of the 'Bohemian Corporal', but the fact was that they had worked on his war plans, that with them he had gone from one adventure to another, driving millions of people senselessly to their deaths. In that lay the historical and human blame of the generals in the Second World War.

I have been rushing ahead with this recognition of my own development.

In those days of October 1942 I was still a long way from such a recognition. I had a feeling that something was not quite right about the whole mechanism of the Wehrmacht command. Sometimes I became angry about so much amateurism, sometimes quite depressed by it. But I did what I took to be my duty. Having myself started off with a military tradition and education, the thought that Paulus as commander-in-chief of the 6th Army had initiated disaster through his own independent decisions was then far from me. One of the explanations for this was that in October 1942 I had hardly yet reached Hell's front door. I had to go right through the inferno of Stalingrad to obtain a deeper understanding. But I will discuss this later.

Among the supply problems that the 6th Army had to concern itself with as the 1942/3 winter approached was the securing of fodder for the thousands of horses. General Paulus decided therefore that all dispensable horses should be moved to the rear army area west of the Don. Only those absolutely necessary for the artillery regiments, the infantry gun companies and the medical services would remain. All the rest were marched off to the west and stabled in villages in which sufficient supplies of food, stalls and barns were available. This was a risky business. The divisions lost their essential transport. But what else could one do if one was not to leave the animals to starve! That these measures might later contribute to our starving thousands of German soldiers no one considered at the time.

In order to save transport space, most of the tanks were also brought to the army's rear area. It had been shown that they were not suitable for the house-to-house fighting within the city. The northern and southern fronts were stuck in a battle for positions. Almost all the tanks, those that had not been totally destroyed, needed major repairs. In order to reduce the demands on fuel, spare parts and equipment, the army headquarters had ordered that the tanks be pulled out of the front and moved back to the area west of the Don for restoration. The workshop companies had already taken up their assigned winter quarters. In view of the bad omens on the northern and southern fronts there were no more transfers of the Panzer regiments.

In the pincers
At the end of October the land between the Don and the Volga lay under thick fog all day long. The reconnaissance activity of the Luftwaffe was completely immobilised. We had no exact picture of what the enemy was up to. At last came a few clear autumnal days, offering good visibility. The first flights over the area on the northern flank confirmed what our divisions had reported from their observations. Excitedly we pored over the aerial photographs. The Red Army had strongly extended their bridgeheads over the Don, especially in the area of Serafimovitch, Several new bridges had been erected, some of them 'underwater bridges' whose surface lay beneath the water level so as to reduce their visibility.

We were standing near Colonel Elchlepp in front of the big situation map. From the north, from about Voronesh, the front line followed the Don generally eastwards, crossed it south of Shishiskin and reached the Volga north of Rynok. This enormous, 600-kilometre long flank was held by just two of our corps and the badly equipped armies of our allies. The run of the front south of Stalingrad looked no calmer. A mighty hole gaped between the 4th Panzer Army and the Rumanian 4th Army, the right-hand neighbour of the 6th Army, and the German units in the Caucasus. On a front-line sector of about 400 kilometres stood the widely dispersed 16th (Motorised) Infantry Division. Not unjustifiably, it bore the nickname of the 'Steppe Fire Brigade'.

Parallel to this the enemy front was shown as a red line on the map. In front of the 6th Army's left flank and the Rumanian 3rd Army, as well as in front of the right wing of the 4th Panzer Army, was shown a mass of Soviet units. General Paulus put one hand on the northern mass of enemy troops, the other on the southern, and then he pushed his hands together as if shutting a trap. What lay inside the trap, what was cut off by the arms of the trap, was us, our 6th Army.

Elchlepp commented laconically: 'If Hitler whistles at our proposals again in this dangerous situation, the catastrophe is complete.'

The nervous tension among the army staff increased. After supper I escorted Paulus to his quarters. Both of us hardly noticed when we left the village street. Nevertheless a little later we were standing on the bank of the Don. For a short time our eyes roved over the surface of the water, then Paulus broke the silence. 'You know my requests, Adam. Hitler has rejected everything: the suspension of the fighting in Stalingrad, and the release of the XIVth Panzer Corps from the city. He went through the orders given to me at Vinniza on the 12th September and demanded the speeding up of the taking of the city by all means. That way we bleed. But that is not all. Stalingrad could become the 6th Army's Cannae.'

The last sentence seemed as if he had spoken to himself. For several minutes he stood sunk in thought, as if he had forgotten me. Then he stroked his brow with his right hand as if he wanted to brush away the tormenting thoughts. His thin figure stretched itself: 'Let us concern ourselves with what we can do. When will the first young officers be available? You know how urgently we need them. Dozens of companies are being led by NCOs.'

'I was in Suvorovski yesterday. At first the young cadets were not happy about being transferred to the infantry. But now their hearts are all for it. Captain Göbel also reported that they were making good progress. I can confirm that from my own impressions. Unfortunately the course had a late start. We can finish at the end of the month at the earliest. In addition, the taking over command by Colonel Abraham at Suvorovski has worked out well. His original humour and his rich experiences are priceless. With this he has regained his health himself.'

'I regret today that I agreed to a later ending of the course. See to it that whatever happens, they are ready by the 30th November!'

We directed our steps back to the village. It was becoming frosty. Was this only due to the cool of the evening, or was this a terrible warning?

At headquarters the usual reports were set out. Nothing unusual there, still nothing. At 2200 hours the connection to the corps became available. There were casualty reports, decorations, promotions, officer postings. Always the same, I thought.

Among the ruins of the Volga city

In the middle of November I had some business to do with the 71st Infantry Division. One of its regimental commanders, Colonel Roske, was an old acquaintance of mine. Until the outbreak of the war we had both been teachers of tactics at the War School in Dresden. Now Roske was with his staff in Stalingrad, his regiment right on the bank of the Volga. I accompanied him there. Seeing the devastated state of the city for the first time from bombing and close-quarter fighting, Schiller's words came to me: 'Horror lives in the empty window frames.'

Ruins, nothing but ruins. In the cellars among them huddled soldiers. Bomb craters and heaps of rubble made the once smooth street virtually impassable. Glass splinters, window casemates, bits of machines, wrecked cars, bedding, remains of furniture, cooking utensils, stoves, electricity cables, tram cables – an inconceivable jumble of destroyed and damaged objects of all kinds. Roske and I moved forward only with difficulty. No one could say exactly where the front line ran in this rubble. Enemy troops could appear suddenly behind our soldiers at any time. Death lay behind every ruin and at every crossroads.

Roske was a good guide through the rubble, dust and glass splinters. After about half an hour the view opened up. We were standing in a covered trench on the western, steeply falling bank of the Volga. The mighty stream was here more than two kilometres wide. It looked almost like a lake, and was a bit misty. Only if one strained one's eyes hard could one faintly see the outline of the far bank. To the right of us a big wooded island appeared in the middle of the powerful stream. Its southern end attracted our attention.

Roske said that during the night our sentries had been pushed back to the Volga bank. Now there was no ship, no boat to be seen on the water. Some German pilots who were keeping a watch over the river had nothing to do. The dive-bombers had more to do, diving steeply on the east bank and the island, their targets being enemy mortars and troop concentrations. They fired their cannon as they dropped their bombs. I stood astounded at the enormous dimensions of the river landscape. After the broad expanse of the steppe came the width of the river, then the city. It had had 600,000 inhabitants, the factory workers alone amounting to ten thousand. What a life there must have been here on Europe's mightiest river between the Caucasus and Moscow.

The tacking of machine-gun fire interrupted my thoughts. Hand grenades exploded to our left and then, with dull thuds, the artillery joined in the battle. While we were standing here in the protection of the trench, bodies were being torn apart by the shelling only a few dozen metres away.

Suddenly all was quiet again. 'It is often like this,' the regimental commander's voice sounded next to me. 'A short exchange of fire, mostly in connection with some troop activity or other. Complete silence reigns over the Volga by day, but it becomes much livelier as dusk approaches. With the field glasses you can see Krasnaya Sloboda over there. Our bombers have blasted the village umpteen times, but no sooner do the first signs of dusk appear on the river than the boats are loaded with men and supplies. The Russians try to cross over to the west bank in the darkness of the night. Then comes a tremendous spectacle: flares throw their magical light over the water, and searchlights slide their beams over the surface of the river. Should a ship or a boat be discovered, it is bathed in light and shot at by machine-guns and guns of all kinds. Aircraft appear, drop their bombs and dive down firing their cannon. Nevertheless, most boats reach the bank. From prisoner-of-war statements we know that in the middle of October a whole rifle division was transported across in a single night. The Russians only reduce their river traffic in bright moonlight.

Roske's regiment was involved in the close-quarter fighting, together with the whole of the 71st Infantry Division and its neighbours to the left and right. While returning to his command post, my companion described the struggle: 'Assault troops from the division to our left forced their way into a building and threw the Russians out of the ground floor. The enemy is still sitting in the floor above today. For days now our people have been pursuing the fighting with all their might, but have been unable to drive Ivan out. It is puzzling how he is supplied. He should have been starved out long ago and shot himself, but no! That handful of Russians has no interest in surrendering!'

They did not even think about it in the following weeks. This small, brave garrison held out until the German troops in this part of the city had been smashed or taken prisoner. We later discovered, from the Soviet history of the war, that this was Sergeant Pavlov's team.

The Army High Command permits defensive measures on the northern flank

Paulus had applied yet again to the Army High Command for permission to abandon Stalingrad and withdraw the 6th Army behind the Don. Again his application was rejected. The attack to the death of the exhausted divisions was gradually assured. Our troops had reached the end of their strength. The last attacks in November had had to be paid for with the lives of thousands and further thousands were crippled. Only a few square metres of ruins had been gained by these attacks. The taking of the city was postponed indefinitely.

But the repeated requests obtained one result from the Army High Command, which at last approved some defensive measures on the 6th Army's northern flank. The XXXXVIIIth Panzer Corps, inserted on the 6th Army's right wing in the city, finally handed over two of its divisions to the LIst Corps. With its three divisions, the 29th (Motorised) Infantry Division became the reserve for Army Group 'B'. Its now superfluous corps headquarters was moved to the rear of the Rumanian 3rd Army, and the 22nd Panzer Division and the Rumanian 1st Tank Division were placed under its command.

The looming catastrophe

The commanding general of the XXXXVIIIth Panzer Corps was Lieutenant-General Heim, the former chief of staff of the 6th Army and an officer with whom I had long enjoyed working. Heim was to act as a corset to the Rumanian 3rd Army threatened by the enemy's attack preparations. General Paulus did not expect much from this. His mistrust lay not with the commanding general, but with the troops under him. 'The Rumanian 1st Tank Division', he said to me, 'is equipped only with light French and Czech tanks, the men are not fully trained and have never been in battle. The German 22nd Panzer Division was badly decimated in the consequent fighting. Heim can only have part of the remainder. Half of the Panzer regiment has been deployed elsewhere by Army Group 'B'.'

Obviously the limited protective measures from Führer Headquarters could in no way banish the most earnest worries of the commander-in-chief and the chief of staff. I discussed this with Paulus on the 15th November. The chief of staff was again referring to Lieutenant-General Heim's task: 'I regard it as more than superfluous if anyone believes that Heim can prevent a breakthrough by the Russians with his two half divisions. When will the Wehrmacht High Command and the Army High Command finally learn to gauge the strength of the enemy correctly!'

'Then you too regard as insufficient the defensive strengths that you, General, have placed ready behind our left flank?'

'Of course they are insufficient. That is why I sought permission to extract the XIVth Panzer Corps from the Stalingrad front. The Army High Command also turned that down, even though the tanks in the city are virtually unused.'

'I simply don't get it, General. Such false decisions are already provoking a catastrophe.'

'Don't condemn so harshly, Adam! The XIVth Panzer Corps has received orders from me to pull back the Panzer regiments and anti-tank battalions of the XVIth and XIVth Panzer Corps so that on demand they can immediately go to the left flank west of the Don.'

'And what is going to happen in the south? Would the 4th Panzer Army hold if the Russians break out? Apparently there is hardly anything left of the Panzer army. It also has had to give up all its tanks and its infantry division. It still has the Rumanian infantry divisions, which have fought bravely several times, but they are poorly armed and equipped.'

'Everything depends upon the strength of the enemy. Should he attack with large battle-strong units, it could also be catastrophic in the south. I too fear the worst if the High Command does not produce battle-strength divisions as soon as possible. But we cannot let any panic break out.'

'I fully understand that, but are we going to look on while doing nothing as the noose is drawn around our necks, General? Our divisions simply cannot do any more. Many of them do not even have half their fighting establishments.'

'All these statements are of no help to us, Adam. Think of the many different situations we have already been through this year! Above all you know the orders of the Army High Command. They are binding for me as a soldier. From my subordinates I too demand that they carry out their orders unconditionally.'

With this our talk came to an end. Our concerns remained, especially for Paulus. He worked restlessly, checking, visiting, speaking. He demanded the utmost from himself, but did not change his mind in doing so. The fate of the 6th Army was decided at Fuhrer Headquarters, and Paulus had accepted his orders.

The tragi-comedy of winter clothing

The first snow fell on the 16th November. The wind whistled icily over the steppe. It found no resistance in our light field-grey coats. Forage caps and 'dice boxes' were not suitable protection against the cold. Really one should have learnt from the nasty experiences of the winter of 1941/2. But by the middle of November the 6th Army still had no adequate winter clothing.

Paulus had already ordered it, as he had known that operating within the city would not be complete before the cold set in. The army's quartermaster-general shared the view of our commander-in-chief. On the other hand, Hitler was of the opinion that normal winter clothing would suffice on the eastern front, especially since the National Socialist People's Welfare was ready with a grandiose collection of winter items, to which every member of the public had contributed, to be sent through to the soldiers on the eastern front. In fact, the population was prepared to contribute anything, no matter what articles of clothing, against the cold and icy wind. Enormous crates were filled with them, but the cold period had come to Stalingrad so suddenly that hardly any of the collection had reached the front, and not much got to the rear areas either. The army quartermaster-general tried to get the delivery expedited, but with little success, the transport facilities being so limited and the overwhelming distances so great. From Millerovo, the main source of supply for the 6th Army, it was reported that a paradoxical picture had emerged when the first wagon of winter clothing was opened. Instead of the requisite woollen and knitted items there were hundreds of ladies' coats, muffs, Persian capes and other fur items, including some very expensive ones, that were, however, completely useless at the front. Apparently the items of clothing handed in by the civilian population had not been secured and checked, but simply despatched without evaluation. Did the troops want to see what they could get?

Schmidt exploded over this mess-up but he could not change anything. Those responsible were somewhere warm at home, 2,000 kilometres away from Stalingrad. The divisional quartermasters received instructions to issue the few good items available to the fighting troops. This barely sufficed to clothe even a fifth of our soldiers huddling in the shelter trenches and bunkers of the northern front without stoves, without fuel, in the middle of the snow-covered steppe swept by the biting north-easterly winds.

While this was going on, the alarming reports arriving at army headquarters were growing. Our nerves were stretched to breaking point. There was no doubt that the Soviet offensive was imminent. What would happen if the XIth Corps and the Rumanian 5th Army failed to hold their positions?

Chapter 3

Counteroffensive and Encirclement

The storm breaks

The telephone rattled – storm! I was shaken out of my sleep. But before I could grasp the telephone I heard a distant rumbling. Drumfire, I thought. The duty officer called: 'Alarm, Colonel. To the chief of staff immediately!'

That was the beginning of the Soviet counteroffensive. The calendar showed 19th November 1942. I put on my uniform tunic and boots, and rushed to the headquarters section. Officers and soldiers were already gathering as if they had been torn from their sleep. The chief of staff, Major-General Schmidt, had already put the whole army on alert. It was extremely serious. The tiring days of waiting, during which our gunners and tank crews lay beside their guns, were over; our infantry loaded their machine guns for automatic fire and grasped their hand grenades, which lay ready within reach.

Shortly afterwards the army commander-in-chief appeared beside Schmidt. The telephone rang. General Strecker, commander of the XIth Corps, reported: 'All Hell's broken loose! An unimaginable drumfire is falling on our positions. The ground is being literally ploughed up. We have enormous numbers of casualties. The main blow appears to have hit the Rumanians. I telephoned my left-hand neighbours, the Rumanian IVth Corps. Their commander was really pessimistic. He fears panic breaking out among his troops. Our divisions are at their posts but can see hardly anything through the snow. We will keep army headquarters informed.'

Paulus gave Strecker the following briefing: 'To ensure the safety of your left flank, send the 14th Panzer Division southwest of Mal-Kletskaya. Go as close as you can as soon as the direction of the enemy attack is identified.' Paulus put the telephone down, looked at us silently for a moment, then picked up the telephone again: 'Connect me with Army Group "B".' An officer on the staff of the army group took the first report from the 6th Army about the enemy's artillery preparation.

From then on the ringing of the telephone in the chief of staff's room hardly stopped. Reports, questions, orders chased each other. The withdrawal from the city of the XIVth Panzer Corps was prepared. The Army High Command was informed by its liaison officer to the 6th Army, Major von Zitzevitz, who had relieved Major Menzel. But as yet we still did not know enough about the enemy's intentions and direction of attack.

Breakthrough at the Rumanians

At about 0700 hours General Strecker reported again. 'The enemy has gone into the attack from the bridgehead. We have been able to hold on to our positions so far. The thrust is directed at the Rumanian 3rd Army. The 376th Infantry Division informs us that the Russians have broken through the positions of the Rumanian IVth Corps and are pushing south with tanks. The situation with the Rumanian 1st Cavalry Division is completely unknown. It no longer has connection with its left-hand neighbour. I will pull back the 376th Infantry Division and put it to protect our flank with its front facing west. The telephone connection with the 44th Infantry Division has been destroyed. A motorcyclist reports that the shelling has almost destroyed the foremost positions. The Red tanks have crushed everything the Rumanians had.'

Paulus authorised the withdrawal of the 376th Infantry Division to a flanking position, ordering cooperation with the 14th Panzer Division, and attached the Rumanian 1st Cavalry Division, which had been pushed eastwards, to the XIth Corps.

From Army Group 'B' we learned that the Soviet artillery had been firing thousands of tons of steel at the Rumanian 3rd Army's positions for hours. Then two shock armies broke out of the bridgehead near Kletskaya and Serafimovitch. The Rumanians had defended themselves bravely, but were overrun and forced to flee. At this moment Soviet tank units carrying infantry and some cavalry units were thrusting unstoppably further south. Neither German nor Rumanian command posts could say where the enemy spearheads were. Only one thing was certain: the 6th Army was already under threat from the rear.

My attempts to get an idea of how many casualties the XIth Corps had suffered were equally unsuccessful. The corps adjutant informed me that the telephone lines had been almost continuously broken since very early morning. In his opinion the 44th and 376th Infantry Divisions must have suffered severe casualties.

For the army headquarters staff the 19th November passed in anxious waiting. Catastrophic reports piled up hour after hour. Although by evening we still had no precise knowledge of the extent of the Soviet success, it was obvious to all of us that we were in deadly danger. At about 1900 hours I went to Paulus for a conference. He was pacing back and forth, bent over, across the room. That he was more nervous than usual showed on his face. He stopped in front of me. 'Now has happened what I have been forecasting for weeks. Hitler does not want to accept as true what every simple soldier can see. Keitel and Jodl have supported him in this. For weeks we have had nothing but empty words. Now we have to dish out the soup. We have no idea if it is possible to stop the Russian counteroffensive.'

I nodded wordlessly, tormented by the same thoughts. Angrily Paulus went on: 'The danger confronting us is gigantic. I see only one way out of this situation: turning away to the southwest. The fastest action is necessary!'

This was also my opinion, so I asked: 'In this case must the army really ask for a decision from the Army High Command? Here we are talking about the lives of almost 330,000 men!'

'Even if it is to be or not to be, the whole of the 6th Army goes. I have, as you know, asked to abandon Stalingrad. That was refused. There is still the order whereby no commander of an army group or an army has the right to relinquish a village, even a trench, without Hitler's consent. Of course the decision of every army commander has been paralysed. But how will we get through the war if orders are no longer complied with? What effect would this have on the troops? However large the command of a general is, the men must be given an example of his soldier's obedience to orders.'

This basic attitude also determined Paulus's conduct in the weeks to come. Even though the necessity of independent action was still compelling, Paulus did not even consider it. He remained an obedient general. In this he was backed by his temperamental, but also fanatical, chief of staff, Major-General Schmidt, and most of the commanding generals. I too, despite many inner conflicts over these painful but also consequential considerations, failed to stand out.

Our first countermeasures

During the night of the 19th/20th November the army staff obtained a clearer picture of the situation. The 14th Panzer Division reported that the enemy had thrust about 30 kilometres into the hinterland with tanks and cavalry. Their artillery regiment had repulsed several strong attacks. Fresh news from the XIth Corps indicated that the Rumanians had been attacked by strong tank units without offering any serious resistance, the tanks simply mowing down anything that stood in their way. Those Rumanians still alive fled desperately to the south and east. The Rumanian 3rd Army did not appear to exist any more. Also many of our rear services had suffered a hard shock from the enemy storming south before them.

Clearly no one on the staff could think of sleeping that night. All the section heads were assembled in Schmidt's office. Without any sign of internal excitement, he described the new situation west of the Don and finished with these words: 'The move of the army headquarters to Nishne-

Chirskaya is to be prepared. Orders have yet to come about the destruction of dispensable files, especially the secret ones.'

Schmidt's optimism and bubbling energy in this situation contrasted especially with Paulus's heavy sense of responsibility. To the chief of staff, the internal conflict of his commander-in-chief was alien. Schmidt was in his element, making decisions, issuing orders and controlling their execution. He was convinced that it would be possible to defeat the enemy despite the Russians' considerable initial success on the battlefield. He spread out General Paulus's proposal, which he had worked on with the 1st general staff officer. It went:

The XIVth Panzer Corps with the Panzer regiments of the 16th and 24th Panzer Divisions must reach the west bank of the Don, then strike the forces of the Red Army advancing from the heights west of Golubinskaya in the flank and destroy them. The staff of the XIVth Panzer Corps will take over the army's command post in Golubinskaya. The 14th Panzer Division will also be attached to it. The assault troop activities in the city are to cease immediately.

All available troops on the fronts of the VIIIth and LIst Corps will be withdrawn as reserves for the 6th Army.

The bridgehead on the west bank of the Don west of Kalatch will be reinforced by the engineer and anti-aircraft artillery courses with all dispensable troops from the rear services and placed under command of Colonel Mikosch.

The officer cadet school in Suvorovski is to be ready to move.

Army headquarters will move on the 21st November to Nishne-Chirskaya. Colonel Adam is responsible for the move.

Wounded and not-required supply troops will be moved to the area south of Chir, where the Russian attack is threatening the railway line and with it the main supply route.'

Paulus approved this proposal. The orders were prepared and distributed to the units.

Hope and highest decisions
Midnight was long past, and no new reports were expected before daybreak. For the moment there was nothing to do at army headquarters, so I escorted Paulus to his quarters. On the way he started talking: 'If Führer Headquarters had allowed my proposal to withdraw the 6th Army behind the Don, we would have been spared this difficult crisis. Hopefully Hitler and his entourage have now at least some understanding and will order the city to be abandoned. That is no longer easy today with the whole of the Rumanian 3rd Army knocked out of the Don front. The Russian tank and

cavalry units have practically no one in front of them. I have little faith that Heim's XXXXVIIIth Panzer Corps can bring this thrust to a halt.'

'If you are expecting such an order from Führer Headquarters, General, it would be expedient to start preparatory measures.'

'Temporarily I have proposed to army group pulling out all the troops from the city. Obviously I cannot let this intention become known to the troops yet. That would only cause panic, and at the very least lead to a reduction in the will to resist. The corps staffs are already busy dealing with this question. At least it must be clear to them that the orders signed by me previously have the aim of extracting the army from the threatened encirclement.'

We had reached the commander-in-chief's accommodation. I excused myself and went back to my section. When I entered the room, Senior-Sergeant-Major Küpper got up from his desk. The other clerks were already asleep.

'So, Küpper, you are already up. We can get on with the work.'

'It is already done, Colonel.'

'You think so?! You will be surprised. We will prepare all the dispensable files, especially the secret ones, for destruction. The remainder will be packed. The staff moves to Nishne–Chirskaya tomorrow.'

'Ah, so that's the truth of it. Yesterday I heard of it from various corps despatch riders. One from the XIth Corps said that the Russians had overrun the Rumanians and pushed suddenly to the south. I took that for just a latrine rumour. But when I heard an hour later that you were still with the chief of staff, I sensed nothing good. That is why I am still awake. It must look very bad if we are already burning the files.'

'Don't throw the flint into the corn yet! First of all we must be careful. We will wait to see what today brings. Let the others sleep in peace. We will do the work ourselves.'

The senior-sergeant-major pulled the steel box containing the secret files from under the camp bed, opened it and gave me the papers one by one. I divided them into two heaps: papers that had to be destroyed when danger threatened, and those that were less secret, such as recommendations for awards, leave approvals, and so on. After this the stacks of paper were bundled up and put back in the box. As we were finishing, the day was already beginning to dawn.

'Go and get some sleep now, Küpper! I am going to my quarters to wash and shave myself. I will be back here at 0800 hours at the latest.'

Attack also from the south

Half an hour later I was standing shaving in front of the mirror in my bedroom. The telephone rang. 'The Ia, Colonel.'

What could have happened, I thought, as I pressed the telephone to my ear. 'Come immediately to the chief of staff! General Paulus is already here.'

I quickly finished shaving and hurried to the command section. The wind was cutting in my face and into my skin under the not winter-proofed clothing. Individual snowflakes settled on the field-grey or ran down the chin and cheeks. In Schmidt's room a large white-chalked clay farm stove maintained a pleasant temperature. The commander-in-chief was standing with the chief of staff, Ia and Ic before the map hanging on the wall. The depiction of the latest situation had begun. I stared bewitched at the entries. In the 4th Panzer Army's area was a thick red arrow going through its forward positions. The Soviet Army had also entered from a southerly direction.

Paulus pulled it all together: 'The enemy early this morning, after a strong artillery preparation, attacked the positions of the 4th Panzer Army and the Rumanian 4th Army. The situation there at the moment is not clear. The Red Army is pursuing its attack from the north here. Its left-hand group is going in a south-easterly direction on Verchne-Businvka. We must therefore reckon that the XIth Corps' route to the south will be blocked within a few hours. The greatest danger lies here with the railway line from Morosovsk to Chir Station.'

So we were right up to our necks in it! The Soviet High Command was pressing both fangs together. We tried to prevent this with a counterattack by the XIVth Corps and the XXXXVIIIth Panzer Corps. But what if this attempt failed? What if our armoured forces proved too weak? Then the enemy would tighten the noose and the 6th Army would be caught in a cauldron.

A general reports sick

I paced my little office restlessly, three steps forward, three steps back. When I tried to relax, my thoughts immediately returned to the situation map. The red attack arrows threatened nightmarishly. Upon extension they would meet near Kalatch. But something must happen! Would our Panzer regiments attack in time to remove the threat to the rear of the 6th Army? What would the next few hours bring?

The answer came more quickly than I would have liked. Paulus had me summoned. I entered a room that was dense with cigarette smoke and hung with thick blue clouds. The ashtrays on the tables were full to the top. Among them, still untouched, stood a cup of black coffee. The commander-in-chief was lighting a new cigarette. 'You know, Adam, that Major-General Baessler took over the 14th Panzer Division a few weeks ago. Today the general has reported sick. Apparently it's an old heart problem that has come up again. He asked my permission to drive back to the homeland. I have agreed. A commander who reports sick in this situation is useless and becomes a burden to the troops.'

'This well nourished gentleman was already unsympathetic when I saw him for the first time. Nevertheless I would not have believed that he would leave his troops in the lurch in this dangerous situation. That is desertion.'

'This is to make it clear that we must leave it to the army group. I have informed them of the foregoing. General Baessler was in such a hurry that he should soon be with them. The Ia of the 14th Panzer Division reported to Schmidt that Baessler was already on the way in his car to Chir Station. He has not even considered it necessary to wait for the arrival of his replacement. A shame that he should be a general!'

'Baessler is not only an officer who forgets his duty. The day before yesterday, with the first reports of enemy activity, he became already afraid and failed to spare his troops unnecessary casualties. A courier officer from the 14th Panzer Division told me that a hard dispute had occurred between Baessler and his Ia. I am not taken in by his sickness. In soldiers' language this rates as cowardice. The gentleman is concerned about his precious life.'

'Do we wait for the investigation? The personnel office will see to it. I want to know from them who the successor is to be. The division must still have a new commander today.'

'Presuming that Major-General Schmidt is agreeable, I propose Colonel Lattmann, commander of the armoured artillery regiment of the 16th Panzer Division. I consider him one of the most capable officers in this army. He is clever, agile, circumspect and energetic. Lattmann knows the armour to his fingertips, which in this complicated situation is especially important.'

Once Schmidt had accepted my proposal, Paulus too gave his approval. The Army Personnel Office was requested by teleprinter to permit this change of command of the 14th Panzer Division.

A few hours later Colonel Lattmann reported to the army staff in Golubinskaya. The chief of staff briefed him on the situation. The new divisional commander was not envied his task. The 14th Panzer Division had already suffered considerable losses in the defensive fighting. Above all, its artillery regiment had been literally shot up by the enemy's tanks.

Hours of unrest and uncertainty
We lived through hours of unrest and uncertainty. Rumours of all kinds were circulating. No one knew where they came from. No one knew what was really happening. Had the enemy really interrupted the Don High Road to Chir Station? Was it correct that he had reached the railway line from Morosovsk to the Don, that the 4th Panzer Army had been defeated? What measures had the Army High Command initiated to fight the rear of the 6th Army free? Where was the XXXXVIIIth Panzer Corps hiding? Had it attacked? With what results?

Our nerves were at breaking point. At last, on the evening of the 20th

November we had some information about the situation with our right-hand neighbour, the 4th Panzer Army. The enemy had broken through its defensive line from the south and was thrusting westwards towards the Don. The 29th (Motorised) Infantry Division was tasked by the army group with blocking the breakthrough, but was incapable of stopping the attack. The IVth Corps and the Rumanian 20th Infantry Division had been brushed aside and were now positioned with their front facing south. Nothing was known of the other Rumanian division in the south. According to the latest reports the Soviet tanks were standing close in front of the 4th Panzer Army's headquarters.

That was a fine mess: a gaping hole on our left flank and now also on the right! The enemy thrust with ever stronger forces through our shattered front. His attacking spearheads were rapidly getting closer. And we had no reserves with which to repulse this deadly danger.

From army group we learned that the counterattack by the weakened XXXXVIIIth Panzer Corps under Lieutenant-General Heim had been easily checked. Our Luftwaffe, which perhaps could have relieved the situation, had been rendered inoperable by snowfalls. The Soviet tanks had reached the Liskatal from the north and were storming towards Kalatch. Another group was rattling further south. The only supply railway coming from the west via Morosovsk to the Don and ending at Chir was under immediate threat. For the enemy the way south as far as the mouth of the Don at the Asov Lake was virtually open. That meant nothing less than that sooner or later the Russians would find themselves in the rear of Army Group 'A', which was composed of the 1st Panzer Army and the 17th Army, and was operating in the Caucasus. Every one of us knew that we were confronting a catastrophe of inconceivable extent if the German side did not act quickly and powerfully.

How could it be managed?

Paulus applies again to abandon the city on the Volga
How could the situation be handled? Paulus requested permission from the Army High Command to abandon Stalingrad and break through to the southwest with the army and so avoid the threatened encirclement. Army Group 'B' supported this request at Führer Headquarters.

In waiting for the reply, minutes seemed like hours, hours like eternity. Meanwhile our troops were fighting a desperate battle without being able to stop the enemy. Some of the rear service units had fled in wild panic to the east as the tanks with the five-pointed stars approached.

The commanders of the 6th Army and Army Group 'B' waited obediently for the Supreme Commander's decision. The longed-for decision finally arrived that evening. The breakout was refused. Stalingrad was to be held – that was what Hitler and the Army High Command wanted.

Paulus, Schmidt and all of those who, because of our military appointments, knew the catastrophic situation the 6th Army was in, were bitterly disappointed. But all obeyed.

That night Major-General Schmidt briefed all section heads on the latest developments. More messages full of alarming news. It had meanwhile been established that the Rumanian 3rd Army had been completed smashed. The gap in our left flank had become larger. The XIth Corps and the 14th Panzer Division were bleeding to death in defensive fighting. Rear service units of all possible kinds were fleeing from the Soviet armoured spearheads. How long would it last before the enemy stood near Golubinskaya?

These questions, and the acute danger posed to army headquarters, made its move a matter of the utmost urgency. The army headquarters was no longer secure in Golubinskaya. Therefore Schmidt ordered, with Paulus's agreement, a change of position for the 21st November. Until dawn the bundles of sealed items and dispensable files flamed in the fire. Even then the Red Army allowed us no rest. Suddenly several army staff trucks raced into the village. They were to drive on the Don High Road via Chir Station to Bishne-Chirskaya. Apparently they were only a few kilometres from Golubinskaya when they ran into enemy troops.

We were completely surprised, but this report seemed to us a fantasy. The Ia, Colonel Elchlepp, said: 'In their fear, they saw ghosts.'

They were no ghosts. A motorised scout troop under the command of an officer immediately sent off by Schmidt clarified the situation. With their lights off and muffled engines, the few jeeps and motorcyclists moved slowly southwards. Not an hour had passed before they returned, the scouts reporting that the Red tanks were just 20 kilometres south of Golubinskaya and standing on the Don High Road. The shortest way to the new headquarters location in Nishne-Chirskaya was also blocked. With mixed feelings, we reinforced the guards. A few anti-tank guns took up positions on the Don High Road.

Transfer to Nishne-Chirskaya
Even nature seemed to have turned against us. On the night of the 20th/21st November the temperature sank to minus 20 degrees. The blanket of snow that had fallen the previous day was stiff with ice. The connecting road from Golubinskaya to the railway track on the Don heights was mirror smooth. I was apprehensive at the thought of our heavy vehicles having to climb up this steep slope. But we had not got that far.

Paulus had decided to set up a forward army command post between the Don and the Volga in order to conduct a secure and friction-free command. It would be occupied by the Ia, the Ic and a quartermaster with the necessary orderly officers and requisite vehicles. For its location he chose a point west of Gumrak, near the railway station.

In the early hours of the morning General Hube, commanding general of the XIVth Panzer Corps, arrived with his staff at Golubinskaya. He reported that the tanks of the 16th and 24th Panzer Divisions had been withdrawn from the front and would arrive at about midday or in the evening at the Don. This news filled us all with confidence. Hube enjoyed great esteem among the staff for having broken through the enemy front from the Don to the Volga with his 16th Panzer Division back in August. Naturally I knew that the tanks had suffered considerable casualties in the city. But, almost like a drowning person grasping at straws, I pinned all my hopes on Hube.

Paulus described to the general the situation on the west bank of the Don. Then he assigned him his task of attacking the enemy thrusting south with the 14th, 16th and 24th Panzer Divisions. This would release the 6th Army from the threat to its rear.

The staff of the XIVth Panzer Corps took over our headquarters in Golubinskaya. The wireless net was not dismantled, so that Hube had contact with all the corps and divisional staffs as well as the new army headquarters.

Towards noon on the 21st November I escorted Paulus and Schmidt to the airstrip in Golubinskaya. There stood only the two 'Storks' that the generals and their personal orderly officers would fly in to the new headquarters. The other aircraft belonging to the army's courier service had already moved to Nishne-Chirskaya that morning. As Paulus shook my hand upon leaving, he said to me: 'Start moving out straight away. You must cross the Don near Perepolni and drive south along the east bank. We will see each other again at the latest early tomorrow morning in Nishne-Chirskaya.' Hardly had the aircraft lifted off the ground than heavy fire broke out from the Don Heights. I hope all goes well, I thought. The 'Storks' could only fly at a low height.

There was no time for pondering. The car took me back to the village, where several dozen loaded trucks were waiting. It seemed to me advisable, in view of the nearness of the enemy, to form five convoys. Each column came under the command of the head of a department, including the army's chief of engineers, Colonel Selle, and the army's chief of signals, Colonel Arnold. I took over the last convoy. After crossing the Don, we wanted to assemble in Peskovatka at the VIIIth Corps headquarters and from there on continue the journey together.

Only with care could we climb the steep bank of the iced road. In some cases the escorts had to provide mutual support. Finally it worked for all of us. The Don High Road was almost completely empty. We moved forwards quickly. The nearer we got to the bridge near Perepolni, the slower we went. More and more tipped-over vehicles or horse-drawn carts narrowed the way through. Often boxes of all kinds and sizes lay in the middle of the road and obliged us to avoid them to the left or right. There were also rifles, steel helmets, various guns with broken wheels, and even three tanks with the Balkenkreuz, all marking the retreat of Rumanian and German units. This debris openly indicated flight. From the west streamed vehicles from the railway. Wherever they saw the smallest gap they tried to squeeze themselves in. So it was hardly possible to keep one's own convoy together. In the immediate vicinity of the bridge chaos threatened to break out.

Night had fallen. With dipped headlights, our truck jolted along behind the others in second gear. Suddenly we heard shouts and swearing on the road, then we came to a complete stop. Nothing was moving. As I climbed out to discover the reason for the blockage, I met Colonel Selle. He had set off with his convoy half an hour ahead of me. With his companion, Captain Dr Gottsmann, Selle was trying to untangle the confusion ahead of us. This was not easy as we had come up against the contrary movement of the 16th Panzer Division. Their steel giants were crossing the Don from east to west in order to occupy the assembly area allocated to them by the army. The immediate reason for the blockage was a tank that had slipped on the deadly smooth road and now stood across it. Selle had quickly got to this position. Captain Dr Gottsmann had already climbed on the vehicle when another tank rolled up. As this too started to slide, its tracks caught the captain's leg and injured him so badly that he died shortly afterwards.

After this shattering experience we drove at a very slow speed along the iced track. It took hours for all the vehicles to get across the bridge. After a short break with the staff of the VIIIth Corps, during which the convoys assembled, we set off on our journey to the south on the east bank of the Don. A gentle blanket of snow lay over the steppe. It also covered the convoy's route so that we had to drive by compass. We drove into Kalatch at about 0500 hours on the morning of the 22nd November. Apart from the sentries here and there everyone was fast asleep, as if the enemy was a long way off. Likewise, deep peace reigned in the village somewhat further to the southeast, where the army's senior quartermaster's department was accommodated. Completely frozen through, we rested here for an hour, enjoying the warm room, the hot coffee and the wonderful taste of freshly baked bread.

I had the senior quartermaster woken up. I showed him that the danger of the situation was not realised everywhere. Now he raised the alarm and took measures to change location. This was easier said than done. The camp with its supplies, clothing and field post office required thousands of tons of transport space. Two days later I discovered that a considerable amount had had to be destroyed.

From the senior quartermaster's department to the Don Bridge near Verchne-Chirskaya was no longer very far. But what we now experienced was much worse than everything up to now. It was a picture of horror.

Whipped on by fear of the Soviet tanks, trucks, command vehicles, cars, motorcycles, riders and horse-drawn vehicles raced westwards, bouncing off each other, becoming stuck, tipping over, blocking the road. Between them thrust, pressed, shoved and wriggled those on foot. Anyone who tripped and fell on the ground did not get back up. They were trampled, driven over, crushed.

In the hunt for saving life, everything was left behind, hindering the runners. Weapons and equipment were thrown away. Fully loaded ammunition trucks, field kitchens and horse-drawn carts were left behind, but one could get forward faster on the backs of unharnessed horses. Verchne-Chirskaya offered the worst chaos. To the fleeing troops of the 4th Panzer Army was added from the north the soldiers and officers of the Rumanian 3rd Army and the rear services of the XIth Corps. All looked alike in their panic, and all were streaming towards Nishne-Chirskaya.

Paulus and Schmidt fly into the cauldron
On the 22nd November at about 0900 hours I met the last convoy in Nishne-Chirskaya and reported to Paulus the completed transfer of the headquarters. He was sitting with Colonel-General Hoth, the commander-in-chief of the 4th Panzer Army, and some of the staff were briefing them on the situation.

Shortly afterwards I had to return to the conference room. I handed Paulus a radio message that had been received from Hitler. He read out aloud the short text. According to it, Colonel-General Hoth and his staff were required for other tasks. Paulus and Schmidt received orders to fly into the surrounded cauldron immediately and establish the army headquarters near Gumrak Station.

Perplexity could be read on all their faces. While Hoth appeared to be happy to get out of this dilemma, Paulus and Schmidt had become very thoughtful. And no wonder: the High Command was burdening them with a catastrophic situation and an enormous responsibility. Already fresh and alarming news was arriving. The XIVth Panzer Corps under General Hube, which should have stopped the enemy advance with a flank attack, had almost run out of fuel. An attack was out of the question; it could not even hold its position but, like the XIth Corps, was being driven back eastwards to the Don. The especially important Don Bridge near Kalatch was lost without a fight. The way south – the 6th Army's eventual retreat route – was for the most part in the hands of the enemy. Only a few kilometres separated these spearheads from Kalatch. There were no forces to stop them. We therefore had to reckon that the encirclement would be completed during the course of the day.

Colonel-General Hoth wished General Paulus 'Soldier's Luck' on leaving – a more than doubtful wish in this damned situation. Two Fieseler 'Storks' stood ready for Paulus and Schmidt. Already prepared for their trip, the commander-in-chief summoned me to his office. 'We now have to part, Adam. I don't know when we will see each other again. As the most senior officer, you take over command of the staff. As soon as the Red Army reaches the Lower Chir, move the headquarters via Tormossin to Morosovsk and combine with the quartermaster's department, which is already on its way there.'

The cars had driven forward. I escorted Paulus and Schmidt to the airstrip that had been established on edge of the town. Hardly a word was exchanged. A last handshake, then they both climbed aboard.

The propellers began to turn, soon running at full speed. The machines rolled forward, lifted up from the ground, turned to the east, flew over the Don and quickly disappeared behind the wooded bank opposite.

Driving the five or six kilometres back to my quarters took over an hour. The car stood still more than it advanced. The roads were blocked with men and vehicles of all kinds. Nishne-Chirskaya had become an army camp.

As fast as a bushfire spreads, the news was out that the army staff had taken up quarters here. And where the army headquarters is, one is safe – so thought thousands of soldiers, who stayed in the little Cossack town on the Chir.

Combat teams out of scattered soldiers

At dusk I telephoned the commander of Chir Station and asked him: 'What do you know of the enemy? Where are their spearheads?'

'That I cannot say, Colonel. I only have a few men with me; all the others have left during the course of the day with the fully laden trucks. There are still hundreds of tons of foodstuffs, ammunition and fuel lying here. I don't know how I can move them on. The few vehicles I still have will not suffice.'

'There are many hundreds of trucks here. I will try to send you some of them. Keep in contact with me under all circumstances! Should something new happen, then please report to me immediately. Colonel Mikosh's combat team is in Verchne-Chirskaya. I will send it to you as soon as the station is threatened. But take all the weapons, all the machine guns with you!'

Hardly had I put the receiver down when the telephone rang again. To my delight I heard the voice of Paulus. 'We have already landed. How is it with you?'

'Chir Station is still in our hands. Thousands of vehicles are blocking the streets in Nishne-Chirskaya. But I am amazed, General, that we can telephone each other. The line goes through territory that the Russians have already taken.'

'Perhaps it has not been discovered yet, or perhaps he wants to listen in. Certainly it will not last much longer. Keep us in touch by radio. All the best. Out.'

Colonel Abraham and Captain Göbel came into my room. They reported the arrival of the officer cadet school that I had ordered to Nishne-Chirskaya.

The telephone rang again. Colonel Winter, the 1st general staff officer of Army Group 'B', enquired about the situation on the Lower Chir. From him I also discovered that not a single German soldier stood in the area between Verchne-Chirskaya to east of Morosovsk any more. That was miserable news. Something must be done immediately. I suggested that a battle group should be set up from the soldiers camping here to secure Nishne-Chirskaya and the bridgehead east of the Don. Its nucleus should be formed by the officer cadet school. Winter was very agreeable to this suggestion. Nevertheless I could not undertake much more in the night. So I tasked the temporary Captain Göbel with sending strong reconnaissance units north to Chir Station and northwest to the mouth of the Liska on the Chir river, to make contact with Colonel Mikosch, and organising the guarding of Nishne-Chirskaya. The town commandant was ordered to put together a truck convoy and send it off to Chir Station.

Towards 2300 hours army group rang again and passed the following order: 'The bridgehead east of the Don and the railway line are to be prepared for defence by combat teams in order to hold the way free to the south for the 6th Army when Stalingrad is abandoned.'

I breathed out with relief. So the army group expected an order from the Army High Command to break out. I immediately summoned the staff officers to me to discuss measures for the 23rd November. First, the traffic jams in the streets of Nishne-Chirskaya had to be sorted out. As day dawned, all the officers of the staff and of the local headquarters were detailed for this task. At the same time they had orders for all soldiers and officers – with the exception of drivers – to assemble at the school with their weapons and ammunition. There they were to be sorted into combat teams.

At last it became quiet. Dead tired, I lay down on a mattress, but was unable to sleep. The events of the last three days were still too pressing. Inwardly I swore at Hitler and the Army High Command. They had put us in this hopeless situation because they had thrown all requests and warnings into the wind. The first requirement for commanding troops is a correct assessment of the enemy. The High Command had cast off this basic tenet in an irresponsible and reckless manner. What could actually now be done when the army was practically already surrounded? Actually only one thing: to break through to the southwest. It must succeed if the bridgehead over the Don east of Verchne-Chirskaya was held. I was firmly determined to set all forces to this in the coming day.

Hitler orders the Volga city to be held
Renewed ringing got me up from my mattress. The Ia of the army group

wanted to know what was new around Chir. 'Situation unaltered,' I replied,'
and how does it look on the rest of the army's front?'

'The XIth Corps and the XIVth Panzer Corps are fighting with their
backs to the Don. The IVth Corps stands at Stalingrad with the front facing
south in hard defensive fighting. Since his arrival Paulus has been
consulting with all available commanding generals. Unanimously they
propose to revise the appeal to bring the 6th Army back over the Don. The
army group also sees no other way out and has strongly supported the
proposal. A short while ago the answer came from Führer Headquarters.
Listen well: "On the orders of the Führer, the 6th Army has to hold
Stalingrad and the Volga front under all circumstances. Should, through an
opening-up of the flanks, a position of all-round defence become necessary,
this will result in the holding fast of Stalingrad. The army headquarters is
to move to the area northeast of Kalatch. The IVth Corps (297th Infantry
Division, 371st Infantry Division and 29th Motorised Division) of the 4th
Panzer Army will come under the 6th Army!"'

Colonel Winter, the speaker at the other end of the line, left a short
pause as if to give me time to digest the Führer Order. Then he went on:
'The Army High Command has even raised objections to the order that
the necessary troop movements cannot be carried out for the forming of
the cauldron. The necessary troops for closing the gaps between the right
and left flanks of the army are not available and it first has to be checked
how far units can be extracted from the city front, there being no positions
available to form a front, and wood for the construction of positions and
bunkers is lacking.'

'This order to a whole army is nonsense,' I said. 'What happens then to
our divisions still fighting west of the Don?'

'According to Hitler's order they should be led over the Don to the east,'
said Winter. 'But in spite of the Army High Command's attitude, Adam, see
to securing the bridgehead and the Chir front.'

With that our conversation ended. It was obvious that my forces would
be insufficient to hold the battle sector handed over to me. But what would
happen to the surrounded 20th German and 2nd Rumanian divisions? That
was another dirty trick of the Army High Command. Had Paulus really to
obey Hitler's orders? Should he, supported by his much better knowledge
of our situation, not simply handle the matter independently, and break out
to the southwest before it was too late?

The more I thought about it, the more certain I became: Paulus was a
through and through disciplined and obedient soldier. He would rather
perish with his army than become a mutineer. To me inwardly General
Paulus represented a superior and humane being. I was very sorry for him
in this deep conflict. I regretted not being able to be with him in his advance
headquarters at Gumrak.

The telephone sounded once more in this midnight hour. Paulus announced himself over the still intact telephone line. Resignedly he replied after my report: 'The encirclement is already closed, Adam.'

'But, General, individual soldiers are still coming to us from the area east of the Don. The ring cannot be so dense.'

'What use is that to us when we are firmly nailed to the city?' he replied bitterly. From some of our exchange I gathered that the headquarters of Army Group 'B' also shared Paulus's view on the necessity of a breakout, but no one there was willing to take responsibility. They had been more inclined to await new instructions than go against the Army High Command's orders.

Chir railway station is no longer responding
My fatigue finally won over my tormenting thoughts. But the sleep bringing forgetfulness did not last long. About two o'clock I was woken up again. Standing in front of me was Colonel Arnold, the army's intelligence chief. 'The commandant of Chir Station is not responding any more. My radio troops report heavy rifle and machine-gun fire from the direction of the railway line. I don't yet know what is happening there. The Mikosch Combat Team have sent scouts off to Chir Station.'

I jumped up off my mattress. 'Get the local commandant of Nishne-Chirskaya as well as Göbel here immediately!' Burning inside me was the need to look after the harassed soldiers streaming into the town, and their weapons and equipment; also the responsibility towards the heavily threatened 6th Army.

Both the officers I had ordered came in. I briefed them on the latest developments. 'Captain Göbel, send out new scouts immediately. I must know precisely what the situation is at the railway station, where the foremost enemy elements are. Tell your scouts that the Mikosch Combat Team has also been sent towards Chir Station!'

I ordered the local commandant to increase the sentries at the town exits and to patrol the ground between the town and the station with scouts.

A call from the Mikosch Combat Team reported that there was still no news from the reconnaissance team. The colonel feared being surrounded by the enemy pressing forwards and southwards. I told him that at daybreak we would deploy a strong combat team on the flat ground west of Verchne-Chirskaya about two kilometres south of the railway line. I further told him to cooperate closely with Colonel Tschöckell's combat team in the Don bridgehead. Both combat teams concerned themselves with the railway bridge over the Don.

Alerting the army staff, reporting to Army Group 'B', and reconnoitring and marking the route to Tormossin were the next measures that I took. Meanwhile the scouts reported that the enemy's foremost elements had reached the railway line either side of Chir Station and were sending out scouts southwards. However, these had already withdrawn when we opened fire on them.

The new day, the 23rd November, was dawning in the east. Officers from the staff were there, already disentangling jammed vehicles at the town's southern exit. The drivers were sullenly, reluctantly, complying with their orders. Then like a blow an officer cadet remarked that the Russians had already reached the railway line. Dull apathy turned into hectic activity. More than any order, fear drove the utmost haste. Captain Göbel had established a collecting point for stray soldiers in the Nishne-Chirskaya school. From all sides large and small groups marched in under the direction of our officer cadets. They had arms and ammunition with them, so that they could immediately be formed into companies and battalions. The instructing officers from Suvorovski were deployed as battalion commanders, the pupils as company and platoon commanders. The new formations were immediately sent off to their set positions. By midday the first battalions were ready for action west of Verchne-Chirskaya. Captain Göbel took over their command. He could never have dreamed of having to command such a colourfully varied and thrown together collection of troops. Most of his soldiers came from the rear services, the field post service and the Organisation Todt. In addition, there were a few strays from the attacking divisions and men returning from leave. Their arms consisted of rifles and pistols, as well as three light machine-guns. That was hardly very encouraging. But all had the earnest wish to help their comrades surrounded in the area between the Volga and the Don. The second quartermaster of the 6th Army, Captain Tümpling, confirmed to me that the cauldron was complete. He had taken part in a defensive fight in Kalatch and then observed during the flight in the Don bridgehead how the Soviet pincers had closed east of the town.

Within a few hours Nishne-Chirskaya had emptied. The main roads were free again. I handed over the command of the staff to Colonel Selle and tasked him with moving to Tormossin. I remained in Nishne-Chirskaya. My main concerns were anti-tank guns, mortars and tanks for the fighting units. Without these weapons they were unable to offer the enemy any earnest resistance. Early that morning I had already instructed our workshops in Tormossin by telephone to get all serviceable guns, tanks and machine guns ready as quickly as possible, latest by evening, and send them to Nishne-Chirskaya. In fact the first arrived at noon. Colonel Selle supported this action energetically after his arrival in Tormossin. He literally cleared out the workshops, supervised the repair facilities day and night and produced arms and ammunition almost daily.

Driven by fear

I was driving to visit the combat teams, travelling in a jeep back along the same route I had come by more than 24 hours before. Already on the day before one could talk of there being order on the road. Now I found no trace of the wild confusion of the headless flight that had occurred.

The stream of shocked soldiers was not over. Now a group of about twenty German and Rumanian soldiers approached my car. All were without weapons, unshaved and tattered. 'Where do you come from, what unit do you belong to?' I asked a German NCO.

'We are from the 4th Panzer Army. We have lost our units. The Russians are right behind us, Colonel.'

'That is nonsense. You can see that I am driving to where you came from. A new front has already been established there. Why did you not join their ranks? Are you going to leave your comrades in the lurch? And where are your weapons?'

'We are drivers, Colonel. Our weapons are in the vehicles.'

'And where are your vehicles?'

'We had to leave them behind in a village, otherwise we would never have got through. The Russians were already everywhere. We have been on the way now for two days without getting anything to eat.'

'Report to the town commandant in Nishne-Chirskaya, which is the place behind the strip of woodland. You will get rations there. And do something to smarten yourselves up first, then the world will look different again.'

Astonished looks met mine as my vehicle drove off again towards Verchne-Chirskaya. Apparently it was baffling to them how one could overcome the horrors. For my part, on the other hand, I found it incomprehensible how quickly the morale of our troops could have sunk so low, how soldiers could let themselves become so low who only a few months before had gone victoriously through the Don steppe. Was it only fear of life in the raw? Was it the dread of imprisonment? Was it the question of the sense of this war?

Defence without heavy weapons

I met Colonel Mikosch in Verchne-Chirskaya. His battle group lay only 1,000 to 1,500 metres from the enemy. But they had well built bunkers and trenches. The off-duty men could rest and sleep in houses behind the fighting line, although occasionally fired on by '*Katyushas*'. Mikosch had hardly a gun or a mortar with which to reciprocate.

Next I finally sought out Colonel Tschöckell's battle group in the Don bridgehead. They had occupied positions on the edge of the woods and were constantly being attacked by weak Soviet forces, so that the soldiers were getting no respite. The lack of heavy weapons was even more alarming here than with Mikosch.

'Without artillery support this cannot last any longer,' said Colonel Tschöckell, 'and even better would be some tanks.'

'The workshops in Tormossin will send all serviceable heavy weapons with ammunition to Nishne-Chirskaya. Tomorrow I hope to be able to help you a bit,' I assured him and made a few remarks about the defensive measures encountered earlier on. Then I drove on to the newly established Battle Group Göbel, dug in, in accordance with orders, west of Verchne-Chirskaya, about two kilometres south of the railway line.

Captain Göbel had only one field kitchen for about 1,500 men. This was far from adequate, but there were several field kitchens on the road back. I authorised Göbel to take all that he might need of the vehicles, equipment, ammunition and weapons. The situation was tricky on his left flank. His scouts had reported not encountering any German troops for far and wide. 'The enemy has only to advance along any road to the Chir and we will be sitting in a mousetrap, Colonel.'

'Immediately upon my return I will call upon the army group for support. You will then get immediate support from me. Have you telephone contact with Nishne-Chirskaya?'

'All in order, Colonel. I spoke with the switchboard an hour ago.'

I drove back somewhat calmer. Our situation without heavy weapons was naturally scary, but if the enemy would only leave us in peace for a few days, we could strengthen the front. To this end it occurred to me to give the battle groups a joint command. This would increase their punch should there be a Soviet attack. I decided to speak to army group that same day.

During my absence one of our training officers from Suvorovski had organised three further companies out of stragglers. These I immediately sent off under his command. In connection with the Göbel Battle Group they secured the roads running along either side of the Chir. Another danger point had been reinforced. This relieved my concern somewhat.

I also provided another welcome addition to the front. The town commandant reported that on the 22nd November a complete bakery company and a butcher platoon had arrived in Nishne-Chirskaya. They had escaped from the enemy tanks, a situation they should not celebrate too soon. Now I incorporated them into my battle groups.

Battle commandant of Chir

Time for yet another talk with Army Group 'B'. The connection succeeded after a few minutes. Colonel Winter was on the telephone. I reported to him the insertion of eighteen companies west of Verchne-Chirskaya and the other measures I had taken. 'The enemy has not crossed the railway line to the south. I visited several battle groups today. Of considerable concern to us is that we have hardly any heavy weapons. I can tell you too that it is troublesome that the three battle groups have no united command. I suggest that you attach them to a divisional battle group.'

'Agreed. Who should take over these battle groups?'

'I still have Colonel Abraham of the 76th Infantry Division with me. Four weeks ago we withdrew him from the front as he was ill. Meanwhile he has recovered really well. I regard him as completely suitable.'

'Agreed. You know Abraham better than I do. But he is helpless without a capable staff.'

'We have the staff of the army's artillery commander here. The general is not here, so the staff can go complete to Abraham. May I go ahead with this?'

'Of course, Adam. Have you any other questions?'

'I should say! What does it look like to the left of us? Our reconnaissance troops report that there are no German soldiers to be found there.'

'Unfortunately that is correct. The front has been torn apart for several hundred kilometres. We still do not know how to block this vast gap. Should I get a division from somewhere, somehow I will send it to your left. Until then we can only help you with battle groups of stragglers.'

'Yes, that is a bad aspect. If we only had a few anti-tank weapons with sufficient ammunition! And several dozen infantry officers. Most companies are led by NCOs.'

'I have noted everything. We will help as much as possible. But you know that with us too the blanket is too short. Where do you want to set up your headquarters?'

'I have moved my staff to Tormossin today. I am staying here myself until the situation at Chir and in the Don bridgehead has settled down a bit.'

Following this conversation I asked Colonel Abraham to come and see me. I presented to him the proposal that he take over the divisional battle group and told him that army group had approved this.

To my great astonishment he turned it down, as he was still ill. I have never been so surprised about a comrade as I was with Abraham at this point. We demanded the very last effort from our simple soldiers, and how did an active officer and regimental commander behave? He reported sick, although nothing noticeable in his condition had arisen during the last few weeks at Suvorovski. It seemed to me that the behaviour of my old comrade was due to depression. This did not alter the medical condition that affected him. Nevertheless I had to react according to service regulations.

I rapidly decided to take over the command of the battle groups myself. General Paulus, with whom, surprisingly, I still had telephone contact, approved my decision. 'Hold the line of retreat open for me, Adam! The Army High Command has to approve the breakout if it hasn't lost its senses.'

Army Group 'B' also approved. Its Ia told me that, on the orders of

General von Sodenstern, the chief of staff, I was now under the immediate command of the army group.

I called the staff of the army's artillery commander and gave them a stack of orders on the strict organisation of the battle groups. Alone again, I went over some of my thoughts. It was already dark outside. The electric light on the table threw a circle of light whose outermost edge hit the thickly frozen-over window to the street. It was bitterly cold; already by midday the quicksilver had sunk to 15 degrees below zero. Tonight it could reach a good 25 degrees below. And the majority of the troops lay in the icy wind on the open steppe without winter clothing. Had there been any sense at all in forming a line of defence with such thrown-together units, without anti-tank guns, without artillery, without mortars, without tanks, yes, even without a sufficient number of machine guns, a line which must surely break apart with any strong attack from the enemy? Did it make sense to sacrifice soldiers to no purpose? But there was that last telephone conversation with Paulus: 'Hold the line of retreat open for me, Adam!'

So I had to do everything to keep this last chance open for the twenty-two surrounded divisions. This was now my most important duty, the day's challenge. It concerned the lives and fates of about a quarter of a million surrounded troops! I was responsible for them too. Thus all my thoughts and strength were concentrated on the defensive capabilities of the combat teams.

It was as if this painful inner conflict gave me new additional strength to make the harder decisions. An officer reported the arrival of heavy weapons from Tormossin: two 88mm anti-aircraft guns, four 105mm howitzers and four 55mm anti-tank guns. Some tanks would also arrive the next day. My heart beat faster: if the army group supported us now, we could stop the enemy.

During the night of the 24th November Captain Göbel reported lively Soviet scout activity. In the following days the enemy attacked our defences repeatedly with weak forces. Without doubt he was testing our front. Gradually the Soviet attacking forces became stronger, the fighting harder and more costly in terms of casualties.

Army Group 'Don' under von Manstein

The Army High Command had made some organisational alterations on the Don and Stalingrad fronts shortly after the beginning of the Red Army offensive. The 6th Army, the battle groups on the Chir and the remains of the Rumanian 3rd Army were put under the newly formed Army Group 'Don'. The command was assumed by Field Marshal von Manstein on the 28th November. My battle group was allocated to the XXXXVIIIth Panzer Corps, whose staff moved to Tormossin. This corps had been posted under Lieutenant-General Heim behind the Rumanian 3rd Army at the beginning of the offensive. Its task was to check the enemy attack. General Paulus had told me many times that this was one of the most dangerous illusions entertained by the Army High Command. This was where misfortune really struck. Heim was surrounded with his two badly weakened divisions. Only with some short breaks was he able to break through to the west. Hitler made him a scapegoat and relieved him of his position. Despite the obvious lack of fighting experience, equipment and strength in Heim's Rumanian and German divisions, the blame for the Soviet breakthrough was placed on him and he was thrown out of the army, although he was later rehabilitated. His successor was General of Panzer Troops von Knobelsdorff, who arrived at Tormossin on the 1st December.

The situation at this critical point could not be improved with these organisational and personnel alterations alone. On the whole Chir front from the mouth to the upper course of the river it was catastrophic. The enemy only had to attack with stronger forces and our battle groups would be unable to stand up to them. Our front had ever deeper dents in it. We urgently needed reinforcement.

In the first days of December the 336th Infantry Division took up position next to my battle groups. In addition to this, several companies of a Luftwaffe field division were attached. They were extremely well armed and equipped, especially with what our soldiers needed most: winter clothing. The mood of my men was understandably not enhanced when they saw the piles of fur coats, fur waistcoats, fur hats, felt boots, winter gloves and padded camouflage suits, with which Göring's Luftwaffe warriors were equipped. On top of this, the Luftwaffe men refused to fight. It was not their fault. Their officers kept their noses in the air but had no idea about fighting as infantry.

Hoth's relief army
At this time General von Knobelsdorff visited me in Nishne-Chirskaya. He confirmed what I had already heard: the new 4th Panzer Army under Colonel-General Hoth was standing ready in the area of Kotelnikovski east of the Don. In the next days it would break through the enclosing forces and roll forward on a wider front. At the same time an army detachment under General of Infantry Hollidt would thrust from the area west of the Upper Chir into the flank of the enemy attacking south. The XXXXVIIIth Panzer Corps under General of Panzer Troops von Knobelsdorff had to lead the attack out of the bridgehead east of Nishne-Chirskaya with the newly met 11th Panzer Division and some still-expected units. The commanding general inquired about conditions in the Don bridgehead and our knowledge of the enemy situation.

The appearance of German tanks in our immediate vicinity gave the soldiers and officers considerable impetus. They had endured days of bloody, casualty-expensive fighting under the worst of conditions against a strong, bitter and bravely fighting enemy. Many of my men had friends and relations in the cauldron. They regarded it as a point of honour to make a contribution to their release. But all of them were extraordinarily worn out physically and emotionally very exhausted. This was not insignificant in how they reacted to the gradual realisation of the stubbornness with which Hitler and the Army High Command responded to all rational proposals to break out of the encirclement.

What do we want here on the Volga, Colonel?
I went to the foremost positions every day. I was often asked: 'Why must we hold these positions if the army has to remain in the cauldron?' Often I spoke with an old soldier who had taken part in the last year of the First World War. One day he said to me: 'Colonel, I don't understand what we really want here on the Don and Volga. When I think that I can be killed today or tomorrow, my wife and my children will not know what I was fighting for. And in all honesty, I don't know either.'

It was immediately clear to me that an earnest question had been touched on here. If this mood took a wider hold, we would disarm ourselves. So I had to counter it. I tried with the words: 'Think about our surrounded comrades! If we don't hold the bridgehead, if we abandon the defence of the Chir line, our front line will fall back many kilometres. That is as good as not thinking about establishing a connection to the surrounded troops. We remain here now for the sake of our 330,000 comrades.'

My opposite number was silent. Therefore I went on after a short pause: 'I don't know what our High Command intends. But it's clear enough that we mustn't throw our flints into the corn. We must do our duty as soldiers.'

Inwardly I was not comfortable with my reply. It did not hit the core of the question that the soldier had thrown at me. Why actually were we standing here on the Don and the Chir? Why did we want to take Stalingrad? To what purpose was it that here and in the cauldron hundreds, thousands were killed or wounded, hungry and frozen? The basic, decisive answer I had tried to find with my words, but they were not enough. They were not overpowering, led to no consequences. Tradition, doing one's duty and sympathy for one's surrounded comrades prevailed over the voice of reason. In addition came the intensive preparations for attack by our immediate neighbour. They gave hope, uplift. Perhaps the whole misery will have passed in fourteen days! 'After every December comes May again' said a soldiers' song that no one among us sang anymore, though it was broadcast almost daily.

New storm on the Chir
We all longed for the day when the relief army would set off. 'May' under

these circumstances was a long way off. We first experienced literally the arrival of December and what came afterwards. Once the 336th Infantry Division had occupied positions on our left, but strong Soviet armoured units stormed their sector and the division was pushed back. Thus our left flank was threatened. The 11th Panzer Division restored the old situation. But meanwhile things flared up elsewhere. Here too the 11th Panzer Division had to put out the fires. It immediately became the front's fire brigade, which had to be everywhere where the thin line of defence threatened to be torn apart by the enemy attacks. In these day and night engagements it too was hard hit. We hardly saw its tanks in our sector any more, although we urgently needed tank support in the increasingly stronger attacks. The situation was not good at the Don bridgehead. It was being ever more reduced so that an evacuation was becoming imminent. This all hit our morale hard. Even though a few days earlier we had been given fresh impetus by our tanks, now our spirits sank even deeper than before. It became normal for soldiers to leave their positions without permission. All sat in fear of imprisonment and a bullet in the back of the neck. Even officers had the desire to get out of this mess as soon as possible.

Meanwhile the telephone connection with the cauldron had been broken. Consequently there was constant radio communication. Major-General Schmidt requested officers and clerks from the staff. They flew from Morosovsk to the cauldron in supply aircraft. One radio message from the chief of staff read: 'The commander of the army signals regiment, Colonel Schrader, is to fly in immediately. He has to take over the duties of the sick army signals officer.' As our staff had moved meanwhile from Tormossin to Morosovsk, I gave the radio message to the army's senior quartermaster to pass on. Only an hour later the radio announced that Colonel Schrader had reported sick. That was the third time in fourteen days that a senior officer of the 6th Army had become a coward. The chief of staff, Major-General Schmidt, ordered a court martial for Colonel Schrader. I have never discovered what the outcome was.

Chapter 4

Between Hope and Destruction

Lieutenant-General von Gablenz relieves me

Another radio message came to Nishne-Chirskaya from the cauldron. It concerned me personally. General Paulus wanted me to fly in urgently. It was quite clear that I must go as soon as possible. I asked Army Group 'Don' by telephone for my relief. But this was turned down at first. Only when the army commander-in-chief had given the reason why I was so urgently required in Gumrak was it agreed. The condition was that a divisional commander in the cauldron who had become free was available as a replacement. The Army High Command was agreeable to this.

With a heavy heart I said goodbye to my battle group. I had come to know the officers and soldiers in the two weeks of combined leadership of the fighting and I had won their confidence. Would they understand me giving up the command when the situation at the mouth of the Chir was coming ever more to a head with wide-ranging decisions involved?

Captain Göbel assured me that they were all reluctant to lose me. But none raised the idea that I was leaving the combat group in the lurch in a difficult situation. Certainly I was not leaving personal security behind, especially with an uncertain future in the cauldron. I myself was completely clear about the uncertainty. Possibly there was no escape from the iron ring between the Don and the Volga.

On the 10th December Lieutenant-General Freiherr von Gablenz, commander of the 384th Infantry Division, entered Nishne-Chirskaya with his headquarters staff. We knew each other well. Gablenz was a friend of Paulus's and had often visited us at army headquarters. He said, 'I have to greet you on behalf of General Paulus. He thanks you for arranging things on the Chir. But now the 6th Army needs its 1st Adjutant back, which is why I am relieving you, Adam.'

'That is excellent, but what has become of your division, General?'

'Right. You don't know everything that has happened in the cauldron since the 22nd November. I hardly know where I should begin. On the 23rd

November we were so hard-pressed by the enemy that the army decided to send the XIVth Panzer Corps and the XIth Corps to the east over the Don to get them away from the destruction. My division received orders to form a bridgehead west of the Don to secure the crossings near Perepolni and Akimovski. The position was to be defended until both corps had crossed the river. It was a bitter, costly battle. When we reached the east bank of the Don on the evening of the 24th November my division hardly existed any longer. We were incorporated into the new West Front, but our fighting strength was just about zero. General Paulus therefore decided to disband the division. Those remaining soldiers and officers were shared out among other infantry divisions. Things did not go much better with the 376th Infantry Division, which was covering our backs on the east bank of the Don. It still exists but its fighting strength is not much more than that of a regiment. As a result of the swift Russian advance on the 19th and 20th November, the divisions of the XIth Corps have lost their rear services, along with their rations, ammunition and clothing. My quartermaster informs me that most stores fell into the hands of the enemy intact. Even the few deliveries of winter clothing that had arrived by then could not be issued in time. The rations in the cauldron have been handed out. But I won't tell you the worst. You will soon find out for yourself.'

'Apart from the 384th, were any other divisions disbanded, General?'

'Yes, the 94th Infantry Division was wiped out while clearing its former position. The 79th Infantry Division has had such severe losses that it will probably be disbanded in the next few days, as Paulus told me. The commander of the 94th Infantry Division is to fly out and collect those men of the 6th Army returning from leave.'

The handover of the battle groups went quickly and smoothly. Once I had given a summary of the situation and condition of the troops, we drove to the individual commanders. I used this opportunity to say farewell and thank them for their preparedness for action.

In Morosovsk

The next day a jeep took me to the quartermaster department of the 6th Army at Morosovsk. Here too were the headquarters of the Rumanian 3rd Army, which had been supporting my battle group during the last days. As I reported my departure, Colonel-General Dumitrescu invited me to lunch. There I met the Rumanian and the German chief of staff, Colonel Wenk. From him I learnt that the whole front north of Morosovsk was on the move. Our arriving transport was hardly sufficient to eliminate the existing breaches.

The difficult experiences of the previous three weeks and the current seriousness of the situation meant there was no proper conversation among the high-ranking officers sitting at the lunch table. Now and then there were a few words between people sitting next to each other. Otherwise there was an oppressive silence. Unspoken questions hovered in the room: what alarming news will the next hours bring? How long will we be in Morosovsk? When will the Hollidt replacement army be formed?

After the meal I went back to the quartermaster department. I hoped to be able to talk to some of my old comrades and fellow workers before my flight into the cauldron. Unfortunately I did not meet my friend Colonel Selle. He had taken over a combat team at Chir, near Surovikino. The few present seemed to pity me, which annoyed me. Naturally it was no pleasure to fly into the cauldron, but in a difficult situation every officer belonged to his unit, which for me was the surrounded 6th Army.

Late in the afternoon I met our quartermaster, Colonel Baader. A few days earlier Paulus had sent him out of the cauldron so that he could conduct a better and more continuous resupply for the army. The colonel handed me a telegram from Major-General Schmidt in which he requested that three regimental commanders be flown in. That seemed a bit odd to me; hadn't Lieutenant-General von Gablenz said that two infantry divisions had been disbanded? Shouldn't there be sufficient commanders available?

I cautiously directed an appropriate inquiry to the army. The reply came promptly: three regimental commanders were to be flown in. It was not difficult, as there was an officer reserve in Morosovsk. From them I would select three staff officers to go to Gumrak the next day.

Once this business had been resolved, I discussed a few supply problems with the quartermaster. 'How will the army actually be supplied, Baader?'

'By air. A supply base has been established here. Every day – weather permitting – aircraft fly uninterruptedly into the cauldron with food, ammunition, fuel, medical supplies and bandages. They bring back the severely wounded. Tomorrow they will also be landing on the big airfield at Pitomnik. There are still some fighters there to escort the transport aircraft.'

'I don't understand this. The army has a ration strength of about 330,000 men, and you have to supply all of them by air?'

'Although three divisions of the 4th Panzer Army and two Rumanian divisions are included, this is not too many. According to yesterday's reports the supply strength in the cauldron is only 270,000 men now. But even with these numbers the supplies flown in are widely insufficient. The army only gets a fraction of its minimum requirements. The whole thing is a big mess for which Göring is primarily responsible. He assured Hitler in his big-mouthed way that the Luftwaffe could fully supply the army. According to our calculations, the army needs normally at least 700 tons of supplies a day. Should the fighting strength be maintained to any extent, no less than 500 tons is required. But this target has not been achieved on any day. The result is an ever-growing deficit in supplies, ammunition and fuel. In addition, eight of the surrounded divisions have lost their camps and rear services. Already these divisions, who have hardly any winter clothing, for which naturally transport is also lacking, have to occupy the new southern and western fronts, where there are no trenches or dugouts. The army is confronting the worst hunger catastrophe and mass freezing if the connection with the cauldron is not established very soon.'

'Tell me, Baader, why didn't the army break through the weak encirclement right at the beginning and escape to the southwest? Certainly it would not have been possible without casualties, but the majority would have been saved.'

'I only know one thing. The commander-in-chief had again requested a breakout, but Hitler turned down his requests every time. Paulus can perhaps tell you more about it.'

'You take it to be impossible for the army to be supplied by air for much longer?'

'I repeat once more, such thoughts can only be born in the head of a dreamer. Even my fellow workers, who all have rich experience in this area, are of the same view as me,' replied the Colonel.

'May I convey your opinion to General Paulus?'

'But of course.'

It was nearly midnight as I walked back and forth in the room that had been allocated as my accommodation. Despite my sense of duty, and all the courage that I still retained, I was already none too happy when I thought that not for the first time in 24 hours I was sitting in the damned mire. I had seen that the situation was not much better outside the cauldron. Before our ravaged front west of the Don stood the well equipped armies of the enemy ready to make the breakthrough. They had been attacking our battle groups and the Rumanian 3rd Army ceaselessly for days. I could also not believe that the advance of our new army under General Hoth near Kotelnikovski would remain concealed from the Soviet High Command. Certainly strong defensive forces had gathered on the Kalmuck Steppe between the Don and the Volga. And our front on the Lower Chir; how long would it hold? The 11th Panzer Division and the 336th Infantry Division had been badly hit and had their hands full repulsing the enemy. No support could be expected from them in the relief attack by Hoth's army.

But what use was this brooding? Next morning I would finally meet Hoth's tanks. A big convoy with supplies for the 6th Army would follow them.

Before lying down to sleep I called the Morosovsk airstrip. The commandant himself came on the line. 'Tell me, exactly what time I am flying tomorrow?'

'The first three machines are starting at 0400 hours. With you are flying two of the requested regimental commanders. You yourself follow in one of the next three machines, which apparently will be taking off at 0800 hours. The situation could force us to change the schedule at short notice. Therefore it would be useful if you could be here already at 0700 hours.'

I promised to be punctual.

I fly into the cauldron
The weather on the 12th December was frosty, and dawn had yet to break when I arrived at the airstrip. The commandant was restlessly awaiting the return of the aircraft that had taken off at 0400 hours. Then at last, when it had become light, one of them landed. Where were the other two? The pilot reported that the three aircraft had encountered hefty flak shortly after leaving the cauldron. Apparently the two missing *Ju 52*s had been shot down.

This was no good omen for me, nor for the three regimental commanders who were supposed to fly with me. But after shaking hands with the commandant, we hurried to the three waiting *He 111*s. We climbed into two different machines. Clambering over sacks and boxes of foodstuffs, I wriggled into the seat behind the pilots, next to the radio operator. Immediately after taking off, the aircraft climbed steeply into the sky. The altimeter soon showed 4,000 metres. Then we began to fly east.

We crossed the Don far to the south of Nishne-Chirskaya. Under us the sunshine glistened on the Kalmuck Steppe. Above us smiled a cloud-free blue sky. I recalled my first flight, which took me to Vinniza in the summer, also in the finest weather. Then too I scanned the sky with my eyes peeled for Soviet fighters. But then there had been German fighters in the sky. Now there was no fighter protection and the sky was open to the '*Yaks*'. 'What should I do if enemy fighters attack?' I asked the pilot in front of me.

He laughed. 'Stay sitting quietly, Colonel. We'll do everything ourselves.' He shouted back over the sound of the engines.

The youngster annoyed me a little, for I had no parachute. 'And if we get hit?' I shouted forwards.

'Then we are wiped out,' he answered at the same volume but with the greatest calm, as if he was dealing with the most natural thing in the world. He pointed downwards. 'There is the Red Army position.'

I recognised vehicles in a settlement. 'Tanks, Colonel.' Like a tour guide he explained everything that appeared in our view. Puffs of cloud – once near, once further off, once over us, once under us – showed that the flak had opened fire. But my guide was not disturbed in his loud presentation. Was he trying to help me to overcome my uneasy feeling, or even more my anxiety? I wondered about this young officer who had to fly this death-surrounded stretch several times a day. He turned to me with his smiling face. 'We have made it, Colonel, down there is Pitomnik.'

I really felt relieved. Helplessly watching the enemy shells without being able to avoid them was an unpleasant feeling.

The machine glided down, crossing over the airstrip several times. This way I got the first impression of what was happening here. The place was overflowing with crashed aircraft and destroyed vehicles: there a '*Condor*', here a '*Focke-Wulf*'. Among the wrecks were several *Ju 52*s and *He 111*s – the work of the Red bombers and fighters!

The two other aircraft kept close to us. My pilot, who had been the quietest on the way, pressed for haste. The supply items were quickly unloaded. Then came the 'return freight': wounded men crawling out of holes in the earth, creeping and hobbling, or carried on stretchers. An officer and some soldiers, apparently a control team, braced themselves against the group of humans trying to force their way onto the aircraft. They were only flown out if they had a chit from the army doctors.

'Alarm!' was sounded in this confusion: Soviet bombers at a great height. For a moment everyone thought of the approaching danger and sought cover as well as they could. I went straight into the bunker of the airfield commander as the bombs started exploding. The ground shook, the strong planks shivered, earth trickled through the wooden roof and onto the table standing in front of us. There were several dozen hits, then it seemed to be over.

'There is little to celebrate here,' I said to a Luftwaffe second lieutenant who belonged to the airfield commander's staff. 'Do you get such visits often?' 'We are used to them, Colonel. There is hardly an hour during the day that Ivan leaves us undisturbed. As long as there are no losses, it is not too bad.'

The airman had not yet completed this sentence when the call for help came: 'Medic! Medic!'

'Are there doctors nearby?' I asked concernedly.

'There are some roomy medical tents on the edge of the field. All badly wounded are brought here on the orders of the army to be flown out by the supply machines. The army doctor, Doctor-General Professor Dr Renoldi, is stationed here. He is responsible for the loading of the wounded. In fact he is almost powerless, as so many lightly wounded come here. They hide themselves in unused trenches and bunkers and are the first on the spot, and ruthlessly drag the badly wounded away. Some manage to smuggle themselves aboard despite the controls. We often have to empty the aircraft again to find room for the badly wounded. The paintbrush of a Höllen-Bruegel or the eloquence of a Dante would be necessary to illustrate the cruel scenes that I have experienced here in the last ten days.'

We went up out of the shelter. Our three *He 111*s had already started up for the return flight. Meanwhile it had become clear to me why the pilots were in so much of a hurry to leave Pitomnik again. Destruction and death lurked in the air.

Coming to meet me were two older officers. It appeared that they were the regimental commanders who had left Morosovsk at 0400 hours and had been awaiting my arrival in a bunker. Talking to them, I discovered that they were former E-Officers – officers who in peacetime worked in local district headquarters or on the staff of higher staffs. They had asked the army staff about their role but no one could tell them where they had to report. I telephoned Schmidt, who had ordered their flight. He referred me to the adjutant of the VIIIth Corps, from whom the request had come. But the latter told me in reply to my call that all posts were taken in the VIIIth Corps. He had never requested any such replacements.

This was a strong blow, letting old commanders be flown into this precarious situation unnecessarily. What should I do? They could only fly out again on Schmidt's orders. I was not authorised to give such a solution, but I wanted to get Paulus to approve the flight. I therefore invited these two gentlemen to await a further decision at the airport.

A car took me to the headquarters near Gumrak station. Already four weeks previously I had driven along this road. Then supply vehicles were rolling day and night to Stalingrad, signs gave clear directions, military police regulated the traffic. Now the same road had a completely different aspect. Hollow-cheeked figures with heads wrapped in blood-soaked bandages and feet bound in cloths tottered along. The road signs had long since been burnt, the military police had vanished. Now shot-up vehicles and discarded helmets, gas masks and weapons marked the road from Pitomnik to Stalingrad. Ghostly skeletons of fallen horses protruded from their thin covering of snow, showing where hungry soldiers had hacked the flesh off them with hatchets.

A hectic, hyper-nervous atmosphere reigned at army headquarters. I wanted first to arrange the flight out for the regimental commanders and so went to Schmidt. He categorically refused. 'In this situation we cannot let any officer fly out unless he is severely wounded,' he countered.

I had made a tactical mistake that was almost impossible to correct. General Paulus would certainly have approved my proposal. From experience, however, I knew he would never countermand a decision made by Schmidt. Nevertheless I decided, after a short reflection, to see the commander-in-chief and ask about the return flight of the regimental commanders. I reported to Paulus and made my request. 'Who asked for these officers?'

'In Morosovsk Colonel Baader gave me a radio message signed by Schmidt, General. All corps adjutants have confirmed that they have not asked for any regimental commanders. I have been unable to establish in my short time here who made this nonsense.'

'Then Schmidt should give the order to have them flown out of the cauldron.'

'That is why I went straight to him. Nevertheless Schmidt refused. I don't regard this as being correct.'

'Hoth's relief army has set off today. Let us wait until contact has been made with us, then we will place all three men back in the commander reserve. Until then, they will be placed at the disposal of the VIIIth Corps.'

That was how the decision about these old officers was made. Uselessly they sat with the VIIIth Corps and were finally sent to the slaughter with thousands of others in the cauldron.

A bunker in the steppe

Apart from this sad episode in military bureaucracy, I was pleased to be back with Paulus again. He had greeted me especially heartily. Already my first critical view had shown me how much the catastrophic situation of his army was consuming him. The nervous sucking-in of his face seemed no longer to be heard. Head and shoulders were more strongly bent forwards than before. There was bitter disappointment in his words. He was unhappy with himself and his dealings. Tired and stressed from his just-ended journey to the hard-pressed western front of the cauldron, he asked me where I was accommodated. When I told him that I had had nothing from the chief of staff as yet, he told me to go and look around and to come back at 1600 hours. He hinted that I would have a lot to do in the days to come. Neither recommendations for awards nor promotions had been worked on during the past three weeks. That is why he had asked for me.

I went back into the open. A few dugouts lay half underground on the open steppe. No tree, no bush to provide cover. All vehicles had to park several hundred metres away. Lieutenant Zimmermann told me that this had previously been the headquarters of the 295th Infantry Division. Round about were similar clusters of bunkers, all interconnected by tracks and footpaths. Would I find my way around in this labyrinth?

Next I had to go to Major-General Schmidt, whose bunker lay close to that of the commander-in-chief. 'May I ask where my section is accommodated, General?'

'There was no room for you here. Your clerks are in a bunker about 1,000 metres away. Lieutenant Schatz will take you there.'

Together with Schmidt's orderly officer I trudged across the steppe for ten minutes, fifteen minutes. Finally we stood before a hole in the ground. My eyes gradually picked out the outlines of Staff-Sergeant Küpper and Senior Corporal Dr Asch. Both were delighted to see me again. I brushed the tears from my eyes and a dry cough from my chest. I could hardly breathe and had to go out into the open with both of them. 'It is impossible for you to live here, Colonel. We have hardly any room in this three-metre square hole. We can't even put a typewriter on the little table. One cannot talk of doing proper work here. We have to open the door to be able to see, but then the cold makes our fingers clammy and immobile.'

'Na, na,' I countered. 'We will get things going somehow.'

The smoke had dispersed a little so that I could see the accommodation a little better. Two wooden stretchers on which blankets lay had been fixed one above the other along the long wall. There was no room for another bed. The floor of firmly stamped earth was frozen. As I lit a cigarette, ice crystals in the walls glittered in the shine of the burning match.

No, three men could not really be accommodated in this hole. We needed some other accommodation. That Schmidt saw too when I reported to him. I myself was provisionally given space in General Paulus's bunker, and a small room was provided for my staff in the big headquarters. Already next morning work started on a new earthen hut.

Meanwhile it was 1600 hours, the appointed time for me to go to General Paulus. Although in the last two or three days I had heard something from General von Gablenz and Colonel Baader about conditions in the cauldron, I was now concerned with a fully open question. Next in turn came Paulus with questions. He was mainly interested in conditions outside the cauldron. 'How goes it then on the Lower Chir and north of Morosovsk? What was your battle group's task, Adam?'

I reported fully on the development from the 22nd November to the 10th December, finishing with the following hint: 'The army group expected me to hold the bridgehead over the Don east of Verchne-Chirskaya under all circumstances in order to ease the way of the 6th Army to the west or southwest. Soldiers and officers of the battle group were very disappointed when they discovered the army was digging in and making no effort to break out of the encirclement. I too expected daily that the army would break out to the southwest. During the last days the soldiers asked me often why the stream of blood had to flow if the army was not to break out.'

As I was finishing my report, the 1st general staff officer entered. Colonel Elchlepp shook my hand firmly. 'Lucky that you should be here at last. I have been carrying out the most urgent of your tasks for the past three weeks. It went, however, more badly than correctly.'

Paulus interrupted him: 'Adam, I owe you yet another answer. The best thing for me to do is to describe to you the whole debacle since the 22nd November, so that you understand things better.'

Breakout forbidden

After several seconds of reflection, Paulus spoke again: 'That I had already ordered the withdrawal of the army behind the Don on the 21st November you already know. Shortly after my flight into the cauldron I summoned the commanding generals together to a meeting. In full agreement with them, I repeated our conclusions on the 22nd November and several times in subsequent days to the Army High Command. The orders for the breakout were to be issued early on the 24th November. There was nothing else to do. But in a conference with Hitler, Göring said that he was in a position to supply the 6th Army by air. Consequently the Führer decided to turn down my request. Despite the orders for the breakout, I received this radio message.'

The commander-in-chief handed me a sheet of paper. Attentively, I read the following text: 'The 6th Army is completely encircled by Russian forces. I intend the army to surround the area Stalingrad–Nord–Kotluban–Height 137–Height 135–Marinskovka–Zybenko–Stalingrad– South. The army can be assured that I will take all appropriate measures to care for and timely replace it. I know the brave 6th Army and its commander-in-chief, and know that they will do their duty. Adolf Hitler.' I returned the paper without a word.

'You see, Adam, I could not handle things differently. Since the arrival of that message I have called back all the commanding generals, including also those of the XIth Corps and the XIVth Panzer Corps, which meanwhile had carried out the change of banks on the Don and with part of their units had taken up the new western front. All expressed more or less concern about the possibility of air supply. The last ends all my proposals under the prevailing conditions of making a breakout from the pincers. Only one man energetically expressed another opinion: General von Seydlitz.'

'I understand that Hitler's order weighs heavily, General. But I know that Colonel Baader as well as other senior Luftwaffe officers are of the opinion that it is impossible to supply an army of about 330,000 men by air.'

'Seydlitz has demanded that we act contrary to the Führer Order. I have no suggestion to make about this. Seydlitz himself has given a clear example of what happens when commanders manage things their own way. Without our knowledge he took the 94th Infantry Division back from the north-eastern corner of the cauldron. The enemy recognised the move and immediately attacked. The division was completely wiped out, and we were forced to disband it. I let the divisional staff be flown out. Our handling can only be successful when it is in harmony with the intentions of the High Command.'

The telephone rang. Since the 12th December connection with Army Group 'Don' had been by the Decimetre apparatus. Manstein was on the line. Paulus waved us out. There was no longer an opportunity to learn more about the tragic fate of the 94th Infantry Division. Months later, in captivity, General von Seydlitz told me that in giving the order for the division to retreat he had firmly believed he was acting in accordance with the Army Command's proposed breakout. That Paulus two or three days later submitted to Hitler's order was not Seydlitz's fault. In fact, he could not have held on for much longer on the strongly endangered north-eastern front to the Volga with the widespread and very weak 94th Infantry Division. In the operation ordered by Seydlitz the defence sector would have been reduced to 15 kilometres.

Paulus, as a well educated officer of the general staff, assessed the situation soberly. He was thoroughly aware of the deadly danger. But going against a given order went against his military upbringing. So with Paulus – as with many older officers – from the very beginning their responsibility for the soldiers and military obedience were in strong conflict. After some difficult inner conflict, military obedience won.

General von Seydlitz resists

I accompanied Colonel Elchlepp to his quarters, where we continued our discussion. 'Do you know, Adam, our senior quartermaster has behaved completely correctly. Lieutenant-Colonel von Kunowski, whom Baader has now replaced in the cauldron, was worried from the start. On not one single day have the minimal essential number of tons of supplies been flown in. Hunger is increasing. If the liberating offensive from outside fails to break through, things look very black.'

'Would it not be right to get out of this damned mess against Hitler's orders and break out?'

'No. We know neither the intent nor the possibilities of the High Command. Schmidt and I have strengthened Paulus in his final decision. You would have behaved exactly the same if you had come here.'

What should I say to that? It was particularly difficult for me to put myself in the situation with which the commander-in-chief was confronted. For I knew for certain how carefully General Paulus considered things.

Elchlepp went on: 'The conversation with the commanding generals finally broke up dramatically. All turned sharply against Seydlitz. Colonel-General Heitz threatened to shoot him if he continued to demand disobedience of Hitler. Seydlitz then laid a memorandum before Paulus, the original of which was sent on to Army Group 'B'. Should you visit the LIst Corps in the next few days, which is not far from here, you can familiarise yourself with this memorandum. Seydlitz has, with the opening of the Demyansk cauldron last year, amassed various experiences that he brought to our attention. What he writes is not uninteresting.'

An orderly informed the Ia that he should go to Schmidt. I too burned, despite or because of the inner unrest that gripped me after this account, so I went quickly to my section. Küpper had already prepared something. I wanted an overview of the personnel strengths of the divisions and army troops as quickly as possible. That was not at all easy. Many units had been torn apart. There the remains of a battalion had been extracted to block gaps in the western and eastern fronts, here alarm units had been set up and thrown into battle. Often an officer did not know his unit's soldiers. The soldiers frequently did not know their officers or even the name of the man next to him. Losses in killed and wounded were reported only in numbers, not by name. Usually only the names of senior officer casualties were given. Under these circumstances it was very difficult to obtain realistic results.

Is Hoth's army strong enough?
By evening we had brought at least some order to the confusion. About 1900 hours we were called to supper, which we took in Paulus's bunker. With the commander-in-chief were the chief of staff, the 1st general staff officer, the quartermaster, the Ic, the 1st orderly officer, his personal orderly officer and me.

At first I had to talk about what was happening outside. Then events in the cauldron were discussed. With this opportunity I discovered that only in recent days, after its formation by the release of senior officers, had Army Group 'Don' obtained a true picture of the situation in the cauldron. At the end of November its chief of staff, Major-General Schultz, and shortly afterwards its Ia, Colonel Busse, had flown in for a few hours. Since then contact was generally being maintained by radio. General Paulus had no possibility of speaking personally to Field Marshal von Manstein. Nevertheless the mood in our group that evening was quite high. Hoth's army had started opening up the cauldron and by evening had come forward a considerable distance. 'If the army keeps up this pace, contact will have been made at the latest in a week,' said one of the junior orderly officers.

Paulus damped down this optimism a bit. '*If* the 4th Panzer Army maintains its pace! Good, that you make this limitation. It must be obvious to you, Zimmermann, that Hoth has been thrown back by the Red Army's most forward forces. The combined thrust with the main forces has yet to come. Let us hope that Hoth's army has sufficient breakthrough power!'

I recalled a conversation I had had in Morosovsk the day before with Colonel Wenck, the German staff officer to the Rumanian 3rd Army. 'If I am not wrong,' I commented now, 'the LVIIIth Panzer Corps with the 6th and 25th Panzer Divisions, as well as the 15th Luftwaffe Field Division, form the spearhead of Hoth's army. Rumanian infantry and cavalry divisions follow as flank protection. Apart from the 6th Panzer Division, which has just come replenished from France, all the divisions no longer boast their complete fighting strength. This applies especially to the Rumanian divisions, which were scattered by the Red Army attack on the 20th November and put to flight.'

'That's right,' agreed Schmidt. 'But in the next days Hoth will get the 17th Panzer Division.'

Paulus looked pensively in front of him. When the orderly officers left the room and only the department chiefs remained, he said: 'I don't understand the Army High Command any more. It seems that nothing has been learnt from the heavy blows of the last weeks. The composition of the

Hoth army is a shattering example that the strength of the Red Army is irresponsibly underestimated. Adam tells me that the few advancing divisions are hardly sufficient to close the new gaps appearing daily on the Chir front.'

'I am of the opinion, General,' I added, 'that our troops on the Lower Chir cannot hold their position. Until now the Russians have felt their way forward with security forces. We could only repel them with the utmost effort. With a main enemy attack the Chir front will soon collapse. This threatens the Hoth army's flank. It no longer has a chance of retreating.'

Paulus nodded. 'Let us trust, gentlemen, that the Army High Command will bring forward reinforcements in time.'

Then he turned to me: 'The Army High Command has already ordered Army Group "Don" to take up positions for a relief attack. Elchlepp will inform you of the details.'

With these words Paulus stood up. We parted from him. I accompanied the Ia to his dugout only a few steps away. As we stepped out into the cold winter night, Elchlepp said sceptically, 'Quite honestly, I too have only the slightest confidence in Hoth's mission.'

'But you were here from the beginning, Elchlepp, in immediate proximity to the troops. I can still not understand why the army did not set off immediately to the southwest. That was certainly possible in the first two or three days.'

'Yes, we wanted to. But we had not experienced these nerve-racking days. Day after day we asked permission by radio to break out. Army Group 'B' supported our requests, Hitler and the Army High Command turned them down. Finally army group confirmed the Army High Command's orders. It was the most obvious tug of war between the army and the superior commands. As the weaker ones gave in we were overwhelmed. The Army High Command presumed that it could assess the situation in the cauldron better than the 6th Army, which was sitting in the mess. Hitler had fixed the course of the western and southern fronts precisely. No ditch, no village, no piece of soil of the ordered ground was to be given up without his permission. We are now just better paid NCOs.'

In his office the Colonel showed me a file: 'Here, read it!' It was Paulus's selected positions for the army. I read something like the following:

1. The 4th Panzer Army does not appear to be strong enough to be able for certain to break out of the Stalingrad ring. Should it not, however, attain its goal, the chances of a breakout are worsened. Already on supply grounds the 6th Army is unable to maintain resistance much longer.

2. At the moment it is not possible to see how and when the Don Front broken through by the enemy can be stabilised. Even should

the thrust of the 4th Panzer Army succeed, Hoth's troops are threatened by the danger of being cut off.

3. From this assessment of the situation, the 6th Army Headquarters proposes a breakout from the cauldron to the southwest, in timely accord with the 4th Panzer Army's attack to the northeast with which it will combine on the high ground southwest of Stalingrad. Strength-wise the 6th Army is capable of taking all the wounded with it. In this way the fighting strength of the 6th Army will be maintained. The High Command will thus have reserves for the construction of a new front in its hands.

In my estimation this was a fundamentally correct and realistic assessment of the situation. I spoke to Elchlepp, expressing the following thoughts: 'Whether Point 3 can be realised today, I would doubt.'

'This question is certainly difficult to decide,' he replied. 'With our proposal we want above all once more to achieve an exact check of all planned measures. I simply cannot believe that the High Command can play so casually with an army of twenty-two divisions. Nevertheless I am impressed that Hoth's army was not reinforced by a single battalion and we here have to keep on holding out. As a soldier I will always obey the orders of my superiors, but I want to be able to understand them. That has become somewhat difficult recently. I had the greatest confidence in Manstein, but isn't it laughable when the Field Marshal in this desperate situation comes out stereotyped with the announcement that the Führer has ordered so and so! Should he not be more in tune with our army headquarters? Now read this too!'

'Fortress Stalingrad'
He handed me several radio messages from Führer Headquarters. From the date stamps it could be seen that they had arrived immediately after the formation of the cauldron. Hardly believable was what was there: the 6th Army from then on was to call itself 'Fortress Stalingrad'.

Elchlepp saw my startled face: 'That astonishes you, does it? But now at least you know where you are: in "Fortress Stalingrad".'

'If I had not read it myself, I would have doubted you. You would be pulling my leg. Stalingrad a fortress! What does Paulus say then, and Schmidt and the other generals about this nonsense?'

'The same as you: it's nonsense. The description "Fortress" does not only apply to the city itself. Even here a comprehensive system is lacking. No bombproof dugouts nor constructions with tank turrets, no underground communication passages nor barricades and obstacles are available. The ruins of the buildings and cellars offer some protection against splinters, perhaps even from the weather, but one cannot speak of preparation for a long period of time. But you know that from your own experience.'

'And how does it look on the new western and southern fronts, Elchlepp?'

'That is where the description "Fortress" sounds exactly like a joke. There are neither trenches nor dugouts, only holes in the hard-frozen, cut-up ground. Just holes in the snow. They are our soldiers' fighting and resting places, offering them a little protection from the cutting steppe wind, but nothing more. A strong attack by the Russians and our hungry, half-frozen and overtired soldiers would be unable to hold. These all', closed the Ia, 'are things that I can only describe with difficulty. But in the end we are soldiers and we know what orders are.'

It had become late. I reached out my hand to shake his. Outside the icy northeast wind blew in my face and through my uniform. Shells were exploding in the distance. The sound of vehicles came from the Pitomnik–Stalingrad road. In the air throbbed some *Ju 52*s or *He 111*s, which unfortunately were bringing us only a fraction of the things we needed to live and fight.

Uneasily I churned in my first night in the cauldron, the night of the 14th December, tossing to and fro on my straw sack. I got up while it was still dark. The orderlies had already prepared the sparse breakfast. There was a slice of bread more than usual from some loaves that I had brought from Morosovsk. I sat at the table with General Paulus. Each of us had a cup of hot black coffee in front of us. Slowly we chewed the three slices of bread allotted to us. Paulus's eyes were directed at the situation map on the wall. The front at the big breakthrough position west of the Don was shown as I had indicated. From Kotelnikovski thick blue arrows pointed north.

'Have we any news about Operation Hoth, General?' I asked.

'As Schmidt informed me by telephone earlier, the attack is going according to plan. Since yesterday we have had verbal communication with Army Group "Don" through the Decimetre apparatus, so we can actually be informed earlier than before. For the time being I am not very confident. Their report yesterday on the situation outside the cauldron was more serious than I thought. Look at the map! The Italian 8th Army is threatened in the flank and rear. They are almost just battle groups that should be securing the wide breakthrough points. If the enemy attack here again the catastrophe will be even greater than it is now.'

'I simply cannot understand, General, how we can stabilise the front. Have we still no troops to form a new army? Won't all the Army High Command's measures come too late? Will the Italians hold their sector of the front on the Don?'

'Should the Italian 8th Army be thrown back then the Hungarians will also be forced to give up their positions. Then even the German 2nd Army on the Voronesh front sector will be threatened on its flank. It is presumed that it is possible to stabilise the whole Chir–Don front, and that the Army

High Command has operational and strategic reserves and has already sent them marching to the threatened places. I cannot be certain about this with you. After the bad experiences of the last three weeks I have become somewhat sceptical about the decisive and resolute capability of the Army High Command.'

'Only a question, if you will permit, General. Elchlepp showed me a radio message from Hitler ordering that Hoth should re-establish the old front. That would mean we would have to remain here. With the current uncertain situation outside the cauldron, in my opinion such an order would be nonsense.'

'The order really reads like that. Nevertheless we have made preparations to enable Hoth to make a counterthrust. I hope that the Army High Command recognises at least at the last minute that my proposed abandonment of the city and breakthrough to the southwest is the only possible way of saving the army.'

General von Seydlitz's memorandum

I was not making much progress in my efforts to keep a realistic picture of the fighting strength of our divisions and units. Therefore I decided to visit some of the corps adjutants to speak to them about how we could more precisely establish the strengths of their many elements. I began with the nearby headquarters of the LIst Corps. The corps lay mainly in the city. It had, apart from the defeat of the 94th Infantry Division, suffered least from the beginning of the enemy offensive. The city had become the quietest fighting front of the cauldron.

'How is the atmosphere among the staff?' I asked the adjutant.

'Not good,' he replied. 'The older ones complain like mad. It is annoying that Paulus looks inactive while the 6th Army slowly but surely goes to earth. Seydlitz regards it as irresponsible waffle by Göring that twenty-two divisions could be supplied by air. He must know about Demyansk. Would you like to read his memorandum, or do you know it already?'

'I have heard about the memorandum at our headquarters. It interests me very much indeed. Have you the text there?'

'But of course, Colonel.' The adjutant went to his file chest, took a folder out and handed it to me. I read it ever more intently. Precisely, matter of factly, irrefutably, Seydlitz assessed our catastrophic supply situation, the continuing enemy offensive, the first effective relief measures taken by the Army High Command and the strength situation of the troops. All these hard facts demanded a decision. 'Either the 6th Army defends itself in a hedgehog position until it fades away, that means is defenceless . . . or the army breaks out of the encirclement in active engagement,' concluded the general. He was not afraid of taking the requisite measures against Hitler's orders to hold out, and ended his memorandum with the words: 'If the Army

High Command does not immediately lift the order to persevere in the hedgehog position, arising from their own knowledge about the army and the German people and the obligations of command, they themselves, despite the orders that until now have prevented freedom of manoeuvre, should make use of the still available possibility of avoiding catastrophe by means of their own attack. The complete destruction of two hundred thousand combatants and all of their equipment stands in the balance. There is no other option.'

That was civil courage, daring and decisiveness for independent handling, as I then felt. That Seydlitz's goal was also none other than the army being 'saved' for the continuation of the war, thus for new battles and dying, did not occur to me. A moment later the thought came to me: What would happen if Seydlitz instead of Paulus was commander-in-chief of the 6th Army? I rated Paulus highly. In this case, however, Seydlitz had my full respect.

I asked the adjutant what would happen to the memorandum. 'It will go from the army via the army group to the Army High Command and – now you will laugh – Seydlitz is to take over the whole northern and eastern fronts of the cauldron.'

'How did Paulus react to this clipping of his authority?'

'That I cannot tell you, Colonel. I only know that a discussion took place between Paulus and Seydlitz.'

Once I had obtained the information about the personnel situation with the LIst Corps, I drove back to my staff. I could not work out why Hitler had given Seydlitz command of the most important sectors of the cauldron. Did he want to tame the general? Why should this be at Paulus's expense?

Perhaps Elchlepp could answer these questions. I went to see him immediately after my arrival. He greeted me with the words: 'Have you seen Seydlitz's memorandum? What have you to say to that?'

'I admire the precision and consequence of the judgement. I was naturally puzzled when I read the proposal to act against the Führer Order.'

'We all – Paulus, Schmidt, I and the other commanding generals – disagree with this conclusion. That is absolute anarchy. I acknowledge that an army commander has the right and duty to make individual decisions, but only when he has no communications with the superior command. That is not the case with us. The High Command is scrupulously informed about our situation. It is quite absurd to assume that the Army High Command will sacrifice us.'

Göring's lie about air supply

'Paulus told me yesterday that Hitler had been willing to order the army's breakout. Under Göring's influence he then decided otherwise. Neither Paulus, nor Schmidt, nor you, not one of the commanding generals – none of us – believed in view of the whole war situation that the Luftwaffe could keep an army of some 270,000 men supplied with food, ammunition, fuel and medical supplies. That is Utopia. It may have been possible before the envelopment, when the Red ring around the 6th Army was not yet firm and the enemy anti-aircraft artillery was less effective, but now the enemy's flak and fighters are fully in action and it is completely out of the question.'

'Of course, Adam. Paulus recognised this in the very first days of the encirclement. Major-General Pickert, commanding the 9th Flak Division, regarded it as illusory that the Luftwaffe could keep our army sufficiently supplied. That is why the commander-in-chief let him fly to the army group on the 27th November to speak to Field Marshal von Manstein, without holding anything back, and to orientate him on the maximum possibilities of air supply with the Luftwaffe units available. Pickert was to openly explain and stress our doubts about the reality of air supply, and reiterate that the army could only be saved by breaking out with support from outside. Therefore no time could be lost.'

'A question, Elchlepp. How many machines must fly into the cauldron every day if the army is to remain battle-worthy?'

'You know, Adam, that we need at least 700 tons of supplies, and a *Ju 52* takes two tons. So that means that every day 350 *Ju 52*s must land at Pitomnik. A *He 111* can only carry only one and a half tons. The number of machines thus rises to more than 400 should there not be enough *Ju 52*s available.'

'Colonel Baader gave me a similar answer. And how many machines have actually flown in the last days?'

'Only a small number, a quarter at the most. But let me go on. Pickert returned several days later. He reported to Paulus about his long talk with General Fiebig, the commanding general of the VIIIth Air Corps, whom Hitler had tasked with the air supply of the 6th Army. Although this corps on Hitler's orders was spared from all combat tasks, Fiebig had to declare that he had too few machines to be able to fly the requested tonnage into the cauldron. He was himself in a conflict. He flew into the cauldron on the 11th December and declared before Paulus and Schmidt that he would do everything humanly possible to assist the badly suffering 6th Army. But he was not only lacking aircraft. Sometimes heavy frosts, raging snowstorms and thick fog paralysed air traffic almost completely. As a result of this, on not a single day so far has he been able to deliver more than a quarter of the required tonnage. Within the next few days we will apparently be forced to further reduce the bread ration, which was already reduced to 200 grams a day at the end of November.'

Gnawing doubt

'I have already experienced in Morosovsk several divisions in fleeing retreat losing their whole stores, even their field kitchens, and having to go hungry for several days.'

'That is how it is. Therefore soon after his arrival in the cauldron, Paulus ordered all units to report the precise state of their rations, clothing, ammunition and fuel stocks. Quartermasters and managers were ordered to ensure even distribution. I do not know if all have reported back honourably and truthfully. We cannot check all the reports.'

'We must thus assume that most of the encircled army troops have been hungry for days. The lack of supplies worsens every 24 hours in direct correlation to the smaller number of machines flying in. Where is the way out, Elchlepp?'

'The way out lies in continuous, maximum possible air supply, and in the success of Operation Hoth.'

'Neither of us believes in the reality of the air bridge. Whether Hoth's army will succeed in forming a land bridge to us appears to me also as very uncertain. But are we not falling into an unhealthy self-deception?'

'Naturally a big question mark lies behind both assumptions. But we too are not idle. Although Hitler has ordered Stalingrad to be held, we have made all preparations to be able to thrust towards the Hoth army in the next few days. We cannot give up faith in success.'

This general staff officer, Colonel Elchlepp, was a one in ten thousand honourably believing officers and soldiers. Their loyalty rested in their trust in the High Command, for which they were ready to risk their lives, and they were also firmly convinced that their trust with deeds and decisions was in accordance with their responsibility. Trust for responsibility, responsibility for trust – that certainly was the formula to which military thinking and dealing conformed. Brought up in this spirit, most of us lived and fought by this principle. What, however, if the High Command misused this trust, so that this responsibility on whatever grounds, perhaps even carelessly, was illegal?

This doubt nagged at me. This obvious belief, this unshakeable trust in the responsibility of the Wehrmacht command was strongly embedded in me. The formal trust regarding responsibility, responsibility versus trust, seemed questionable to me, simplified, somewhat naïve after the bitter disillusionments of the last weeks. Might not General von Seydlitz be right? For the moment I went on with other everyday matters.

'I have yet another question, Elchlepp. Can we look after the wounded and sick, especially the badly injured, in orderly fashion?'

'Unfortunately not. You know that all the big hospitals lie west of the Don. There are a few field hospitals on the edge of the city and in the steppe. These have long since been overflowing, although we pack every returning aircraft with badly wounded. It's not only places that are lacking, but especially dressings, narcotics, medicines, surgical equipment. The supply is minimal. Doctors and medical staff are vastly overworked and are falling out in growing numbers. Army doctors and quartermasters can tell you all about that.'

The conversation with the Ia had made me wiser, but not more comfortable. I made my way to my office in the commander-in-chief's dugout. Only a few courier post items were there. While I was giving Senior Sergeant-Major Küpper instructions to deal with, the door opened and Paulus entered. 'Much work, Adam?'

'Nothing worth mentioning, General. Some recommendations for the Knights' Cross and the German Cross in Gold have been approved. I will pass them straight on to the corps.'

'A Knight's Cross for a lost battle! Comical, don't you think?' Paulus smiled and then went on: 'You were at the LIst Corps headquarters this morning. Is there anything new there?'

'No, General, or actually, yes. There was something new for me. The corps adjutant told me that some of the divisions on the northern and eastern fronts of the cauldron are backing General Seydlitz. I did not know that.'

Paulus nodded his head lightly and spoke in a somewhat lower voice. 'Yes, that is how Hitler's radio message went. You can read it later at my office. I myself do not know what it means. It could be that Hitler is testing whether Seydlitz really has the courage to go against a Führer Order. It could also be that Seydlitz stands high in Hitler's estimation.'

'I don't understand it, General. On one side Hitler says he is leaving things to the commander-in-chief of the 6th Army. A day later he places most of the divisions under General Seydlitz. But that is a contradiction, especially as Seydlitz has requested freedom of action despite the Führer Order. What does he really mean now at this point?'

'I asked him about it in the presence of General Strecker. He answered me with: 'Under the circumstances, I must naturally obey.' Come with me, I will show you Hitler's radio message.'

In his office Paulus took a sheet of paper from his briefcase and handed it to me. I read the following sentences signed below by Hitler: 'Breakout out of the question, supply by air assured. New army is being assembled under General Hoth for opening up the cauldron. All divisions on the Volga and northern front come under the command of General Seydlitz.' A supplement noted that General Paulus retained responsibility for the general command of the surrounded troops.

Later, when I was alone again, I had time to think about the Paulus–Seydlitz relationship. Two opposing characters: Paulus, the knowledgeable, careful general staff officer, the thinker but also the hesitant one; Seydlitz, much less well trained and knowledgeable than Paulus, but nevertheless a decisive daredevil. Seydlitz, in also having his own opinion regarding Paulus's frank presentation, was defiant in contrast to the other generals.

Hitler's order with the personal distinction of giving him higher powers of command had also turned him silent. General von Seydlitz too obeyed, despite his divergence of opinion. How often, as the army adjutant, had I been able to observe how higher positions, promotions and higher decorations at least influenced the behaviour of several officers! How they were linked through thinking and dealing in selected ways. Even Seydlitz had given up.

The army eats its horses
The days after the 12th December were especially exciting. Army headquarters prepared the breakout. Operation Hoth had the codeword 'Winter Storm'. With 'Thunderclap' the 6th Army would break out of the ring and march towards Hoth. It was planned that we would take out all the wounded on trucks. If only the food supplies were better! Of food supplies, fuel and ammunition up to the 12th December per day on average not once was 100 tons flown in. In response to the incessant call for help from the army there was a slight increase thereafter, but even then the minimum request of 300 tons was not attained by far. Hunger increased and bored even deeper into the bowels of the surrounded. The number of those debilitated through hunger already exceeded the number of wounded. In every bunker, in every trench, at every main dressing station lay wasted soldiers and officers no longer able to stand on their feet.

In this emergency situation the army took back the horses of the Rumanian cavalry division that were already half dead from lack of fodder. The army quartermaster, Captain Toepke, gave four thousand horses up for slaughter. Their flesh and bones enabled the rations to be improved at least temporarily. Not much was gained, however, as on the 15th December the bread ration had to be reduced to 100 grams. Two slices of bread per day, a thin soup of horse flesh and some cups of herb tea or malt tea was what the soldier had to fight and live on, and withstand frost, snow and storm!

Understandably the quarter million encircled men fervently awaited Hoth's approaching army. With the arrival of the 4th Panzer Army a wave of relief, returning self-confidence and a new will to resist swept through the cauldron. Holding on seemed to make sense once more. A few days more and the deadly surrounding ring could be prised open. The high morale lasted two or three days, but then, as day after day stretched into futile waiting, shattering disappointment and bitter resignation took over.

General Paulus drove every morning to the divisions standing at the critical point of the battle. Early in the morning of the 16th December the thermometer was below minus 30 degrees as he set out for the hard-threatened western front of the cauldron. When he returned towards midday he looked as if he had experienced something serious.

'You were at the 44th Infantry Division today, General. According to yesterday's evening report they have had large losses. Have the Russians attacked again?'

'You know that there is constant simmering in this sector. But the casualties from combat are not the worst. The divisional commander and divisional doctor report ever more cases of severe freezing in recent days. Without adequate winter clothing the soldiers in their holes in the snow are unprotected from the ice-cold steppe winds. By day they cannot leave their trenches and holes to perform their necessary functions at all. When they try to, most of them have to pay with their lives. There are none that can rest in their narrow holes, inevitably they freeze.'

'How can the wounded and sick be removed from the front lines?'

'That is just about an insoluble problem. The enemy fire at any movement. Only with the arrival of darkness can the wounded be carried off and the frozen treated. That means too often that the medical assistance comes too late.'

'Yesterday an orderly officer from the 44th Division was here. He said that at night on both sides the fighting comes to an almost complete stop. We only leave weak security in the positions. Is there at least time for the possibility of providing accommodation for the resting troops, General?'

'The few settlements on the steppe were strongly shot up by us in the summer, and now by the enemy. There are some bunkers among the ruins, mostly constructed by our rear services in the autumn. They are partly occupied by staffs. They are naturally far too few. During the night everyone gathers around the fires and stoves. The firewood has to be brought with difficulty from Stalingrad.'

'What will happen then when the fighting strength of the divisions sinks further at this pace? How will the front continue to hold out?'

'It is imperative that we soon have a connection with the outside world. But tell me, Adam, what suggestions can you make to me?'

New hope of a breakout
Paulus went off to see Schmidt. I went to my office, taking the divisional and army unit figures with me. The tank and artillery units that had lost their tanks or guns were already disbanded, those of their officers and men who were still fit for fighting being deployed as infantry. One could still comb the rear services and the higher staffs, whose work was diminishing. Also officers and soldiers were being released from our divisions in the city to reinforce the endangered sectors of the front. I proposed speaking to Schmidt about it at the next opportunity. While I was still going through this, an orderly entered and asked me to attend a conference in the chief of staff's room. General Paulus and Elchlepp were already present. Right behind me came the Ic and the deputy quartermaster. Major-General

Schmidt was standing in front of the situation map. At a wave from the commander-in-chief he reported: 'I have just now spoken with the chief of staff of Army Group "Don", General Schulz, by the Decimetre apparatus. He told me that early today the Red Army went into the attack against the left flank of Army Group "Don" and the right wing of Army Group "B". Apparently the enemy has the intention of breaking through towards Rostov. The situation at the moment is unclear. The LVIIIth Panzer Corps of Hoth's army is engaged in bitter fighting with strong enemy forces and is advancing only slowly. Its foremost elements are struggling near Verchne-Kumski, Vertianski and Krugliakov, which means about 50 kilometres from the southern front of our cauldron. Army Group "Don" has been tasked by the Army High Command to assist the 6th Army in breaking out of its encirclement. We must reckon that in this exceptionally critical situation the Army High Command has at last shown some consideration. I ask the Ia and the quartermaster to report on the state of our preparations.'

The voice of our chief of staff trembled somewhat excitedly, but by the end of his presentation it was sure and firm again. The Ia said: 'Our forty or fifty still-serviceable tanks are gathered near the ordered breakthrough point. The fuel supplies are sufficient for at least 30 kilometres. The commanding general of the panzer corps has been given the task of breaking through the enemy defence lines and establishing contact with the LVIIIth Panzer Corps. The breakthrough point is to be secured on either side so that the 6th Army can slip through. The withdrawal of our divisions is ready on all fronts.'

Then the deputy senior quartermaster, Lieutenant-Colonel von Kunowski, reported: 'Captain Toepke is in Karpovka as ordered. He has assembled there trucks with a load capacity of 700 tons, with which he will follow our attacking tanks. His task is to take over the supplies from the Hoth army and to drive as quickly as possible to our advancing divisions. The VIIIth Air Corps has orders to drop fuel and ammunition to the tanks thrusting south. Guns and field kitchens will be towed by the trucks. The necessary number is ready.'

Schmidt now remarked that all superfluous apparatus should be prepared for destruction.

Paulus was looking at the map during this report. Now he turned round to us. 'Hopefully the order will come very soon, or there will be the danger of us not being able to carry it out any more. Every day gnaws at the strength of our soldiers, reduces our food supplies, ammunition, fuel and medical supplies. Today there is still sufficient fuel for a 30-kilometre attack, but in four or five days our reserves will have shrunk to the extent that we will no longer be capable of carrying out an attack.'

After this most serious, although not so surprising, appraisal of the situation, we were dismissed.

Naturally the measures taken by the troops in the Karpovka area could not remain concealed. The simple soldier in these respects was especially alert. Just as the slowness of the advance of the Hoth army brought a certain depression, so the news of an impending breakout spread with the speed of the wind, bringing new optimism. The simple soldiers just wanted to forget the stresses and victims of the past weeks if they got out of this mousetrap. Breaking out of the cauldron meant regular and sufficient supplies, release from the fighting front, rest and long-overdue leave, seeing wives and children, parents and relations. What illusions these over-excited, fought-out, emaciated soldiers had!

Our clerks and orderlies beamed in expectation of the forthcoming change of luck. They no longer sat apathetically and indifferent at their desks. When towards evening on the 16th December I went to see my clerks in their dugout, I found Senior Sergeant-Major Küpper smiling. 'It will soon be over, Colonel. How we will celebrate when we get out of this damned hole again! Those at home don't know anything about how it is with us. Only yesterday I had a letter from my wife in which she asked for at least the tenth time when I was coming on leave.'

'You lucky chap! I, dear Küpper, have heard nothing from my family since the 19th November. But one can only hope. – Prepare for me all the paper rubbish that you have collected for destruction! We will not encumber ourselves with it in our breakout.'

'Already done, Colonel. Just now there was a clerk from the LIst Corps here. According to what he said, General von Seydlitz is setting a good example. He has literally burnt everything – uniforms, underwear, boots, camera, books – and retained only those things that he can carry on himself.'

I had to laugh. That was Seydlitz, temperamental and basic, and no friend of half-measures.

Manstein gives way
In these days our staff returned to the old life. The apparatus ran full pelt. Orderly officers, telephone conversations, radio communications, orders, reports! Schmidt especially was on form. Almost daily Paulus spoke over the Decimetre apparatus with Field Marshal von Manstein. I listened in to most of these conversations and took notes. They didn't agree with each other. Paulus wanted to know: What is the situation at the Soviet breakthrough point west of the Don? When can we expect the relief army to get near? Is there a comprehensive stable front at the Chir? Has the enemy offensive been checked? Will General Hollidt counterattack soon? But Manstein gave only inadequate, vague answers. Paulus was angered by what he saw as the lack of orientation of the commander-in-chief of Army Group 'Don'. 'How can I make decisions here when I don't know what it looks like outside, what Manstein and the Army High Command are doing and

intending? I only hear the eternal 'Hold on!', which we have been doing for four weeks already and going to the dogs. Certainly it seems that Hoth is making hardly any progress. Parts of his LVIIIth Panzer Corps have gone over to the defensive.'

'Perhaps we can relieve Hoth when we break out and thrust towards him, General. The Russians would then have to fight on two sides and divide their forces.'

'That is quite right, Adam, but until now Manstein has not allowed it. The codeword "Thunderclap" has to be given. Until now he has not thought about it. Hitler and the Army High Command still want us to hold the city. And Manstein is shy of giving such an order, even though he knows our predicament. At the time, right after the closing of the cauldron, the order to hold on was based, among other things, on the contention that an early abandonment of the city would result in the destruction of Army Group "A" in the Caucasus, which at any time could have become impassable because of the autumn rains and mud, as it certainly is today also in the foothills of the Caucasus where the ground is frozen hard. Nevertheless the ban on a breakout for us still continues. What can I do when I don't know the full situation and am not being properly informed by Manstein?'

These last words rang like a desperate cry for help. Paulus seemed to be about to fall apart under the overwhelming burden of responsibility. Hopefully he would keep it together, I thought, as I left the room.

Late in the evening on the 17th December Army Group 'Don' informed us that it had made contact with Hoth's army and had crossed the Axei near Generalovski. 'Hopefully Hoth will now gain some ground, General,' I said when I went to tell him.

'It would be wishing a lot in our interest. Had this division gone into the attack five days earlier, success in my opinion would have been assured. Meanwhile the Red Army High Command has had sufficient time to reinforce its defensive forces. Let us wait and see what happens tomorrow and the day after.'

How this waiting tore at the nerves! How it paralysed! Even the agile Major-General Schmidt showed signs of it. When I suggested pulling out soldiers and officers from the staffs and rear services as infantry, he agreed but wanted to wait until the decision on our breakout had succeeded.

Was the enemy also hesitating? It was hardly detectable. He was active, if only in the form of a '*Sewing Machine*' which circled over our headquarters and dropped bombs. One of them apparently struck quite close to our headquarters dugout. The ground shook and windows shattered.

How long would the enemy hold back his clenched fist? When and how would our waiting end?

Army group sends a major
On the morning of the 18th December the airport commandant rang from
Pitomnik. 'The Ic of Army Group "Don", Major Eismann, has just landed.
He is asking for a vehicle to pick him up.'

Immediately a car from the stand-by pool was sent off. One hour later
the major reported to General Paulus, and then to Major-General Schmidt.
Thereafter followed a detailed discussion in Schmidt's office involving both
generals and the representative of the army group.

I got to know Eismann during our lunch together. My first impression
was that he was still a very young officer, though clever and adroit. What
task had brought him here? No word was spoken about it during the meal.
I only heard that he had orders to fly back to the headquarters of Army
Group 'Don' at Novotcherkask that same day. A flying visit, I thought. After
the meal Eismann wanted to talk with Elchlepp and Kunowski. As usual, I
escorted Paulus to his bunker. The commander-in-chief took me into his
office. 'Go ahead and ask what the short visit by the young general staff
officer was about, Adam. Manstein had tasked him with briefing us on the
overall situation. The Hoth army has come up against a very strong,
overwhelming enemy. It is making hardly any progress. In the opinion of
Army Group "Don" it is questionable whether Hoth can break through the
encircling ring with the forces available to him. Manstein also considers an
increase in air supply as out of the question. Therefore the 6th Army should
prepare itself for a counterattack.'

'I think, General, that we have made all the preparations necessary for
it. When should we start? The most serious thing seems to me to be our fuel
situation. Our few tanks can only go just 30 kilometres with the supplies
available. Hoth's spearheads are, however, more than 50 kilometres away
from us. Has the army group at least arranged for fuel and ammunition to
be flown in? Does Manstein know the fighting condition of our soldiers?
Does he know that most are half-starving?'

'You say yourself that our soldiers have been weakened and most of our
divisions stand about 40 kilometres from the proposed breakthrough points.
Think of the fate of the 94th Infantry Division that Seydlitz withdrew from
the northern front on the 23rd November! Exactly so will the enemy drive
into our emaciated, decimated troops and defeat them. No, under the present
circumstances, giving the order to break out would be irresponsible. I must
be certain that the outside encirclement will be broken or that Hoth is so
close that we can meet up in one day. If anyone can make the preparations
for the breakout possible, it is Manstein. Until now he has kept avoiding
this decisive question. I have explained my position openly to Eismann and
asked him to brief Manstein just as openly. The situation in the cauldron
has basically changed in the last weeks. Our army is now very limited in its
fighting capacity.'

'I don't understand, given our catastrophic situation, why Manstein only sent a major instead of flying into the cauldron himself or at least sending his chief of staff. Our superiors, General, need to avoid a further worsening of the situation.'

'You are absolutely right. Army group headquarters must know what has to be done. Manstein knows the situation within and outside the cauldron. He knows what forces are still coming. Apparently the commander-in-chief of Army Group "Don" is not ready to go against Hitler of his own accord. I have spoken much about the cauldron in my personal talks with Manstein. Now he must lay his cards on the table. Schmidt too cannot understand Manstein handling the 6th Army on the brink this way, sending us his youngest staff officer. Now we have to wait yet again. Kunowski gave Eismann a written report on the overwhelming lack of food supplies and medical equipment. It must be clear to Manstein that the remains of the 6th Army will go miserably to the ground, if not now, then at the last minute. All the forces from outside are concentrated on its relief. For ten thousand even this massive assistance operation is coming too late. Despite everything, I have little hope that Manstein will issue the order to give up Stalingrad. You will see, Adam, that whatever happens here I will be the one made responsible for it. Who will take into consideration that my hands were tied to their orders by superior headquarters! Who will notice that I was hampered by lack of information about the situation outside the cauldron?'

What could I say to our almost baffled general, who day and night pondered how he could lead the army out of this hopeless situation. I could find no words. It was obvious to me that no one would take the main responsibility for the suffering of the 6th Army except those who had sent him with his soldiers into this abyss and then betrayed him. But who were these people? Hitler? Keitel, Jodl and the Army High Command? What blame attached to Weichs or Manstein? Were there more guilty ones? I could find no clear answer at that time.

On the evening of the 18th December the departmental heads met in Paulus's bunker as usual. Schmidt's short report about Operation Hoth stated only what Eismann had said that morning. The 17th and the 6th Panzer Divisions were practically stuck fast.

A Knight's Cross with a horrible background
Finally we shared our meagre supper. The atmosphere was depressed. Then an orderly entered and asked Paulus to go to the telephone for Field Marshal von Manstein. We listened attentively. Was this the saving order arriving? Elchlepp said: 'That worked really quickly this time.'

Nobody took his eyes off the door. Minutes passed, but Paulus did not come. Slowly the old scepticism returned. If the conversation was really about the breakout, Paulus would certainly have called Schmidt. Then,

finally, the commander-in-chief came back into the room, followed by my
Ia clerk, Senior Sergeant-Major Küpper. That was certainly unusual. It could
have nothing to do with the order for the breakout. While I was still
reflecting, Paulus came up to my chair. 'I have for you all, gentlemen, a
happy announcement to make. Today our 1st Adjutant, Colonel Adam, for
his participation in the construction and defence of the Chir Front, his
personal engagement in this, and his bravery, has been awarded the Knight's
Cross.' With these words Paulus handed me the high decoration that Küpper
had brought.

I was so astonished that I remained dumb at his congratulations. All
rushed towards me and shook my hand. For a brief moment misery and
death were forgotten. A great pleasure overwhelmed me, sincere pride in
this decoration, especially since the commander-in-chief emphasised that
it was the first time in the German history of war that an army adjutant had
been decorated with the highest award. But this happy feeling vanished
before it could really spread. Into the celebration cup fell the bitter
remembrance of the heavy casualties on the Lower Chir, of the many
comrades who had then and since lost their lives. At the end of November
the commander-in-chief of the army group had ordered us to keep the line
of retreat open for the 6th Army. It was for this reason that the soldiers who
had fled to Nishne-Chirskaya were deployed. Helping their sorely pressed
comrades in the cauldron was also my duty then. That was why we had
prepared for the fiercest action. But the fact that the lives of the bloody
victims had been thrown away did not change my Knight's Cross that had
come after it.

More than the sad revue of the previous four weeks, the horrible present
prevented this order from going to my head. We staff officers were still
sitting together when Schmidt brought some fresh news on the evening of
the 18th December. The Soviet Army was pursuing the attack begun on the
16th December with growing success. The whole of the Italian 8th Army's
front had been breached. Its units were in wild flight, their positions
abandoned as they set off for the west.

'Thus,' the chief of staff concluded his briefing, 'on the left flank of the
Upper Chir fighting German units and emergency units are being torn wide
apart. The breach is already 45 kilometres wide. Apparently army group has
had to withdraw the whole of the left wing.'

What would happen to Hoth's offensive now? Would his panzer army
be strong enough to launch an attack and quickly make contact with us?

We stood together with Paulus and Schmidt in front of the situation map.
It was incomprehensible. We knew little about which of our own troops
were at the breakthrough points, what their fighting strength was, exactly
how their positions ran. We knew absolutely nothing about the strength of
the enemy and his main direction of thrust. The commander-in-chief listened

Colonel-General
Paulus.

Paulus in his office.

Stuka dive-bombers over Stalingrad.

(*Above and following pages*) Scenes staged and photographed after the Stalingrad battle which give an impression of the conditions and the character of the fighting.

Paulus after the
surrender.

Paulus in captivity.

Paulus at the headquarters of the Soviet 64th Army for a meeting with General Shulimov.

German prisoners being rounded up after the battle.

Marshal Georgi Zhukov at the German surrender at Karlshorst, Berlin.

for a few minutes to our conjectures and then said: 'Everything depends on what reserves the Army High Command can and will deploy. We cannot judge this from inside the cauldron. May the optimists be right!'

Burning questions
Worries upon worries! I went out into the clear frosty night with the Ia and we walked together between our bunkers several times. 'It is all incomprehensible to me, Elchlepp. If I am not wrong, was the German XXIXth Corps not deployed with the Italian 8th Army? It seems as if the German units have disengaged too.'

'Supposedly. Apparently they have been scattered by the fleeing Italians.'

'When I consider, Elchlepp, how we have rushed from victory to victory since 1940. Now defeat follows defeat. There must be a reason for it.'

'I see the main reason being our immovable, stubborn command. We react too seldom and then only reluctantly to the enemy's measures, underestimating him in unanswerable ways.'

'The more I think about it, the more oppressed I am with the thought that we too in the headquarters of the 6th Army have handled things inflexibly and narrow-mindedly in decisive moments. That is naturally easy to say today, looking back. Neither Paulus nor Schmidt, nor the commanding generals, with the exception of Seydlitz, nor you or I in the days before the 20th November were prepared to go against the orders of Hitler and the Army High Command to break through to the southwest and unclasp ourselves from the threatening enclosure. There was still enough time then. We would have saved thousands of lives that have since been lost in a battle that on our side lacked ammunition, fuel and rations, which must be described less as a battle than as an agony. Will not all of us who occupy leading appointments in the 6th Army be allocated a portion of the blame at some time?'

'You know my standpoint in this situation, Adam. We are soldiers and we have to obey. That also applies even if we cannot understand the correctness of an order and perhaps ourselves have to bite the dust. Every soldier has to take this into account, but professional officers like you and me especially so. Not every day is evening now. The leaf can still turn in our favour.'

'We have known each other long enough,' I said, 'to know that neither of us is a coward. If it falls to our lot, we must reckon on having to go to the front any minute. I agree with you completely that it goes with our profession. But firstly, it does not apply just to the two of us, but to about 270,000 soldiers. Secondly I would like to repeat that what is being played out with our units is hardly fighting, but must better be described as perishing. You know that as well as I do. Who bears the responsibility for this silent dying? Only Hitler and the Army High Command? Only Manstein and his staff? Are we completely free of blame? Were we as military leaders completely correct in our responsibility towards the troops? Have we not passed the point in time, without action, at which our officers' honour should have offered to handle matters in the interest of our soldiers ourselves? Please understand me correctly, Elchlepp, I am far from rising up to act as a judge of the army leadership, or making myself a martyr. I myself am not clear about these questions. But I also cannot simply brush them aside. They are there and they bore ever more painfully within me as our situation deteriorates. Your optimism is honourable, old chap. I too am considered an optimist among our comrades. However, today's report about the destruction of the Italian 8th Army has now destroyed my confidence.'

'Let the musing be, Adam, it does not help. We are unable to review the whole situation for the moment. Certainly the southern front is under threat, but the Army High Command will soon get a grip of the situation. A few more days and we can shake hands with the Hoth army. The mess will be at an end. We will be operating on an open battlefield! Today our divisions on the southern front have reported that the thunder of Hoth's guns can already be heard.'

We were now standing in front of my new dugout. Sparks were coming out of the small chimney. Apparently my officer assistant was clever at heating. When I had set off that afternoon, the ice on the walls was shining. 'Have you visited my "villa", Elchlepp?'

'I have had not the opportunity as yet.'

'Come in for half an hour. I still have a bottle of cognac as iron rations in my box. A good slug is helpful against brooding and freezing.'

The colonel followed me down the five steps to the entrance to my bunker. I opened the door. In front of the stove my lieutenant was squatting and stoking the fire. In contrast to conditions outside, the room was pleasantly warm. The walls seemed to have defrosted.

While Elchlepp was exchanging a few words with my lieutenant, I extracted the bottle of Martel brandy from my box and uncorked it. I found a glass for Elchlepp, and Wehrmacht-issue aluminium beakers for the other two. The chairs were brought closer to the stove.

'Here's to a good result to the battle!' Elchlepp raised his glass. We drank with him. With a little jerk we tipped the brandy down our throats. What a treat!

'And if it does not go well, Elchlepp, what then? And if the breach through the Italians can't be sealed? Must not the relief army be pulled back as quickly as possible if it is not to be surrounded? Would our defeat then not finally be sealed?'

'You just can't leave the gloom alone today. What is it? Defeat means death or imprisonment – or to be exact, only death. Imprisonment is the same as death.'

'According to the newspapers and the broadcasts to the soldiers, you could be right. But I was so convinced, quite honestly, about the shot in the back of the neck that the Reds give to everyone, that living in captivity was never advisable. I myself saw several examples with our Ic. He told me that the person signing had actually belonged to the unit concerned and was named as missing.'

'That could be, Adam. I will never go into captivity.'

'According to your opinion, the whole army must be in a hopeless position if it no longer has the least prospect of a breakthrough, only the option to let oneself be shot down by the enemy. How does your thesis differ from the appeal for mass suicide? I too personally fear captivity. But can we take the responsibility for hundreds of thousands being victims of perhaps unfounded anxiety? That is senseless! In my opinion the battle must go on as long as there is any possibility of relief. Otherwise the question arises of the last vestiges of hope having vanished.'

'My dear Adam, you can be assured that I would never agree to a breaking-off of the fighting, when that would be tantamount to captivity. And imprisonment is death.'

'How will you avoid captivity, Elchlepp?'

'I would ask Paulus to permit me to go to the front as a combatant. There I would sell my life as dearly as possible.'

'That is nonsense, Elchlepp, nothing but suicide. You have your wife and your children! It is not dishonourable for a commander to end a battle that has demanded the useless expenditure of the lives of tens of thousands of men. I think that you should go over all of this once more.'

The Ia stood up. 'There is nothing for me to revise. But I hope that all will come out well.' With these words he said goodbye to me and my speechless lieutenant sitting there.

The distress of the wounded
Until now I had had little opportunity to visit the troops on the immediate front line. Today, on the 19th December, I wanted to visit the ones I had missed and see for myself how it really was out there. 'Watch out that you don't end up with the enemy!' said Paulus as I reported to him on my departure.

'I have entered the whole of the front on my map from the latest reports, General. My aim is to visit the 44th and the 76th Infantry Divisions.'

We started off at about 0900 hours. I did not know the driver. He had been commandeered from a division by our staff. On the way via Gontshara to Rossoshka I witnessed the shattering scenes that were played out every day at the dressing stations, sick bays and in the field hospitals. I got out in front of a hospital. In September I had visited a main dressing station near Gumrak, where the impression had dug deep into my consciousness. But what I saw in this hospital this day was even more shocking, absolutely dreadful, ghastly. Half-debilitated orderlies were taking the badly injured out of the many waiting vehicles around and taking them on stretchers to medical tents. There they lay on some bloody, dirty blankets until there was room for them on the operating table. The room was in a house about 15 metres long on whose entrance hung a Red Cross flag. In order to get in I had to push my way through a number of lightly wounded, all wanting treatment. One of them begged me: 'Help us, Colonel! We have been here three days without any attention. Most of us have frozen hands and feet. Forward of here all the collecting points and dressing stations are full. The doctors sent us on here.'

Out of a dirty, stubbled, staring face blinked a pair of tired, feverish eyes. The hands of the soldier were bound with strips of a woollen blanket. I told him that I had come to speak to the doctors. Then I turned back into the building.

Through an open door I was able to look into a room full of wounded. These were tended cases waiting for transport: a shivering collection of white bandages and dirty uniforms, laid closely together in rows on the ground, more or less covered in greatcoats or scraps of cloth. In the adjacent room was the operating theatre. As I appeared in the doorway, a man rushed towards me from those standing around the operating table. It was a doctor. Hollow-eyed, pale, tormented, he stood in a blood-soaked smock and smeared apron. 'For three weeks now we three doctors and twenty medical orderlies have been working day and night. Once, when a bomb ripped off half the roof, about thirty wounded and nine of our people were killed. Another time the Russian artillery had similar success with two hits. Now we cannot move any more because all our vehicles are out of action. We are completely full. Of course we help all the newcomers. We give them a plate of hot soup or a cup of tea, change their dressings and send the vehicles on to the city. Emergency hospitals have been set up there in the remaining buildings and cellars of the ruins, where these poor chaps at least have a protective roof over their heads.'

'What do you do with the severely wounded, doctor?'

'We send them on by divisional ambulances to Pitomnik airfield. The army surgeon arranges their flights out of the cauldron, Colonel. With our capacity here there is nothing much we can do about healing. It is a misery. If you drive on you will unfortunately see much worse than here.'

And so it was. On the road were stopped vehicles fully loaded with the wounded. But their wounds did not bother them any more: they were, literally, frozen. The vehicles' fuel tanks were empty. Until the driver, usually the only one capable of driving, returned with his fuel canister after hours of seeking and begging, such misfortune was inevitable, the fierce cold extinguishing the little life left in the weakened bodies. Nobody was looking after this dead freight. Usually they were mercifully covered in a white blanket of snow.

The light wounded and sick gathered everywhere where there were buildings, tents or dugouts. In small groups they trailed tiredly along by foot to the city. A few had the rare luck to get a ride on one of the vehicles that were still moving. During the heavy fighting of the summer and autumn the city had been avoided by everyone who was not ordered to go into it; now it was like a magnet that drew everyone. There they hoped to find shelter in a cellar, assistance from a medical unit and perhaps even a plate of soup.

Napoleon's beaten army must have looked similar when it withdrew to the west wrapped in blankets and bits of tent, with sacks and bandages on their frozen feet instead of boots. They were hardly soldiers any more. They were a broken, disarmed mob. If they were to be saved, immediate medical help, food and warm accommodation had to be ready for them. Every day's delay meant that it was too late for many.

The adjutant of the 76th Infantry Division complemented my own impressions with a detailed report on the personnel situation. 'The casualties, especially sick and completely exhausted people, have been catastrophic for several days! The gaps among the infantry are ever larger. Those reporting sick are mainly too late, so that there is nothing that can be done for them.'

'How can that be explained? Until now we have taken immediate countermeasures. Many soldiers report themselves sick for the slightest reasons – just sick enough to get out of the combat zone for a few days,' I interjected.

'That's right, Colonel, but it is different here. Not a few shy off from reporting sick because they fear being left behind in a fighting retreat. I think that most of the infantrymen not in the front line are sick.'

'What is the mood among the troops?'

'That is hard to say, Colonel. They were depressed when the cauldron was closed. When it became known that Hoth had started a relieving attack, it raised their courage and hope. We believed that the encirclement would be quickly broken. Since then eight days have passed and there is understandably deep disappointment. There are individual voices harshly criticising the High Command, Hitler, the Nazi Party and the whole war. Even some officers do not understand the sense of this sacrificial holding on and the long wasting away of our army.'

'But until now the 76th Infantry Division has shown steadfastness in every situation,' I interrupted the divisional adjutant. 'The symptoms you have described contrast with the behaviour of the troops in battle.'

'That is so, Colonel. When the enemy attacks, those who were cursing the Führer only a few minutes before pick up their weapons. They fight sometimes because they have a panicking fear about captivity, at other times because they are waiting for Hoth to open up the cauldron. How far has Colonel-General Hoth got towards the enclosing ring?'

'From what I heard before coming to see you, the relieving army is engaged in strong attacks by the enemy. They are only slowly gaining ground. But we hope that they will be advancing again in a few days.'

On my journey on to the 44th Infantry Division I witnessed the same terrible scenes. I soon had the vehicle full of wounded. Mouths and eyes peered out of the blood-soaked bandages. The second one had his shot-through arm in a sling. I had taken in the third because he was staggering all over the road so that one feared at any moment he would fall and never get up again. Full of fever, he sat between the other two wounded on the back seat of my jeep.

'Where shall I drop you off, comrade?' I asked the one with the injured arm.

'When it is possible for you,' – he saw my badges of rank – 'Colonel, at a hospital where we can be taken in.'

'We will try in Gumrak. There is a proper hospital there. We will see if we can take another two comrades.'

My driver threw a disapproving look at me when I took in two more soldiers with head injuries who were looking for help on the side of the road. They sat on the rear of the backseat. As it was already quite late, I abandoned the intended visit to the 44th Infantry Division once I had got enough of an impression. I told the driver to turn eastwards. After a long journey, going past army headquarters, we eventually reached Gumrak. Although this hospital was already overfull, I was able to hand over my five passengers.

No orders for a breakout, but fortress battalions
I reached headquarters later than intended and reported my return to Paulus. There was still no order to break out. 'Headquarters Army Group "Don",' said the commander-in-chief, 'is keeping quiet.' The only reply I have received to my questions ran: 'Wait, implement Operation "Thunderclap" only on explicit orders!'

'How long is this going to go on, General? The adjutant of the 76th Infantry Division reported to me today that the gaps in the infantry will soon be so big that the front will no longer be able to be manned throughout.'

'The LIst Corps has received orders to extract companies from the city front and give them to the divisions of the western and southern fronts. Have a look at the allocation plan at Elchlepp's. Apart from that we have decided to remove soldiers, NCOs and officers from staffs, rear services, panzer regiments and artillery battalions. We are calling them fortress battalions. The various regiments have released their third battalions, there are enough battle-experienced commanders there. Give me proposals for the personnel appointments!'

'Has someone been made responsible for the setting-up of these fortress battalions, General?'

'Not yet, Adam. Who do you suggest?'

'I am thinking of the commander of the 14th Panzer Division, Colonel Lattmann. He has a capable staff. His division exists only as small combat teams that are individually deployed.'

'Good, agreed. Lattmann has the makings for this role. Schmidt too values him and will say nothing against this proposal.'

In fact Schmidt immediately approved when I took the matter to him. 'Yes, indeed, Lattmann is the right man for these emergency units.'

'Will he too be delighted, General? From what I know of the mood of the troops, there is no great desire among either the officers or the soldiers to play a role in such a thrown-together fire brigade.'

'If it goes as it is, we won't need Lattmann. He will soon come to order,' said the chief of staff laconically.

I was not happy about the business. 'Fortress Battalions!' Really a nonsense when one thought how many of these soldiers had no experience of infantry combat. Most of them had been vegetating until now near the stoves in some bunker or other. Now they were being chased out into the icy cold and raging storms. Would they really be of any assistance in the hard fighting on the front?

Medals and propaganda instead of bread
Back in my bunker I went through the courier post. It consisted of the usual: promotions from the ranks for bravery before the enemy, awards of Knight's Crosses and German Crosses in Gold. The Army Personnel Office gave notice of a consignment of decorations, Iron Crosses Ist and 2nd Class as well as appropriate clasps, Knight's Crosses and German Crosses. In addition, almost unbelievably, there were two cases of Croatian medals, when we had only one Croatian artillery regiment in the cauldron, under the 100th Jäger Division. This regiment was at the same time already being taken care of with the same medal in generous quantities, so that it had no further requirements.

Already the next day the medals arrived by courier aircraft. It needed four soldiers to move the vast container into a workroom. The boxes took up so much space that I could hardly turn around in the room. Senior Sergeant-Major Küpper opened them with a hatchet. They were filled to the brim with Croatian war medals. 'It would be best, Colonel, if we send the boxes as they are to the 100th Jäger Division,' said Küpper.

'That makes no sense. They don't rightly know what they should do with them. I will talk to General Paulus about it.'

At supper I talked about the awards that had been bestowed on the army. My description brought general laughter, but also anger that valuable cargo space had not been used for foodstuffs.

'I can give you further hair-raising examples,' said the senior quartermaster. 'With the last machines came a dozen cases of prophylactics, 3 tons of sweets, 4 tons of marjoram and pepper, and 200,000 knapsacks of Wehrmacht propaganda. I therefore wish the bureaucrats responsible only had eight days of experience in the cauldron. Then they would no longer do such imbecilic things. I wonder too that Colonel Baader has not prevented this when we have sent out so many requests for this purpose. I immediately protested energetically to Army Group "Don" and begged that in future the persons responsible at the despatching airfields are better instructed and supervised.'

'That is good, Kunowski,' intervened Paulus. 'I will also ask Manstein to ensure that such misdemeanours cease in future. Baader seems to me no longer to have any influence on our supplies. We should transfer suitable officers to take command at the despatching airfields who have their own experience of our situation. I ask you, Schmidt and Kunowski, to check over the problem and make me proposals.'

Codeword 'Thunderclap' does not come
The following days passed without the awaited codeword 'Thunderclap' from Manstein. Paulus and Schmidt spoke daily on the Decimetre apparatus with the army group. As on previous days, I listened to and recorded in shorthand most of the conversations that Paulus had. As before, Manstein put aside all questions about the situation outside the cauldron. On the 22nd December connection with the outside world was lost when the Decimetre apparatus fell silent. Our troops on the Lower Chir must have been wiped out.

So went our days: days of useless discussions and inactive perseverance. The 6th Army headquarters waited for the redeeming orders from above. Meanwhile fell, froze and hungered ever more thousands of soldiers, their vitality becoming ever weaker with this delay. Paulus and his staff saw that the main reason for the growing catastrophe lay in the stubbornness and lack of care shown by Hitler and the superior headquarters. Doubtless they bore a considerable part of the blame. But did this not prove that our army headquarters, by dutifully holding out, was nothing but a well functioning cog in the whole people-killing machine? Was it not thus also guilty?

We were a product of Prussian military training, accustomed to obeying orders and ourselves then passing on a given order even if it made no sense, was murderous, barbaric towards our own troops. Above all, we were not educated in critical political thinking. We thus thought at that time that the catastrophe of Stalingrad was essentially a result of decisive military errors by the High Command. That the Second Word War started by Hitler's Germany was a crime not only against the peoples attacked by us, but also against the German nation, did not occur to us. And because of this, we did not recognise the deeper reasons for the defeat on the Volga, which lay not in individual strategic or tactical errors, but in the superiority of the socialist state and social system, whose sharp sword was the Soviet Army. We wondered about the strength and bravery of the Soviet soldiers in front of and within Stalingrad, and were astonished at the precision with which the Soviet operations were conducted, but we did not understand what drove them.

Christmas in the cauldron

It was a gloomy Christmas festival. Towards 1800 hours on the 24th December came the news by radio that Hoth had been obliged to retreat. We were as if stunned when a little later we gathered for supper with General Paulus. In his short speech the commander-in-chief touched on Hoth's shattered relief attack and the collapse of the whole southern front. He spoke of the now severely threatened Army Group 'A' in the Caucasus, and the seriousness of our own situation. Despite everything, we should not give up hope. After a few words on the meaning of Christmas, he concluded: 'And so we too have gathered together under burning candles to think of our families back home, as they think of us at this time.'

The crass contrast between the brutal reality of the war and the Christmas message could not be glossed over by words. Everyone realised this on this evening. There was some very quiet thinking, almost the quiet of the grave. Some lit candles on the table had been decorated with balls and tinsel, and next to each plate lay a couple of cigarettes and two or three chocolates, which General Paulus had brought in a large confectionery box that had been sent to him from Rumania.

There was no post at all from home. No parcels, no letters were distributed. Heavy snowstorms had almost immobilised air traffic. My wife and daughter had sent me a lovingly packed Christmas present some fourteen days, if not almost three weeks, earlier, by post. It never reached me. I had not written about our hopeless situation to my relatives, realising how much my wife was suffering over the death of our son Heinz. But nevertheless they surely knew that a disaster was looming over the area between the Volga and the Don.

Despite this, several items that were flown in reached us very soon after supper that evening. Everyone wanted to be alone with their thoughts or to sit together with their closest colleagues. I too was expected by my staff in the room which served as our office. The brightly burning fire in the stove gave a little cosiness. I had prepared a small present for each of them: some cigarettes or a cigar, a few slices of crispbread and biscuits wrapped in newspaper. The army group adjutant, Colonel von Werder, had sent me two bottles of brandy, which I now placed on the table. Best of all was a small Christmas tree that one of the NCOs had made from a package from his wife that had reached him three days earlier. To all this Senior Sergeant-Major Küpper had contributed some candles on a carefully shielded stand.

They all looked expectantly at me. What should I say to these four comrades with whom I had worked for over a year, and who had been soldiers long enough not to let me make a fool of myself. All were married, all had families. I told them truthfully about the events outside the cauldron. Then we talked about our homes. The four of them had received mail during the last eight days. Letters and photographs made their rounds. We forgot everything outside in this conversation. We chatted together happily for hours.

The candles burnt themselves out, the bottles were empty. Towards midnight I entered my adjacent room and office. My driver added some sticks of wood to the crackling stove. I pulled off my boots and jacket, extinguished the light and lay down on my camp bed. Thoughts went round in my head for a long time until I finally fell asleep without having come to any conclusions.

Activity should distract you
When I entered the office the next morning, the first day of Christmas, my colleagues were seated at the table drinking a dark brew that called itself coffee and chewing the crispbread and biscuits I had given them the previous evening. They wished me a happy Christmas, and Senior Sergeant-Major Küpper was the first to shake my hand. With his pale, sunken cheeks, he seemed even thinner and taller than usual. During the night the hope of seeing his wife again had almost expired. And with the other three, things looked no better. I attempted to boost them up, but not at first. To do this I had to lie. We had to have more work so that there was less time to think. I turned to Küpper, 'When you have finished your breakfast, come to me.'

Seeking distraction with work seemed to me to be the best, perhaps only, way. There was not much more for an adjutant to do, yet something of an occupation could be created. 'Küppel, put together the figures of how many soldiers and officers of the 6th Army were away at the time of the stopping of leave on the 19th November, thus were unable to return to their units at the end of their leave. Further, how many should have returned daily.'

'That will soon be done, Colonel. From our army's daily orders we can ascertain how many men went off on leave daily. We only have to ask IVth Corps for their figures.'

'Give yourself time and make it exact!', I repeated as the telephone rang. Schmidt wanted to see me.

When I came to him, he said: 'You know the situation, Adam. We must reckon on strong attacks in the west and south of the cauldron in the next few days. Our weakened fighting strengths will force us to reduce the cauldron. At the moment there is no establishment to deal with our retreating troops. In order to establish it as quickly as possible I must have our chief engineer, Colonel Selle, here. Radio army group with the request to fly in Colonel Selle!'

'It will be done as quickly as possible, General. Selle is leading a battle group at Chir.'

'Deal with the matter urgently. There are enough officers out there to replace Selle.'

Why should Selle have to be commanded to take part in our almost certain downfall? The new position could be taken over by any engineer battalion commander. And how would they dig into the stone-hard frozen earth. That is what went through my head. On the other hand, I would be happy to see my friend again.

I knew Schmidt well enough to know that it was completely useless trying to advise him against his decision. So I went to the signals officer and sent the radio message. Finally I sought out General Paulus. I had not seen him yet that day. Lieutenant-Colonel Zimmermann directed me to his dugout. Paulus was there preparing a message to Army Group 'Don'.

As I entered he was sitting at a desk. My Christmas wishes he returned most heartily and offered me a chair. The question regarding the chance of a breakout was still open, and lay burning in the air.

'I am no Reichenau'
'Hold on, the 6th Army is fulfilling its historical mission on the Volga,' Paulus quoted the first sentence of an order from Hitler. 'My hands are tied in every way.'

'I understand you, General, but what sense does this holding out have now? We will not get out of here any more. Can we reply that the whole army is going under?'

'You know the orders. The formation of a new defensive position in the southern sector depends upon our holding on. I am responsible if Army Group "A" suffers the same fate as us.'

'Six weeks have passed, General, since the order was given. In my interpretation it has long since been overtaken.'

'That is not quite correct. Manstein informs me that Army Group "A" is holding on to its positions in the Caucasus as before.'

'I don't understand that. The Army High Command had six weeks to withdraw the troops from there to shorten the front. That would have freed up panzer divisions to support Hoth's attack.'

'There is no sense in going over these questions, it is too late now. Even if we want to, we cannot now get away from here with our broken, emaciated army. The German main front line is hundreds of kilometres away from us, and it apparently has to withdraw even further. No one will help us out. I spoke to all the commanding generals, divisional commanders and Schmidt at the end of November and recommended we break out on our own, but Hitler was immediately informed by his liaison officer, Major von Zitzewitz, who has his own radio, and introduced his countermeasures.'

Paulus stared for several seconds at the plank wall of his dugout. Then he turned his gaze on me. He saw from my expression that his comments had not removed my doubts. 'You are not happy with our discussion. I know what you are thinking. You are comparing my handling of the situation with that of Reichenau last year when he initiated the attack on Donetz against Hitler's orders.'

When I nodded, he went on: 'It is conceivable with that daredevil Reichenau, that after the 19th November, if the 6th Army had fought through to the west, Hitler would have declared: "Now you can go over my head!" But you know, Adam, I am no Reichenau.'

Paulus had really guessed my thoughts. He spoke the truth as if he himself, as a loyal general, characterised the careful assessor, the over-thoughtful waverer. But even with this self-criticism he did not cut through the vicious circle in which he, I and many others were entangled every bitter day. Whether Reichenau or Paulus, both men's intentions were aimed at the continuation of the war.

A correctly timed, successful breakthrough by the 6th Army would perhaps have postponed the final defeat of Hitler's Germany, but it could not have prevented it. Such a result would not have changed the imperialistic, anti-national character of the war of conquest. Would the 6th Army really be 'saved' if tens of thousands of those who survived on the Volga were slaughtered in the subsequent fighting?

But on the 21st December we were still far from such insights. We simply functioned correctly – and badly – as cogs in the heavily laden German war machine.

When I returned to my dugout, Küpper had laid out the required material. At the beginning of the counteroffensive by the Red Army some 25,000 men were on leave. Every day about 1,000 men had returned to the front.

'What happened to these leave people, Colonel? If they were here, we could close some of the gaps.'

'Presupposing that they are meanwhile not also starving or frozen. Apparently General Pfeffer was to collect them together and make them available to the army. But that came to nothing. On the orders of army group headquarters, all those returning were put into the battle groups.'

'Oddly enough, every day some of those returning from leave are flown back to the cauldron on the supply aircraft. I telephoned several of the divisions today in order to get the precise figures for the information you required. One clerk told me that whenever the aircraft carrying these men arrive, an announcement is made over the loudspeakers instructing every officer and soldier to report to the railway station commandant. Nevertheless, some make their own way and ask for the airport, where the pilots take them on as machine-gunners. If these unsuspecting fellows had known what was happening here, they would certainly have remained outside.'

'I can thoroughly understand that, Küpper. But that is the comradeship that forms in pleasure and sorrow. It brings back many to their units.'

Colonel Elchlepp visited me on Christmas Day. 'Is there anything new?' I asked him, after we had shaken hands.

'Has Schmidt told you about the long-distance telephone conversation he had yesterday with General Schulz of the army group?'

'No; was there anything special?'

'There is nothing new from the Chir front. Schulz said, however, that the 6th Panzer Division has been withdrawn from the Hoth army to protect Morosovsk. The pilots of the supply aircraft report that the left wing of Army Group "Don" has been withdrawn to the west. Until now it has not been possible to check the enemy offensive. It seems to me that the army group wants to keep us in the dark over the whole situation, as before.'

'In any case it confirms that there is no longer any escape for us. The 6th Panzer Division forms Hoth's main striking force. If it is unable to overcome the enemy, then things will not go well. It is clear that Hoth and the two remaining weak panzer divisions will have to withdraw.'

'Doubtless Manstein realised the new catastrophe as early as the 16th, or at the latest the 18th December. It is incomprehensible that he should not have informed Paulus and given the codeword "Thunderclap". The order for the breakout would have doubled the strength of our soldiers. Every following day that uselessly passed, army group told me, we should have initiated "Thunderclap". Fuel and supplies would have been flown in, but only when the weather was suitable.'

'That is clearly a mockery, Elchlepp. What do Manstein and his staff then really think about the state of the 6th Army! That has nothing more to do with military necessities.'

'I share your opinion. Paulus is writing a new report on the pitiful state of our divisions.'

The commander-in-chief writes a new report
The following day this report went to the commander-in-chief of Army Group 'Don'. It ran something like the following lines:

Bloody losses, the cold and insufficient supplies have allowed the fighting strength of the divisions to sink drastically of late. I therefore have to report:

1. The army can repel weak enemy attacks as before and still deal with local crises for some time providing there are better supplies and replacements flown in.
2. If the Russians send stronger forces against Hoth, and with these or other troops proceed to attack the fortress, it will be unable to resist much longer
3. Breakout is no longer possible if a corridor has not been achieved and the army stocked with men and supplies.
I therefore request that higher commands are made aware that energetic measures for the fastest relief of the army are taken, otherwise the whole situation will force them to become victims. That the army will do everything to hold on to the last moment is self-evident.

'The army continues to function. Today only 70 tons were flown in. Bread tomorrow, fat tomorrow evening, no supper for one corps. Drastic measures now urgent.' The commander-in-chief of the 6th Army wrote a new message. Looking back, one must say that at this point in time, on the 25th December, as Manstein's strong 6th Panzer Division was withdrawn from Hoth's replacement army, hardly any more breakout orders could be given from our own resources. The 6th Army was now too depleted, lacking fuel, heavy weapons, tanks and ammunition, to attack the iron ring and the bitterly fighting Russians without substantial help from thrusts from outside, and establish a connection with the forces of Army Group 'Don'. I believed that Paulus was unable to make any reproach if he himself was unable to make any decision of his own at this point in time. But how often had he – and all of us –not done so? All of us had dutifully reported, ordered and kept silent, while there was still time through our own efforts to present the facts to the supreme command and save the lives of tens of thousands of soldiers who were later to be starved, frozen and killed! This question and the resulting responsibility for the defeat of the 6th Army rested with all who had the highest command functions for clothing the surrounded units. The motives and considerations that had been played out in the decisive command posts of the 6th Army could be explained, but not excused. We were prisoners of the Order and Obey system but was not that, when the order apparently went against the traditional Prussian–German military concept, itself immoral according to its moral code. Even more denied to us was the vote for the real alternative to the sacrifice of the 6th Army ordered by German imperialism: the alternative that lay in a timely capitulation. We completely lacked the political insight for doing this.

On Paulus's orders all preparations for the breakout from the cauldron were cancelled in the following days. The assembled trucks were sent back to their units. Captain Toepke resumed his place with the senior quartermaster, but was soon afterwards ordered to the airfields of the supply aircraft leaving the cauldron.

The High Command and the van Hooven report

At the end of December Colonel Selle came to the cauldron. We shook hands with mixed feelings and I escorted him to the commander-in-chief's dugout. After he had given his report, we asked him to tell us how things looked from outside. 'Worse than we had feared, General. Before taking off I was able to take a look at the situation map through my friend Colonel Busse on the staff of the army group. Tazinskaya was lost on the 24th December with the big supply depot. The airfield was taken by the Red tanks in a surprise attack. Almost all the aircraft were captured by the Russians. That will have serious effects on the air supply for the cauldron. Morosovsk is also threatened. The battle is raging west of the Rumanian 3rd Army. Millerovo was already occupied by the enemy, but is back in our hands. Battle groups, here and there whole battalions, were quickly brought forward to stop the enemy. The 6th Panzer Division was taken from Hoth on Manstein's orders. This and the threatened encirclement forced Hoth to retreat. Army Group "A" is still in the Caucasus. On the other hand, the headquarters of Army Group "Don" has moved from Novotcherkask to Taganrog.'

'In other words, Selle, we must finally bury our hopes of relief. Only one thing remains for us: to fight on and hamper as many of the enemy forces as possible, at least to tie up some of the enemy's forces, and enable Manstein to establish a new front.'

Schmidt too had Selle report to him. Much less impressed than Paulus, he acknowledged Selle's account somewhat cheekily: 'The flag will not be lowered, old chap.'

The army commander-in-chief and his chief of staff took course for the defeat of the 6th Army. How much longer could our worn-out, lost mob hold out against the enemy's strong forces? What justified encouraging more than 200,000 soldiers to engage in such a questionable aim?

Army Group 'Don' telegraphed that our future signals chief would be Colonel van Hooven. His predecessor, Colonel Arnold, after being wounded seven times, was no longer fit for front-line duty. On the 28th December 1942 I stood for the first time in my life opposite my new comrade. He was tall and thin, had a clever, small face, and showed himself extremely well orientated both inside and outside the cauldron.

'Tell me, Hooven, how is it that you are so extremely well informed?' I asked him.

'I was commander of the Supreme Command's signals regiment. Naturally I had a complete view of events on all fronts in this position. On the 24th December General Fellgiebel personally briefed me at Führer Headquarters on my new task. On the 26th December I landed at Army Group "Don" in Novotcherkask. There I learnt everything that I did not know until then.'

In the following conversations with Generals Paulus and Schmidt, Hooven confirmed what Selle had already told us. Hooven drew the situation more realistically, using his knowledge of the reports and orders that had passed through his hands at Führer Headquarters. It appeared that the Army High Command still believed in the success of Hoth's action on the 24th December. Then General Fellgiebel had asked Hooven to pass his greetings on to Paulus and let him say that he was hoping to greet him personally soon. Hooven too had believed in the imminent relief of the 6th Army. His stop at Army Group 'Don' quickly dispelled this illusion. Speaking to Paulus, he gave his opinion that an immediate breakout was the only chance of saving at least part of the 6th Army, as there were no more forces available for its rescue.

As I appeared for the conference that afternoon, Paulus confirmed to me once more his standpoint expressed to Army Group 'Don' on the 26th September. 'Hooven's proposal to break out of the encirclement is not achievable. I do accept that he is well in the picture on many things, but the latest intentions of the Army High Command and Army Group "Don" are not open to him either.'

Schmidt was emphatically angry with Hooven and accused him of making a pessimistic assessment of the situation, saying that the will to hold on was paralysed. In fact there was much discussion among the staff about the description by the army's chief of communications. Two groups began to form at about this time. While some of the officers believed that there was no longer any chance of saving the surrounded army, the others did not give up their belief in being liberated.

General Hube flies to Hitler

'If the Führer knew', said some people, 'how it really looks like here, he would certainly take extensive measures. But it seems he does not get sight of our reports.'

Above all, the younger officers led by Elchlepp argued this way. Under his influence, Paulus and Schmidt were persuaded to send an officer to personally report to Hitler. Then I received a radio message from the Army

Personnel Office with the following content: 'General of Panzer Troops Hube is to be sent to Führer Headquarters to receive the award of the Swords to the Knight's Cross with Oakleaves.'

'That is our opportunity,' said Paulus, when he read the message. 'Hube must give an unvarnished report on our situation. Hitler will listen to this highly decorated general. Schmidt, put together immediately all necessary papers on supplies, ammunition, fuel, tanks, guns, especially about the fighting strengths and combat readiness of the troops, losses from gunfire, freezing and sickness, and also about the wounded and the difficulties of medical care!'

The reporting system continued to function relatively well within the war machinery of the 6th Army. As Hube entered the headquarters, precise information lay on the table. Paulus and Schmidt added verbal instructions and asked the general about his personal opinion of being thrown into the scales in order to present a realistic assessment of our situation to Hitler.

Hube flew off the same day by courier machine. 'I am anxious about whether Hube will be able to speak or whether Hitler will interrupt him immediately after the first sentence in order to keep all the unpleasant news from himself,' said Paulus.

These days many officers called in on me and sat around without a function because their units had been smashed. Some sought a new role, most asked for permission to fly out. Every day one of them could board the courier machine to Army Group 'Don'. I had the task of recommending those to be sent out on medical grounds. This concerned, without exception, the older gentlemen who were deemed no longer fit for combat by the doctor. Major-General Schmidt checked every case and decided by name. Only those who had witnessed the pitiless dying in the cauldron could have any idea what feelings of relief these officers experienced when they had the order to fly out in their hands. 'Torn away from death,' said many of them as they reported to me upon leaving. But so many of them had not yet finished with the war in the years to follow until 1945.

One day the battlefield artist from Leipzig, who had appeared during the summer, came to see me. Under his arm was a packet of drawings, sketches for battle scenes. His face bore traces of the distress and suffering of the encirclement. I took the sketches to Schmidt and suggested we let the artist fly out. For us he posed only an unnecessary burden, and was not required as a combatant. Schmidt declined to make an exception. General Paulus, to whom I eventually went for a positive decision, shied away from correcting his chief of staff. So the painter became a senseless sacrifice to the beast of war, which his talent had recorded. He left my dugout completely broken.

Painful recognition

Küpper stood below the entrance. 'Post from the High Command, Colonel.'

'Put it on the table.'

The Senior Sergeant-Major pointed to the letter on top. It was a long, detailed report from the VIIIth Corps about increasing appearances of disintegration among the troops. 'Since the failure of the relief offensive became known, the will to resist has fallen drastically,' I read. The writer quoted reports of breaches of discipline, leaving of posts, going off to Stalingrad, refusal to obey orders, even self-mutilation. Even officers were beginning to act listlessly.

'We must now reckon with such tendencies. The commanders must get a sharp grip and re-establish order' was how the usually strict Schmidt reacted to these signs of decline. Heitz came after with the promotion of Schmidt. I heard of his order to the VIIIth Corps from our Ia. I still remember that every paragraph began with the words: 'Was shot . . .' and then followed the offence: who left the position without an order having been given, who failed to carry out a given order, who made contact with the enemy, and so on.

Paulus was more understanding. 'One should not forget what these soldiers have gone through in the last weeks. If they can only eat themselves full and sleep again, they will see everything with different eyes.'

'Of course, General, this also plays a role,' I interjected. 'But it seems to me that there is much more to it. In talking with young officers and soldiers I keep coming up against deep doubts about the reasons for which they are having to fight. At school, at home, the Hitler Youth, the Nazi Party and in the Wehrmacht was implanted a feeling of the greatness of fighting for an honourable aim. They believed in the Führer, trusted him, put their lives at stake. Now they are discovering that the promises are broken, their trust in the lies was valueless. That is especially painful and leads in many instances to positive breaches of discipline.'

'As far as it goes with the younger men, it applies here and there. But there are also signs of resolve among the older ones.'

'The report still indicates something else. Every night apparently, Germans call through loudspeakers from the enemy trenches for our soldiers to give up the senseless fight. The 6th Army has been betrayed by Hitler. They are to be sacrificed to his prestige.'

'The speakers are German Communists who emigrated to Russia. From pamphlets thrown over, we recognise the names of Ulbricht, a former member of parliament for the German Communist Party, and of the writers Weinert and Bredel, also Communists. I regard this propaganda as being of no great effect. We must watch out, of course, that no radical effects arise. In the meantime it is enough if we keep on being aware that this is enemy propaganda trying to break our resistance. Incidentally, we must keep alive the hope of being released from the cauldron.'

Keeping the hope alive of being released, in which the commander-in-chief himself did not believe! Was that not the same as Hitler and the Army High Command were doing? Lies versus trust? Could an army commander take this course? Had this, in view of the dying and suffering, not something to do with soldiery and obedience? These questions did not only come from me, they also came from Paulus himself. But they led to no consequences. The will to hold on took the upper hand.

In this lay the combined guilt of General Paulus and all the military commanders in the Stalingrad cauldron – an historical, military and human guilt.

Promotions and awards

The Wehrmacht High Command animated Paulus in a way through its decision to hold out. At the end of December came a radio message from the Army Personnel Office. It terminated the commander-in-chief of the army's special authority, which until then only the Army Personnel Office had held, for the promotion of officers up to lieutenant-general, and awards of the German Cross in Gold and the Knight's Cross.

Hitler wanted to relieve the dying. The favoured awarding of the highest German awards and promotion from the ranks should convey the desired physic to the 6th Army. There was another aspect to this that seemed important to me at the time. Promotion to the next highest rank meant the raising of the widows' and orphans' pensions. The divisions were informed of the rising chances of promotion.

In the following period the work in my section returned once more to full speed.

On the 31st December Captain Toepke flew to Army Group 'Don', whose headquarters had meanwhile moved from Novotcherkask to Taganrog, about 200 kilometres further west. On the previous day Paulus had personally tasked Toepke in Schmidt's presence with the task of being the army's supply commissioner. 'You will report to Field Marshal von Manstein personally and tell him that you have received the task from me for purposeful loading and complete use of the cargo space of the supply aircraft. You know what is happening here. Take all the papers on food supplies, ammunition, fuel and medical supplies with you and put them in front of the field marshal!'

Schmidt added: 'Take care that at last all available aircraft are placed at our disposal. The army group must stop sending dozens of *Heinkel 111*s to the abandoned Tazinskaya airfield. Our soldiers are threatened with death by starvation. Report back to us when we can expect a better supply service!'

Manstein appointed the captain senior quartermaster for the air supply of the 6th Army and Toepke energetically applied himself to helping the surrounded army. However, no noticeable improvement appeared. The loading space was far too little. Soviet anti-aircraft gunfire and the winter weather decimated the amount of goods being flown in. The distance from the source airfields and the cauldron was considerably increased following the loss of Morosovsk and Tazinskaya. The airfields at Schachty, Novotcherkask, Voroshilovgrad and Salks lay 350 to 400 kilometres away by air.

In a radio conversation at New Year Hitler repeated that every member of the 6th Army could enter the New Year with confidence, that the Führer would not leave the heroic fighters on the Volga in the lurch and that Germany would see to the needs of their commitment. At the same time General of Panzer Troops Paulus was promoted to colonel-general.

'Loyalty to loyalty' – there was then such an expression of Hitler's which, despite all the agony, was not totally without effect, even if it was also questionably worded like a similar report six weeks earlier. The repeated exchanges, the inhuman privation, the hollow-cheeked dying had brought something to us. But we no longer saw the things as a whole. It was very difficult to see things as a whole. So the disaster continued.

Rumours and a handful of soldiers

1st January 1943. The first morning of the New Year. When I awoke the fire was already flickering in the stove. I thrust my legs into my boots, slipped on my uniform jacket and went into the office. In contrast to the year before in Poltava, my colleagues sat there, downcast, indifferent, dulled. They shook hands silently. I too did not try to liven them up, being myself inwardly torn. The section leaders subsequently met together in Schmidt's office to wish Paulus a happy New Year and to congratulate him on his promotion to colonel-general. I knew that he had been expecting this promotion. Now that it had arrived, he only gave a slight smile.

We had already left the dugout when I realised that I had forgotten to add the third star to his epaulettes. I went back to see to this. To my apology he said: 'Leave it, Adam. Hitler only wants to relieve my end with this promotion.'

The normally withdrawn general started to recount his visits to the divisions. 'You can be pleased that you don't have to drive over the battlefield every day. When you returned from a visit to the 76th Infantry Division one day, I clearly noticed how you had been struck by the experience. Meanwhile everything has become much worse. Hunger is leaving ever crueller traces. At various dressing stations the doctors assure me that the hunger and cold are causing many more deaths than enemy action. Hospitals and main dressing stations are completely full of thousands of wounded for whose attention the necessary things are lacking. In many the will to live has gone. Hopelessness continues to spread. For all of this one only has fine words left.'

'I thought, General, that following Hube's talk with Hitler, much would have changed. As far as I know Hube, he would not have held anything back.'

'Let us hope that he behaved that way! I only fear that it is now too late. I am bound in any case as before by Hitler's order to hold on here.'

'Have you already heard, Colonel-General, of the crazy rumours going all round the cauldron? On our western front the soldiers of an SS division are rumoured to have reached Kalatch. Even the thunder of the guns has been heard. Others are already talking again of a parachute division having landed between Kalatch and Karpova.'

'I know about these rumours and I only want to know who is spreading such nonsense. One regimental commander said Pitomnik airfield is the source of this nonsense. Perhaps he is right. I think it possible that the pilots of the transport aircraft either unknowingly, or perhaps directed from outside, are being set to conceal the fight to the death.'

'Are you thinking of doing something against such rumour-mongering, General? Should we not finally tell our soldiers the truth?'

'Of course we have to. I am awaiting the return of Hube to do so.'

In the first days of January I received a call from the airfield commander. 'Two large transport aircraft have arrived with soldiers. Where shall we send them to?'

I was baffled. What use was a handful of soldiers to us against this deadly threat? Was this the reaction of Army Group 'Don' to the army commander-in-chief's message of the 26th December? We didn't need forty or a hundred soldiers, but fully established divisions. Above all, we needed food, ammunition, tanks and fuel. 'Please wait 15 or 20 minutes. We will check which divisions need reinforcement most.'

I thought it over. The disbandment of the 79th Infantry Division had been ordered the previous day. The still available soldiers and officers had been divided up almost exclusively among the divisions fighting in the city and the divisional staff had been flown out.

The 44th Infantry Division had suffered the most casualties in the last few days. Once Major-General Schmidt had agreed, I told the divisional adjutant and told him to collect the newcomers.

Paulus took this action by the army group as a hollow gesture. He told Army Group 'Don' not to fly in any more soldiers and officers, just more supplies. Finally he had made the bread ration for everyone even smaller. Manstein then forbade the further flying-in of troops.

As he was about to dismiss me, the Colonel-General handed me a letter that he had received from Manstein. The army group commander had expressed his sympathy and understanding in relation to the repeated requests from Paulus to permit the breakout of the 6th Army. However, the superior knew better how to judge the situation, therefore Paulus had to bear the consequences of the orders given. With this, the responsibility for whatever was to happen was lifted from him.

That was interesting. 'Are you not aware, General, that Manstein, from whom we expected so much, is completely bound by Hitler's dictatorship?'

'I have that impression too, Adam.'

Actually this recognition must have arisen earlier. Manstein, outside the cauldron occupied by the 6th Army, must have known much sooner the enormous danger that threatened, and yet in recognising it much more clearly nevertheless adhered to the lack of responsibility that went with Hitler's increasingly betrayed principle of Order – Obedience. His military, moral and historical guilt for the shocking downfall of the 6th Army would clearly be greater than that of Paulus and several other high-ranking officers of this army. But they too were led by the same soulless clichés and contributed to the 6th Army's death sentence.

Again and again we took refuge in the hope that those whom we ourselves had already often had to convince would recognise that they were being unrealistic. So we kept asking ourselves: Where is Hube? We still did not know when something else would disturb the punishing waiting.

Hube's message and the Soviet offer
On the 7th January 1943 the Red Army High Command informed the commander-in-chief of the 6th Army by radio of the appearance of three envoys. The army declared itself ready to receive them. The next day the northern front reported that envoys were approached the fighting line. At the same time Soviet loudspeakers announced the contents of the capitulation text. Pamphlets fell from red-starred aircraft and fluttered from the sky. A little later an officer of the LIst Corps brought the surrender conditions and handed them over to Colonel-General Paulus.

At about the same time it was announced that General Hube had landed at Pitomnik. Tensely we awaited his arrival at army headquarters. Decorated with the Oak Leaves and Swords to the Knight's Cross, Hube drove directly to Paulus. In the presence of Schmidt, he reported on his meeting with Hitler. When I was shortly afterwards summoned to the commander-in-chief, Hube was already on his way to his command post.

'I will tell you the news that General Hube brought, so that you have an idea of the Army High Command's intentions. The Führer is planning a new relief attack with much stronger forces than were available to Hoth. For this tanks are to be concentrated behind a new southern front. Some of them will roll up next. Naturally the assembling of these forces will take some time. The beginning of the attack can be reckoned as the middle of February. Hitler has agreed to renew the organisation of air supply and to improve it considerably. So far one can welcome the High Command's plan. Now comes the great "but": these measures can only be realised when it is possible to form a new southern front and to bring back Army Group "A" from the Causcasus without severe losses. Therefore the 6th Army must continue to tie down as many of the enemy's forces as possible. For us this means holding on. Hitler is merely agreeing to a reduction of the cauldron if it is absolutely necessary.'

'May I now ask a question, General? How do these widespread breaches look from the outside? Where does the fighting front run in the southern sector? What forces will close the outstanding gaps resulting from the defeat of the allied armies?'

'I asked Hube the same question. However, he was unable to give any satisfactory reply. At Führer Headquarters, as at Army Group "Don", one is limited to some general hints. For certain we only know that Army Group "A" is moving towards Rostov, at last one must say. For me this is the bitterest thing that we have to suffer all these agonies any longer. The promise of improved supplies is more than vague. But as you say yourself, Adam, what can I do other than accept the order to fight on?'

'Fighting on requires first of all that the army is saved from starvation, in addition to sufficient ammunition, fuel and medical requirements being flown in. Captain Toepke flew off already eight days ago. I am convinced that he has tried everything to improve our supplies, but hardly anything seems to have changed. We simply lack the basics. Finally the enemy is also on hand. The pilots report that the anti-aircraft defences of the enemy have increased considerably within the last weeks. The shot-down figures increase and the flying distances are longer. Many aircraft have to be repaired after being hit. Excuse me, General, if I say Hitler's renewed promises about the improvement of air supplies can be described not only as vague, but rather more as thoughtless. For me the trust fades away with this eternal putting-off.'

Paulus looked at me with astonishment. 'But you have gone along with it strongly in the last few days, Adam. Where is your usual optimism? Obviously the army can only hold on until Hube's relief date in the middle of February providing the men are sufficiently and continuously supplied with all the necessary items. I do not conceal that I am sceptical in other respects. But firstly I do not know all the Army High Command's air transport reserves, secondly I am not responsible for the fulfilment of the promises, and thirdly my freedom to handle things was taken from me on the orders of the Superior Headquarters. On these grounds I have also requested the decision of the Army High Command on the Red Army's offer of surrender. I presume that the answer will soon arrive.'

Capitulation rejected
Lieutenant-Colonel Zimmermann reported that the commanding generals were assembling in a room nearby. I went to my dugout. Later the army's chief engineer, Colonel Selle, told me that he had taken part in the conference that followed. All the commanding generals already knew the text of the offer of surrender. Paulus told them of Hube's report and asked

them to state their positions. They all spoke against surrender. They assured him this was also the opinion of the divisional commanders. Meanwhile the reply arrived from the Army High Command. It read: 'Capitulation out of the question. Every day that the army holds out longer helps the whole front and draws away the Russian divisions from it.' Paulus's request for freedom of action was again denied. Army Group 'Don' shared the Army High Command's position.

Major-General Schmidt drew up the consequences from Hube's report and the surrender offer to the army, which entailed a further combing of the staff, rear services and hospitals with the aim of establishing more emergency units to strengthen the front line and the further construction of positions for the west front as already marked out by Selle, the army's chief engineer. He went on to say: 'In future enemy envoys are to be driven back by fire.'

'The chief of staff is back on top,' said Selle. 'He has made me responsible for setting out the new line of defence. Where I will get the manpower I have not been told, of course. Have you actually read the offer of surrender?'

'No, I have not received a copy, only heard something about the content.'

'Just concern yourself with it and read it through. There is much in it for you.'

The colonel had hardly gone when Küpper appeared with a leaflet in his hand. There I had the text of the Soviet ultimatum. It began with a detailed analysis of the 6th Army's situation. This fully coincided with my own assessment. It warned of the worst frosts, the icy steppe winds and snowstorms to come. Apart from our hopeless situation and the futility of further resistance, the Red Army High Command suggested that, in order to avoid useless loss of blood, resistance by all the surrounded German troops should cease and that they should organise themselves for surrender. It went on:

All members of the Wehrmacht of these surrendering units will keep their uniforms, badges of rank and decorations, their personal necessities and valuables. The senior officers will retain their daggers and side arms.

The officers, NCOs and men who surrender will immediately receive normal rations. All wounded, sick and frostbite cases will be given medical attention.

We expect your reply in writing on the 9th January 1943 at 1500 hours Moscow Time through your personally appointed representative, who, in a recognisable car with a white flag, must drive along the road from the Konny bypass to Kotluban station.

Your representative will be awaited on the 9th January at 1500 hours by authorised Russian officers in Department 'B', 0.5 kilometres southeast of the bypass.

Should our request to surrender be rejected, we inform you that the troops of the Red Army and the Red Air Force will be forced to destroy the encircled German troops. The responsibility for their destruction will be borne by you.'

The letter was signed by representatives of the Headquarters of the Red Army, Colonel-General of Artillery Voronov, and the commander-in-chief of the Don Front, Lieutenant-General Rokossovski.

I was of the opinion that, with the offer of capitulation, the survivors of the surrender need not fear a bullet in the back of the neck. On the other hand, I was unable to get away from Paulus's arguments.

Looking back at this time, I must say today that the rejection of the offer to surrender was correct at the time, as the commander-in-chief of the 6th Army contested the decision of the Army High Command. On the other hand, it was pointless in light of the miserably dying divisions and the unscrupulous breach of faith by Hitler regarding the 6th Army that Paulus was denied the ability to exercise freedom of action in full agreement with the conventional military concept of loyalty to the loyal. I estimate that far more than 100,000 soldiers and officers would have been saved and able to return to their families at the end of the war.

The argument that the blooded and hungry 6th Army would draw strong enemy forces away from the German southern front was based on scant evidence. The Soviet Supreme Command doubtless also knew that the 6th Army had been forbidden to break out by the High Command, and that its fighting strength was greatly reduced. This knowledge enabled the Russians to seek an end to the Soviet troop concentration on the Volga.

The rejection of the Soviet capitulation offer of the 8th January 1943 is historically, militarily and humanely seen as the greatest cause of blame not only on the part of the German High Command and the headquarters of Army Group 'Don', but also of the commander-in-chief of the 6th Army, its corps and its divisions.

Caught up in illusions and formulas

The Soviet ultimatum was known to practically everybody. The Ia, Colonel Elchlepp, confirmed it to me: 'As among the staffs, it was made known to almost everyone in the army and the pros and cons discussed. Those awaiting the return of Hube and the new plans for liberation were far more excited. The mood pendulum, which in the last fourteen days had returned to doubt and apathy, swung back to the side of hope and courage.'

'Are the poor lads aware of what can be awaiting them with the planned meeting with the relief force in the middle of February? Do you really believe, Elchlepp, that we will get out of this? And that our troops can hold on for another six weeks?'

'Yes, Adam, I really do believe it. You can be assured that Paulus will, as before, definitely carry out the Führer's orders. Schmidt and I will reinforce him in this to the full.'

'I don't understand one thing. Why does the Colonel-General demand freedom of action then? In this present phase one can only understand the suspension of the fighting because further resistance is futile. Breakthrough to the main front about 400 kilometres away is completely impossible from our heap of rubble. There is no difference of opinion between us over this. You say that capitulation does not come into the question. What will happen then? The fighting strength of our army is now sinking rapidly and will soon come to an end.'

'Then we will go down as obedient soldiers. I repeat what I have said to you on other occasions: I will never go into Russian captivity.'

'Do you believe that all soldiers and officers think as you do? I strongly doubt it. What little desire the men have to risk their lives in a more than questionable resistance is shown by a great aversion to the emergency units. Now we want to comb through again and set up more. Consequently they are almost worthless. These men unaccustomed to fighting melt away like snow in the spring sunshine.'

'You should think more about the calls for help from the troop commanders, Adam. The front sector of the 297th Infantry Division is only manned skin deep. There are not the slightest reserves to seal off a breakthrough. Every man that we send them counts. We can't throw in the towel. It seems to me that Selle and Hooven have turned your head. Surrender is completely out of the question. That is all Communist propaganda that they put in their leaflets. I don't believe a word of it. It only remains for us to fight to the last round.'

I could not penetrate such obstinacy. A rational conversation was impossible.

On the afternoon of the 9th January Paulus made an appeal to the troops. In it, the offer of surrender was written off as enemy propaganda aimed at undermining the soldiers' morale. No member of the army could believe the pamphlets. The order of the hour was much more to resolutely repel every enemy thrust until our renewed tank unit attacks had re-established connection with us.

With hope once more revived that the cauldron would be pierced from outside, and the underlying fear of captivity, the will to hold on flared up again. Even the wounded grabbed their weapons once more. In contrast to this, there was an incident of reluctance by the troops, including the generals, to act. General Hube had just resumed command of his panzer corps when the Army High Command ordered him to fly out immediately. He was to reorganise the supply of the 6th Army outside the cauldron. This was a really a paradox. Of all people, the commanding general of the panzer corps was leaving the cauldron to take over a task better conducted by a professional. That was why the army headquarters had appointed the senior quartermaster, Colonel Baader, already weeks before. Was this a consequence of Hube's visit to Führer Headquarters? Why had he already flown out? Similar questions were asked of me repeatedly by generals and officers, making no secret of their anger. I too knew no more than they what was behind Hube's order to fly out.

General Hube climbed into an aircraft flying out on the night of the 10th January. At my suggestion, Lieutenant-General Schlömer, commander of the 3rd (Motorised) Infantry Division, took over the command of the XIVth Panzer Corps.

There were several individual well known cases, in which officers tried to sneak out of the cauldron. One such was the 1st general staff officer of the 14th Panzer Division, Lieutenant-Colonel Petzold. He asked me to obtain him permission to fly out from Schmidt: 'What should I do here now?' he said. 'The division hardly exists any more. Its remains have been incorporated into battle groups. The divisional commander, Colonel Lattmann, is forming new emergency units on the orders of the commander-in-chief. So I am completely superfluous.'

I suggested to Petzold that he take his request personally to Major-General Schmidt, as he came directly under him as a general staff officer. He did that. As was to be expected, the chief of staff promptly kicked him out. But the lieutenant-colonel had not given up. He tried again under a different guise. Promptly next day he put in his application for a transfer to the SS. But he had no luck with Schmidt. His crumpled application ended up in the wastepaper basket.

More cunning was the quartermaster of the VIIIth Corps. Knowing that he would never be permitted to fly out, he went directly to Pitomnik. He said that he had to clarify some supply problems and was thus able to climb into an aircraft ready to take off. When Paulus heard of the quartermaster's clever trick, he applied to Army Group 'Don' for a court martial for desertion. As I later learned, this quartermaster was shot.

But such cases of personal deceit among the officers were exceptional. The majority of officers took the order to fight to the last round seriously, sharing the hunger, pain, misery and death with their soldiers. But what they took as moral duty, loyalty and obedience, was, through the criminal concept of war and the irresponsible conduct of the long-involved highest State and Wehrmacht leadership, nothing but shameless deceit. Their superhuman devotion arose out of a false trust, they were prisoners of military ideology. In this lay the tragedy of many of those German soldiers and officers who fought and died at Stalingrad. And the senior military leaders of the 6th Army contributed to this tragedy.

Chapter 5

An End to the Horrors

A thundering reply

The air thundered, the ground shook. Steel rained down on 'Fortress Stalingrad', savaging people and animals, destroying dugouts and vehicles, tearing apart weapons and telephone lines. The links between army headquarters and the staffs were reduced to a few radio sets that had escaped the shells, mines and rockets. The Red Army was replying to our rejection of the offer of surrender. We are writing of the 10th January 1943.

In the Ia's dugout the wireless operator was trying to reach the VIIIth Corps. At the beginning of the bombardment a message had got through that reported devastating results from the bombardment. Then the corps fell silent – the connection was broken. While we waited feverishly until the repair teams had reconnected the line, the artillery fire eased off. Presumably the enemy's tanks and infantry were going into the attack. Then VIIIth Corps came through again. Soviet tanks had broken through our western front and part of our southern front, simply crushing their way through. Our troops were fighting doggedly, but in vain! They were unable to withstand this attack, especially as few anti-tank weapons were available; even the rifle ammunition was almost gone. There were also no collection points for them. Despite the orders of the chief of staff, Schmidt, it was not possible to dig trenches and bunkers in the concrete-hard frozen ground. Those who did not fall, or fled, were captured in the second or third waves of attacking Soviet units. The armoured attacking wedge was biting ever deeper into our front. We had no reserves that we could throw in against it.

Gradually we gained a clearer picture of the new situation. The main attack had been against the divisions of the VIIIth Corps and the XIVth Panzer Corps. Its goal was the heart of the cauldron at Pitomnik airfield. The 44th, 76th and 29th (Motorised) Infantry Divisions were badly hit. For the moment it was not possible to get an idea of which of these divisions still existed and could be employed in a renewed defence. Bad news arrived continually by radio and telephone. The 1st orderly officer had his hands full maintaining the situation map. There also seemed to be a disaster in the south-western corner of the cauldron. The 3rd (Motorised) Infantry Division had been there since the end of November 1942. Now the districts of

Dmitrievka in the west and Rokotino and Zybenko in the south had been lost. The 1st general staff officer looked at these places. I looked questioningly at him: 'Are you thinking that the 3rd (Motorised) Infantry Division is threatened with encirclement, Elchlepp?'

'Certainly. Until now the division has been able to repulse all enemy attacks. Now, however, since the loss of the Dmitrievka and Rokotino districts, it has become threatened on both flanks. We must immediately retake these southwest-pointing projections.'

He reached for the telephone receiver and had himself connected to the chief of staff, newly promoted to lieutenant-general. Schmidt was already in the picture, as was Colonel-General Paulus, who was with him. The division received orders to get itself out of the encirclement and take up a new defensive position along the line Dmitrievka–Rokotino.

Messengers and orderly officers came and went one after another at the headquarters on this disastrous day. It was hard to distinguish between any of these numbed figures of soldiers. Only eyes, mouth and nose could be seen of these material-shrouded figures, their legs and feet being mainly wound round with cut-up blankets. What remained was dressed in faded, worn-out greatcoats. Only a fortunate few possessed winter clothing, and that was mainly of Russian origin. With their frosted hands they were often unable to unfasten the clasps of their map cases and pull out the messages. Once they had slurped down two glasses of tea, they recounted in spurts their frightful experiences in the past hours, the shot-up artillery positions and exploded ammunition dumps, the panic among the supply troops and the wounded. While their legs still carried them, they were fleeing into the city on the Volga in naked fear, throwing everything away like children.

A second-lieutenant from a division on the south-western front recounted how in the last two days two or three German Communists had called across asking them to give up fighting and go over to the Russians. 'We have heard such propaganda often already. I cannot go along with them. What is new, nevertheless, is that now a German captain and two lieutenants have gone over to the Communists.'

'Do all the soldiers react like you?' I asked him.

'They listen to the words, but they don't believe them either.'

In fact, fear of capture was so great that even in the most hopeless situations, where every minute of continuing to hold on could bring death, only a few soldiers went over to the Red Army. The year-long business of anti-Soviet agitation was fully absorbed in the thoughts and behaviour of most Germans. This disabled the brain and alone drove tens of thousands to their death in the Stalingrad cauldron, when they could have been spared if only they had listened to the voices from the other side.

Back to obedience
Colonel-General Paulus reported the results of difficult breaches on the cauldron's western and southern fronts. He added that 6th Army Headquarters saw no real opportunity of preventing the enemy advance. Nevertheless, thrown-together emergency units had occupied the threatened positions. Although Paulus and Schmidt were clear that a further weakening of the divisions fighting within the city was no longer their responsibility, they ordered the LIst Corps to give up the most available battalions, companies and artillery units to the western and southern fronts. The military machinery groaned but kept going. It obeyed its own laws. Colonel-General Paulus was himself in deadly danger, suffering from the burden of his responsibility. But he, like those around him, believed that the blame for the catastrophe must lie not only with Hitler, but also with the Army High Command and Army Group 'Don'. Meanwhile we went on functioning with bleeding hearts and tormented souls. And this continuation cost many their lives.

I will never forget the talk that I had with Paulus on the evening of the 10th January 1943. It demonstrated our personal conflict but also the fact that we then agreed on all final measures for the continuation of the war. We believed that the 6th Army had to be sacrificed for this.

'My dear Adam, many soldiers and officers are now asking why did Paulus not accept the ultimatum; why, in this hopeless situation, did he not handle it against Hitler's orders? They know that I have no right to go against the orders of the High Command. But it was not only that which prevented me from complying with the capitulation. What would become of the war if our army in the Caucasus was also surrounded? That danger is real. But as long as we keep on fighting, the Red Army has to remain here. They need these forces for a big offensive against Army Group "A" in the Caucasus and along the still-unstable front from Voronesh to the Black Sea. We must hold them here to the last so that the eastern front can be stabilised. Only if that happens is there a chance of the war going well for Germany.'

'If I may be allowed to make a remark, Colonel-General, I too in your place would equally decline to decide upon capitulation. But let us suppose for once: would the Russian armies released from here really not take weeks to get to the front 300 kilometres away?'

'There you are certainly making an error. The Russians are great at improvisation, as the past has repeatedly shown. What seems impossible to us, they make possible. With our dubious situation in the southern sector any strengthening of the enemy forces can be disastrous for us. I will perhaps be responsible should this war be lost. We must fight on to prevent such a catastrophe.'

Neither Colonel-General Paulus nor I then thought that the actual misfortune in starting the war was that it had politically, economically and militarily been an anachronism from the beginning, because it went contrary to the passage of time. The First World War had already shown that the policy of conquest and robbery that had been practised by some imperialist states in the nineteenth century could not be repeated in the twentieth century. The war represented a challenge to other states who united against the German desire for conquest and punished the instigator. Even more anachronistic was the unequivocal starting of the Second World War by Hitler's Germany. It had to be shattered by the will to resist of the people, especially the socialist might of the Soviet Union.

The key questions regarding the character of the war, its historical role and its political-moralistic aim were not challenged by us; we were too far away from this to even recognise it. Brought up in a nationalistic and military spirit, we could hardly challenge it. That was the real key to our misfortune, the door to the abyss into which we were thrown ever deeper through our accepted duty to hold on.

Alarm at Pitomnik

As on the 10th January, so followed on subsequent days one frightful piece of news after another. They were all the same: renewed breaches in the makeshift enclosed defensive ring, flight from attacking tanks, abandoning of positions without orders to do so, the failure of commanders of emergency units, signs of disintegration everywhere. Especially alarming news came on the 12th January: Pitomnik, our only airfield, had been abandoned in flight from Russian tanks.

The chief of staff was enraged. How could such a thing happen? After the last report we had the impression that no immediate danger threatened there. Was this just a rumour? Schmidt wanted to know for certain, as it would have an immediate effect upon army headquarters.

The reconnaissance team returned after a short time. It appeared that our troops – airmen, drivers, medical staff and wounded – had taken to their heels from an enemy reconnaissance troop, which had subsequently withdrawn. This time I could understand Schmidt's scornful outburst.

Paulus ordered the airfield to be more strongly protected and put back in action as soon as possible. Afterwards a staff officer who had driven to Pitomnik to pick up the post reported: 'Within a few minutes it was absolute chaos.' He recounted. 'On the cry "The Russians are coming!" healthy, sick and wounded rushed out of tents and bunkers, everyone trying to reach the exits as quickly as possible. Some fell and were trampled down. Those unable to walk properly clung on to colleagues, stumbling on with sticks or rifles and hobbling in the icy cold towards Stalingrad. Many wounded and exhausted men collapsed on the way. No one looked after them. Several hours later they were frozen. Bitter fighting broke out over places on vehicles. Luftwaffe ground staff, medical orderlies and lightly wounded ran off to the few trucks standing on the edge of Pitomnik airfield, started up the engines and tried to get to the road leading to the city. In a short while men were hanging on to the wings, running-boards and even the radiators. The vehicles threatened to break apart under the loads. Many remained immobile from lack of fuel or engine damage. Those following made detours round them. Those men capable of walking hurried more or less quickly away, the others calling for help. But not for long – their calls soon ceased from the freezing that overcame them. There was only one motto: 'Save yourselves those who can!''

What safety could the destroyed city give that was now also being attacked by the enemy from the Volga? It was not only a matter of physical safety, but more especially was an escape from the fear-driven delusions of whipped, ragged, half-dead men, whose bodies and spirits had been torn apart by the destructive battle.

Although it very quickly became known that the airfield was back in our hands, it had been torn apart by a Soviet reconnaissance party, and only a few of the sick and wounded turned back. The shock was too deeply seated in their bones. On the other hand, most of the pilots and medical orderlies were back in Pitomnik by evening.

Fantastic breakout plans
Fresh plans were being made at army headquarters and especially at the LIst Corps headquarters. Could we not make the cauldron smaller and thus better concentrate our forces and form a proper reserve? 'Impossible,' said Paulus. 'That would mean the voluntary abandonment of the life-essential airfield.'

Should one give up the battle? No, no way. That would be tantamount to imprisonment and would endanger our surrounded comrades outside the cauldron. Perhaps we could break out on all sides in small groups without artillery preparation. This suggestion came from Seydlitz's staff. He foresaw the divisions lying on the Volga bank seeking to cross the frozen river to the south and breaking through behind the enemy lines. There they would have to combine with the divisions fighting between the Don and the Volga and simultaneously pressing south.

All these aims must, according to this plan, make connection with the German troops outside the cauldron. We took into account that the retreating Hoth army was still fighting south of Zimlianskaya.

Schmidt thought that such a breakout undertaking would be very costly for the 6th Army. Nevertheless he agreed to it. Strange, I thought. Until now he had stubbornly demanded that Hitler's orders be carried out implicitly. Now that it was too late, he was going to be disobedient.

But this plan too remained a fantasy. It was just about imaginable for those divisions whose soldiers had been lying in the streets for weeks and whose bodies were somewhat less fit. All others regarded it as completely illusory, as their half-starving, sick soldiers could no longer carry out an attack.

Such considerations showed how much the army leadership was groping in the dark, as in the higher commands too panic ruled. No one knew how the German troops in the southern sector were faring. The Ic believed that they had moved back 400 kilometres to the west, but we did not accept that. That would have meant they had returned to their starting point of the summer of 1942. So the whole of the fighting in the previous year had been for nothing. That could not be!

Manstein, who knew exactly, still gave Paulus no clear information.

Major-General Pickert leaves his division
Yes, Manstein. Although the 6th Army was left in the lurch at a critical time, Paulus and Schmidt once more made an attempt to persuade Manstein to make a decision in favour of those surrounded in this dubious situation. They ordered the commander of the 9th Flak Division, Major-General Pickert, to fly to Army Group 'Don' and to report to Field Marshal von Manstein exclusively over the catastrophic conditions in the cauldron. During the last few days even fewer supply aircraft than usual had landed. Hunger was advancing forwards much more rapidly than before. Pickert was finally to get a better air supply service working, not least to alleviate the 6th Army's severe losses.

Basically this step by army headquarters was exactly as delusive as the several previous attempts. It also had another, unexpected consequence: General Pickert did not return to the cauldron. Before taking off he had assured both his chief of staff and Colonel-General Paulus, in his farewell visit, that he would fly back as soon as he had completed his task. But we waited in vain. Instead a radio message arrived: 'Flew over Pitomnik last night. Attempt to land failed, had to turn back.' That same night other aircraft had landed at Pitomnik. We were furious. Nevertheless, nothing was done about Herr Pickert.

Germans on the other side
I sat in my dugout and leafed through the papers that Senior Sergeant-Major Küpper had left. There were enemy pamphlets among them. I pushed them aside. My thoughts wandered between home and front. If the family at home knew what was being played out on the steppe between the Volga and the Don, if they could only see these hollow traces of hunger, these faces blackened by dirt and frost! But the army's reports still rang full of hope. Not a word about the frightful cruelty of this destructive battle. I had not read a newspaper for weeks, and there had been no news from my wife and daughter for weeks. They would be worried about it! What would become of them when they received the dreadful news about our end?

Mechanically I reached for the pamphlets. Almost thoughtlessly, I passed them one after another from hand to hand. Then I began to read. Various parts were underlined. The names of the writers, Walter Ulbricht, Erich Weinert and Willi Bredel, meant little to me. I only knew that they were Communist emigrants. That was no recommendation for me then. But what they wrote was not meaningless. Their language was clear and impressive, their knowledge of our situation amazing. They knew of our fear of captivity, and of our trust in Hitler's promises to care for our liberation.

In all the pamphlets it was written that Hitler and the Army High Command had lied and betrayed us when they promised to rescue us from this deadly encirclement, as they had no chance of doing so. The writers speculated that the Army High Command had no clear picture of the overall war situation.

One pamphlet contained exact details of losses in war material in the last fighting. Others spoke of Hitler's betrayal of the German people, of the senseless dying, of the purposelessness of further battles. At one point it said significantly: 'We are sitting here together with German prisoners-of-war. Stop the fighting immediately! This is the only way of saving your lives.'

I leafed through the pamphlets again and again. Contemplation on an empty stomach, I must say, in many instances often led to the same consequence. The last promises of Hitler, the Army High Command and Manstein – had they not been empty words? None, or almost none, of them had amounted to anything. What had been set out in high-sounding phrases had simply not been realised.

But could we believe these Germans speaking to us from the enemy side? Were they not Communists who had betrayed our country? Certainly, seen from a military point of view, they were right, as my experience told me, as my understanding told me too. But as a soldier, as an officer, I rejected this propaganda, as it damaged the fighting morale of the troops.

Then another pamphlet drew my attention. Paulus had said that the purpose of continuing to hold on gave Army Group 'A' in the Caucasus the opportunity of escaping from its own looming encirclement. However, here it said that Army Group 'A' was already operating in the Rostov area. Had Paulus been deceived? Was Manstein deliberately not giving him a clear picture?

I saw no way out of the labyrinth into which this reading of the pamphlets had led me. Finally I read the names of three officers who had been captured back in 1941: Captain Dr Hadermann, Lieutenant Charisius and Lieutenant Reyher. I was brought up short: Dr Hadermann, so an officer of the reserve. As I recalled, he came from the Hesse town of Schlüchtern. There I had got to know a scholar at a gymnasium called Hadermann. He was studying late philology. But what this name already meant! The three officers would talk to our troops through loudspeakers at night. That confirmed what the second-lieutenant had told me on the 10th January after coming to see me, frozen through from the southern front.

Damn it! What could one really believe? Had Küpper made a fool of me with this thing? I summoned him. 'Why did you put this pamphlet on my desk?' I asked him as he came in.

'I thought that it might interest you, Colonel,' he said.

'Have you also read what is in it, Küpper? What do you make of it? You can peacefully give you opinion,' I said, as he started to reply.

'Certainly, Colonel, we have read the pamphlet. The order to hand in immediately all leaflets found, according to the messenger, was only followed superficially. Although hardly anyone would have the courage to run over to the Red Army, the opinion gradually gathered that the Russians did not shoot prisoners of war. A messenger from the IVth Corps told me yesterday that during the night a soldier of the 371st Infantry Division, who was well known, spoke from the Russian trenches through a loudspeaker.'

'Has this pamphlet been discussed among the soldiers of the staff, Küpper?'

'Already much has been discussed about this lately. Some reject it, others again think about it and even defend it here and there. In any case hardly any believe any more about being shot in the back of the neck in captivity.'

Küpper left my office. I had almost no more work, but plenty of time to think things over. Equally thoughtful, though perhaps 'angry' was more accurate, was Paulus, who called for me after a while. Lieutenant Zimmermann had given me the wink. The Colonel-General really needed to speak to me. I knocked and entered.

He was sitting at his desk, his arms propped up and scratching his head with his right hand. I knew this movement well already; it came mainly with especially strong sucking-in of his cheeks. What has been happening here? I thought. In front of him lay a sheet of paper. Without saying a word, he handed it to me.

I looked at it. It was another pamphlet, but one directed at Paulus and signed by Walter Ulbricht, a member of the German Reichstag. I read it carefully, sentence by sentence. In clear, logical reasoning Ulbricht said that Paulus, by following the orders of Hitler and the Army High Command, was not acting in the interests of Germany and the German people. His duty was to give up the senseless fight. I looked at the army commander questioningly and gave him the pamphlet back.

Slowly Paulus began to speak: 'Of course the publisher of this is right from his point of view. He sees the whole business as a politician. For my military obedience, for the considerations that led to my decision, he can have no understanding as a civilian.'

'Before you called me, Colonel-General, I had a number of pamphlets from Ulbricht, Weinert and Bredel in my hands. Their language is not what we are accustomed to. Everything in me resists them, but on many points they tell the truth.'

'We could say so, Adam, but they see everything through different eyes from us. I do not deny these men good will in any way. But for me this is undermining the men's discipline, and that I cannot allow. Where will we get to if soldiers in wartime work against the government of their own land?'

'I am myself not certain what is correct and true, Colonel-General. But I have asked myself again and again what sense there is in the dying of tens of thousands. Is the traditional conception of military obedience enough in a situation in which our trust in the High Command has more than once been shabbily betrayed? What compelling military grounds are there today to justify our extinction? May I take it, General, that you know the content of all these leaflets? In one it is said that Army Group 'Caucasus' is already fighting in the Rostov area. In which case the danger of its encirclement must be over. Why then the frightful human sacrifice of the 6th Army?'

'I have read it, but cannot believe it. We cannot be critical enough with everything to do with propaganda.'

'But what if it should be the truth? If we are knowingly or unknowingly being led astray by higher headquarters?'

'I don't agree with everything you say. Manstein knows from Pickert what a desperate situation we are in. I simply cannot imagine that the suffering and dying of our army does not disturb him, that the victims being demanded from us are unnecessary. I stand here as ordered and cannot be responsible for Army Group "A" in the Caucasus.'

So this conversation also ended in a cul-de-sac. It was reflected over and discussed. But the way out of the devil's circle we closed ourselves. We were not capable of extracting ourselves from the formal responsibility against senseless, even criminal orders in the real responsibility to our people. Nothing then could alter the rousing words of German anti-Fascists.

The road of death

Lieutenant-General Schmidt had me call him. 'Adam, you are to reconnoitre the new headquarters. We are intending that the 71st Infantry Division takes over in the city south of the Zaritza stream. As far as I know the dugouts in a gulley near Stalingradski should suit us. Take the advance detachment with you. At the point where the way from the Stalingrad road turns off to the gulley, an orderly officer from the 71st Infantry Division will be waiting for you.'

Upon returning to my bunker, I contacted the divisional adjutant and agreed a time for the meeting with the detailed officer. At 0900 hours on the 13th January my vehicle stood ready to move. It was only a few hundred metres to the roadway. Lines of distressed refugees were still heading towards the city. After just a kilometre my cross-country jeep was full of wounded. Two were even standing on the running boards.

'Drive slowly,' I said to the driver, who was worried about the axles and springs. I decided to make a little detour to Stalingrad and deliver the wounded to a hospital there. Although the car was already heavily overloaded, we took another one on shortly afterwards. From quite a distance I saw him standing, one thickly wrapped hand stretched out in supplication. As we came slowly towards him, I discerned a desperate face. Tears were rolling down his cheeks. He hobbled towards us. 'Please take me to Stalingrad!' My driver and I crushed together to make room for him. The youngster was not yet 19 years old. He had severe frostbite on both hands and feet. He had been hobbling along the street for hours. No one had taken pity on him. He did not know how he should thank me. He kept on trying to shake my hand. Stalingrad seemed to be his salvation.

I put them all down at the hospital in the western part of the city, after having a few words about them with the duty doctor. We almost had to carry the youngster. In farewell he wanted to give me a small, hard sausage. 'It is from Mutti, I have been saving it,' he said sincerely. Naturally I gave it back. 'You need it more than I do, young friend.'

Innumerable dead lay alongside the roadway. Many were the corpses of wounded and sick who had only wanted to lie down for a short rest to try to regain some strength. They had fallen asleep from fatigue and frozen to death. The dead also lay on the street. Nobody made any effort to remove them. Tanks and trucks with unfeeling, stupid drivers rolled over the hard frozen corpses and flattened them, and pedestrians tripped and stumbled over them. The road deserved the description 'Death Street'.

This name applied also to the hundreds of wrecks of all kinds of trucks, cars and special vehicles destroyed by bombs, turned over, the truck beds ripped, the occupants torn apart. In between the smashed tanks and guns, here and there lay a burnt-out aircraft and countless fully intact vehicles lacking only one thing: fuel.

My vehicle stopped. The orderly officer from the 71st Infantry Division climbed in. From the first impression there was no need to talk to me. We were already at our destination.

'Hartmannstadt'

We turned into a deep ravine, at the bottom of which a road ran between the steeply rising walls on either side and a proper bunker settlement had been built. It was called 'Hartmannstadt' after the divisional commander, Lieutenant-General von Hartmann. The bunkers had been constructed in three storeys, connected by steps in the left-hand wall. Steps and pavements were protected by railings. Even a kitchen and a food store had been included in the steep slope.

The 71st Infantry Division had captured the northern forts of Verdun – Vaux and Douaumont – in the Western Campaign. It was known as the 'Happy One', and its vehicles carried a four-leaf clover emblem as a distinguishing mark. But now luck had left it without a trace. I found Lieutenant-General von Hartmann in a very depressed mood. 'What a frightful situation we have been brought to. There is no longer any escape. Of my division, of which I was always so proud, nothing much remains. It will not last to the end.'

I too saw only black on black and told him of my terrible journey on 'Death Street': 'You are right. These frightful pictures are enough to break one's heart and rob one of one's sanity.'

In our further discussion I discovered that he too had lost his only son in the war. Fallen for the Fatherland – as we had believed for so long or at least imagined. After the bitter experiences of the last months this explanation seemed very questionable. But even more frightful was having to say that they had died senselessly. As I was leaving, I had the feeling that Hartmann was more torn and lost than I was.

The adjutant and orderly officer showed me round the well constructed dugouts. There was a sturdily built stove in every one. Beds, tables and chairs were available in sufficient numbers. Curtains and blackout materials hung at every window. All the rooms were illuminated by electric light. How primitive our headquarters had been until now!

The divisional staff intended to leave the next day. An advance party from our headquarters had to take over in the next few hours. Using a sketch map, I divided up the individual dugouts among our staff. Then I set off back.

Once I had informed Schmidt about the events of my journey, I asked him when the move was to take place. 'That depends on how the situation develops further and when the telephone connections are ready to be taken over. As long as Pitomnik is in our hands, we stay here,' he said.

Finally I reported to Colonel-General Paulus about 'Hartmannstadt' and about the ghastly things I had experienced on the way. 'It is really frightful,' he said. 'If I knew that Army Group "A" was safe, I would put an end to it. As no one has authorised me to do so, I must fight on as long as it is possible somehow.'

'Can our troops still fight, Colonel-General? The front in the west will collapse on the first assault.'

'It will close up again. Pitomnik is still in our hands. And who goes into captivity willingly? The soldiers are still hoping for relief and do not want to think about surrendering. This reinforces me in my dealings.'

Captain Behr's task
In fact, a mix of anxiety and hope certainly filled the thoughts of most soldiers. Among the army's staff no one thought seriously of a relief.

However, no one had the courage to tell the troops the truth. It was also clear that we could not hold on to Pitomnik for much longer. Schmidt therefore ordered that the war diaries of our staff (Sections Ia, Ic, QQu, IIa (Adjutant), Army Engineers and Army Signals) should be flown out so that they did not fall into the hands of the enemy. The 1st orderly officer of the command section, Captain Behr, a dashing young holder of the Knight's Cross, was tasked with this. He should next describe the fight to the death of the 6th Army and then fly on to the Army High Command to report personally to Hitler how distressfully the 6th Army was perishing and starving. The army commanders thought that a highly decorated captain would have more influence than a general. Behr did not return to the cauldron. Today I do not know whether he was hindered in this so that the hopeless situation of the 6th Army would remain veiled. From my personal knowledge of the captain, I do not know whether he held things back either with Manstein or with Hitler. But the number of supply aircraft did not increase. The army languished even further. The field kitchens remained cold as there was nothing to cook in them. Even the little evening meal diminished here and there. The front had pressed closer to Pitomnik. Red Army fighters flew over the airfield and shot up many of our unprotected *Ju 52*s and *He 111*s flying in. Others that had been able to land were destroyed on the ground by Soviet bombers or low-flying 'Sewing Machines'. It was no use if Schmidt radioed the detached Captain Toepke: 'Hit them with a cudgel if no more aircraft are employed!'

Gumrak airfield
On the 14th January an advance party from the army headquarters took over the headquarters of the 71st Infantry Division. That day Pitomnik was finally lost. The ground crews were still able to move over to the replacement airfield at Gumrak, which had been prepared in a rough and ready manner in the previous two days. Colonel-General Heitz, the commanding general of the VIIIth Corps, had to clear his headquarters on the edge of Pitomnik in a hurry. He appeared with his staff in the former headquarters near Gumrak. Similarly the headquarters of the XIVth Panzer Corps, until then between Pitomnik and Novo-Alexeievski, had to move to near Gumrak.

On this day Colonels Lattman and Dr Korfes were promoted major-generals. Major-General Lattmann, whose panzer division had been completely eradicated, was given the command of the 389th Infantry Division in place of its former commander, Major-General Magnus, who had proved completely useless in this situation. Perhaps Magnus hoped that Schmidt would let him be flown out, but that was not so.

By the middle of January the cauldron was considerably reduced in size. The new front in the south and west ran along the ring road. It was occupied by the tattered remains of the 44th, 76th, 297th and 376th Infantry Divisions, the 3rd and 29th (Motorised) Infantry Division, the 14th Panzer Division and the so-called fortress battalions. Now army headquarters near Gumrak was under immediate threat. We feared that the new defensive ring would not hold out much longer. The bunkers occupied by our headquarters were required by the fighting troops. Therefore the staff moved on the morning of the 16th January to 'Hartmannstadt'. Again files and pieces of equipment were burnt. Only the absolutely essentials went to the new site. We drove along the roadway in the few remaining vehicles in small convoys past the ghostly starving, sick and wounded soldiers to the new headquarters site.

At Gumrak station we encountered a dense crowd of wounded, who, driven by fear, were leaving the hospital and trying to make their way east. The badly wounded and the very ill remained behind, there being no transport available for them. For most of them the spark of life was about to expire anyway. Paulus had ordered the senior doctors to hand over the hospitals to the advancing enemy. The Russians found heaps of hard-frozen German soldiers' corpses that had been carried out on stretchers or planks from the house of the dying. Themselves weak, the medical orderlies no longer wanted to hack out graves for the dead in the hard-frozen ground. And there were no more explosives available.

No more supply aircraft
In no way could the Gumrak landing ground replace Pitomnik. It lay under artillery fire and the landing strip was cratered by shells and bombs. The heavy supply aircraft could only land at maximum risk. Then the Luftwaffe pilots completely refused to land, having lost dozens of aircraft to flak and fighters, and through bombings and crash landings. Two or three days after the loss of Pitomnik not a single machine landed, although everything had been done from our side to put the Gumrak airstrip in order, and Army Group 'Don' had been told. Apparently they were not ready to persuade the Luftwaffe to fly into Gumrak. Paulus said in a radio message direct to Hitler: 'My Führer, your orders for the supply of the army are not being carried out. Gumrak airfield has been usable since the 15th January, the place faultless, clear for night landings, ground staff to hand, urgent engagement necessary, greatest danger.'

At the army commander-in-chief's hastily summoned situation conference, Schmidt complained angrily about the Luftwaffe. The senior quartermaster was in despair. Through him the demands from the starving units combined in a single cry of distress: 'Don't let us die so miserably! Give us bread!'

Paulus decided to appeal to Manstein once more. Two hours after the transmission of the message to Hitler came a radio message from the commander-in-chief of Army Group 'Don': 'The objections of the Luftwaffe are seen as an excuse, landing possibilities through Luftwaffe organisations and flying units found in every direction. The landing strip is considerably widened. Ground staff faultless with all equipment as was previously at Pitomnik. Commander-in-chief has requested the Führer take radical measures, the present delays by the Luftwaffe having already cost the lives of numerous men.'

Army headquarters believed it had done everything possible to ward off the frightful distress. Hours went past without a reply and not a single supply aircraft appeared.

Once more Paulus radioed Army Group 'Don': 'Still no aircraft arrivals. Army requests aircraft crews to be given orders to land.'

In vain! No reply – either from Hitler or from Manstein. Therefore ever more cries for help stormed 6th Army Headquarters on behalf of the troops: 'Number of casualties from hunger mounting hour by hour. At least minimum rations essential immediately. Suicides from hopelessness and doubt the order of the day.'

Who will be flown out?
The army commander sought yet another means of lessening the distress. He asked Manstein to fly in a Luftwaffe general who could see for himself the landing possibilities in the cauldron. If there is such a general who values his life so little, I muttered, when I heard of this attempt. My scepticism was justified. On the morning of the 16th January a Luftwaffe major, instead of the requested general, reported at our headquarters. It was obviously an indication of the value the 6th Army had among the senior commanders. I controlled my anger over this new betrayal by superior headquarters in accordance with the elementary principles of military propriety.

Into my office came Captain von Seydlitz, a relative of the commanding general of the LIst Corps. As a candidate for staff training, he had been assigned to our army headquarters for part of his practical training. On behalf of the chief of staff he told me that specialists such as tank commanders and staff candidates were to be flown out immediately. 'The Army High Command has also ordered Major von Zitzewitz, Hitler's liaison officer to our staff, to be flown out. Lieutenant-General Schmidt would have you ask the corps and divisions for the names of the officers concerned by telephone. We are hoping that at last another supply aircraft will land tonight.'

'And what happens to the severely wounded?' I asked. 'I have heard from the army doctor that all are now being brought to Gumrak. All the dugouts are packed full.'

'The army doctor has been instructed to cease immediately the flying out of the badly wounded,' said Seydlitz.

I had to check myself when I heard this. In every modern army wounded soldiers and officers were given special care and handling. In this case those who were being taken out of the cauldron were those deemed still of value in the continued conduct of the war; the rest were being left to their fate. This could only be regarded as further evidence that the High Command had closed the book on the 6th Army. But the attitude towards this question must also have changed in our army. Until now Schmidt had discarded every proposal of this kind. Why was he not now standing against the orders from the Army High Command? For a moment the thought arose in me that the chief of staff himself might be behind the new order. The general staff officers were also specialists! They were not named in the order. But those who were not might perhaps be included as the situation came further to a head. Then it seemed to me that such an imputation was so low that I should try to knock it out of my head. I turned to the captain. 'Then may I congratulate you, dear Seydlitz. Certainly you belong to the first of those that will leave this death trap. Have you already packed your things?'

'I don't think it will happen, Colonel. Schmidt told me early today that I am indispensable since Captain Behr flew out. Honestly, I don't understand this reason. For days there has been hardly anything to do. I am sent to and from divisions to orientate myself on the situation. But for days it has been the same miserable picture, only the resolution increases. Yesterday I was on the western edge of Gumrak airfield. It was guarded by weak emergency units. Hardly any anti-tank weapons or artillery are available. And where a gun is still intact, it lacks ammunition.'

'Nevertheless the half-dead men act with renewed resistance when the Russians attack. What really goes on in the heads of our men?' I asked him.

'That is strange. Many lie apathetically in their holes, staring ahead of them and hardly answering when spoken to. Others complain like mad. They have been lied to and betrayed. But as soon as there is an alarm they bring their rifle or machine-pistol up to their cheeks, or jump to a machine gun or anti-tank weapon.'

'Apparently the fear of captivity is greater than the anger and disappointment over their plight that we experience here.'

'That certainly applies to the great majority, Colonel. But in the last few days there have been here and there small combat teams who have surrendered with their officers. Eight weeks ago that would have been unthinkable. I see the effect of the enemy propaganda in this.'

Captain von Seydlitz said goodbye. As we shook hands at the open bunker door as he was leaving, I saw the Luftwaffe major escorted by Elchlepp below in the gulley. A vehicle drove up from under cover. The Luftwaffe officer climbed in and saluted as he drove off towards Gumrak airfield.

'This visit did not last long. I am keen to know what has come out of it,'

I said. 'I too, Colonel,' said Seydlitz and headed off to the chief of staff's bunker.

Colonel Elchlepp had noticed me. He climbed up the steps and shortly afterwards came in to see me. 'The pilot had nothing to say in apology. Schmidt addressed him harshly, saying that his arguments did not interest us. The 6th Army expected food, ammunition, medical supplies and fuel. It was a scandal to leave us so much in the lurch. Paulus agreed and said that the Luftwaffe had not kept the promises it had given to the army. The behaviour of the higher commands towards the 6th Army was a breach of trust that nothing could excuse.'

'So this major took the hiding for the generals. We can presume it was all exchanged in words. Do you believe, Elchlepp, that our supplies will be improved by this? Can you hear the shell bursts? The front has come damned near our headquarters. How many more days will it take to eliminate the cauldron? We have not to be honest with ourselves, or we must surrender. Then at least thousands of lives can be saved. All of this no longer makes any sense. The Army High Command has written us off. Now a few specialists will be flown out, the others can perish.'

'I have my nose full like you, Adam. But an officer cannot surrender to the Bolsheviks. He fights to the last bullet and then dies.'

'But those are just empty words, Elchlepp. A meaningless fight is irresponsible, even immoral. In this sense, I will always act like Colonel-General Paulus.'

'Nobody can deny you that. But you will not achieve it. For Paulus military obedience is the highest principle.'

My friend Colonel Selle

In the following days specialists, overwhelmingly from the armoured and motorised divisions, reported to me. After the massive protests from the army's headquarters at least a few aircraft landed again at night with supplies and ammunition. They took these specialists with them to Army Group 'Don'.

I was really pleased that Colonel Selle was flown out. Back in October 1942 our doctor had urgently advised a stay for him at a cure resort, and the application was already approved when the Red Army's big offensive began. Selle immediately declared that he would not leave the troops in the lurch. At the beginning of December he took over a battle group at Chir and later received from Schmidt an unnecessary order to fly into the cauldron. Although a serious health problem meant it was difficult for him to stay on his feet, he made no attempt to fly out. He eventually went several days later, after I had asked him to take a photograph of me with my camera, as I wanted to send the film and camera by the next courier aircraft to my wife and daughter. Afterwards we had had a frank conversation. Selle, an old member of the National Socialist party and holder of the Party's golden badge, told me that he had again advised Paulus to go against Hitler's orders and to do what the responsibility towards his army imposed. But for Paulus, Schmidt's views applied only to tactical matters, and Selle regarded this as disastrous. The Colonel-General, together with his chief of staff, held the joint responsibility for the senseless sacrifice of the 6th Army. In a burst of anger against Hitler and Göring, Selle took the Party badge from his uniform, threw it on the hard-frozen snow and trampled it in.

Although this scene was little more than a gesture without any further consequences, it impressed me then because it at least signified a revolt, where Paulus, Schmidt, Elchlepp and the others demanded unconditional obedience to immoral orders. Possibly the chief of staff would not have placed Colonel Selle on the courier list if he had heard of our conversation. On the 22nd January Schmidt told me that Selle would be leaving the cauldron. I wanted to be the first to convey the glad tidings. When I called, his adjutant answered the telephone.

'Is Colonel Selle there?' I asked.

'A moment, I will give the telephone to the Colonel.'

'What is new, Adam?'

'You are to fly out today or tomorrow!'

There was silence at the other end of the line. Had he lost his voice from shock?

'Are you there, Selle?'

Finally I heard his voice again. 'I hope that you are not playing a joke on me.'

'My dear Selle, I would not think of it under these circumstances. Schmidt only told me a few minutes ago. I congratulate you heartily and am delighted that someone gets out who will not waffle about our heroic battle. I hope that you will not remain silent back in the homeland.'

'You can be sure of that' came resolutely back.

'Don't forget to come by me again before you go!'

While I was speaking the last sentence, Captain von Seydlitz entered the office. 'Excuse me, Colonel! Lieutenant-General Schmidt is asking for you to immediately reconnoitre an emergency landing ground for our supply aircraft near Stalingradski. Gumrak is under strong enemy artillery fire.'

There was not a second to be lost. I set off with some soldiers. We had soon reconnoitred a place and staked it out. It was only a few minutes from our headquarters.

Colonel Selle was waiting for me in my dugout. He had already said his farewells to Paulus and Schmidt and he told me of his talks with both of them. I still remember his words very clearly. 'Paulus is really at the end of his strength. As he put out his hand to say goodbye to me, he said: "Go with God and make your allotted contribution based upon which the commanders of the Wehrmacht can return to a really sound basis!" That was very impressive unwritten, but in Paulus's mouth it was a destructive sentence, don't you think? You can imagine how difficult it was for me to say anything at this point. I did not once look him in the eyes. With the words: "May the cross on our army's grave not be the death memorial for all of Germany!" I left the dugout.'

'Paulus has in the last weeks withstood indescribable agonies. His brain has been tormented every day. But he cannot free himself from Hitler's and Manstein's orders. What impression have you of Schmidt?'

'I had not seen him for several days and was surprised by his appearance. He no longer looks like the victorious, self-assured chief of staff he was. The man who until now strongly reproved any negative remark now sharply criticises the High Command. He released me with the words: "Say everywhere you go that the 6th Army has been betrayed by the High Command and left in the lurch!" It is very regrettable that he did not realise this sooner; he could have saved the 6th Army much misery.'

Colonel Selle had just left when I had a telephone message from the adjutant of the IVth Corps that their commanding general, General of Engineers Jaenecke, had been wounded in the head and shoulders in an enemy bombing attack. Dutifully I immediately telephoned this on to Army Group 'Don'. Several hours later came the decision from the Army Personnel Office to fly out the wounded general on the next machine to land in the cauldron. By this time the enemy had already occupied our last airfield at Gumrak. The aircraft flying in were instructed to land in Stalingradski, although no landing ground was yet marked out. General Jaenecke was flown out of the cauldron from here together with Colonel Selle on the 23rd January.

It was one of the last aircraft to land. Most pilots, those who managed to break through the enemy flak belt, simply threw out supply packages, not a few of which fell over the Soviet lines. What did arrive was fallen on by the starving soldiers. The commander-in-chief's order to report all supply packages and deliver them to an established central point was ignored, and most of the contents were shared among the men who found them. Could we blame them for dealing with these things in this way? For weeks they had had hardly anything to eat. The tearing hunger drove them to the edge of insanity and swept aside their orders on discipline so they themselves forgot their helpless, wounded comrades.

What does Lieutenant-General Schmidt want?

On the 23rd January the commanding generals gathered for a talk by Paulus. In place of the wounded General Jaenecke, Lieutenant-General Pfeffer, commander of the 297th Infantry Division, was tasked with the command of the IVth Corps and simultaneously promoted to General of Artillery. At the centre of the conference stood the question: How should we continue? Generals von Seydlitz and Pfeffer asked for a suspension of the fighting, while Heinz, Strecker and Schlömer persisted in holding out.

Finally Colonel-General Paulus spoke to Schmidt, Elchlepp and me about the same problem. I referred to the senseless dying and suggested surrender, looking at Schmidt. How would he react? I was fully expecting an outburst of rage, but Schmidt remained quiet, seeming to approve the proposal. Only Elchlepp was still decisively against it. The commander-in-chief had become uncertain, but he could not yet jump over his shadow. He decided once more to radio our superior headquarters with a detailed report on the situation within the cauldron and to request permission to capitulate.

On the evening of the 23rd January two *He 111*s landed on the provisional airstrip only a few hundred metres away. Shortly afterwards Lieutenant-General Schmidt summoned me to his dugout. He went over the talks that we had had that afternoon with Paulus and did not conceal the fact that he was very disappointed about the holding back by the superior headquarters. 'What does he want now?' I was thinking. 'I know that as well as he does!' His following sentence made it clearer. 'Until now neither Hube nor any of the other officers has achieved any improvement in our situation, although they were all tasked with reporting the army's disastrous situation. I have the impression that none of them had the courage to tell the Führer the naked truth. I have myself long wanted to fly to report in person at the headquarters.' Now my ears pricked up. 'The catastrophic situation forces us to take a last step to finally achieve freedom to negotiate. I must ask you to suggest to the commander-in-chief to let me fly with one of the machines waiting in Stalingradski to Führer Headquarters to report to Hitler. You can be assured that I will immediately return to the cauldron.'

That was too much! This bad spirit of the army, who until now had not only acknowledged the order to hold out but wanted to put anyone who mentioned capitulation in front of a court martial, now wanted to desert. One could not interpret his demand any other way. Every simple soldier on the staff knew that by the next day no further machines would be landing in the cauldron.

Laconically I answered him: 'I suggest, General, that you present this proposal personally to the commander-in-chief.'

Angry, but still in control, he glared at me as I left his dugout without another word.

I briefly informed the 1st general staff officer, Colonel Elchlepp, about this episode. He angrily jumped up from his chair: 'That's a mean trick! You must tell the commander-in-chief immediately!'

'I am on my way to him, but wanted to make sure of your support.'

Then I went in to see Paulus. Shocked, but also disappointed with his chief of staff, who had always demanded that we fight to the last bullet, he accepted my information. 'Just let him come. I know now how I am with him.'

Soon there was a knock at the door and Schmidt entered. Perhaps he thought Paulus was alone and did not expect him to be already informed of our discussion. Almost with the same words that he had used with me, he sought to justify his flight out.

The commander-in-chief – quite contrary to his normal manner – answered immediately, clearly and unequivocally: 'You stay here! You know as well as I do that it can end any time. No one is prepared to help us any more. I think that any further discussion is unnecessary.'

Under control of himself, Schmidt stood there, and left the room without a word after Paulus had tasked him with describing the situation in writing and drafting a request to Hitler for permission to capitulate. Then the pilots of the two *He 111*s received permission to take off. They had been waiting for hours in the orderly officers' dugout, held back on Schmidt's orders. A few minutes later their machines rose up in the frost-clear night sky. Another turn around our headquarters and they vanished from our view in a westerly direction.

Colonel Elchlepp's plan
Colonel Elchlepp was waiting for me in my dugout. The question was pressing: what should we do when the end comes?

'You have repeatedly said, Elchlepp, that you would never become a prisoner of war. You will have to decide soon now.'

'As I see it, nothing has changed. A senior officer does not surrender. When it gets that far, I will take my place in the front line, and there I will shoot to the last bullet. The last bullet I will keep for myself.'

'You are talking about suicide. Has that anything to do with a soldier's honour? That cannot be a solution. Paulus told me that various generals have requested an order from him that no general or senior officer can go into captivity. Every officer should use his last bullet on himself. The commander-in-chief has dismissed this as cowardly avoidance of responsibility. He has taken the standpoint – and I have supported him in this – that in our catastrophic situation the officer belongs to his troops and must share their fate once the fighting ends.'

'I don't contest that the officer has to persevere to the end of the battle. But he can turn the weapon on himself when he has no more to lead.'

Elchlepp seemed incapable of being turned away from his suicidal decision. I reminded him of his wife and his children.

'I want to see them again. So I have initiated a plan, better said, plans, that have been outlined by various officers.'

I knew what was coming now. For some time now Elchlepp had been hinting at the intentions of some officers who wanted to fight their way through to the west. I had not taken them seriously until now. This night Elchlepp spoke in detail about these plans. 'It is time, Adam, to get you involved in our plans. I calculate that it will be barely more than a week before the cauldron is liquidated. Together with Lieutenant-Colonel Niemeyer, Lieutenant Zimmermann, Lieutenant-Colonel Heitzmann from the 9th Flak Division and some young flak officers, I will go to the fighting front in the next few days. There we will conceal ourselves from the attacking Russians, let them roll over us and then march off to the southwest behind their front line. The route has been carefully worked out. We have informed General Hube of our intentions and asked him to have supply packages dropped at specific points. I have drawn the places concerned on a map that one of our courier officers has already taken out with him.'

'But that is nonsense, Elchlepp. Even if you were able to get through the enemy lines, you would never reach your goal. Remember that our whole southern front has been drawn back some 400 kilometres westwards. You would have to creep for weeks through enemy territory. It is impossible.'

'We have prepared ourselves thoroughly. Our rucksacks are fully packed with woollen and fur items. Bandages and medicines have also been considered. For days we have been saving up crisp-bread and some conserves so that we will have the necessary supplies at the beginning.'

'Have you also thought that this is desertion, Elchlepp? A flight from responsibility? Your plan contradicts your own demands to hold on.'

'We will not be deserters, rather we are requesting Paulus to release us from our duties. We will only go ahead with it if he is in agreement with our intentions. Incidentally, Colonel Clausius, the LIst Corps' chief of staff, is going to break out of the cauldron with his orderly officer on skis. We hope to meet up on the way. Individual groups from the 71st and 371st Infantry Divisions will travel away from the Volga to the south to break through to the 1st Panzer Army near Terek.'

'Don't get me wrong, but these are dangerous fantasies. You know that the 1st Panzer Army is now apparently in the Rostov area. Haven't you told the group? And do you really believe that the enemy will secure their rear areas so badly that they cannot pick out such crazy travellers within a few kilometres? Be reasonable, Elchlepp!'

'You can save any further words; my decision is irrevocable.' With these words he left my dugout.

Our penultimate headquarters

In the early hours of the morning of the 24th January the following radio report was sent by Colonel-General Paulus to Hitler: 'The army reports on the basis of reports from corps and personal messages from commanding generals, as far as they are still obtainable, the following situation report:

Troops without ammunition and supplies. Elements of the 6th Division still reachable, indications of disintegration on the southern, northern and western fronts. No unified following of orders possible any longer. The eastern front only slightly changed. 18,000 wounded without the slightest aid of bandages and medicines. 44th, 76th, 100th, 305th, 389th Infantry Divisions destroyed. As a result of strong breaches, the front has been torn apart at many points. Strongpoints and possibility of cover only available within the city. Further defence futile. Collapse imminent. Army requests immediate capitulation in order to save remaining lives.'

The reply came promptly. It was as unscrupulous as ever. The sense was conveyed in Hitler's radio message: 'Capitulation out of the question. 6th Army is fulfilling its historical role by fighting to the last round to enable the construction of a new southern front.'

I told Paulus many times that I regarded this order as criminal and, as a result, not binding on us. Lieutenant-General Schmidt, who was hardly 'weak' regarding the army's fate, demanded further holding on. Paulus remained an obedient soldier and facilitated Hitler's criminal destruction of the 6th Army.

Towards 0900 hours we heard rifle and machine-gun fire, and the explosions of hand grenades. During the night the front line had withdrawn to the immediate vicinity of the gulley. All the members of the staff stood in front of their dugouts, the drivers ready by their vehicles. Would we come out safely from our bunker village? The 71st Infantry Division had prepared a new headquarters for us in the cellars of a former hospital in Stalingrad-South. Already Schmidt's cutting voice sounded: 'Get everything ready for moving headquarters.'

The remaining files and all disposable personal items were quickly destroyed. Two blankets and a briefcase containing underclothes and toiletries comprised my entire possessions, apart from what I was wearing. It was high time for us to leave. Already rifle bullets were whistling over the ravine. The windows of the dugouts splintered under the pressure of exploding grenades.

When we had occupied the headquarters eight days earlier, I had been tasked by the chief of staff with marking out a defensive line on either side of the ravine. But who was going to occupy it? The handful of people on the staff? The enemy had taken further advantage of us. He had used the cover of darkness to push forward to within several hundred metres of the headquarters. Our 'line of defence' was already in his hands. Schmidt gave the order: 'To the vehicles!' All took their places in flying haste, the engines howling away. We left the bunker village in a rush, hearing the shouts of the Red Army soldiers from the other end of the gulley. A few minutes later and the army headquarters would already have gone into captivity on the 24th January. Today I can say that it would not have been a bad thing for us and the whole army, cutting short the final act and saving many lives, but it gave us a powerful shock at the time. The drivers pressed down their accelerators until we reached the first buildings in Stalingrad, then they had to slow down in order to get through the rubble. Slowly we went round bomb craters, rubble and stones and chunks of concrete, past the remains of walls and chimneys. What shellfire had not destroyed our troops had dismantled to provide building material for positions and dugouts, or, as long as it was combustible, for heating purposes.

An officer of the 71st Infantry Division was waiting for us at the Zaritza Bridge. He led us to the designated cellar rooms. There was not much to put up, as we had left most of our equipment behind in the gulley. Would this be our last headquarters? Our poor cellar holes made a mockery of the term. The person who seemed the least annoyed was Lieutenant-General Schmidt. Soon after our arrival he ordered me to find out how the surrounding ruins were defended. With this there also had to be a landing strip for a Fieseler 'Stork'. Paulus shook his head at this order. 'What a nonsense! Where can the 'Stork' come from? But carry out the instructions if it pleases the chief of staff.' Elchlepp complained about Schmidt's latest whim, but was hardly interested in what we were doing.

My impression was that Schmidt had not given up hope of being flown out. Possibly he had established contact with his friend General Hube, either by a letter that he had given to a pilot on the night of the 23rd/24th January or by radio.

About a hundred metres from our headquarters cellar was a level area of open land that appeared suitable for landing a 'Stork'. Lieutenant-General Schmidt ordered me that afternoon to make the landing strip identifiable by landing lights, as he expected two of these aircraft that night. They would be towed in by two larger machines as they themselves did not have sufficient fuel to fly so far.

Was Schmidt really so naïve as to believe that General Paulus would allow him to fly out? Demanding that soldiers and officers should fight to the last man, but wanting to save his own life: what behaviour was that for an officer who shared not a little of the blame for the 6th Army being crucified!

The night passed. The chief of staff waited in vain. His orderly told me that he had not closed his eyes all night long. Aircraft did fly over the considerably shrunken cauldron, but they were supply machines randomly throwing out foodstuffs. The pilots could no longer tell where friend or foe were located. But no Fieseler 'Stork' landed.

General von Hartmann seeks death

My occupation as adjutant of the 6th Army was at an end. I only had a pencil and writing pad, an official rubber stamp, about a dozen Knight's Crosses and the same number of German Crosses. Sitting around in the cellar with nothing to do was not for me. I therefore took on the role of a liaison officer and drove first to the 71st Infantry Division, which lay several streets further south, its headquarters fired on by enemy artillery at irregular intervals. On the previous day Captain von Seydlitz, on attachment as a potential staff officer candidate, had been killed by a direct hit. Just as I entered General von Hartmann's office, several shells exploded again right in front of the building. Among the victims was the chief of staff's personal orderly officer, Lieutenant Schatz. He had come in a jeep and had been killed by a shell as he was directing the driver.

The general briefed me on a city map about the deployment of the forces still available to him. His voice was calm and relaxed. 'I intend to go to my infantry in the front line by the morning at the latest. I will seek death among their ranks. Captivity for a general is dishonourable.'

'I am of another opinion, General. Most of our soldiers still living will become prisoners. In our exceptional situation capitulation and captivity are not dishonourable. We have long had to take this step. I see it as our duty to share the bitterness of captivity with our soldiers. We should say this openly to the troops and not commit suicide in front of them. Permit me to speak openly as I have done so often in these last hours. You too, General, should face the question of responsibility towards our soldiers openly, and also towards your wife and your daughter, who already grieve over their son and brother. The order of the hour cannot be suicide, but rather the will to survive!'

It was in vain. 'I know that you mean well, Adam. But I will go my own way.' And that is how he said goodbye to me.

Colonel-General Paulus was shattered when I reported to him my conversation with Hartmann. He immediately telephoned him, but he too was unable to persuade the divisional commander to change his mind. 'I will be with my soldiers in the last hours and therefore will go into the front line' was how he responded to all the reproaches that Paulus made to him. And that was how it remained.

My next route took me to Colonel Roske, who was lying with his staff in the cellars of a department store north of the Zaritza. The upper storeys of the building had been destroyed. But there was plenty of room in the underground storerooms, so that even the headquarters were well accommodated. Roske was prepared to let us have part of the cellar for ourselves.

In the course of the conversation with Roske I discovered that he too was against going into captivity. He was planning a breakout. In the yard of the department store he showed me a captured Russian truck. It stood there fully tanked up and laden with petrol cans. Roske commented on his plan: 'I have three surplus Soviet prisoners-of-war in the headquarters that are assigned to my plan. As soon as the enemy breaks in, we will mix in with their victorious troops and leave the yard in the vehicle in the resulting confusion. We can hardly fail. Everyone will think that we are carrying fuel. As soon as we have the city behind us we will drive on to the west without stopping until we reach the German southern front. Join us, Adam! We will hide ourselves behind the barrels.'

'For goodness sake, Roske, have you lost your senses? You cannot believe that I would take your plan seriously. You would never be able to get out of the yard. And what of your soldiers who have believed in you until now and held on with you! Are you going to leave them in the lurch? I cannot believe this of you. Forget these figments of the imagination!'

My impulsive appeal seemed to have made an impression on Roske. He looked at me in astonishment, then gradually became more thoughtful. 'Thank you for your words. You are obviously right. A commander really belongs with his men now. I will seriously think over the matter again.'

We went back into the cellars. I was convinced that Paulus and Schmidt would approve of the change of accommodation, so we went ahead and marked the rooms that our headquarters would occupy.

The return journey to headquarters was conducted under enemy artillery and mortar fire. The rubble-strewn streets were almost free of people. Everyone was seeking shelter in the cellars and ruins. Only here and there tottered or crept a few mummified figures, half-starving, frostbitten or wounded soldiers looking for their unit or a cellar hospital. What had become of our proud 6th Army! Why did it have to perish so cruelly on the Volga, 2,000 kilometres from home?

I was so sunk in my thoughts that I hardly noticed when my vehicle turned off the main road behind the Zaritza bridge. Suddenly it stopped in front of our headquarters.

Capitulation refused

Paulus and Schmidt agreed to have the army headquarters moved into the ruins of the department store. The timing was left up to Schmidt, depending on how the situation developed.

Once I was alone with Paulus he told me that Seydlitz had sought him out again. Once, in Schmidt's presence, he had demanded an army order to capitulate in view of the risk that the commanders might negotiate individually.

'He was quite right there, Colonel-General. Everything has turned out as he forecast in his memorandum of the 25th November last year. Let us now put an end to this pointless holding on! No one can justify it.'

But Paulus refused even now, when the cleft between orders and conscience had been irrevocably torn apart. He did not want to follow the voice of reason. 'You must understand, Adam, that I cannot handle things any other way.'

I could not understand this any longer, but further words were superfluous.

In view of the apparent inability of the army headquarters to operate effectively, individual units decided to handle matters themselves. For instance, a IVth Corps order said: 'With concern for the wounded, the battle can no longer continue in the city centre. The present fighting lines are to be held. Where further resistance is senseless, it can be abandoned and this made obvious to the enemy.'

In practice, this order opened the way to a partial surrender, thus contradicting the interpretation of the army headquarters. Nevertheless the latter took no action against this. Derisory contempt for the dying army was expressed in a broadcast from the Army Personnel Office, in which it was said that the awarding of the Iron Cross 2nd Class could be made immediately by company commanders, and of the Iron Cross 1st Class by battalion commanders. What companies, what battalions still had commanders? And to whom could these crosses be awarded on the verge of death?

The army staff were aware that Soviet envoys had appeared before the 297th, 371st and 71st Infantry Divisions in the south of the city requesting an avoidance of further bloodshed. They promised food and medical attention for the wounded of all surrendering units. The commanders received the Russians, contrary to Schmidt's orders, but sent them back without having reached a decision. Paulus and Schmidt took note of these measures without comment.

The 297th and 371st Infantry Divisions came under the IVth Corps. I was curious to see if the corps orders opened the option of laying down their arms, but for the moment we were unable to find out.

The Elchlepp breakout team had completed their preparations. The 1st general staff officer asked Paulus and Schmidt to relieve his and his comrades from their posts. Permission was given. Shortly afterwards the troop set off with a hearty farewell. It would subsequently be run over by the attacking Red Army soldiers in the 297th Infantry Division's area.

In place of Elchlepp, the Ia of the 71st Infantry Division, Lieutenant-Colonel von Below, was taken on the staff. In all, we were now down to only twenty of the original sixty officers and soldiers. The little group melded together again. In an outburst of despair Colonel Elchlepp's batman, an old man and head of a family, took his own life. He could not get over his colonel having left him in the lurch. Distracted, he sat silently among his companions. No one took any notice of him when he left the room until the hand grenade exploded outside. We found him lying dead in a pool of blood.

Similar reports came from the units with which we still had contact. Suicides increased as the end drew near. In several places an epidemic of suicides threatened to break out, especially among the younger officers and soldiers.

Major-General von Drebber writes from captivity

Late in the evening of the 25th January we received a message that the 297th Infantry Division had surrendered, together with its commander, Major-General von Drebber. The complete collapse of the army had begun.

Early the next morning I was sitting with Paulus at a small table in front of the cellar window when an orderly entered and handed the commander-in-chief a letter. 'Sender Major-General von Drebber' read the General in surprise. He did not open the letter immediately. Suddenly a bomb exploded on the street directly opposite our window. The window shattered and shards of glass and bomb splinters swept over our heads. Gunpowder gas blew into the room and the air pressure made the door burst out of its frame. My first thought was for Paulus. Once the smoke had dispersed, I saw that he was bleeding from his head, but it was not serious. I too had had the skin on my head torn in various places. A medical orderly was called in and applied light bandages to both of us. Once more we had been lucky.

After this shock, Paulus could at last open the letter. He buried himself in the content. Then he shook his head. 'That is hardly believable. Drebber describes how he and his soldiers were well received by the Red Army troops, being correctly handled. We are all victims of Goebbels' propaganda. Drebber asks me to give up the useless resistance and to surrender with the whole army.'

Meanwhile Schmidt had entered the room. His face darkened when he realised what was happening. He raged: 'Drebber never wrote that willingly; he must have been forced to do it. We are not surrendering! We will move this morning to the department store to better control the divisions.' As no 'Stork' was now expected to take him away, Schmidt had reverted completely to his former role.

On the same day we received the news that General von Hartmann had fallen. Standing upright on the railway embankment, he fired shot after shot from his rifle before collapsing. A bullet to the head killed him instantly. Colonel Roske was tasked with the command of the 71st Infantry Division.

More bad news reached us on the 26th January. 'General Stempel, commander of the 371st Infantry Division, has committed suicide,' reported a staff officer. His son, who was a second-lieutenant on his staff, had attended the same class as my son at a Dresden gymnasium. His father had written in his farewell letter to him that he was going to shoot himself as he could not endure this misery. The youngster wanted to make contact with Army Group 'A' towards the Volga with a group of like-minded troops. He did not get far before being captured.

Several other IVth Corps divisional commanders fell this way.

By chance Schmidt discovered on the 26th January that Seydlitz had given his regimental and battalion commanders the right to surrender at their own discretion. Angrily he asked Paulus to relieve Seydlitz of his position and put his three divisions (the 100th, 71st and 295th Infantry Divisions) under Colonel-General Heitz of the VIIIth Corps. Unfortunately the commander-in-chief let himself be taken by surprise and gave his consent.

I was astounded that Paulus had taken such a heavy measure against a general who in principle had judged the situation from the beginning onwards more correctly than the Army High Command. Paulus subsequently saw that he had handled the matter too hastily, but he was not prepared to recall Schmidt to cancel his consent.

Paulus by now was in an indescribable condition. As a 'simple soldier' he was completely helpless to act, unable above all to do something to recover from the unscrupulous Schmidt's act. It seemed to me that he realised he had made a mistake at the decisive moment. But this recognition only weighed him down and paralysed him further. He was physically and emotionally at the end of his strength.

The tragedy of the wounded
The army staff now consisted only of the commander-in-chief, the chief of staff, the Ia, the army signals officer, the 1st adjutant and some orderly officers. With two cars and a truck, we drove at about noon on the 26th January to our last headquarters. Rifle bullets and machine-gun bursts were already striking the streets around the hospital ruins. An officer of the 371st Infantry Division reported that enemy tanks were advancing.

The streets were busier than on the previous days when I was on my travels. Wounded and sick were making their way to the local district headquarters 'Mitte'. There, according to the army order, they were to assemble and be attended to. But a district headquarters no longer existed there. They had to make room in the hospital. Sick and wounded lay under a tattered roof. Those who could not be accommodated in this building sought shelter in the cellars around until they too were full to bursting.

As we crawled into the department store there was not a cellar left in the part of the city still occupied by us that was not completely full. The divisional surgeon of the 71st Infantry Division told Paulus that only a fraction of the wounded and sick were getting medical treatment. In most hospitals it was pitch dark. At best the doctors and medical orderlies working in various corners had a few candles or trench lights. Nobody knew how many dozens or hundreds of men lay pressed tightly together on the bare ground. If one did not move for a few hours, the man next to him would call out: 'There's a dead man here!'

Perhaps they hardly noticed any more, because the one opposite was also dead. The doctors were almost helpless, having run out of medicines, dressings and drugs. Often they had lost all of their medical equipment in the retreat, because their vehicles either ran out of fuel or were hit by bombs. In addition to this, the doctors and medical orderlies could hardly stand on their feet from exhaustion. But they did whatever was humanly possible and were supported by the chaplains. There were unimaginable scenes as the command post buildings that had become hospitals were hit by artillery fire. Hundreds were crushed in the crowds, engulfed by the flames and buried under the collapsing rubble.

Typhus
A malicious danger appeared during the last days in the cauldron: typhus. It followed the surviving men of the 6th Army into captivity and swept away tens of thousands of them. At first hardly any were affected, but here and there a soldier was very tired and breathless, shivering and with pains in the limbs; then he became delirious and suddenly died. There were also other sicknesses with similar symptoms. But typhus was by far the most serious. The virus, conveyed by lice in the clothing, led to a more than 80 per cent death rate among those affected within one to three weeks. More than 90 per cent of the remaining troops were infected. It was impossible to hunt for the quickly spreading lice in an ice-cold hole in the snow or a dark cellar. Almost everyone who staggered into the prisoner-of-war camps at the end of January and the beginning of February carried the germs of the deadly epidemic in their bodies. Only a few had been vaccinated, and very few in their half-starved state could withstand the day-long tormenting fever of more than 41 degrees. Despite the selfless commitment of Soviet doctors and nursing sisters, typhus deaths reaped a frightful harvest in the prisoner-of-war camps. It continued the cruel game of German militarism with the 6th Army further, leaving only a few thousand alive. The blame was borne by the same forces that had chased the 6th Army to the Volga, keeping them there in inhuman conditions with orders to hold on, until only the wreckage of humanity survived.

Last post: the department store
I shared a room in the cellars of the department store with Colonel-General Paulus. Opposite, separated by a passage, sat the chief of staff with the Ia. The remaining members of the staff camped in two or three other rooms.

It must have been a vast department store, I thought, when I made a tour around it. Through the solidly built cellars ran a road-wide passage, into which one could drive from the yard in a truck. There were storage rooms on either side that once had been lightened by large windows. Now piles of sandbags towered in front of the windows. Our vehicles stood in the passageway, protected by strong walls and ceilings against splinters and direct hits from lighter calibre weapons. The roof and upper storeys were destroyed. The whole building had been burnt out down to the ground floor. Only the stone staircases remained that had once led to the roof. They seemed to sway, but could still be climbed in the gaps between shots. From the second storey one had a good view over the wide square. Opposite lay the ruins of a theatre, and there, between the ruins in the east, gleamed the glassy water of the Volga. To the right of the theatre curved the view of the Zaritza, a deeply cut tributary of the Volga.

Army headquarters lay in the 71st Infantry Division's area. Colonel Roske, who had been tasked with its command following the death of General von Hartmann, was promoted to major-general on the 27th January. The soldiers of this division were in far better condition than those on the western and southern fronts. Since the beginning of the encirclement they had always had well constructed positions and even now still had heated accommodation, and – particularly astonishing – apparently sufficient provisions.

What was the explanation? In my travels through the cellars I came across several doors from which hung thick bars. I ordered the NCO escorting me to open them. He obeyed my instructions unwillingly. The reason for his reluctance immediately became clear when I saw that the rooms were richly stacked with foodstuffs. Obviously the quartermasters and paymasters, and apparently also the responsible commanders, had not reported these in November as they should have done. What a filthy swindle! If the other divisions on the northern and Stalingrad fronts – even if only in individual cases – had acted in the same way, one could easily imagine what huge quantities would have been withheld from the hard-fighting divisions on the western and southern fronts. Roske admitted that he had let the reports of the responsible army officials go uncontrolled.

The generals demand surrender
On the 26th January the Soviet units attacking from the west had linked up with elements of the 62nd Army advancing from the bank of the Volga at Mamai-Kurgan. This hill, so bitterly fought over back in the autumn, was finally retaken by the Red Army. The cauldron was now split into two parts. There was no longer any telephone connection with the northern part. The VIIIth and XIth Corps were on their own.

Almost every hour the enemy attacked from all sides, narrowing down the two cauldrons. Several generals without commands sat in the former city jail north of the Zaritza, among them von Seydlitz, Pfeffer, Schlömer, Deboi, Leyser, Edler von Daniels and Colonels Steidle and Beaulieu. These senior officers, assembled by chance, had lived with the horrors of the battle, the gradual wasting away and dying of their troops from the very beginning. Now they saw no sense in continuing the fighting any more. Their consciences warned them to request the destruction to cease fighting, even at the last minute.

On the 27th January the telephone rang near me. General Schlömer wanted to speak to the commander-in-chief. I asked him to wait a minute as I had to call Paulus to the telephone. It was a short conversation. Schlömer described the situation and the state of the troops, who were totally exhausted and no longer capable of resistance, and asked permission to surrender. The commander-in-chief reminded him of the order to hold on and put down the receiver.

About half an hour later Lieutenant-General Schmidt entered the cellar room that I occupied with Paulus. Angrily he reported a telephone conversation he had had with Colonel Müller, the chief of staff of the XIVth Panzer Corps: 'General, the XIVth Panzer Corps is considering surrender. Müller says that the troops have come to the end of their strength and no longer have any ammunition. I have told him that we are aware of the situation but that, as before, we still have our orders to fight on and that surrender is out of the question. Nevertheless, General, I suggest that you seek out this general yourself and talk to him.'

Paulus agreed. The journey to the city prison under enemy artillery fire was a risk, but they got through safely. Upon his return, Paulus told me that all the officers present had complained about Schmidt. To their quite justified questions and requests, they got only harsh words from him. They pointed out that their divisions were completely exhausted. The battle groups were already individually making contact with the enemy and surrendering. No one knew if their neighbours were still holding their positions. So it repeatedly happened that individual units were being attacked by the enemy from the flank and the rear and were destroyed. They were asking for orders to bring the unnecessary blood-letting to an end with the army's complete surrender.

'What answer did you give them, Colonel-General?' I asked him.

'I referred the generals once more to Hitler's orders. Every day and every hour counts in tying down the enemy's powerful forces,' countered Paulus.

'"The enemy's powerful forces!" Do you really believe, Colonel-General, that the Soviets are still using all the armies that we identified at the end of November within the city area? The cauldron is now completely shrunken. A fraction of the original troops is enough to eradicate us with a death thrust. The enemy knows our situation full well. The way in which he is conducting the battle shows that he is not prepared to sacrifice lives unnecessarily.'

'Naturally the enemy will have withdrawn some of his forces. But the fact is that he still has some here. At any rate the generals and colonels were of another opinion. "Hitler is a criminal" was one of the tamest expressions. As I was leaving the cellars of the town prison, I heard someone behind me say: "Just as we have been lied to, so will the German people be lied to. No newspaper, no radio will report the horrors that we have been experiencing for weeks. Goebbels will glorify our defeat.'"

Innumerable victims

Paulus heard and knew all this. Nevertheless he remained an obedient general. A new radio message from the Army High Command reinforced him in holding out further. It said that in case of the splitting of the cauldron, each part of the cauldron came personally under Hitler.

On the 28th January the northern cauldron was again split. The army reported that evening to the Army High Command: 'Strong enemy breach along the Gumrak–Stalingrad railway line split the army's front: in the northern cauldron XIth Corps, central cauldron VIIIth and LIst Corps, and southern cauldron XIVth Panzer Corps and IVth Corps without units. Army seeking to form a new defensive front along the northern edge and western frontage. Army calculates final collapse of its resistance by the 1st February.'

When dusk fell I was sitting alone in our cellar. Paulus had gone over to Schmidt. The artillery fire had become so strong by day that we hardly dared venture into the yard. Now too the sounds of fighting were coming from all around. I lay down on my bed. The pitiless fighting continued outside. Every hour demanded new victims. No one counted them. For days now I had been unable to gather definite reports of losses. They ran only approximately: 76th Infantry Division on the 27th January severe losses; 44th Infantry Division completely beaten; 371st, 305th, 376th Infantry Divisions wiped out; 3rd (Motorised) Infantry Division reduced to only very weak combat teams; 29th (Motorised) Infantry Division no contact any more.

How many soldiers were still alive? How many combatants did we still have? How many wounded and sick were there in the cauldron? The doctors I had come across in the last few days spoke of 40,000 to 50,000. Did the combatants still have any ammunition? Were there still rations available? Were the wounded and sick being cared for? Apart from a few individual cases, these questions had to be answered with 'No'.

On the 29th January came the news that Lieutenant-General Schlömer and other generals had received some Russian envoys and were negotiating a surrender with them. Schmidt threatened them with court martial. At the same time Colonel Steidle appeared at the department store. He wanted to speak to Colonel-General Paulus personally. He had been involved in the heavy fighting retreat from the west bank of the Don, when the new southern front of the cauldron was established, and lost almost a whole regiment of the 376th Infantry Division in defensive fighting. His soldiers regarded him as a brave and fair commander. Paulus treasured him for his reliability and frankness.

Two days earlier, on the 27th January, Steidle had said during a talk with the commander-in-chief that our responsibility to the soldiers and to the German people demanded the immediate cessation of the fighting. He had now come to ask Paulus to give the order to surrender. In doing so he first spoke with Schmidt, who knew full well what was going on. Schmidt gruffly turned down the colonel's request for permission to speak with General Paulus, and ordered him to go back to his troops immediately. Steidle had to leave the department store without having performed his task.

Was Lieutenant-General Schmidt playing a double game?
In these last days Schmidt also developed a lively busy-ness in other respects. Thus he ordered Colonel von Beaulieu, commander of an infantry regiment of the 3rd (Motorised) Infantry Division, to see him. This man, who had spent a long time in the Soviet Union during the 1920s, spoke the Russian language, knew the country and the people and – as he stressed – was familiar with the Red Army. I had met him frequently since the beginning of the Eastern Campaign. Astonished, I greeted him as he left the chief of staff's room. 'Schmidt had me tell him about the Russian Army. He was particularly interested in the question of what one could expect from their soldiers and officers. I had no idea that your chief of staff could be so friendly.'

Likewise, the interpreter of the LIst Corps was repeatedly called to headquarters to report to Schmidt. He was a Czarist emigrant, a former landlord and ensign in the Czarist Army. With him too Schmidt discussed the land and the people, and the soldiers and officers of the Red Army.

What was causing the chief of staff to have these discussions? Could it be a preparation for captivity? Was he playing a double game? Already he had instructed Roske to prepare the department store for all-round defence – was he also preparing himself for captivity?

It was late evening on the 29th January and I was walking in the dark passages of the cellars when someone tugged my sleeve. I thought at first that it must be one of the wounded, who had sought shelter here in the last few days. But by the light of my pocket torch I recognised Schmidt's orderly. The general himself was with Roske, discussing defensive measures for the headquarters. The senior corporal led me into Schmidt's living room and pointed to a corner where a little suitcase stood. When he opened it, I bent down and then looked at the soldier in surprise. Then he said smiling: 'He orders all his subordinates to hold on, surrender being out of the question, while he himself is equipped for captivity.'

I thanked him for this very informative exposure and went to my room. So that is what it was all about. Schmidt was not applying to himself the order to fight to the last man. Paulus shook his head as he heard my observations. 'I would never have thought it possible. The man who has been spreading the rumours about prisoners being shot in the head carefully informs himself about the expected handling by the Red Army. He is reckoning on captivity but lets no one else know about it.'

'Schmidt was never my friend, but I took him to be consistent in his ways. But in the last few days he has shown his true self. His words and deeds are incompatible. It's a pity that you took his advice, Colonel-General.'

'Now it is too late to talk about it. We have reached the end. Perhaps another chief of staff from the general staff would have helped to make better decisions. But let us leave it.'

Suicide or captivity?

Yes, the end was near. A comprehensive defensive position was no longer available. There were now only strongpoints that could be defended by battle groups. Such a strongpoint stood opposite the department store near the Zaritza, which had already been crossed by the Red Army. It was occupied by Colonel Ludwig's battle group, for which the remains of the 14th Panzer Division were grouped as the army's reserve.

The battle group had set itself up in the ruins of a shop. On the ground and first floors the window spaces had been barricaded with sandbags and bricks. This was now the forward position. The Red Army was already sitting in the Gorki Theatre opposite. Colonel Ludwig regarded this as the last line of defence before the last 'headquarters'. The building was already under direct fire from the enemy's infantry weapons. To the west of us the red-starred tanks were only a few streets away. We really were coming to the end!

Before us now stood the question: suicide or captivity? While Paulus had previously dismissed the notion of suicide, he now began to waver. After a long deliberation he said concernedly: 'Hitler expects especially from me that I commit suicide. What do you think about that, Adam?'

I was angry: 'Until now we have tried to prevent suicide in the army. This is and remains the right thing to do. You too have to share the fate of your soldiers. Should a shell hit our cellar, then we are dead. I would, however, regard it as shameful and cowardly should we end our lives by suicide.'

Paulus seemed to be freed from pressure by my words. He basically thought the same as I did, but wanted to check the consequences of my argument once more. That was his way of doing things.

Lying glorification

Paulus's silence was now at an end. He began to recount his experiences and events in the Führer Headquarters. As deputy chief of staff of the army, subordinate to Colonel-General Halder, Paulus had witnessed many of

Hitler's outbursts of rage. In his presentations, Halder hardly ever got beyond his first sentence before Hitler overwhelmed him with words and went on talking. Paulus described how Hitler's greatest delusion was strongly reinforced by those subservient, praising people around him, with Field Marshal Keitel in the forefront. In the main, as seen through these accounts, Hitler's role and character stood out flashily and naked, and it was barely understandable, even unpardonable, that a person with such intimate knowledge of him had continued to be a follower. This was the 30th January 1943, the tenth anniversary of Hitler's 'seizure of power'. Schmidt had prepared two radio messages to Hitler, which Paulus had signed unaltered. The first read: 'The 6th Army has, faithful to its oath of allegiance, in view of its high and important task, held its position to the last man and the last bullet for Führer and Fatherland. Paulus.' The second radio message included best wishes for the 30th January:

On the anniversary of your seizure of power, the 6th Army congratulates its Führer. The swastika still flies over Stalingrad. Our battle has given the living and coming generations an example, also in the hopelessness of never surrendering, that Germany will win.
Heil mein Führer
Paulus, Col-Gen.

Was that not a mockery of the 6th Army's dreadful fate? Army headquarters could not have done Goebbels, as Reichs Propaganda Minister, a greater service. This radio message gave him an opportunity to glorify the senseless deaths. Hitler replied immediately:

My Colonel-General Paulus!
Already today the whole German people look upon this city with deep emotion. As always in world history, this sacrifice will not be in vain. The creed of von Clausewitz will find its fulfilment. The German nation now understands the whole difficulty of this battle and will make the greatest sacrifice.
With thanks to you and your soldiers,
Your Adolf Hitler

Similar deceitful pathos filled Göring's speech of the 30th January 1943. Cynically he reached out to the still living in the outermost lying cauldron, but also in the homeland: 'It is at last the end that sounds so hard, it is all the same to soldiers, whether fighting at Stalingrad, at Rshev, or in the deserts of Africa, or over in the ice of Norway, who fight and fall.'

I was overcome with disgust as I listened to the fat Air Force marshal. But my anger at Hitler's unscrupulous riff-raff grew, that after his shameless betrayal they now also expected those of us still alive to listen to our own obituaries.

Colonel Ludwig negotiates with the enemy

Towards evening, Schmidt came excitedly to Paulus. 'It has just been reported that Colonel Ludwig is dealing with the Russians. I have ordered his court-martial.'

'Poor Ludwig' was my first thought; it will not be easy for you! As soon as the chief of staff had gone away, I expressed my concerns, but Paulus calmed me down: 'I will not tolerate Ludwig being punished for his individual negotiations.'

Ludwig was taken away by an officer with a steel helmet and slung machine-pistol. This looked very much like punishment and fitted the formula that Schmidt had been using until now: 'Whoever makes individual contact with the enemy will be shot.' Later Ludwig told me that he had expected the chief of staff to have him court-martialled. But something else happened. Schmidt first asked about the securing of the southern front, for which Ludwig was responsible. Then he asked him to sit down. Then came the question that Ludwig was expecting, cool and direct: 'Tell me, I am listening. Have you been dealing with the Russians today?'

The colonel reported how and why it had come to negotiation. He had taken this step because of the falling strength of the troops, and the tens of thousands of unattended wounded and sick. Schmidt watched him attentively as he was speaking. He did not interrupt him with a word, but simply paced to and fro restlessly in his cellar room. Several minutes after Ludwig had finished speaking, he suddenly came to a halt in front of him. 'This is not easy for me, you going straight over to the Russians, negotiating surrender, and nobody comes to us, to headquarters!'

Ludwig did not quite understand this. This was one thing he had not considered. The pigheaded holding-out general was suddenly in favour of surrender. Did he now want to save his own life after having for weeks followed Hitler's and Manstein's strictest orders, and in doing so contributing considerably towards the downfall of the 6th Army?

'If that is all, General,' answered Ludwig, 'I believe that I can promise that early tomorrow, at about 0900 hours, a negotiator will be standing here in front of the cellar.'

'Good, Ludwig, just do that – now, good night.'

Colonel Ludwig had never been so bewildered as he was after this conversation with Schmidt. The latter, following his conversation with the colonel, came to Paulus but did not tell him about the conversation, merely reporting that he had tasked Ludwig with negotiating the surrender of the army headquarters.

This event rounded off the picture of Lieutenant-General Schmidt. Only the day before he had been threatening execution by shooting, and now he was prepared to go into captivity. His life was apparently so precious that he did not want to fight with a gun in his hands. Naturally the contradiction between fighting to the last round, as the troops had been ordered to do, and the generals and senior members of the staff giving up without a fight, did not occur to Schmidt. But this was particularly stupid of Schmidt, who as the army's bad spirit, more than any other, had reacted fanatically and inexorably against any reasonable thinking.

This made his military failure also a deeper failure of his human character.

Red-starred tanks before the department store
After the chief of staff had left, Major-General Roske appeared. Briefly and precisely he reported to Paulus: 'The division is no longer in a position to resist any further. Russian tanks are approaching the department store. This is the end.'

'Thank you, Roske, for everything. Convey my thanks to your officers and soldiers. Schmidt has already asked Ludwig to negotiate with the Red Army.'

I threw the few last remaining pieces of paper into the stove, as well as the dozen Knight's Crosses and German Crosses. But my conscience would not let me part with my duty stamp. I threw it into my briefcase together with the ink pad. Then I went to my assistant, Lieutenant Schlesinger, and the clerks, to bring them up to date on the situation and check to see if everything had been destroyed here too.

For an hour or more I sat with the army commander-in-chief in our narrow room. A candle flickered between us. Not a word was spoken. Both of us were busy with our own thoughts. Finally I broke the silence: 'Colonel-General, you must get some sleep, otherwise you will not be able to stand all day tomorrow. It is going to cost us the rest of our nerves.'

Midnight was past when Paulus and I stretched out on our mattresses. I jumped up once to see Roske. 'Is there anything new?' I asked him as I entered. Roske was destroying the last of the disposable items. He asked me to take a seat, handed me a cigarette and lit one for himself.

'A Red tank is standing in a side street quite close to here with its gun aimed at our ruins. I immediately reported this to Schmidt. He said that the tank must be prevented from shooting, as this could mean death for all of us. That is why an interpreter with a white flag should go over to the tank commander and start surrender negotiations. I will deal with them myself.'

When did the tragedy on the Volga begin?
So, the decision would be made within a few hours. I quietly crept into our room. Paulus was breathing deeply and quietly. I could not sleep. I

frantically sought to bring order to the thoughts revolving in my head. They centred around Paulus, who was lying only an arm's length away from me on his camp bed. He qualified first as a talented general staff officer, for whom a marvellous career was predicted. And where had fate brought him! Fate? Was it really fate that had sentenced him and his quarter of a million-strong army to defeat? To what extent were one's own faults, military and human, attributable to misfortune? Was not the cause of our debacle to be found much earlier, long before the battle on the Volga? I recalled several remarks Paulus had made about his role as deputy chief of the army staff when he had participated in the planning of the war against the Soviet Union. Would it not have been much better not to have begun the Eastern Campaign, indeed the whole war? Was there actually a war aim that could justify these streams of blood, these mountains of rubble, these tears of pity? The war against Soviet Russia was begun on necessary preventive grounds, we were told, necessary to protect us from the threat of Bolshevism. Actually I could never believe it. What I personally experienced on the 22nd June 1941 and in the following weeks of the Eastern Campaign gave absolutely no indication that the Red Army was prepared for a war of aggression, but much more showed that it was no way ready for war, nor sufficiently prepared for defence. In the year and a half of engagement on the Eastern Front I had gained the impression that in former Tsarist Russia, whose hopeless backwardness I knew from the First World War, forces were now at work that wanted to make something new and big, but the difficulties still had not been overcome. Was it really illogical that the ruler in the Kremlin first chose to develop the enormous possibilities of his powerful land, instead of playing with the questionable idea of overrunning Germany? But why, if that was so, if this war from our side was not worth defending, had it been necessary at all?

Terrible! Then all the blood and frightfulness of this war remained clinging to our fingers.

Could I continue living under such a terrible burden? Would I ever get a clear answer to my question of the sense of our downfall after the justification of this war?

What was my life?
I was as if bewitched. During these hours of the night I sought answers, clarity. Instead of finding them, I became involved in further questions and ever more lack of clarity. It soon seemed as if in the forty years of my conscious life I had asked too few questions, as if too much had seemed too clear and problem-free, as if too much had seemed important that in fact was not. Was this really my life, running on what tracks?

I saw before me my parents' farm in Eichen, near Hanau am Main, the pride but also the burden of my clever father and my hardworking mother, who died much too young. Their whole love and concern were for their two sons, my older brother and I. Our parents did everything to give us a happy childhood. They – as well as our grandparents – set us certain standards and norms for life. Thus my father was connected with his home earth, a capable farmer honoured and respected in the village. The word 'Germany' had in his mouth a high, self-conscious sound. That was much like my grandfather on my mother's side. He was mayor at the head of the Eichen community for over twenty-five years. He sat as a member of the provincial parliament in Kassel and was an ardent admirer of the old Reichs Chancellor Bismarck. A Wilhelm von Bismarck, as district president of Hanau, was for several years his immediate superior.

It was in this atmosphere that my brother and I were brought up to love our homeland and be faithful to our ruling house. My parents' upbringing had a substantial influence on my life, which was further developed at school and later at the teachers' training college with a number of illustrative materials and slides. For instance, from 1910 to 1913 I had a geography teacher who could not give a lesson without making some hateful remark about England. Deep into our minds were sown the roots of sources of German arrogance, German nationalism, even chauvinism. The love of Germany, love of our country, was for my grandfather and my father, for myself and most of my generation coupled with a feeling of German superiority, a claim to superiority in the world, the need to fight and exploit a legitimate right and our holy duty. The First World War was a logical consequence of this. There was nothing frightful about it for me. Like many tens of thousands, I marched off inspired to protect throne and altar.

I came back bitter and disappointed that Germany had lost the war. At odds with the injustice of fate, I sought forgetfulness in studying and teaching. But soon my pleasure in the teaching trade faded. I was teaching at the school in Langenselbold, a working community near Hanau am Main. In my memory appear many blond, brunette or black heads. How the faces glowed with zeal when we opened a tumulus, laid the ground for a specific local museum, or improved our strength with sport and games! The older ones among my then pupils must have long since donned military uniform. How many of them had fallen or been wounded? I did not now know; following my return to military service as a teacher of mathematics at the Weimar army trade school in January 1929, and my enrolment as a captain in the Wehrmacht in 1934, I maintained only a loose connection with my previous work as a teacher.

One face from that time which had especially imprinted itself on my mind was Röder's. He was a Communist, apparently the only one that I had got to know then. I had two of his sons in my school. The father willingly assisted us as a hard worker and gave us various plans and projects. I got on well with him. However, when it came to talking about politics, I waved him off. I was not interested. I left him with the phrase that one was hearing more and more: 'Hitler means war!'

When the First World War had ended with the defeat of Germany, I was annoyed that I could no longer remain an officer. The desire to be an officer increased in me during the whole time of the Weimar Republic. In 1934, the second year of Hitler's rule, came fulfilment. I forgot the Communist Röder almost completely, and was proud of the successes that Hitler obtained: general conscription, the air force, a U-boat fleet, the occupation of the Rhineland, the return of the Saar, the acquisition of Austria, the occupation of the Sudetenland, the formation of the Böhmen-Mähren protectorate.

Did these successes not confirm our right and our claim to leadership? And all without war! With it came the ending of unemployment, and the arrival of the autobahns. Hitler was indeed a genial leader – which was how I saw him then. My grandfather was still living, having also replaced Bismarck with Hitler. Certainly he had done some unpleasant things: the arrest of Communists and some others. They were isolated in camps, one was told. Humanly regrettable, I said to myself, thinking of Röder. But why did they oppose a development that made Germany unmistakably stronger and mightier! I felt myself remote from *Kristallnacht* and other repressive measures against the Jews. But in the end I was not responsible for it. And moreover one should not forget the great results that National Socialism had brought to the German people – so I sought to unburden myself. A little thorn of doubt remained within me, but what significance did it have in contrast to the unending appearance of Hitler's chain of happy accomplishments?

Germany's luck or misfortune?
Then came the 1st September 1939 and war against Poland. I detected then that a new section of Hitler's policies had begun, a more earnest section. The Communist Röder had been right so far. But the Polish campaign was over in just eight days, a great victory obtained. During this time France and England had stood by with their weapons ready. Denmark and Norway were also occupied only half a year after Poland. Then the strongest military nation on the continent, France, was overrun in six weeks and forced into unconditional surrender, 'the insult of Versailles' eradicated. The British 'learnt how to run', as we put it, at Dunkirk and were quickly chased into the sea. Another great victory, perhaps the greatest in the comet-like rise of the Third Reich. Unfortunately it had demanded a hard sacrifice from my wife and I. Our son Heinz fell on the 16th May 1940. That was a hard blow, a pain that others attributed to the 'unpleasant aspects' of the Nazis. He was my own flesh and blood, my only son. My wife never recovered from this loss. This too gave my heart pain when I thought about it. But as a soldier

he was prepared to die for Germany, for the fatherland, as I believed, as a sacrifice.

Again the fanfares sounded for victories, announcing successes in the U-boat war, in Africa and in the Balkans. Despite a few minor setbacks, the German chain of luck seemed to grow to broader, more handsome bounds.

Then came the 22nd June 1941. The German Wehrmacht advanced along a front of some 2,000 kilometres against the Soviet Union, supported by Rumanian and Finnish units. The world held its breath. I, who crossed the Soviet border towards Kovno that day with the XXIIIrd Corps, was not quite in the mood. This was the feared 'war on two fronts'. And we had put ourselves in this position with an attack on a vast enemy about whom we knew very little. But at first it all seemed to go surprisingly well. The fanfares of victory sounded every day. The chain of luck was extended by new important links. Then something happened that we had not experienced in the eight years of Hitler's reign. Next to the chain of luck began a chain of misfortune. And it began with the massive links formed by the German defeats at Moscow and Leningrad, in Kalinin, Smolensk, Oriol, Kursk, Charkov, Stalino and on the Kertch peninsula in the winter of 1941/42. But these links were small in comparison to the defeats that followed in the winter of 1942/43, especially that of the downfall of the 6th Army.

I was filled with a fearful anxiety. Who truly understood this disastrous development? What would become of Germany if the enemy approached the German borders at this rate? How long would the other fronts hold out? What if the destruction of the 6th Army anticipated the destruction of Germany?

These tortuous questions continued to persecute me in the troubled dreams of a short nap.

'The Russians are here'
31st January 1942, 0700 hours. The day dawned pale and hardly noticeably. Paulus was still asleep. It took quite a time before I found a way out of my tormenting thoughts and confused dreams. Then I could have gone to sleep, but it could not have been for long. I already wanted to get up without making a noise when someone knocked at the door. Paulus woke and got up. The chief of staff entered. He handed a piece of paper to the commander-in-chief with the words: 'I congratulate you on your promotion to field marshal. The radio message was the last to arrive early in the morning.'

'That is just an order to commit suicide, but I will not grant this favour,' said Paulus after he had read the message.

Schmidt went on: 'At the same time I have to tell you that the Russians are outside.' With these words he took a step back and opened the door. A Russian general walked in with an interpreter and declared us his prisoners. I laid our pistols down on the table. 'Get ready to leave. I will take you from here at 0900 hours. You will drive in your own vehicle,' said the interpreter, translating for the Soviet general, and they left the room again.

It was just as well that I still had my official stamp. I performed my last official duty; I entered in Paulus's pay book his promotion to field marshal and applied the official stamp, which I then threw into the burning stove.

Then I went to Roske, wanting to know what had happened during the night. He reported as follows: 'As I told you several hours ago, Schmidt had tasked the interpreter to go over to the Soviet tank commander with a white flag. After you had left me, I went over with the interpreter. I could see the tank from the yard entrance, and I could see it clearly, as it had meanwhile come closer. The hatch was open and a young officer was looking out. Our interpreter waved the white flag and approached the tank. I heard him speaking to the Russian. Afterwards he told me that he had suggested to him: "Have the firing stop! I have something quite big. Promotion and awards! You can come with me and take the commander-in-chief and the whole of the 6th Army's staff prisoner." The young officer sent a radio message to his commander. Two other officers and some soldiers appeared. They came up to the yard entrance, where I received them. We went down into the cellars by a nearby entrance, which was near Schmidt's room. It had been shut off with sandbags until then, but Schmidt ordered it to be cleared.

'The negotiations were then conducted in my presence. I suggested that the commander-in-chief be called, but Schmidt refused. Apparently he wanted it documented that he had conducted the army negotiations in accordance with his wishes. The chief of staff tasked me with conducting the negotiations. He himself would only intervene if he thought it necessary. Meanwhile a general and several officers had appeared from the Soviet side. After a formal greeting, he tasked me with negotiating the surrender conditions. In doing so he left no question or proposal to me. When I wanted to agree, Schmidt joined in the talking that he had been holding back from until then. He wanted to introduce some unclear questions. You, Adam, would have been as astounded as I was when I heard:

"Firstly, whether the field marshal could retain his personal orderly; secondly, whether he could take some foodstuffs still in his possession with him; thirdly, whether it was not possible for the field marshal to have a Red Army bodyguard for his personal protection on the journey to captivity". Quite clearly I was ashamed at this point. I had seen Paulus often in the last weeks and spoken to him. I could not accept that he had given Schmidt such instructions.'

'I have been with him for the last few days and gained some insight into his inner self. I also regard this as out of the question. If he had been concerned with such things, he would have discussed them with me and not the chief of staff. But what did Schmidt want to achieve with these demands? Much of his stubborn behaviour has also trickled through to the troops. He seems to have a bad conscience. How did the Soviet general respond to these questions?'

'I had the impression that he was as surprised about them as I was. Instead of an answer, he asked the question, where actually was Paulus? Schmidt replied with a smile: "The field marshal did not want to become involved in the negotiations but to be handled as a private person." That was absolute nonsense, as this phraseology was contrary to what had only shortly before been asked of Paulus.'

'The Soviet general must have had a fine impression of German generals. I take this as being a secret of Schmidt's with which he perhaps wanted to gain advantages for himself. Paulus had never charged Schmidt to obtain special conditions for himself.'

Major-General Roske concluded his report with: 'The last radio message was sent at 0545 hours: "The Russians are standing at the door. We are destroying . . .". Several minutes later the radio station was destroyed.'

Deeply ashamed about what I had heard, I went back to my room. On the way I decided not to tell Paulus about it. I wanted to spare him any further stress at this time. I sat at the table completely indifferently. I got up as the time to leave came nearer.

'Prepare the staff transport to leave, Adam. Have two cars and a truck made ready!'

The big entrance to the cellar was closed and guarded by Red Army sentries. The duty officer permitted me and the driver to enter the yard where the vehicles were parked. I stopped in surprise.

Soviet and German soldiers, who had been shooting at each other only a few hours ago, were standing here in the yard together peacefully, their weapons in their hands or slung. But what a shattering contrast! Here the German soldiers, ragged, in thin greatcoats over shabby uniforms, as lean as rakes, emaciated, exhausted figures with hollow cheeks and stubbled faces, there the Red Army soldiers, well kempt, vigorous, in wonderful winter clothing. It made me think back to the chain of luck and the chain of misfortune that had not let me rest the night before.

The appearance of the soldiers of the Red Army seemed to me symbolic of the changed conditions of victory and defeat. I was deeply gripped by another observation. Instead of beating our soldiers or even shooting them in the back of the neck, the Soviet men in the midst of the rubble of the city we had destroyed were digging in their pockets for their last pieces of bread, their cigarettes and their tobacco to offer to the human wrecks of German soldiers.

Punctually at 0900 hours the chief of staff of the Soviet 64th Army appeared to take away the commander-in-chief of the defeated German 6th Army and his staff. We climbed into our ready vehicles. Paulus and Schmidt took seats in the first vehicle, the Soviet general sitting next to the driver. I went in the second one with a Red Army lieutenant. The remaining officers and men of the staff followed in the truck.

The sounds of fighting had completely died away. The southern cauldron had ceased to exist. The central cauldron, commanded until the last by Colonel-General Heitz, also surrendered on the 31st January 1943.

Paulus, still bound by the Hitler Order, did not feel himself empowered to order the commanders of the other cauldrons to surrender, as Hitler had appointed them personally. For the troops in the northern cauldron the inferno went on for another two whole days. Despite the pressing representations of Generals Lattmann and von Lenski, the commander of the northern cauldron, Colonel-General Strecker, refused to give up the fighting. Finally, on the morning of the 2nd February 1943 the two generals themselves gave the order to surrender. The battle on the Volga was over.

Chapter 6

New Shores

The train of the defeated

At the head and tail of our small convoy drove a Soviet truck occupied by submachine-gun troops. Tightly closed up, the vehicles drove at a slow speed past the snow-covered and still-smoking ruins of former housing blocks, administrative buildings, schools, hospitals, theatres and factories. An immense mixture of German war material of all kinds, destroyed or still intact, crowded the icy streets. In between the remains of the 6th Army dragged themselves into captivity in larger or smaller groups escorted by Red Army troops. Many of the exhausted and emaciated soldiers were supporting each other. Often two half-starved men carried along a wounded man, who clung to them. Many cursed us, as the shamefully betrayed soldiers recognised the 6th Army's commander-in-chief and his escort in the overtaking vehicles.

In the last frightful weeks in the cauldron Paulus had begun to grasp what a vast personal responsibility he bore through his unconditional obedience to Hitler and the Army High Command. But this reinforced his resignation to the situation and on the other hand enabled his essentially active chief of staff Schmidt to send his last forces senselessly into the fire. Now it was all too late. So much was clear to me on the 31st January 1943 that the question of blame for the defeat of the 6th Army, for all the generals and high commanders, was that they only surrendered when the Soviet troops appeared right in front of their own bunkers. It need not have come to this picture of distress that we now saw through the windscreens of our vehicles. Accepting the Red Army's offer of surrender of the 8th January 1943 would have spared these thousands of men some three and a half weeks of hunger and icy cold. Their state of health would have been considerably better at the beginning of their captivity when the typhus had not yet broken out so strongly. I found our involvement a great crime. Its exponents were Hitler and the Forces High Command and the Army High Command, but also Manstein and his headquarters at Army Group 'Don'. That there were deeper roots of guilt, that these persons functioned as representatives and tools of pernicious forces and sinister mental attitudes in German history, I did not then suspect. I was generally physically and mentally so empty and burnt out that I could hardly bring myself to think.

To me it was like awakening from a frightful nightmare when the vehicle left the city centre and drove across open country in a southerly direction. We were moving forwards quickly now. The Volga soon appeared on our left. After a short stop at several new-looking buildings that apparently served as quarters for a high-ranking staff, the drive went on parallel to the river. Two hours later we entered Beketovka.

Meeting the victors
We stopped in front of one of the dominating wooden houses. My eyes fell on artistically carved window frames and gables. Then our escorting general was already asking us to enter the building. After we had left our coats and hats in an entrance room, we were led into a larger room. What was going to happen next? As if he wanted to take his leave, Paulus reached out his hand to Schmidt and myself. Goebbels' propaganda had hit us even deeper in the bones than we ourselves wanted.

A Soviet general had sat down on the opposite side of the T-shaped table. As it soon turned out, this was Shumilov, the commander-in-chief of the 64th Army. Next to him now sat his chief of staff Major-General Laskin, the general who had brought us here, and an interpreter with the rank of major. I was directed to a seat on the long side of the table. Schmidt had shortly before told me: 'Apart from giving our personal details, keep quiet about everything else.' I found this warning superfluous and tactless.

Shumilov addressed our commander-in-chief as 'von Paulus', whereupon the latter said: 'I am not of the nobility.' The Soviet general looked at him disbelievingly. When Paulus was asked for his rank, he said: 'Field marshal', which only increased the mistrust. Then Paulus took his pay book from his inside breast pocket and handed it to the Soviet army commander. He soon understood it through the interpreter and gave it back with a short '*harasho*'.

As the interview continued, General Shumilov asked Paulus if he had given the northern group the order to surrender. Paulus denied it, as this group came immediately under Hitler. Now something will happen, I thought. Our propaganda had always insisted that the Russians would torture anyone who did not meet their demands. Discreetly I considered the Soviet commander-in-chief. Shumilov spoke quietly and pertinently. Nothing happened. While I was still in a state of surprise, the general stood up. The interpreter translated his last words: 'Tell the field marshal that I am asking him to take a drink with me before I drive off to my headquarters!'

Was this really meant? Outside, Soviet soldiers helped us into our coats. Excitedly we moved towards the entrance, where Shumilov, wearing a tall fur hat on his head, awaited us. He crossed the road and signed for us to follow him. Was this far enough? I looked around me. No execution squad in sight. But perhaps they were waiting behind the wooden building to which the general was walking?

Nothing like it. Shumilov opened the door to a lobby in which an old woman was housekeeping. On footstools stood basins of steaming water and alongside each was a piece of real soap – a luxury I had not seen for a long time. A young girl handed everyone a white towel. Washing was a delight. For days we had only been able to wash our faces and hands in thawed snow water, damply rubbed off.

Afterwards we were invited into the next room. There stood a covered table with various things to eat. I was ashamed as I sat down at Shumilov's request with Paulus and Schmidt. What lies had been told to us about the bloodthirsty Bolsheviks! And we were so primitive as to believe them! I must think about more generals of the Red Army that had passed through our headquarters as prisoners of war. Only the Ic responsible for intelligence about the enemy was interested in them. We other officers of the staff found it beneath our dignity even to say a word to them. They were given only a meal from the field kitchen before being sent back further to the rear.

The gentlemanly behaviour of the victorious Soviet army commander had made no impression on Schmidt. He whispered quietly to me: 'Take nothing, if they offer us something to drink; it could be poisoned.' This spoon-feeding of instructions was repulsive and annoying. I gave Schmidt an angry look to make him understand. If General Shumilov had understood it! He said quietly: 'It would be much more pleasant if we had got to know one another under other circumstances, if I could greet you here as my guests and not as prisoners of war.'

Vodka was consumed by all from the same bottle. The general invited us to drink with him to the victorious Red Army. But we remained sitting motionlessly. After the interpreter had said a few quiet words, Shumilov laughed: 'I don't want to upset you. Let us drink to the two brave enemies that confronted each other in Stalingrad!'

Now Paulus, Schmidt and I raised our glasses. Not long afterwards the vodka began to take effect upon our empty stomachs. I felt a light dizziness. This vanished, however, when I took a small bite of bread. Paulus and Schmidt also tucked in.

We sat together with General Shumilov for more than an hour. I took in keenly everything I saw and heard. The major spoke very good German. For the first time I heard that the Soviet people well knew the difference between the Hitler system and the German people. The Soviet officers assured us that despite everything that had happened, trust in the German worker and the German scientist had not been lost. They were nevertheless surprised that so many Germans had let themselves be misused by Hitler.

Paulus asked for special attention for the wounded, sick and half-starved German soldiers, and the Soviet army commander assured him it would be given to the utmost possibility.

'Do you still have a wish, Field Marshal?' asked Shumilov as the time to go approached. Paulus said briefly: 'I would like to ask you to let my adjutant, Major Adam, remain with me.'

General Shumilov gave an instruction to an officer, who immediately left the room. Shortly afterwards he got up and escorted us to the vehicle waiting to take us further on. He said goodbye with a handshake, saying to Paulus: 'Your wish will be fulfilled.' He stood saluting on the edge of the road as the car moved off. He was a truly noble opponent.

In a village near the Soviet front headquarters
As our next destination Shumilov had allotted the front headquarters, which roughly compared with our headquarters. Our vehicle rattled over the battlefield between the Volga and the Don, the night shrouding the horrors of the scene as an icy wind penetrated our vehicle. Hunched together, I sat in a corner of the rear seat next to our staff interpreter, with two Soviet officers in front of me. I was able to orientate myself from the starry sky. We were driving in a northerly direction, but not for long before the vehicle stopped. Pocket torches flashed at a checkpoint. Our escorting officers answered the questions asked. Everything was in order. The vehicle drove on. We experienced these stops and starts several times during the night's journey. The roads were constantly blocked with barricades. I had to think about our officers' escape plan. They would have no chance with such rigid controls.

Our small convoy stopped again and I heard my name being called. An officer entered our vehicle and asked me to accompany him. His tone was less friendly. I followed him with my heart thumping. At the head of the column I was told to get into a small cross-country vehicle and I had hardly sat down, squeezed in between two officers on the back seat, when it drove off again. There was soon nothing to be seen of the other vehicles. Despite the experience with General Shumilov, I was uneasy. I felt better again when several vehicles appeared behind us at the next stop, in one of which I recognised Paulus.

We had been under way in this cutting cold since 1500 hours, crushed and half-frozen in these vehicles without being able to move much. It was coming up to midnight when I was finally able to climb out in front of a small wooden house. While I was getting out of the vehicle, I noticed that Paulus and Schmidt had left their vehicle. Together we approached a Soviet staff officer standing in front of the building, which was guarded by sentries at each corner.

The door opened from inside. The first thing I noticed in entering was a comfortable warmth. A young senior lieutenant greeted us in German. He explained to Paulus and Schmidt that they should occupy a large room in which there were two beds, a table and several chairs. My sleeping place was in the first room opposite the door of the bricked-in stove, which extended deep into the room allocated to the two generals.

While our frozen bodies were slowly thawing in the pleasant warmth, a senior officer entered the room and asked Paulus and Schmidt to go with him to the front headquarters, where they were expected by Generals Rokossovski and Voronov. Meanwhile the senior lieutenant talked about Moscow, his home city, in which he had studied architecture. He talked about the Kremlin, the Metro and the theatres. As I expressed my wonder at his command of the German language, I received the information that was later even more frequently encountered in similar form: 'Many of us learn German, the language of Marx and Engels. I would like to recommend to you that you learn Russian during your captivity.'

Shortly after 0200 hours a car brought Paulus and Schmidt back. I learned from them that the interview had followed the same formalities and questions as had occurred with the staff of the Soviet 64th Army. As before in Beketovka, Paulus asked the commander-in-chief of the Soviet front for the utmost possible help and care for surviving German soldiers and officers. The Soviet general replied: 'Of course there is not for today or tomorrow sufficient supplies for 90,000 additional mouths. But we will do everything humanly possible for them.'

We were dead tired and sought to go to bed as soon as possible. I was the first awake in the morning when the senior lieutenant gave me a shake.

On the morning of the 1st February we were able to walk around a bit with the senior lieutenant. We did not learn the name of the place that we were in. Our questions about it were met with a shrug of the shoulders. It was unimportant. We were much more interested in the fact that all the surviving generals of the 6th Army would assemble here in the next few days. We were separated from them by a field so we did not get together with them, but we could watch them taking a daily walk from our little house.

During our first days as prisoners of war, the unusual peace and regular meals, I gradually lost the stupefaction and tenseness that had crippled me during the last days in the cauldron. Much more I felt the burden of being hemmed in. Here in this village we had no newspapers or books available. We sat at the table for hours, each busy with his thoughts. Even a look through the window at the level, single-coloured snowy landscape could not lighten our dreary mood. Paulus was at the end of his strength.

Railway journey to an unknown destination

On the 5th or 6th February we were moved, but only for two or three days, then we had to prepare to travel again. Trucks brought all the 6th Army's prisoner of war generals to one of the railway lines passing near the place. On an open stretch by a stationmaster's house was a train, in the middle of which a carriage had been kept free. We were somewhat astounded at the bed sheets, blankets and white-covered pillows in the sleeping part of the carriage.

An old woman acted as interpreter. Through her the train commandant greeted Paulus and informed him about the situation at the front. We also discovered that there were officers of our army in the other wagons, but nevertheless we were not allowed to make contact.

Where were we going? We dared not ask. During the night I stood for some time at the window of our darkened compartment. Larger and smaller settlements went by. They showed no signs of destruction. Only the many troop transports rolling to the front reminded one of the war. Our train rolled along slowly and was often shunted into sidings.

Things came alive early in the generals' wagon. The washing and shaving took longer, then the attendant brought hot tea into the carriage. I took breakfast with Schmidt in Paulus's section.

When I looked out of the window again, my eyes found a changed landscape. The dirty grey snow-covered steppe had vanished. Vast woods in their proud winter clothing extended far off on either side of the railway, frequently broken by settlements at whose stations business activity was being conducted. Women in long rows offered the products of the countryside: bread, chickens, milk, butter and many other things needed by people on long journeys. Soldiers on the troop trains and travellers on the regular train services had brisk need for the items on offer. Every stop at the stations was used to obtain hot water in the tea urns at special taps. Unfortunately I was unable to decipher the place names at the stations, as I did not know the Cyrillic alphabet.

Now and then curious civilians tried to get near our train when we stopped, but they were held back at a respectful distance by our guards. I observed a few scowls from this or that Soviet citizen at those who had devastated their country and brought death to many, but I noticed no offensive gestures against us. How long we travelled I no longer know, but it could have been two or three days and nights. One morning we stopped at a station and were told to prepare to leave the train.

Krasnogorsk prisoner-of-war camp

'Another short journey by bus and you will be at your destination,' said the train commander to the field marshal. And so it was. We drove through a town, but there was not much to see. My general impression was of a little country town, like many I had got to see during the war. After a few minutes our bus stopped before a closed high wooden gate. To the right of it stood a little wooden house. A high barbed wire fence stretched away on both sides. We were in front of the Krasnogorsk prisoner-of-war camp near Moscow. Proper camp life was about to begin.

The camp commandant and duty officer emerged from the guardroom and asked us to follow some of the guards along the road through the camp. On the right side were three long barrack huts, on the left was a small hut, the cookhouse, which we soon came to. Beyond the cookhouse were another log hut and a barrack hut. Some shelters could be made out further along.

The arrival of the 'Stalingrad Generals' naturally caused a sensation among the 'old' prisoners of war. Curiously they stood in aprons and white caps in front of the kitchen or leaned out of the barrack hut windows. The camp did not seem to be strongly occupied.

On the third hut on the right of the street was the word 'Ambulatorium'. It seemed that this housing even had back doors. We entered one of them and waited in a large room for further developments. This gave me an opportunity to look around. On the door was a notice in the German language. Under the heading 'Extract from the orders of the People's Commissar for Defence', I read: 'Hitlers come and go, but the German people remain.'

I had heard similar words on the 31st January during our interview with General Shumilov. Somehow it impressed me more at that time. Now I believed, just as the generals also did, that it could be dismissed as propaganda. Had I been influenced by being together with them every day, usually sounding arrogant and dismissive? Apparently. In any case these words would haunt me during the coming months and years.

After bathing and delousing, we were divided up among the barracks. Paulus, Schmidt and I were allocated a room in the log hut. In a large room of this building lived six Rumanian generals, and in a smaller room were three Italians. Apart from them, the camp also housed further officer prisoners of war as well as other ranks. German doctor prisoners of war worked in the Ambulatorium under the charge of a female Soviet doctor.

At first captivity encompassed a kind of stress and expectation. With a certain agitation we regarded the unknown and the uncertainty. But this feeling vanished quickly in the sense of regularity: getting up, three meals a day, walks, afternoon and night sleeps, gave the day its pattern. Early in the morning and late in the evening the duty officer went through the accommodation. Once a week we went to the baths to bathe. Hygiene and cleanliness were especially important; '*giasno*' (dirty) was one of the first Russian words I learnt, from a Soviet doctor's assistant who expected painful cleanliness in the rooms. Even the generals took this young woman seriously when she entered the rooms and looked at the floors, beds and windows with critical eyes.

Our conversation in the first days and weeks turned overwhelmingly to everyday camp matters, to individual episodes in the cauldron battle on the Volga, to previous personal experiences and to families back home. Everyone tried to grasp the concept of imprisonment. Deep discussions about the causes of the catastrophe on the Volga, about blame and guilt, and about its effect on the further progress of the war were temporarily avoided, perhaps because we were all in a kind of mental paralysis, a kind of trance, after the frightful experiences we had gone through, or because our individual consciences were switched off from any connection with Stalingrad and the tragic German defeat in the war against the hated Bolshevism.

The camp library
But life went on, the war too. After the inferno of the destructive battle, a person with the least spiritual substance could not just dream about food and revel in memories. He needed a new sense of life, a new support and a real hope. He needed to escape from the relentless honourable self-respect in personal ways and in the ways of our people that had led us to defeat. It applied too to any dealings with the Soviet state, with its social order and its goals, especially with the sources of its might and strength that we had apparently so rudely underestimated. In this concern with understanding oneself, books were valuable assistants.

In the camp there was an extensive library equipped with the finest fiction and political literature in the German language. The library came under a German NCO called Beyer. No one was obliged to serve themselves, nor did anyone have to sign for the books taken out.

Once our lives had begun to take on a regular pattern again and the usual sources of conversation were exhausted, I went to the library to find my way around. For over a quarter of an hour I leafed through the registers, and then I selected several German classical romances and books for Paulus and Schmidt. Almost all the prisoners were then asking for fiction.

One day, when I had already become a keen user of the library, the librarian offered me some of the brochures lying on a display table. These were explanatory texts against Hitler. I knew that these were hardly ever read by the officers, but nevertheless I picked up several copies and read the titles and some extracts here and there. I did not like the language at all; it was full of fascism, imperialism, militarism, revenge. It seemed to me as if some things were simply asserted but not proved. I did not feel interested and therefore did not take the brochures with me. But I went off with a blue-bound book entitled 'The Land of Socialism – Today and Tomorrow'. It contained the Central Committee's report on the XVIIIth Party Day of the Communist Party of the Soviet Union, the 10th March 1939.

The book fascinated me because it gave me for the first time a representation of the development of society, economy and culture in the

Soviet Union. This brought comparisons with Ukraine, whose backwardness I had got to know during the First World War as a young second lieutenant and orderly officer of a German infantry brigade. I took the book in order to learn more about the Soviet Union, especially about Socialism. I also wanted to concern myself with the works of Marx and Engels for the theoretical basis of Socialism. I had heard their names at school in connection with the 1848 Revolution. Otherwise I knew only that Karl Marx had written a thick book about Capitalism. So I asked for *Das Kapital* at the camp library. I read some of it but did not understand the meaning of it. There were ideas in it that I had never heard of before in my life. I lacked not only the knowledge but also the will to conduct a successful study of this work. Disappointed, I returned the book. I got on better with the works of Friedrich Engels. I followed his historical works, especially his military historical dissertation, with great interest.

Hitler and the Red Cross postcards
By then I was not far from a new, firm, mental point of view. But from the first day of captivity I did not count myself as one of Hitler's obstinate, inveterate followers. Full of indignation, I saw how those officers and generals who I knew had condemned Hitler and his system in Stalingrad now appeared to have forgotten everything. When one day I heard two officers greet each other with 'Heil Hitler!' loudly and demonstratively on the camp road, I was at first glance inclined to think it had been a mental derangement. Soon, however, I had to accept that there were many among the generals and officers who remained fanatical adherents of Hitler, despite their experiences on the Volga. Among them were Colonel-General Horst and Lieutenant-General Artur Schmidt, the 6th Army's former chief of staff. Some of the stress that I had felt in living together with him was rooted in his radical approval of the war.

My hatred of Hitler and his rule was reinforced when I discovered that the 'Führer' had forbidden the despatch of Red Cross postcards written by members of our families. How happy I was, like all the other occupants of the camp, at last to receive the first card in March 1943. Thus within a few weeks my wife and daughter would be relieved of their worst concerns. And we could write a card every month. In fact the next card arrived in April.

Then came a rumour that shocked me: Hitler had declared in a radio address to the German people that the Stalingraders were dead. We wanted to know for certain, so we asked both the Soviet camp commandant and the German anti-Fascists who visited our camp. Hitler's betrayal of the members of the 6th Army was confirmed by both parties.

To Susdal Monastery
We had already been two months in Krasnogorsk when the Soviet duty

officer and an interpreter appeared in our cabin one afternoon and announced the camp commandant's orders: 'Get ready! The generals and Colonel Adam are being moved to another camp. Rations to be collected immediately!'

This was on the 25th April, a warm spring day. We were ready to go within half an hour, but we had to wait for the order to go outside. The day was already coming to an end when we assembled with our baggage at the barrack gate. We were called forward by name and climbed into a bus, only Paulus taking a seat in a car. The escort was divided up between two trucks. Then we set off for Moscow.

It was dark when we neared the outskirts. On the right side of the street ranged multi-storeyed houses, some only partly completed. Most still had scaffolding around them. The interpreter explained to me that the building work had had to be abandoned on the outbreak of war.

During the night we crossed Moscow from west to east. The broad streets were unlit and almost empty of people. In one square the interpreter indicated the large buildings of the Belorussian railway station.

At last we left the sea of buildings behind us. We were so strongly bumped about on the rough country roads that sleep was out of the question for a long time. Finally fatigue overtook us and conversation died down. I too dozed off until a loud snore behind me woke me with a start. I looked at the time. Midnight had passed. Somewhere between sleeping and waking I noticed we were passing several large villages and later a town. Day was beginning. I was finally awake.

'Where are we?' I asked the interpreter. He gave a sleepy reply: 'In Vladimir', which did not stop me asking: 'How much longer will it take until we reach our destination?'

'You will soon see for yourself,' he said.

Our vehicle was fast approaching a small town. The copper roofs of numerous towers were visible from afar in the spring sunlight. This was Susdal, an old prince's and bishop's seat. We went through the massive open gate of a fortress wall with its loopholes and defensive towers to a long building complex, whose centre point was a church with five onion towers and a bell tower standing before it. Along the sides crouched long buildings of one or two storeys used as accommodation for officer prisoners of war. The commandant, Colonel Novikov, a wiry officer with a light but ringing commanding voice, took us to our quarters. I was allocated a room with Schmidt.

As in Krasnogorsk, the first days in Susdal were taken up with adjusting to our changed circumstances. Susdal offered material for several interesting studies. It was the former capital of the Susdal kingdom, one of the three Russian principalities after those of Novgorod and Kiev. Its fortress-like appearance was due to the former danger from the Tartars. Until the fall of the Czars it had formed, with its vast acreage, one of the trading bastions most closely connected with the Czar and the church. It had become a dreamy country town. And now it housed within its walls prisoners of war, officers of the Rumanian, Hungarian, Italian and German armies.

In the months of June and July I experienced the famous 'white nights' here. Up until midnight it was so light that one could read outside. Equally wonderful were the early morning hours and the time shortly before sundown. Nature, buildings and people took on such splendid colours under the flood of light as I have never experienced before or since.

Dispute over German history

Looking back, the stay in Susdal left a lasting impression on me. On one of the warm summer evenings of 1943 I had an encounter with Professor Arnold. He had come to Susdal from Moscow and was expressly at the disposal of the generals and officers. Most of us had questions and problems enough. Arnold seemed to me to be small in stature but soon after his first words I noted that I had a spirited, extraordinary, highly intellectual man in front of me, a clever, kindly person to converse with, who had an exceptional command of the German language. Our conversation quickly revealed the character of an informal conversationalist, although our talk soon became heated when we spoke about German history of the last 150 years. History had always interested me, and not only professionally as a former teacher. I had worked my way through the works of Treischke, Sybel, Ranke and many others. I was proud of my knowledge of history and imagined I had a firm view of it.

Professor Arnold proved that in the disastrous course of German history, in the decisive points of 1813, 1848, 1870/71, 1918 and 1933 it was not the German people, not the democrats, but the anti-democratic forces that had won. The people had fought well and made sacrifices, but politically they had always been defrauded of the fruits of their fighting. And further, the German people had been misused, unlike any other people, for a war that was not in the national interest, but for the self-seeking conquests and goals of its ruling elite.

'Please understand me correctly,' said Professor Arnold, 'I am far from contradicting the German people's great humanitarian traditions, their towering contribution to the spiritual treasure-chamber of humanity. Already we Soviet people treasure the greatness of those German spiritual giants, Goethe and Schiller, Kant and Hegel, Bach and Beethoven, Kepler and Einstein, not to mention Marx and Engels, who have really become the teachers in our country. But think of Bismarck, the Prussian Junker, who had boundless contempt for democracy and the will of the people!'

'Excuse me,' I interrupted him, 'but Bismarck was the blacksmith of Germany unity, the creator of the Reich.'

'Certainly Bismarck had shown an understanding of the historical necessity that German unification had long since put on the agenda. But please consider how and by what forces the German Kaiser Reich of 1871 was grounded. When Bismarck became minister president of Prussia in 1862, he proclaimed that the problems of the time would be decided not by liberal ideas, but by blood and iron. The Reich came about as a result of three wars. It was founded in the Hall of Mirrors at Versailles, not by the German people but by the German princes. The princes, not the then already economically leading burgers, had the political power of the Kaiser Reich in their hands. They were, however, ultimately responsible to God for their deeds.'

'I don't understand your criticism of Bismarck's politics. He was all for good neighbourly relations with Russia and concluded the German–Russian reassurance agreement.'

'Let us leave open the question whether Bismarck really wanted good neighbourly relations with Russia,' said Arnold, taking up my objection, 'and let us look overall at the motives for his Russian policy, which for me seem to have been dictated more by fear than by friendship, for one has to recognise certain realistic aims of his foreign policies. Bismarck as a statesman was in this aspect much more far-sighted than that lunatic Hitler. Had Hitler learned from Bismarck at this stage, all of us would have been spared much suffering. Apart from this, Hitler has taken many negative things from Bismarck's policies: the hatred of democracy, worker mobility and Socialism, the struggle for power, war-lusting National Socialism, social demagogy. From the Bismarck era a straight line leads directly into the Chauvinism of Wilhelm II and to the excessive conquest plans of Hitler, with which you too, Herr Adam, have been involved.'

'You are talking about the same things in German history, Professor Arnold. It so happens that I have studied history myself and believe that I know at least something about it. For me Bismarck is the outstanding statesman of his time. Perhaps your criticism has a touch of envy? And Hitler may have made some bad mistakes, but as a German I cannot describe everything that has happened in Germany in the last ten years as bad.'

'Certainly not everything has been bad in Germany in the last ten years. There are Germans too, who with commitment, and often at the cost of their lives, fight against Hitler. What, however, has been very bad is that Hitler's Germany has assaulted other people and taken them over by war. Now that has to be bitterly paid for.'

We parted without having agreed. But still it was beginning to dawn on me that we were operating from different basic positions. Professor Arnold considered historical development and historical events strongly from the standpoint of the masses. He saw the true driving force of history in the workers, farmers, businesses, manual labourers and other working strata of the people. He assessed at the same time a scale for the evaluation of historical precedents and the historical acts of individual persons – even the acts of German generals and officers, including mine. The professor said that in this war we were pursuing a bad thing, that we were conducting an illegal war. Rights, morals and historical precedent were not on our side, for some 2,000 kilometres from Germany's borders we were trying to deliver a deadly blow to the Soviet Union. Rights and historical progress stood and remained on the side of the Soviet people and its Red Army, which was defending its homeland and its established order of society with its blood sacrifice.

The words of the Soviet professor worked within me like a thorn. I tried to wipe it away, but the thorn did not weaken, just bored deeper in. The questions raised occupied me day and night. I was angry with myself because I had been so arrogant in my conversation with him and had not simply accepted the arguments of my partner in our discussion, but I really wanted to investigate his point of view. No real opinion can be formed with a dour rejecting attitude. Counterargument must be thought through much more fundamentally and critically.

'Remember, Colonel Adam!'

Following our argument, Professor Arnold invited me to pursue our talk several days later in my room, should I so wish. In fact he appeared one afternoon in our room. Schmidt was already in the garden. I asked the professor not to take amiss my vehemence from before. Whereupon he said, smiling: 'Don't worry about it. No grown-up person finds it easy to separate himself from thoughts and opinions that he has grown accustomed to over the course of many years. But think of the sources you have formed them from! Treitschke especially was no people's historian; he was a Hohenzollern historian and monarchist through and through. The main thing is that you do not persist with false conceptions, which can only bring you personally and your German people new misfortunes.'

We then turned to questions about the Second World War. I had once honestly believed in Hitler's plan for a new order in Europe. Absolutely convinced by it, I had gone into France to resolve the insult of Versailles. Equally honestly had I gone into the Eastern Campaign, albeit with some inner unease, because the Soviet Union appeared to me to be a power with so much unknown about it. I first had serious doubts about it in the cauldron on the Volga. Nevertheless my doubts hardly touched the question of whether the war was correct or incorrect, but rather formed a criticism of Hitler's strategic concept not just of a two-front war but in arousing the hostility of almost the whole world.

My interlocutor referred to the German–Soviet non-aggression pact, which was confirmed for ten years on the 23rd August 1939 and was extended on the 11th February 1940 with a commercial agreement between the Soviet Union and Germany. Arnold cited from the text of the non-aggression pact:

1. Both the contracting parties are duty bound to abstain from all forcible acts, all aggressive dealings and all attacks against each other, either individually or together with other powers.
2. . . .
3. The governments of both contracting parties will in future remain in constant consultation with each other in order to keep themselves informed reciprocally on questions that concern their joint interests.
4. . . .
5. In case of dispute or conflict between the contracting parties or questions about this or anything similar arise, both parties in this dispute or conflict will settle them exclusively in the way of a friendly exchange of opinions or if necessary by an arbitration commission.

'The socialist Soviet Union faithfully complied with this agreement, while Hitler's Germany on the other hand broke it outrageously and attacked us,' said the professor. 'Do you consider this correct?'

I was now able to follow the vocabulary of preventative war. But I had never believed it so correct and in the last minutes I had become convinced that it was only needed by Hitler as a propaganda tool in order to justify the breach of the agreement and give the war against Soviet Russia a moral appearance. As I had undertaken to listen to my interlocutor's arguments and not to squash them with my know-it-all attitude, I kept quiet.

Arnold, taking my silence as unspoken contradiction, then continued after a short pause more sharply than before: 'With your interest in historical questions, you have surely read Hitler's *Mein Kampf.* Remember the place where he said: "We stop the German march to the south and go over to ground policy in the east." In more accurate German that means: we will rob the Slav peoples of their territory and their natural treasures and turn them into our working animals. Look at the tirades of hatred and abuse that were delivered against Bolshevism at the Nurenberg Party Days! Think of the practice of plundering and especially the mishandling of people that during your membership of the German Eastern Army you cannot have missed! Or remember Goebbels' speech in the summer of 1942 in which the Reich's Propaganda Minister proclaimed the robber character of the war, when he spoke of the lining of pockets, but he was not speaking of some ideal or other but rather of wheat, coal, ores and oil. Remember, Colonel Adam!'

Yes, I remembered. I also wanted to admit it. But then everything we had striven for and believed in, and for which we had been ready to put our lives at stake in this stream of blood and tears, would become evil and false. I wanted to talk to Professor Arnold about these doubts, but Schmidt then entered the room. He must have heard the last words and immediately joined in the talk. As formerly so often in the cauldron, even now he wanted to dominate the course of the conversation. In his arrogance he lost all proportion in his performance and was on the verge of insulting the Soviet professor. Arnold smiled, sucked in his cheeks, rose, nodded slightly at Schmidt and left the room. I escorted him to the door of the block and apologised for the unwelcome incident. We parted with a hearty handshake.

Unfortunately there were no more chats with Professor Arnold as soon afterwards he left Susdal. He had helped me take the first steps on the stony, difficult path to new shores by giving me valuable assistance in opening up new problems, understanding and feeling for certain ways, but ripping up false trails. Schmidt's entrance had made me realise that the clarification process would be associated with conflicts in our own ranks. Obviously it would lead firstly to a dispute among the Germans themselves. Even the older ones in the order of rank known to me for decades, from the highest commander or highest war lord, from the field marshals, generals, staff officers, captains and lieutenants down to the lowest soldier, all was up for discussion, by rank, authority and obedience to duty precisely classified. It did not apply to the position within the military hierarchy; the question was what goals the individual objectives served. Was each man just a tool, the foil of an unjust, immoral war of conquest; did he remain a staunch follower of a leadership that did not hesitate to commit crimes, or did he say away with it and go against it. From these questions arose the separation between Fascists and anti-Fascists, which the experiences of the Krasnogorsk camp and Susdal, and also from leaflets of various propaganda works in the camp library, had not rendered so intelligible. Accordingly, I then thought, Schmidt's behaviour was that of a Fascist. Where then did I, Wilhelm Adam, fit in, who had been promoted to colonel by Hitler and decorated with the Knight's Cross? These questions remained. Months went by before I finally cleared them up.

Wilhelm Pieck

One day in 1943 Colonel Novikov announced through an interpreter that there were some Germans come to visit the field marshal. Hardly had I informed Paulus when the camp commandant and the interpreter were already on the steps of our accommodation. In their company was an old man with white hair.

With the words: 'This is Herr Wilhelm Pieck, who wants to talk to you, Field Marshal,' the Colonel introduced the visitor. Wilhelm Pieck supplemented this. He was a member of the German Reichstag and wanted to speak to Paulus about the fate of the German people. As I was about to excuse myself, he smilingly waved me down. 'Stay here! What I have to say to you, you should quietly listen to, it concerns you too.'

With a certain reticence, Paulus invited his visitor to sit down at the table near the window. I sat down to the side with Novikov and the interpreter.

This then was the Communist Wilhelm Pieck. I had never seen him before. Only faintly could I remember his name from the time before 1933. He had a worthy enough appearance, I thought, as I looked on. Goodness and understanding came from his eyes. What would he make of Paulus?

The field marshal looked at him silently. Apparently he wanted to offer the visitor no bridge to a conversation, but rather wait. Wilhelm Pieck then opened the conversation: 'I wanted to ask about you, Field Marshal. Apparently you are surprised that I, a Communist, who must have emigrated from the homeland, should come to you. But I really need to talk to you.'

This sounded so natural, so sincere, that Paulus's voice took on a warmer tone. 'I thank you for your interest, Herr Pieck. As you can see, I am well accommodated. My health has considerably improved in the last weeks. Colonel Novikov looks after us. We have German and Russian doctors. The food is good and sufficient. One could not expect more as a prisoner of war.'

'You, Field Marshal, and many other Germans would have been spared imprisonment if you had not let Hitler and his team lead you,' retorted the visitor.

'You can see, Herr Pieck, that I am a soldier. As a soldier I have to fulfil the orders of my superiors. I have never concerned myself with the political aspects.'

'Field Marshal, you are a clever and well educated officer. You must have known that Hitler had led our people astray and betrayed them. Or do you really think that the Soviet Union wanted to conquer Germany?'

Paulus appeared to be getting excited: 'I cannot imagine, Herr Pieck, that a head of state could betray his people and his army. Like millions of others, I believed Hitler's words when the general staff was tasked with the preparation of the attack plans against the Soviet Union. I also had faith in the High Command when the catastrophe of Stalingrad was already well under way.'

This admission of disillusioned trust had not come easily from Paulus. I could see in his face how it affected him.

Wilhelm Pieck was also lively: 'You were the army commander, Field Marshal! Your military career and position gave you a deep insight into war matters, into Hitler's methods of leadership and his war aims. You must have already thought about the critical development. The lives of hundreds of thousands of German soldiers were entrusted to you. Why did you fight on for so long at the Volga in a hopeless cause? Why did you believe Hitler's lies more than your conscience and your judgement? Why did you dismiss the Red Army's honourable surrender offer? Hitler is a criminal who never represented the interests of our nation. We Communists recognised this from the very first and told the people. You and your generals also recognised it at the last in the Stalingrad cauldron and consequently had to deal with it, Field Marshal.'

Paulus replied dismissively: 'I have already said once, Herr Pieck, that we soldiers never concerned ourselves with politics; we dared not involve ourselves. Our basic principle is that the German soldier must not be political! I have remained faithful to this motto. Hitler was for us not just the Head of State, he was also the commander-in-chief of the Wehrmacht, with whose orders we have to comply unconditionally. I did not know the plans and possibilities of the Army High Command outside the cauldron. That is why I could not simply give in.'

The conversation had come dramatically to a head. Two men who were diametrically opposed to each other were sitting at the table: there the field marshal, a simple non-political soldier, for whom blind obedience to the orders of the superior was his ethos, and there the Communist workers' leader, whose dealings regarding spiritual sovereignty and the highest responsibility were certainly to the people.

Wilhelm Pieck did not let go: 'So, almost all officers maintain like you, Field Marshal, that they have become non-political and want to continue being so. What does non-political mean then? Do you not realise that you have played a not insignificant role in politics? Unfortunately, a role of a negative nature. You were pliant tools in the hands of the spoilers of our people, whose goals were the exact opposites of our national and socialistic ones. War of conquest, war of exploitation was their goal! And you, the generals and officers of the Wehrmacht, have obediently served their criminal policies.'

In a clear, unpolished way the chairman of the German Communist Party showed that we had done some very damaging things for our people. In the end we had become Hitler's pacemakers and made ourselves equally responsible for all the wrongs, damage and suffering that other peoples had experienced through Hitler's war. Regretfully he continued: 'As already in 1914–1918, so in this war our gifted, industrial German people, our working people, above all the workers and farmers, have to pay the bill. Consider for once in whose interest this war has been conducted. Think of the 6th Army's catastrophe! You have to go way back in history to find such an example of our people's misery and misfortune. Believe me, the whole of Germany's picking a war is a crime. It serves a handful of German monopolists and militarists, who out of the blood and bones of the German soldiers, and out of the distress of the conquered peoples, have made vast profits. Should a few marks fall to the population or to the soldiers, they are but tiny proportions of the stolen profit, mere pence for the participants. My party had warned even before 1933, 'Hitler is war!' Unfortunately we were unable to prevent the Fascists taking power and the disaster they caused. We can and must avoid plunging the German people into a national catastrophe. That is why we Communists are fighting together with all those who hate the Fascist criminals and love the German people.'

Wilhelm Pieck then expressed the wish to speak to Paulus alone. Later I learned from Paulus that the chairman of the German Communist Party had developed plans for the founding and leading of a national German committee that would conduct the fight against the Hitler regime on the widest front and for the speedy ending of the war. Emigrant workers' leaders and writers would work closely together with officer and soldier prisoners of war. All differences of opinion would have to be withheld in the interests of the German nation. To the fore must come not the divisive elements but rather the unifying aspects in view of Hitler's conjured-up, immense threat to the existence of the German people. They both, the Communist and the field marshal were German. The history of their homeland moved them both deeply. If they united, Hitler must fall into their hands. Pieck called on Paulus to openly turn against Hitler and to cooperate on the planned committee.

The field marshal was as horrified of the consequences as I was when I heard this. Pieck's proposal seemed unheard of at that time and we wanted nothing to do with it. On the other hand we had to agree with the Communists in their assessment of the situation and the nature of the war. Above all, Pieck's personality influenced us, as did the simplicity and convincing power of his speech and his glowing patriotism. This was no 'landless fellow', as the Nazis would say, and he stayed in our imagination and even haunted us.

Looking back at these days in June 1943, I would like to say that Paulus and I appeared a get a strong impulse for our own understanding as a result of our talks with Wilhelm Pieck. The talk stimulated us to cross over from the traditional area of military thought, the officer's oath and military discipline, to examine the question according to its political aspects. For the first time it opened our eyes clearly to the importance of active resistance to Hitler and the pursuit of the war.

Pieck stayed in Susdal for more than a week. He and his escorting poet, Johannes R. Becher, had numerous conversations with generals and officers, among them von Seydlitz, Lattmann, Korfes and von Lenski. At a full assembly of the camp's prisoners of war, but which the generals did not attend, Pieck asserted that the war was no longer able to be won by Germany. The Allies were also not thinking of seeking peace with Hitler. Thus there was only one way of saving Germany: overthrowing Hitler and ending the war immediately. This was what the Communist Party was fighting for, but they were not alone. They called upon all honourable Germans at home, at the front and in captivity to conduct this war with them. There should be no political, ideological or professional differences to hamper the vital chance to unite all the opponents of Hitler.

Only a few of the prisoners of war at Susdal Camp approved of such speeches and talks at that time. The later development showed, however, that the German Communist Party's solution provided a real alternative to the catastrophic policy of Hitler's regime. The Communists grasped the decisive initiative to form a German anti-Fascist fighting front. The seeds that were planted in July 1943 among the prisoner-of-war officers and generals would at least soon germinate and in some instances come to fruition.

Rents in the generals' front

Our stay in Susdal was about as long as the one at Krasnogorsk. After two months or so, at the beginning of July 1943, the order came again: 'Generals to make ready for the transport!'

Towards evening Colonel Novikov came to say goodbye to us. Provided with supplies, we climbed into our bus, happy to be outside the barbed wire again. A car was ready for Field Marshal Paulus. After a journey of several hours through a light, mild summer night we came to a camp gate for the third time in the first six months of our imprisonment. We had arrived at Voikovo, the prisoner-of-war camp for generals. The camp commandant was an old colonel who spoke German; unfortunately I have forgotten his name. His deputy was a quite young lieutenant-colonel named Pussyrov. The camp doctor was Dr Morov.

The nucleus of the camp was formed by a large former farmhouse built of stone. Opposite lay a second building, whose ground floor was also of stone, and a single-storey administrative building. The finest thing was the laid-out park with an old stand of trees and a linden alley, which went right through the park and past the living accommodation that had until recently served as a nursing home for the Ivanovo railway workers.

As in Susdal, there were here at first thirty-one generals in the camp: twenty-two German, six Rumanian and three Italian. Together with Field Marshal Paulus, I occupied two rooms, while for the generals there were single, double and several bedded rooms. I was pleased with the well set-up dining room and lounge.

There was also a well kept library here. Several generals had given up their rejection of political books and others had started thinking about it. Even if unanimity was displayed to the outside, the increasing schism in the generals' front could not remain concealed. There were divided opinions about Germany's war aims, about the National Socialist German Workers' Party, and about the Soviet Union. Three groups formed in the first weeks after our arrival in Voikovo. To the first group belonged the generals who were looking for new ways forward and were considering how to turn the German people away from Hitler's catastrophic operational policy. The most advanced of these were Lattmann and Dr Korfes. The second group had inwardly turned away from Hitler and his system, but they were dithering, had many reservations and saw no new way ahead. Among this group at that time I would like to count von Seydlitz, von Lenski, Wulz and myself. To the third group belonged those who obstinately clung to the old ways. They were led by Generals Heitz, Rodenburg, Schmidt and Sixt von Arnim. They represented the point of view that as long as we remained together, we would ensure that everyone stuck to it.

Finally there were some generals whose behaviour was difficult to identify. They mainly held back from the discussions. Field Marshal Paulus tried to keep out of all the discussions. He wanted to smooth down the ever-more-frequent high waves.

During the first days after our arrival in Voikovo Schmidt was transferred to another camp. This was regretted by the Heitz, Rodenburg and Sixt von Arnim group. Apart from Rodenburg, Schmidt had no real friends among the generals. Consequently his departure did not affect those remaining much.

A labour company belonged to the Generals' Camp, as Voikovo was called, consisting of one-third each of German, Rumanian and Italian prisoners of war. They acted as kitchen staff, labourers and batmen for the generals. Among the German prisoners of war there was a whole number that had not only turned away from Hitler, but were of the opinion that we should openly oppose Hitler and his war. These soldiers formed the anti-Fascist group in the camp. They not only won over the majority of their comrades to their opinion, but especially called on the generals to fight against Hitler and his system. This raised a cloud of dust. How could such soldiers dare speak to generals like that! Above all Colonel-General Heitz raged and complained about these Communists, as he called them. But the anti-Fascists did not let themselves be intimidated. As workers, farmers or labourers in soldiers' uniforms they realised sooner than we did that Hitler's war brought only distress and suffering to the German people, while some fat-cats did well out of it.

Discussion about the National Committee 'Free Germany'
In the middle of July there was a storm of indignation in our ranks, brought about by a new newspaper in the German language being distributed in the camp: this newspaper was the *Freies Deutschland* ('Free Germany'). There it stated in black and white that on the 12th and 13th July 1943 in Krasnogorsk the National Committee 'Freies Deutschland' had been founded by German emigrants, German officer and soldier prisoners of war,

and surviving Stalingrad fighters. The few examples of the newspaper that we had received were passed from hand to hand. The main interest was not in the content of the manifest to the Wehrmacht and the German people, but in the names of those that had signed it. Every one of us found the names of officers and soldiers that we knew and that we had once treasured as friends. How could they have done something like this with the Communists! That was enough to bring about a damning condemnation of them all. At the same time it was satisfying that it involved only young officers who had 'frivolously broken their oaths of allegiance'.

The first waves of excitement had the generals packing their bags. I was no exception. It appeared as if there was real unanimity in the condemnation of the sheet. Then even the emotional ones calmed down. Several of us began to consider the events more soberly. We studied the contents of the National Committee 'Freies Deutschland's manifest to the Wehrmacht and the German people. I deeper I got into it, the more I had to say to myself that the signatories of this appeal had done so out of deep concern and responsibility towards the German people with this extraordinary publication. It continued that Hitler was leading Germany to destruction. It said in the manifest:

No foreign enemy has brought us so much misfortune as Hitler.

The facts prove that the war is lost. Germany can only drag on at the cost of inhuman sacrifice and deprivation. The continuance of this pointless war means the end of the nation. But Germany must not die! It is now a question of being or not being our fatherland . . .

If the German people take courage in time and demonstrate by their acts that they want to be a free people and are determined to free Germany of Hitler and win the right to decide about its future fate and its place in the world, that is the only way to save the existence, the freedom and the honour of the German nation.

The German people need and want immediate freedom. But Hitler concludes peace with no one. No one will also deal only with him. That is why the formation of a true German government is our people's most urgent task.

Every evening von Lenski, Wulz, Roske and I took a walk along the camp road. We discussed the war situation and the National Committee. In our opinion of the war situation we fully agreed with the manifest and the reports in the *Freies Deutschland* newspaper. In the half year that had passed since the German defeat on the Volga, Libya and Tunis had been lost, but most of all we had lost the battle of Kursk. Seventeen German panzer divisions, reinforced by the 60-ton '*Tiger*' tanks and the 70-ton '*Ferdinand*' assault guns, attacked along a 70-kilometre front. That was a panzer division every four kilometres! Never before had the Wehrmacht concentrated so much attacking strength in such a crowded area. But the German summer offensive of 1943 was beaten back by the Red Army within a few days. In their counteroffensive the Soviet troops were able to regain the cities of Oriol and Belgorod. And their attack rolled on further to the west. How much longer would it now take before it reached Charkov or even Kiev? We knew that Germany had no more reserves available that could be set against the enemy armies storming forwards. The manifest was quite correct when it said: 'The armies of England and America stand at Europe's door. Soon Germany will have to fight on all sides. The weakened German Wehrmacht, ever more closely surrounded by overwhelming enemies, will not and cannot continue to withstand them. The day of collapse draws near!'

The war is hopelessly lost
There were generals in the camp who believed that there would be a draw in this war, because the German army was strong enough to repel an invasion in the west. In this case the Soviet Union would be left on its own and thus would be obliged to come to some arrangement with Hitler's Germany. It was also possible for an understanding to be reached with the Western Powers at the cost of the Soviet Union. Both opinions came from the group of unteachables. Already in August/September 1943 I had not accepted them, but the wish was all too often the father of the thought. The Teheran Conference in December 1943 and developments in 1944 had finally put paid to such thoughts.

After some earnest checks I came to the conclusion that the war was hopelessly lost. Since my talks with Professor Arnold I was of the opinion that Germany had begun the war without compelling reasons and thus burdened itself with a gigantic guilt. Following my own bitter experience, I had trusted Hitler and his clique when they had begun their crimes against the 6th Army without thought that they would affect the whole of the German people. I could agree completely with the conclusions which ended the manifest of the National Committee 'Freies Deutschland':

For the people and fatherland! Against Hitler and his war!
For immediate peace!
For the salvation of the German people!
For a free, independent Germany!

'More civil courage, Colonel!'
So I joined the National Committee 'Freies Deutschland' though I had yet to take an active part. I did not do so, as I was still not quite ready. I was especially strongly moved by the question of whether prisoners of war should be allowed to deal with the political and military leadership. Would

this not increase the chaos, would it not involve the disintegration of the German front, would it not endanger the lives of many of their still-fighting comrades? My oath of allegiance and the traditional concept of an officer's honour prevented me from taking this step. An important role was played by my relationship with Field Marshal Paulus, whom I honoured as a man and whose conduct I esteemed. Could I attack him from behind? I did not feel myself especially personally bound to the signers of the manifest, most of whom I did not know. Despite the deep impression that the personality of Wilhelm Pieck had made on me during his visit to Susdal, I was now reserved with the Communists in the National Committee.

These then were some of the thoughts and problems that concerned me during the weeks after the founding of the National Committee. The grounds were basically a similar conflict to that during the battle for the cauldron on the Volga. Should I follow the voice of reason and actively oppose the apocalyptic developments? Or should I follow Hitler and the oath of allegiance – and in doing so participate in the catastrophe threatening my people? After the inferno of Stalingrad I must yet turn to all the consequences of Germany's next and greatest misfortune, against Hitler and his war. But, apart from the understanding about the foregoing question, there was still something needed: a lot of civil courage. I had it, but not enough to be without regard for the attitude of others and my own responsibility to the National Committee 'Freies Deutschland'.

Thus my thoughts went here and there. Evening after evening I discussed it with the generals standing nearby. I pondered and read, but came to no final decision.

A guessing game with four generals
It was mid-August and I was taking a walk in the park. There I encountered Roske. 'I have been looking for you, Adam. Do you know already that Seydlitz, Lattmann and Korfes are leaving us today?'

'Leaving? What has Paulus to say about that, Roske?'

'I have not seen him yet. But you can best ask him that yourself.'

Paulus already knew about it. 'I presume', he said, 'it has something to do with the National Committee. Seydlitz's memorandum and his behaviour in the cauldron must be known not only to many of our soldiers and officers, but especially also to the Russians and apparently also to the German emigrants. However, I am convinced that he will remain faithful to us. A tradition among old military families is that in captivity no one ever goes against the head of state.'

Someone knocked. Colonel-Generals Heitz and Strecker entered. Heitz came straight out with: 'We must form a circle around the three of them. Especially is this necessary for Seydlitz, as he already in the cauldron demanded Hitler's orders to be disregarded.'

Paulus agreed to the proposal. He did not mistrust Seydlitz, but regarded a discussion as irrelevant.

The opportunity for one occurred. On the 22nd August von Seydlitz had his 55th birthday. I had prepared for him a cut-out relief of a tower of Susdal Monastery. Paulus wanted to present him with this gift on behalf of all the generals, including the Rumanians and Italians. Now he decided, at the suggestion of von Heitz and Strecker, to give it to Seydlitz before his departure and to add some meaningful words.

Seydlitz was delighted with the gift. He said it was especially well done and assured Paulus that he could leave those remaining to him. 'This tower', he concluded, 'will be for me the tower of truth.'

Generals von Seydlitz, Lattmann and Dr Korfes had already gone. A new discussion arose among us as to where they could be going, and what drove them? Would they keep on maintaining a distance between themselves and the National Committee 'Freies Deutschland'. The same question arose again about fourteen days later when Lieutenant-General Edler von Daniels left the camp.

Meanwhile three new officers had joined us, Colonels Boje, Schildknecht and Petzold. They came from a camp near Moscow and were bitter enemies of the National Committee. They were of the opinion that should it really be necessary to overturn Hitler, it would be the task of the German people back home and the soldiers at the front. They argued that 'if we prisoners of war rose up against Hitler, it would be a betrayal'.

That was naturally water under the bridge for the holding on with Generals Schlage and Heitz, who still had a strong influence on the thoughts of the whole group of generals. With this assertion, it was easy to call upon such actions from the safe basis of captivity to try to discredit the aims of the National Committee. Paulus too had similar reservations that he expressed in the following manner: 'Must the impression not arise that such steps come from Russian pressure? Goebbels would not find it difficult to discredit the activities of the National Committee 'Freies Deutschland' as collaboration or a stab in the back.'

On the 22nd August we had been thinking about Seydlitz. Where would he be spending his birthday? If in the past the relationship between Paulus and Seydlitz had been troubled by individual episodes, the field marshal felt himself closely bound to the general through the old cavalry school. Standing together in this difficult time, the corps spirit showing itself in every situation, that was Paulus's motto. Hampered by one jumping off, making a breach in the generals' front, with his inbuilt old officers' corps snobbery Paulus said 'Seydlitz will keep to his word' several times to Colonel-General Heitz, who, as former president of the Reichs War Court, had seen in Seydlitz a potential traitor since his revolt in the cauldron.

Fear of a new 'stab in the back' legend
It was a very complicated, boring and difficult process reaching the new embankment. The expression 'stab in the back' was used by a field marshal. He said it not to demonstrate any personal dislike of the men of the National Committee, but because he was so inclined.

The 'stab in the back' legend, derived from the peculiar German responsibility for the First World War, and from the shame of the November Revolution and the preparations for the war of revenge, took a central position in the more-than-decisive political-ideological standard equipment of a staff officer of the Weimar Republic. The old generals, from Hindenburg as Reich President and others occupying decisive positions of power in the Reichswehr, were not interested in the truth. They wanted to forget that the First World War had been lost for Germany through military and economic exhaustion and implied the blame lay in the 'betrayal of the homeland'. I too during my early studies of history had, for example, never come across the text of a record of a conference at the Great Headquarters on the 14th August 1918, in which the State Secretary for Foreign Affairs, in the presence of the Kaiser, Hindenburg, Ludendorff and other leading personalities in the retinue of Wilhelm II, had stated the following:

> The Chief of the General Staff of the Field Armies has defined the war situation, that we can no longer hope to break the will for war among our enemies through warlike negotiations, and that our war leadership must set the goal of gradually paralysing the enemy's strategic defensive. The political leadership bows before this declaration by the great generals who have conducted this war, and draws from this the political consequences that politically we will be unable to break the enemy's will to wage war, and that we are therefore obliged to bear the cost of the war situation under the leadership of our politicians.'

These words indicated quite clearly that a quarter of a year before the November Revolution Germany was militarily and politically no longer in a position to win. To conceal the fact, the 'stab in the back' was officially sanctioned in the Third Reich. It went into the history books and professors' colleges. The 'November Criminals' were in essence 'national' betrayers abandoned with the greatest contempt.

This whole tangled mess of systematic drummed-in opinions and condemnations had first to be swept aside before a new way could come into sight. Certainly there were the great historical examples of Stein, Arndt, Clausewitz and Boyen, who appealed to the German people over the heads of treacherous despots and called for a fight for freedom. There was the Convention of Taurrogen of the 30th December 1812, in which the King of

Prussia's General von York, without asking the king, agreed with the Russian General von Diebitsch to cease all hostilities between the Prussian corps and the Russian units.

The National Committee's manifest pointed to these historical examples. In fact, it then dealt with the essence of the same problems and similar conflicts now confronting us in 1943. The men of 1812/13 renounced their head of state and his followers, and fought on their own responsibility in accordance with their knowledge and historical necessity, and the people's and Fatherland's wishes. The group of stubborn ones in Voikovo did not want to let it pass: 'These men were not prisoners of war. And anyway, they allied themselves with the Tsar and not with the "Reds".' This last argument was what it was really all about. The eternal conquerors and militarists among the generals did not want to have anything to do with the Communists. They hated them on principle on the basis of their own class distinction. They also did not think earnestly about concerning themselves with the Communist conceptions of nation, fatherland, state and war.

In the end, all went with the 'corps spirit' and 'officers' honour' that Field Marshal Paulus, strictly within the net of his conservative upbringing, swore by. I, the colonel among generals, was caught in this jungle. Only a millimetre at a time could I extricate myself.

An apparent victory over the Seydlitz delegation
One evening during the first days of September 1943 I was sitting reading in my room. Suddenly someone stuck their head through the door and asked me to come quickly. I threw on my uniform jacket as I went along. On the ground near the steps I came across a group of generals, among them – I could not believe my eyes – von Seydlitz and Lattmann. The thought shot through my head that they had returned to Voikovo. But where was Korfes? I could not make him out; instead I saw Colonel Steidle and a Luftwaffe major unknown to me, whom Steidle introduced as Major von Frankenberg.

Although I greeted both generals and Steidle effusively, I had the feeling that the whole group standing around, among them Colonel-General Strecker, were in a state of uncertainty. General von Seydlitz asked me to report his presence to Field Marshal Paulus, which I did immediately. The conversation between Paulus and Seydlitz did not last long. When I was called back by an orderly and entered the room, the field marshal was irritably striding up and down with long steps.

'Has there been another clash?' I asked.

'No, not that, but in the few days that Seydlitz has been absent his attitude has completely changed. He is talking about new realisations that he has had in conversation with Stalingraders, but also with recently captured officers, with German emigrants and with high-ranking Soviet officers. He is talking about the founding of a League of German Officers (*Bund Deutscher Offiziere*). I cannot make him out. Finally Paulus asked that all the generals be summoned so that he could tell them what he had said to me. I agreed to his request. 'Go personally round to all the generals; I ask that they meet in the dining room in half an hour.'

The generals of the former 6th Army were punctually on the spot. General von Seydlitz sat at his usual place, which went with the seniority of the former commanding general. Paulus asked him to speak. It was as if the dominating gold and red on the generals' uniforms crackled in the assembly, as if at any moment a dangerous explosion would occur. Colonel-General Heitz looked around him with an angry face. Colonel Steidle and Major von Frankenberg seemed ready for him to start.

General von Seydlitz went over the rapidly worsening war situation for Germany since the battle on the Volga. He referred to the long-expected landing of the Western Allies and concluded that the war was no longer winnable by Germany. I noticed how at this point a murmur went through the assembly, and had the feeling that Seydlitz, who was speaking freely, was now coming to the point. One could sense that he was trying to bring his talk quickly to an end. When he called for opposition to Hitler, there was a massive counter-cry of 'Unheard of!' and 'Stop!', forcing him to break off his speech. Resignedly he sat down again, while uproar broke out around him, in which he was shocked by some personal abuse. Some generals ran to the door and wanted to leave the room.

Paulus remained quiet and relaxed through all of this. With some appeasing words, he was able to calm down the noise and enable Major-General Lattmann to speak. He too recalled the German defeat at the front and the air war against the homeland. Then he recalled his own experience on the Volga. Generals and troops had no longer believed overwhelmingly in the highest commander. Hitler had sacrificed them soullessly, coerced them with lies and unrealisable promises in the painful defeat. I knew that Lattmann had previously been a convinced adherent of National Socialism. Now in his words was the time for the settling of accounts, the way to self-understanding. He spoke very emotionally: 'Hitler's brutal power that brought us and our families to the tragedy of Stalingrad will plunge the whole of the German people into a vast Stalingrad if we do not stop him. That is why generals must leave behind their reserve and involve themselves with those who think the same in the fight against Hitler.'

In contrast to Seydlitz, Lattmann was able to end his short speech without a row, although the faces of the generals remained as grim as ever. But when Colonel Steidle then initiated the creation of the League of German Officers with the goal of Hitler's downfall, in order to bring about a cessation of hostilities, the orderly withdrawal of the Wehrmacht to the Reich boundaries and renunciation of all conquered territory, there was a real eruption. Any understanding was unthinkable. Colonel-General Heitz even threatened to box Steidle's ears. He shouted at Major von Frankenberg too. Next to Heitz, Rodenburg, Sixt von Arnim, Strecker and Pfeiffer had the most to say. Seydlitz's group was accused of being traitors. Without even casting them another glance, the generals left the room complaining.

Paulus was especially pained by this incident. Kitchen staff and orderlies had also heard the noise. Must they, must the camp administration be offered such a display? 'What was played out in the dining room was more than unworthy,' he said, when we returned to his room. Then the door opened and Heitz, Rodenburg, Sixt von Arnim and Strecker entered. One of them said: 'We refuse to exchange another word with Seydlitz or his companions.'

'We are not going to be taught by young people like Lattmann, Steidle or even this Frankenberg,' added Heitz. 'We would like to continue the conversation not in your room but out in the park.' The generals left the room with Paulus. I remained alone and thought about this lesson on 'corps spirit' and 'officers' honour'. After a quarter of an hour an orderly appeared, Corporal Erwin Schulte:

'The field marshal asks you to come down.'

Despite it being evening, the camp was like an agitated swarm of bees. Everything was busy. The generals were moving and gesticulating in small groups up and down the camp road. Paulus was only a few paces from me. 'The generals are proposing to conduct an internal discussion on the steps behind the park after breakfast tomorrow morning. All are to attend, without exception.'

A disturbed night followed this announcement. Next morning I was up earlier than usual. All the generals assembled punctually for breakfast. A stormy atmosphere reigned. The meal was quickly consumed. Without exception all reached the appointed place in the park.

After a short, angry discussion Sixt von Arnim put together the following text:

1. We refuse to have further relations with Seydlitz and his companions. No one will talk to them. Those who are accosted will go on without answering.
2. Contact between Paulus and Seydlitz will be maintained by Colonel Adam.
3. The camp administration will be written a letter, in which we will protest the sojourn of the Seydlitz group and against further advertising for the German Officers' League as well as that of the National Committee 'Freies Deutschland'.
4. Lieutenant-General Sixt von Arnim is tasked with the writing of this letter.
5. The letter will be signed by all the camp's officers.

In fact all the generals signed the petition. I too added my name below theirs. I was then given the unhappy task by Paulus of handing over the petition personally to the camp commandant. I reported to him via the duty officer and was taken straight to him. The Soviet colonel took the paper without a word and I was dismissed.

On my way to the camp commandant it had dawned on me that our declaration was in fact a provocation. From Paulus too, one could see that the previous proceedings had not been pleasant. I had spoken quietly to Major von Frankenberg for a few minutes immediately after the tumultuous assembly. We also knew that members of the Seydlitz group, including such men as von Lenski, Schlömer and von Drebber, had had short but pertinent discussions. And now this collective condemnation, this attempt at a warning to General von Seydlitz and his companions!

'I keep going over, Field Marshal,' I said to Paulus, 'whether we handled the matter correctly. Seydlitz had assured you and all of us that he had come to us on his own initiative, only following his conscience and his deep concern for Germany. No one had tasked him to do it. But we, the prisoners of war, turned in this provocative way to the Soviet side!'

'You are right, Adam. I too have been thinking it through again. We handled it too hastily.'

'How would a German camp commandant react if a Soviet prisoner-of-war officer brought him such an aggressive demand?'

'Let us wait and see what happens,' said Paulus, tired by the repugnant quarrel.

It came to nothing. Apparently this display of arrogance and obstinacy by the pro-Hitler German generals had been filed with a pitying smile.

For the benefit of Paulus and the decent ones among the generals, it must be said that the field marshal was later able to get the regrettable pamphlet back. It remained the only reminder of how the matter would be decided politically.

General von Seydlitz and his companions left two days later. They were unable to enlist further generals for the League of German Officers. Even the catastrophe on the Volga had not yet enabled these gentlemen to distance themselves from Hitler. They still bowed down before a criminal supreme commander-in-chief and excused the betrayals that enabled further crimes. However, it was wrong to consider this leading group of the League of German Officers as crazy. The unanimity, the 'corps spirit', was only skin-deep. Already the hysterical way in which the stubborn ones were proceeding gave rise to new doubts along the sober-thinking generals and myself. Who should I actually hate? Hitler and those who, after the 6th Army had been hunted to extinction, were now preparing to lead the whole German people to the slaughterhouse? Or those who demanded that Hitler must fall so that Germany might live?

My 'straight way'

I had always gone my own way. I had never forced myself, but rather set my mind unreservedly to doing what I considered necessary. I had also helped others in a comradely manner whenever I could. Coming from a simple farming family, I had pursued my military career not through nepotism or intrigues, but rather through diligence, punctuality, reliability and efficiency. I believe that I always had a heart for subordinate soldiers and officers and I was also no coward when things were hard. This all belonged doubtlessly to my 'straight way'.

Since the battle of destruction on the Volga, especially after the talks that I had had in captivity with men like Professor Arnold, Wilhelm Pieck and Lieutenant-Colonel Pussyrov, not least through my studying of literature, thinking and pondering, the realisation grew that in my 'straight way' my self-deception had reached an important point. I had been cheated of any real goal along this route, over the 'for what' and the 'where to'. As I soldier I obeyed orders blindly. My supreme commander, however, was Adolf Hitler, in whose hands lay immense power – an abundance of power that no German head of state had held since Kaiser Wilhelm II. This power was enforced by violence, through which the political enemies of National Socialism – Communists, Social Democrats, Liberals and Christians – were locked up in concentration camps, liquidated in cold blood or brought to the scaffold. The majority of the people were, with the help of a cunning national and social demagogy, participating in a coordinated economic phantom existence aimed at armament. Guns, tanks, bombers, fighters, submarines and battleships were sprung from the ground. The army, air force and navy were growing, and Hitler was becoming ever more arrogant, threatening and powerful.

Germany was spreading an atmosphere of fear and horror in the world. Never was the *Furor Teutonicus* as much feared by other peoples as in the first ten years of the Third Reich. When Hitler's Germany believed itself militarily strong enough it overran neighbouring countries, conquered them, utilised them to the utmost and annexed them. Then came the change, which started with the defeat of the Wehrmacht in the Soviet Union during the winter of 1941/2 and was completed with the destruction of the 6th Army on the Volga and the defeat at Kursk in the summer of 1943.

No less than half a year had now passed since the last night in the cauldron, the night of the 30th/31st January 1943, when I had brooded over the questions: 'When did the tragedy on the Volga begin?' 'What was my life?' 'Germany's luck or misfortune?' Now I saw things much more clearly. Above all, it was clear that Hitler's unscrupulous power and war policies were only possible because his generals had served him faithfully, obeyed him blindly and actively assisted him, as I had done on my 'straight way'. Thus Hitler had been able to continue the pitiless war of conquest that was now striking back at the German people in frightful retribution.

Hitler and his regime had undermined all the ethical and lawful practices of conduct between state leadership and the people, between the command of the Wehrmacht and the Wehrmacht itself. While Heitz, Schmidt, von Arnim and other generals still regarded him as the 'faithful one', they were bringing severe blame on themselves, not only for the disaster that could already be seen, but for everything in particular that the Moloch of war had conjured up.

My 'straight way' now obliged me to distance myself from the generals, who had produced such an undignified paper, and whose anger against the search for a new evaluation and a new orientation was out of all proportion; in their inflexibility, it seemed, they would rather leave the world in rubble than deal with it realistically.

I was ashamed of myself after the event for having signed the 'Corps spirit' under the damned collective condemnation against the leading speaker for the League of German Officers. I would never do that again. I undertook basically as before to engage myself with the work and aims of the proposed League of German Officers.

The Soviet war aims
Unfortunately, at this time my health was somewhat unstable and I was in the care of the doctors because of a circulatory problem. As therapy, I would have to do some light work, I thought. But that was not so easy for a staff officer or a general. The Soviet Union adhered to the Geneva Convention of 1929, according to which officers were exempt from physical labour. The Soviet camp doctor, Dr Morov, understood my reasoning and arranged for me to have an area of grass in the park, which I then dug up with some of the generals. The doctor provided some seeds. Soon I was able to supplement our meals with salads, carrots, cucumbers and herbs. The gardening helped inasmuch as I regained my body weight, which had been considerably reduced as a result of the troubles and deprivations in the big battle. Mainly I thanked the quiet care of the camp doctor, Dr Morov, for getting me through my health crisis.

But as an allotment gardener I did not lose out on the spiritual role. In this I got myself into many controversies. I remained a busy user of the camp library. A great impression was made on me by Lenin's work *Imperialism is the highest stage of Capitalism*, Nikolai Ostrovski's *How the Steel was Hardened*, Sholochov's *New Land under Plough*, Alexei Tolstoy's *Bread* and Gladkov's *Energy*; all these helped me to recognise the deeply affecting upheavals which the Soviet Union had allowed to evolve from the rubble of the old Tsarist Russia.

These books answered several of the questions that had arisen in my mind during the advance of the 6th Army the year before, concerning the scientific laboratory in the steppe village, the mighty factories in Stalingrad, the fighting workmen of the Tractor Factory. Above all, the question that I had often asked myself: what gave the Soviet soldier so much steadfastness, courage and fighting spirit, and the attributes that so astounded us and demanded such heavy casualties. Gradually I understood that the Soviet man was conscious of the need to defend his fatherland, of conducting a justified fight against the enemy who, without declaring war, had breached a treaty and fallen on the Soviet Union on the 22nd June 1941 in order to annex the socialist state and society.

In all these deliberations I found in Lieutenant-Colonel Pussyrov a ready conversationalist and patient teacher. From him I learned that Soviet soldiers and officers alike were on the whole brought up with political knowledge. They should know the whole truth about what was happening in the world around them. 'Every Red Army soldier', said Pussyrov, 'knows, for example, the Soviet Union's war aims. The Red Army is fighting to drive the German invader out of our land and to free the Soviet soil. Our fight for freedom mixes with the fighting of the people of Europe and America for their independence, for their democratic freedoms. Our war will lead to the destruction of the Hitler clique. We Soviet people nevertheless differentiate between the Hitler system and the German people. Hitler will and must be destroyed, but we hope to be able to live in friendship with the German people once more. Understand, Colonel Adam, that this is our policy.'

I nodded without a word.

'But what are the war aims of Hitler's Wehrmacht? They want not only to rob our land and our riches, but are destroying hundreds of thousands of women, children and old people. The Soviet man is to be a sub-person, stamped as of a lower race. Think of the Commissar Order! Think of the Fascist mass murders that have been organised in the Soviet Union, in Poland and in other countries, and that millions of our people have been transported to Germany to do forced labour. In view of such Fascist crimes, is it not obvious where the sub-humans are to be found?'

'It is terrible, Lieutenant-Colonel Pussyrov. How can we Germans get out of this filth, out of this wrong?'

'You can do it, you too, Colonel Adam. But you must change your views radically and not just think differently. You must fight for it, so that this filthy episode in the history of the German people at least ends quickly and a new, better Germany can be formed. I think you should begin with your own responsible political thinking and dealing to learn, and not wait for a higher rank or for orders.'

'That is easier said than done. Do you know that in the Kaiser's Army, as in the Reichswehr and the Wehrmacht, the soldier had to be unpolitical? Every political activity was forbidden to him.'

'I know that. Many Germans say that politics will ruin a man's character! You have hit upon a remark by the great Goethe: "Political song, a ghastly song!" But I believe that in this case one leaves Goethe well to one side. Perhaps you are now thinking about the role of politics in your life, especially in the battle of destruction at Stalingrad. You have experienced the consequences of Fascist politics painfully in your own life.'

Was it not a paradox that I should be taking such lessons from a staff officer in the enemy army? I admit openly that I am still thankful today to Pussyrov and to all those who helped me to sort out my problems and to get involved in thinking in a new way. Without them the way to the new shores would have been tedious and painful. By means of such talks and through studying the literature I gradually saw that the series of German defeats in the Soviet Union were not primarily the result of strategic and tactical errors by the German military command – although there were errors in abundance – but rather were the lawful result of the overwhelming Soviet war leadership and the fighting morale of the Red Army, as well as the patriotism of the Soviet people and their determination to defend their homeland, who won the fight through their increasing output of weapons, ammunition and supplies for the front. These factors began to play an ever greater role during the winter of 1941/2 as the Soviet Union overcame the surprise of the German onslaught. So from 1942 onwards they were able to exploit the full mobilisation of all their forces. The first great result of this was the German defeat on the Volga and the collapse of the southern front in 1942/3.

The founding of the League of German Officers
Again the waves rose in Voikovo Camp as the news spread of the founding of the League of German Officers. On the 11th and 12th September 1943 more than a hundred delegated officers from five countries, as well as members of the National Committee 'Freies Deutschland' and a row of guests, gathered in Luniovo near Moscow. The severe German disasters on all fronts had given a group of senior officers the last incentive to take part in the 'Freies Deutschland' movement. The initiative of the German Communist Party and its central committee, as well as the National Committee, had enabled the officers to found their own organisation attached to the 'Freies Deutschland' movement; this had given their movement a wider basis, and it had fallen on fruitful ground.

In Voikovo, following the visit of Generals von Seydlitz and Lattmann, Colonel Steidle and Major von Frankenberg, we were not unprepared. The condemning verdict had made things quite clear. Now it was known that General von Seydlitz had been voted president of the League of German Officers, with General Edler von Daniels, Colonels Steidle and van Hooven as vice presidents. Major-Generals Dr Korfes and Lattmann were also on the committee. In order to ensure constant cooperation between the National Committee and the board of the League of German Officers, a few days later General von Seydlitz was voted vice president of the National Committee. Apart from this, the National Committee 'Freies Deutschland' was enlarged by Daniels, Lattmann, Dr Korfes and a few other officers.

As we discovered this from the newspaper *Freies Deutschland*, the cries of the leading group in Voikovo broke out again. They arranged a fresh statement about Seydlitz, Daniels, Korfes and Lattmann. Old Pfeffer burst out angrily: 'By doing so they have finally distanced themselves from us. We will have nothing more to do with them and will boycott them should we meet them.'

Paulus, von Lenski, Wulz and I did not agree with this complaining. Paulus looked through it to ensure that he and Pfeffer were not shown as in agreement with the threatened boycott.

The League of German Officers turned to 'Tasks and Target Setting' so that a deep consciousness of duty and feeling of responsibility for our people towards every German officer might check the catastrophe threatening Germany. In conformity with the analysis of the National Committee, the League of German Officers declared:

> The war has become meaningless and hopeless. Its continuance lies exclusively in the interest of Hitler and his regime. Consequently the National Socialist government, which is acting against the will of the people and the nation, will never be ready to allow the opening of the way that alone can lead to peace.
> This recognition forces us to declare a fight against Hitler's criminal regime and for the creation of a government with sufficient means of power with which, as seen from our side, peace and a happy future for our Fatherland can be assured.

With this special appeal, the 6th Army's surviving combatants turned to the German generals and officers, the people and the Wehrmacht:

> All Germany knows what Stalingrad means.
> We went through Hell.
> We were declared dead and have arisen to a new life
> We can no longer say nothing!
> We have more than anyone the right to speak, not only in our own names, but in the names of our dead comrades and all the victims of Stalingrad. That is our right and our duty.

The oath of allegiance

In the newspaper *Freies Deutschland* I read with close attention the speech that Major-General Lattmann had made at the founding conference of the League of German Officers. He spoke about the oath of allegiance. Like so many others, this question had greatly moved me at the time. Generations of German officers had sworn the oath to the head of state as the highest attribute of a soldier's honour. Were there any grounds that vindicated breaching the oath? Lattmann went from the ethical content of the oath, to the relationship between the Führer and the follower that the oath made reciprocally binding. He recalled the order by a commanding general not long before the conclusion of the fighting in the cauldron: 'The Führer has ordered that we should fight to the last. God orders, my men!' In this way tens of thousands fulfilled their oath to the utmost. But how far can this 'loyalty' be taken?

'If one thinks this loyalty through to the end,' said Lattmann, 'then one comes to the conclusion: "Even if Germany goes under, the oath of allegiance remains undamaged!" In this extreme consequence lies the justification for describing the further binding of the oath as immoral. As we are of the view that any further fighting will lead to the destruction of our German people, we see under quite different conditions the oath to the person of Adolf Hitler to be null and void.'

While Hitler knew that our promise bound us to him, he could contrive plans that must make him 'the greatest of all Germans'. It was for this idea that the expensive blood of our comrades had been sacrificed, not for Germany any longer! Was this not an abuse of our loyalty, was it not the abusing of a right that he was exploiting from our ethical belief in the wording of the oath?

Lattmann continued: 'We never took this oath to make him or ourselves "Lords of Europe"! We swore by God to be entirely loyal if a war for Germany arose. He, however, whose loyalty we praised, turned this oath into a lie; now, however, we ask our people to be even more compliant.'

It was a clean, earnest discussion that impressed me deeply. The speeches by Colonel van Hooven and Steidle, as well as that by General von Seydlitz, also had the honourable intention of saving Germany before it was too late.

Solution: withdrawal to the Reich borders
A few days later the resolution of the National Committee and the board of the League of German Officers was published: 'Orderly retreat of the army to the Reich boundaries under responsible leaders contrary to Hitler's orders!' This meant that the Wehrmacht should return to the Reich's borders under the command of its generals against Hitler's orders, thus making it known that they distanced themselves from Hitler's plans of conquest, and as the strongest bearers of arms in Germany wanted to thus return to peace.

The National Committee and the League of German Officers constantly repeated their demands of September 1943 by means of loud-hailers, leaflets, personal letters, broadcasts and the newspaper *Freies Deutschland*. The following appeared in a central leaflet of October 1943:

> The National Committee has come to the following decision. There is no way of saving the army other than by an orderly withdrawal to the Reich boundaries. However, there can be no orderly withdrawal without the removal of Hitler as supreme commander. The Wehrmacht will pull out of Hitler's army, without and against Hitler, or they will not return at all.
>
> Therefore the leadership of the National Committee 'Freies Deutschland' turns to the generals: Demand and proclaim Hitler's removal, the criminaliser of the Reich and Wehrmacht, as commander-in-chief! Take your troops back in an orderly manner. Take care that your soldiers do not take matters into their own hands and flee home demoralised.
>
> To the officers and men: Demand the immediate withdrawal of the army! Be conscious that you are to be the weapons-bearers for the freedom of our new Germany.

Complying with this solution meant, both politically and militarily, a great chance for Germany. A national catastrophe would be averted, millions of human victims spared, the destruction of German cities avoided. The world had evidence that in Germany itself there were the strongest forces that could, albeit belatedly, end Hitler's regime and policies. The starting point for a peace treaty and the formation of a new Germany would be incomparably more favourable than would be the case if the war continued.

In vain! The National Committee 'Freies Deutschland' and the League of German Officers were heard on the German front and partly also in Germany. Certainly their admonishing words demanded thought, prevented several soldiers and officers in hopeless situations from dying of despair, and refuted both the big-mouthed war reports of the Fascist propagandist General Sittmar and Goebbels' lies to the effect that the Soviet Army took no prisoners. Yet no great success occurred. The German generals knew as well as the leaders of the National Committee that Germany's military defeat was inevitable, but they continued to follow Hitler's orders, out of either fanaticism or a lack of civil courage.

Lack of civil courage, political illiteracy and other dross from the past stopped me too from following my conscience and taking up an active role in the League of German Officers. Just like the Major-Generals von Lenski and Wulz, with whom I was becoming quite friendly, I agreed with the aims of the National Committee. But we had reservations about the all-encompassing way in which we were being encircled.

Lieutenant-General Schlömer left Voikovo Camp at the beginning of September. This did not come as a surprise to most of us. Schlömer was inseparable from Daniels day after day in imprisonment. We called them 'Max and Moritz'. Apparently both generals had been in sympathy with the 'Freies Deutschland' movement and the League of German Officers for a long time. General Schlömer, as well as General von Drebber, participated in the founding assembly of the League as guests.

More generals travel to Luniovo
The autumn had started cold and unfriendly. Only seldom could one now sit on a bench in the park. Our daily walks became shorter. The gardening work for this year was also over. Therefore to fill my time I carved chess figures, cigarette holders, tobacco pipes and other things that gave small pleasures here and there. Out of the paper from cigarette packets we made playing cards so that we could play Skat or other card games in the long evenings. Several hours of the day were spent on books, including well spirited and political literature, as well as on learning the Russian language, to which the Soviet camp interpreter gave us a friendly introduction.

However, the question that was burning in my soul found no answer that way. What was happening at home; what about our loved ones? My fundamental mood was perfectly summed up by these lines from Heinrich Heine: 'I think of Germany in the night/And then I fall asleep.'

General Hans Wulz, the former artillery commander of the IVth Corps, left us at this time. He had disconnected himself from the false community of resisting generals in Voikovo and went to Luniovo, the seat of the National Committee *Freies Deutchsland*. Surprisingly Generals Roske and Rodenburg also went off on journeys. I learned from Roske that he too had decided for the League of German Officers. Nevertheless in our talks within a small group he maintained a pertinent, reasonable behaviour. Actually he had also made contact with the National Committee, but then became sick and returned to Voikovo. He also confirmed that Rodenburg had joined the League of German Officers and was working together with Seydlitz in Luniovo. That hit the camp like a bomb. Rodenburg, a bastion of the 'war extenders', a member of the League of German Officers! Had he really made up his mind? Later Lieutenant-General Rodenburg turned out to be an accomplice of SS-Obersturmbannführer (Lieutenant-Colonel) Huber, who had been taken prisoner as commander of a unit on the Volga. He had stood out at the Yelabuga Camp as a member of the National Committee. Rodenburg and Huber in the summer of 1944 had wanted Captain Stolz and Lieutenant Dr Wilimzig, who had been given a National Committee document, to be released to go over to the Wehrmacht. They were to give the Gestapo details about the work, composition and location of the National Committee. The next well camouflaged attempt, which could be covered through the regard the Soviet government had for the National Committee, was able to be foiled. The main responsibility for this attempted diversion fell on General Rodenburg, and he was banished from the League of German Officers.

Fully unexpectedly, the group of obstinate generals lost their spokesman. Colonel-General Heitz, the tough soldier with the sound appetite, who covered five kilometres every day in the camp, some of it at the trot, had become ill. Following a temporary recovery, his condition deteriorated. He became completely emaciated. Professors from Ivanovo and Moscow were summoned. They confirmed cancer. The colonel-general was conveyed to a hospital in Moscow, but he could not be saved; the disease had already spread too far, and he died soon afterwards.

My friend Arno von Lenski

In the spring of 1944 I got to know my friend Arno von Lenski in the League of German Officers. He was generally, and by me particularly, regarded as a man of outstanding character. Always open-minded and warm-hearted towards those who found themselves in real difficulty, he was also sincere and open in his assessment of those who remained overbearing in age, lies and perniciousness, and misused the real arguments. A former cavalry officer, himself coming from an old officer family, and often connected with the Prussian–German army, Major-General von Lenski had found it particularly difficult, as a man of strongly rooted beliefs, to take such a revolutionary step. That he did so underlined, however, his spirited nature, his worldliness and his critical ability. For me, Arno von Lenski was the best of comrades in the spiritually difficult moral conflicts of this time, a man whose participation and sympathy I could depend on in every difficult situation.

He, like me, had watched the war situation for Germany constantly worsening since the founding of the National Committee and the League of German Officers. On the 6th November 1943 Kiev, the capital of Ukraine, was reconquered by Soviet troops. Italy had already surrendered unconditionally on the 3rd September 1943. On the 26th November 1943 a salute was fired in Moscow to celebrate the liberation of Gomel. In January 1944 the Red Army broke through the German front in great depth near Leningrad, at Novgorod, on the Ilmen Lake and at Volchov, respectively.

Walter Ulbricht's comparison with 1918

At the end of January 1944 the National Committee 'Freies Deutschland' had analysed the situation at the front in detail in a full session. Together with Lenski, I studied the speeches and resolutions of this meeting. What enlightened me above all was Walter Ulbricht's shrewd comparison with the situation in 1918, which I essentially already knew from his October

1943 article in the *Freies Deutschland* newspaper. 'How is the situation with the German army at the beginning of this winter?' he asked. 'Hitler has almost run out of reserves . . . In addition to this, the Luftwaffe is so weakened that it is completely incapable of protecting the German industrial areas. Without doubt, Germany's situation and that of the German army are worse than in 1918.'

Then he cited a description that Field Marshal von Hindenburg had given in his book *From my Life*. The then chief of the general staff of the field army had written: 'Ever smaller is the number of German troops, ever larger are the gaps in the defensive positions. . . . We have no new forces to deploy like the enemy. Instead of a fresh America, we have only exhausted allies and they are close to collapsing. How much longer will our front be able to bear this vast stress? I ask the question, the most difficult of all questions, "When must we come to an end?"'

Hindenburg saw no more possibility then of winning the war. He also knew that the Allies were declining to conduct negotiations with Kaiser Wilhelm II and the then war government. Together with Ludendorff he demanded the immediate formation of the new government, which he confirmed in his book with the following words: 'All of this compels me and forces the decision to seek an end, that is an honourable end. No one will say "Too soon".'

The retreat of the Kaiser's government in 1918 had to wait some time. Meanwhile the military collapse was ever more obvious. Walter Ulbricht established that Hindenburg, who was thoroughly loyal to the Kaiser, still had the courage to show his supreme commander the bankruptcy of his war policy, and to demand the formation of a new government that Germany's enemies would be prepared to deal with. The same demand had already long stood before Hitler's army leaders, who had the power in their hands to tumble the Hitler government in accordance with the will of the people and the army.

Walter Ulbricht concluded his contribution with the words: 'The united and courageous people and army are dealing through the National Committee 'Freies Deutschland' in order to make it possible to overturn the Hitler government and achieve peace on the basis of freedom and the national independence of our German people.'

Solution: going over to the National Committee's side

As little as von Lenski, or even Paulus, could I talk about Ulbricht's comparison with 1918, to close this argument. We were painfully disappointed at not detecting any strong echo, nor any earnest consequences on the part of an army commander or other high Wehrmacht commander. They seemed to want to go on serving Hitler to a total catastrophe for the people and army. This fact must also have an effect on the work of the

'Freies Deutschland' movement. The generals who remained openly faithful to Hitler did not think that it was possible for the Wehrmacht to make an orderly withdrawal to the Reich borders to enable a ceasefire.

The former solution could therefore not be repeated. In order at least to save the lives of many officers and soldiers, and to shorten the hopelessly lost situation, while daily streams of blood and millions of material assets still contributed to the continuation of the war, the National Committee 'Freies Deutschland' set up a new resolution: 'Suspension of the fighting and defecting to the side of the National Committee "Freies Deutschland".'

At first glance I was alarmed when I read the National Committee's altered resolution. Did it not mean a disbandment of the front, a call for disintegration, the creation of chaos? I bore these questions day and night around with me and spoke to Lenski and Paulus about them, but then came to the conclusion that this solution of the National Committee offered a practical way out for the comrades at the front. Chaos and the disintegration of the Wehrmacht had been going on for a long time. This was not because of the National Committee, but was exclusively the fault of Hitler and his holding-on generals. Whoever wanted to save themselves on the Eastern Front must break through in the way advised by the 'Freies Deutschland' movement.

The Teheran conference

Yet another question concerned me. In December 1943 the heads of state or heads of the governments of the Soviet Union, the USA and Great Britain met in Teheran. The determination of the Allies to fight on until Hitler's Germany surrendered unconditionally drove the diehards of Voikovo into a fury once more. On revised grounds they sought to shift the blame for this decision from the German Fascists to the National Committee. But who was actually conducting the war? The Hitler Wehrmacht or the National Committee 'Freies Deutschland'? Who had changed its whole character, Goebbels or Weinert?

Gradually, such stupid, hateful blackening of the last remains of traditional cohesion tore a rift between von Lenski, me and several other searchers on one side and the majority of the incorrigibles among the generals in Voikovo on the other. Certainly it was not easy for us to look stark reality in the eye. But what else could we expect after all that had happened? We also had no rights or guarantees to demand.

I myself was nevertheless of the firm opinion that unconditional surrender did not mean the destruction or enslavement of the German people, but rather getting rid of the Hitler state, the Hitler Wehrmacht and Hitler politics for ever.

In Krasnogorsk a second time

After von Lenski had left Voikovo, Paulus said to me: 'Now I am anxious to know what you are up to. Actually you should have gone with von Lenski. I know, though, why you are staying. I too have become cleverer during the last year. If you want to join the League of German Officers, then don't let me hold you back. We will always remain what we were in the years of fighting and conflict together: good friends.'

'I would only leave you, Field Marshal, if I was urgently required elsewhere.'

For both of us it came sooner than expected. At the beginning of July 1944 I was taken to Krasnogorsk. A few days after my arrival, a transport arrived with officers who had been captured in the Crimea. Among others I got to know the 1st general staff officer of an infantry division, whose name I have since forgotten. Above all I wanted to know from him what effect the fall of the 6th Army at Stalingrad had had on the German people.

'Officially you are all dead. Hitler himself has said that often enough. At the beginning of February the year before last there were three days of general mourning. The state radio broadcast the report of a German pilot who had flown over Stalingrad in the last hours. He had observed how the department store in whose cellar Paulus was sitting with the army's staff had been blasted to pieces. A further visible explosion had darkened the sky. In illustrated newspapers there appeared drawings of Paulus and some staff officers, surrounded by the dead, joining in the fight with machine-pistols to the last bullet. Your superior was depicted in many speeches, press reports and radio broadcasts with a halo around him. We all wanted to avenge your deaths.'

'Yes, so you say. But did word not trickle through that Paulus, Seydlitz, Daniels and many others were still alive?'

'Yes, of course,' replied the Ia, 'but first gradually and only one at a time. The whole truth about the fate of the 6th Army is hardly known by anyone at home today. What is known comes from the activity of the National Committee "Freies Deutschland".'

'But we have been writing regular postcards home for one and a half years,' I returned.

'I happen to know that they do arrive in Germany. Perhaps you can remember the former adjutant of the XIth Corps. He was head of the final staff in Stalingrad. In confidence he told me that on Hitler's orders the postcards from the Stalingrad prisoners of war may not be delivered to their relatives. They are lying in a Spandau fort.'

'That is indeed a complete secret. I am very sorry, but you cannot say anything about this in Voikovo Camp, where some of the generals obstinately assert that the Russians would hold back the cards.'

During the time of my stay in Krasnogorsk there also occurred a personal encounter with Otto Rühle, my later friend and co-author of this book. I was on a stroll through Camp 27 when I was greeted by a young officer. From his dialect I believed I recognised a fellow Hessian, and I asked him where he came from. He announced that he was a born Schwabian. We had often been not far from each other in the cauldron, he being at the main dressing station of the 305th Infantry Division, the Bodensee Division, later at a LIth Corps field hospital in Stalingrad-Centre, myself at army headquarters. From Otto Rühle I then discovered that on the 30th January 1943 he had been taken prisoner on the other side of Red Square about 300 metres from the department store. He had already joined the National Committee 'Freies Deutschland' a year ago. I was happy to get to know this sympathetic Württemberger, not knowing that four years later he would become a close friend.

The assassination attempt of 20 July 1944
I was waiting for a talk with my friend Arno von Lenski, with whom I wanted to discuss briefly my joining the League of German Officers. During a year and a half of captivity I had learnt that many apparently simple things needed his attention. '*Budiet*' was the often-heard Russian expression for it. So I was patient, spending my time reading, going for walks, chatting.

On the 21st July 1944 I was already sitting at the open window of my room when I heard that the prisoners of war were to assemble on the camp street. I went out into the open air and sat on a bench next to the entrance to the blockhouse in which I lived. The interpreter excitedly appeared with a copy of *Pravda* before him and read with a loud voice that on the 20th July a bomb attack had been made on Hitler. During a conference at the headquarters near Lötzen, Colonel Graf Schenk von Stauffenberg had detonated a bomb. Hitler and several generals were lightly wounded. General Schmundt was dead.

Like all the assembled prisoners-of-war officers and soldiers, I held my breath. Stauffenberg I knew fleetingly from a visit to the staff of the 6th Army. At the mention of his name, I jumped up and got closer to the interpreter so that I did not miss a word. So, the thought went through my head, there are forces in the homeland who are drawing conclusions about Hitler's catastrophic policies and are taking action. I was inwardly happy that resistance against Hitler should become apparent in the homeland in this way, and at the League of German Officers I waited intently for further news. Moreover I was happy that among the rebels, in addition to Stauffenberg, were such men as Field Marshal von Witzleben, Colonel-General Beck, Generals Fellgiebel and Olbricht, and Colonels Finckh, Mertz von Quirnheim and others. I was disappointed that Hitler, with those generals and officers, as well as the SS, hit back so relatively weakly at the resistance and dealt with the conspirators bloodily. The rebels' main error was doubtless that they believed they could dispose of Hitler in a small coup, in contrast to the National Committee 'Freies Deutschland' which saw in the mass of the people and the army the forces to overthrow Hitler and form a truly national, peace-loving and democratic Germany.

Member of the League of German Officers

Shortly before the 20th July I had sought out General von Seydlitz in Krasnogorsk. He briefed me on the developments in the central sector of the eastern front. In fourteen days the Red Army had pushed more than 350 kilometres to the west along a front some 300 kilometres wide. At the beginning of the offensive they had conquered territory the size of Holland, Belgium and Switzerland. Up until the 9th July a further fourteen German generals had been captured and four had fallen. Worth knowing was that for the first time a large formation, the remains of the XIIth Corps under the command of Lieutenant-General Vincenz Müller, had laid down its arms. By the middle of July 1944 the number of generals taken prisoner in the central sector had risen to twenty-six, and at least fifteen others had fallen. Army Group 'Mitte' had been defeated. From Lake Peipus to Galiz, the Wehrmacht was fleeing back westwards under the blows of the Red Army.

Arno von Lenski, who sought me out the next day, took on the formalities of my acceptance as a member of the League of German Officers. I was inwardly relieved that I no longer had to take this step. Looking back to clarify my way from the end of the cauldron battle on the Volga, it seemed that as an active enemy of Hitler's I had been tardy and resistant. It was a fact. I had had many hurdles to cross to get through to the right theoretical acknowledgement of the military, political and moral situation of Hitler's Germany.

In Stalingrad Hitler and his regime were unveiled as representing a system of cynical contempt and common betrayal. But I personally believed that I had gone the 'right way'. Would I now be a traitor? Could I endanger my family in the homeland? Could I separate myself from the honoured Field Marshal Paulus? The answers to these questions needed time to mature. A further way must be found for answering the question how I, as a prisoner of war, could contribute to the overthrow of Hitler, and what would happen afterwards.

And for me then, just as I had achieved theoretical clarity over these conflicting problems, something else was necessary. The decisive, perhaps also the worst: civil courage. That was not like bravery in war. Behind bravery in war stands either directly or indirectly the order of the superior commander. The civil courage necessary for Germany to rise up against Hitler could not be based on that kind of order. Quite the contrary: it means the rejection of such orders. It conflicted with the voice of conscience and reason.

During the next days I went to various discussions together with Generals von Seydlitz, Lattmann, Dr Korfes and von Lenski. I was particularly delighted when I heard that Field Marshal Paulus was on his way from Voikovo to Moscow. Several days later I visited him, together with von Seydlitz. Our conversation was especially friendly. Paulus was happy to have got away from the grumbling atmosphere of Voikovo. The news of the assassination attempt on Hitler had provoked indignation from most of these generals, although some of them had become uncertain. Paulus spoke openly of his sympathy for the National Committee 'Freies Deutschland' and the League of German Officers. When I left him, I was convinced that we could soon reckon on his cooperation.

The men of the National Committee 'Freies Deutschland'
Luniovo had been the seat of the National Committee 'Freies Deutschland' and the League of German Officers for two years now, and my abode and workplace. There I came into close contact with generals and officers whom I already knew: General Walter von Seydlitz, a soldier through and through, who had already come out against Hitler in the cauldron; Major-General Dr Korfes, an historian who as early as the advance of 1941 had opposed the shootings of hostages and Jews; Major-General Martin Lattmann, a former convinced National Socialist, who now saw Hitler's ideals as derisory and betraying; Major-General Arno von Lenski, my closest friend and former cavalry officer; Colonel Luitpold Steidle, the Catholic Action supporter and intrepid regimental commander; the Engineer Majors Karl Hetz and Herbert Staßlein; Major Heinrich Homann, son of a Hamburg ship owner; Major Egbert von Frankenberg, a Luftwaffe officer from an old officer family; and Major Hermann Lewerenz, Secretary of the League of German Officers. Among the other members and colleagues of the National Committee that I got to know were the corporals or privates Hans Goßens, Dr Günter Kertzscher, Max Emendörfer, Heinz Keßler, Reinhold Fleschhut and Leonard Helmschrott – workers, officials and farmers in civilian life. An important role in the work of the 'Freies Deutschland' movement was played by a group of Wehrmacht padres, among them the Catholic priests Josef Kayser, Peter Mohr and Dr Aloys Ludwig, as well as the Evangelical priests Johannes Schröder, Nikolai Sönnischen, Matthäus Klein and Dr Friedrich Wilhelm Krummacher. Dr Krummacher was a senior consistorial adviser in the Berlin external office. In the autumn of 1943 he was taken prisoner near Kiev. After the flight of the German troops, a Soviet Union special state commission established that during the occupation more than 195,000 innocent Kiev citizens – men, women, children and old folk – had been shot, hanged or poisoned. Dr Krummacher had seen exhumed corpses from these massacres near Babi Yar in a ravine-ridden area on the edge of Kiev. Shattered by the bestial cruelty of this fascism, the Evangelical

divisional priest Krummacher joined the 'Freies Deutschland' movement. He and twenty-four other padres, before they came to Luniovo, had appealed to the Christians at the front, in which they said:

> Hitler has lit the burning fires of this war with excessive arrogance, he has spread the conquest and rapine of foreign countries with frivolous openness as war aims. For these criminal aims he has let – without any moral rights, but only an extension of his powerful rule – millions of Germans shed their blood at the front, and has brought blooming cities back in the homeland, with women and children, to destruction in the air war. He has shamed the honour of the German name through unprecedented cruelties in the occupied countries, by means of bloody terror against other peoples . . .

Over the course of time I also encountered men who had been threatened with death or internment in concentration camps in Hitler's Germany but had found asylum in the Soviet Union. There was the president of the National Committee 'Freies Deutschland', and the writer Erich Weinert. Their names I had seen on leaflets, together with those of Walter Ulbricht and Willi Bredel, in the cauldron on the Volga.

Attending a session of the National Committee
On the 3rd August 1944 I participated in a full session of the National Committee 'Freies Deutschland'. As guests were also invited sixteen generals who had shortly before become prisoners of war, including Generals Völkers, Freiherr von Lützow, Vincenz Müller, Bamler and Gollwitzer, who had disassociated themselves from Hitler in a proclamation concerning the 22nd July 1944. 'Action against Hitler is acting for Germany!' they called out to the generals and officers on the eastern front.

President Erich Weinert opened the session. Major-General Lattmann analysed the military situation resulting from the defeat of Army Group 'Mitte', which the National Committee had rightly foreseen. The war was approaching Germany's eastern borders with giant steps. The whole German nation was threatened with a Stalingrad if Hitler and his war did not come to an end.

The discussion brought all-round supplements to Lattmann's presentation, including notebooks and letters found on fallen German soldiers and descriptions from the latest prisoners of war of the effects of the air war on the homeland. Under the massed attacks of British and American bombers, German towns were sinking in rubble and ashes. Already many old folk, women and children lay buried under the wreckage. In a robust voice General of Infantry Völkers, the eldest ranking officer among the guests, reported on how the German corps and divisions had been destroyed in the central section. To the acclaim of those present, Generals Völkers, Gollwitzer, Hoffmeister, von Lützow, Müller, Traut, Engel and Klammt announced their joining of the League of German Officers.

My heart bled when I heard these reports, but in Voikovo, a few hundred kilometres away, there were other generals who called these men traitors who had called for the overthrow of the government, but who themselves had inflicted frightful harm on their way and had thrust the people and nation into the abyss.

After this session I had to be alone. I sought out a bench at the far end of the park and went over my thoughts. It pained me to have heard all these things, and reinforced me in my decision against Hitler and for a free Germany.

The consistency of Lieutenant-General Müller

In the coming days I had many talks with the most recently arrived generals. Unfortunately, with some of them I got the feeling that things had happened too quickly for them. They all complained about Hitler, but hardly any of them said a word about having shortly before been obeying his orders. Hardly any of them said anything about how they thought the new Germany should look. One clear exception was Lieutenant-General Vincenz Müller. As a Reichswehr officer in General von Schleicher's department, he had already had insight into the policies of the various national and military groups in Germany and also knew details about the preparations for war and the Fascist conquest aims. Contrary to Hitler's basic prohibition, as deputy commander of the XIIth Corps he had given the order to surrender on the 8th July 1944, thereby saving the lives of thousands of soldiers surrounded east of the Ptitsh river. Honestly and soberly, Vincenz Müller put his own past aside, but did not speak of being free from the co-responsibility for Fascism.

I also came into conversation with General Hoffmeister. By chance he mentioned that he had reported an event to a chief of engineers who had flown out of the cauldron.

'Colonel Selle?' I asked.

'Yes, that was his name. In the officers' mess of his former battalion in Hamburg-Harburg he had described before the officers and guests the criminal flippancy with which the 6th Army had been treated by the High Command in its defeat. But somebody must have betrayed him. He was arrested and sent to Spandau. Nothing further is known.'

I was sorry for Selle. But hats off to him, he had at least tried to call the person responsible by the right name.

Field Marshal Paulus turns against Hitler

On the 8th August 1944, the day on which Field Marshal von Witzleben was hanged on the gallows in Berlin on Hitler's orders, Field Marshal Paulus abandoned the reserve that he had imposed on himself for more than a year and a half. That evening he spoke on Sender *Freies Deutschland* radio. Tensely we sat in front of the radio in Luniovo. Then came the well known voice:

> Recent events have made the continuation of the war a pointless sacrifice for Germany . . . The war is lost for Germany. . . . Germany has come to this position through the leadership of the state and war by Adolf Hitler. From this comes the behaviour of some of his representatives in the occupied territories who have acted against the inhabitants in a way that is abhorrent to all true soldiers and all true Germans, and must have produced the strongest reproaches from the whole world.
>
> If the German people do not dissociate themselves from this behaviour, they must bear the full responsibility for it.
>
> Germany must rid itself of Adolf Hitler and get a new head of government to end the war and bring about circumstances that will enable our people to go on living and enter into peaceful, yes friendly, relations with our present enemies.

On the 14th August 1944 Paulus announced his membership of the League of German Officers. A few days later, on the 22nd August, he added his signature at the full assembly of the National Committee 'Freies Deutschland'.

At this meeting General von Seydlitz reported on the work of the National Committee over the previous year. The multitude of tasks surprised me: front-line addresses by loudspeaker, leaflets and personal letters to the German commanders, discussions with prisoners of war immediately behind the front line, advertising and explaining in all prisoner-of-war camps, distribution of the *Freies Deutschland* newspaper and an illustrated magazine, radio programmes broadcast from Moscow and often carried by various European stations.

The military situation in Germany was approaching complete chaos. Only the day before, Rumania had abandoned the war. The Balkan front had collapsed, the German troops in Greece and Crete were cut off. The Red Army was deep inside Hungary. Army Group 'South Ukraine' was defeated, Army Group 'North' surrounded with 350,000 men. In the west the Allies, following their landing in northern France in June 1944, were advancing. Germany's home territory would become a battlefield in the immediate future. The National Committee, which wanted to hinder this development with all its might, declared once more that only a combined fight by the army and the people could alleviate the catastrophe. With this in mind, the National Committee decided at the 13th Full Assembly, at which Walter Ulbricht, speaking especially on the role of the Wehrmacht in the new phase of fighting, called for 'All weapons against Hitler!' This was, in effect, a renewed demand to form a national people's front. The same theme came through two months later at the 14th Full Assembly, which centred on a report by Lieutenant-General Vincenz Müller: Volkssturm, the ultimate futility of Hitler's bankruptcy.

Study and work

I too had begun working, writing for the *Freies Deutschland* newspaper and discussing various problems on the radio. Because of my inclinations and knowledge, I went on working with the cultural group of the National Committee, in which, among other questions, the cultural organisation of Germany was discussed and clarified. There were similar working groups for the economy, law and social policies. Above all, however, I learnt and studied myself. Every week there was a day of recitals and discussions. German politicians, trade unionists, writers, Soviet university lecturers, professors and officers offered a copious programme.

In Luniovo I had oversight of all the National Committee's activities, as well as the organisational and educational work in the prisoner-of-war camps. There were representatives of the National Committee everywhere. From time to time delegations left Luniovo for several days to assist and instruct in the camps.

But no less important right until the end of war was the work of the National Committee at the front. In every sector of the Red Army front there was an authorised organiser. At his disposal were prisoner-of-war soldiers and officers available at the army and divisional headquarters. They worked on the front line with the spoken and written word, predominantly with leaflets. There were some that explained the aims of the National Committee and called for men to cross over in large numbers. There were others that revealed the nature of the war and the Hitler government, that described Soviet captivity and finally, in view of the local situation, the purposeless of resistance. Also personal letters sent back by captured generals or commanders played a certain role.

A similarly important and effective means was the loudspeaker, in varying strengths and range. The transmissions had a similar effect to the leaflets, taking into consideration the immediate front activity.

Ever more often individual prisoners of war were sent back. Above all, they demonstrated what Soviet captivity entailed and disproved Goebbels' propaganda. Most of them had the task of forming Wehrmacht groups of the National Committee and of leading them to the front commanders at a set time.

The movement's authorities valued the results of these activities highly, conducted talks with new prisoners of war and explained to them at the collecting camps about captivity and the war situation. They carried out all of the work in their front sector and prepared the commissioned pamphlets, radio texts and information. Not last they maintained liaison with the National Committee in Luniovo.

The teachers from Korsun
Several times in special circumstances the National Committee and the Presidium of the League of German Officers sent delegations of their leading members to the front. Thus at the beginning of February 1944 General von Seydlitz, accompanied by Major-General Dr Korfes, Major Lewerenz and Captain Dr Hadermann, went to the Korsun-Shevschenkovski cauldron to support the task of the National Committee's working group under Colonel Steidle and Second-Lieutenant von Kügelgen. Here some 75,000 German soldiers were surrounded and faced certain destruction if they did not surrender at the right time. The generals and officers of the former 6th Army talked to General Stemmermann, the commander of the surrounded troops, whose situation was becoming ever more similar to that of Paulus at Stalingrad.

In the cauldron itself, meanwhile, SS-General Gille had grabbed command for himself. He ordered a senseless outbreak, from which only a few thousand got through. Another 55,000 German soldiers and officers remained dead on the battlefield, and 18,000 surrendered, of whom the majority immediately joined the German freedom movement.

The battle of Korsun-Shevschenkovski played an important role in the further work of the National Committee and the League of German Officers. It showed that Hitler's order 'We never surrender!', from the commander-in-chief of the Wehrmacht, was still being maintained. The sober General Stemmermann was detained by SS-General Gille. He confirmed what the National Committee had already established at its 6th Session in January 1944, that a retreat to the Reich boundaries under the command of its generals could not be relied on. In the last phase of the cauldron battle of Korsun-Shevschenkovski the new password 'Suspend the fighting and cross over to the side of the National Committee "Freies Deutschland"' was used for the first time.

Many prisoner-of-war statements confirmed that the existence of the National Committee and the League of German officers was known to almost all the members of the Wehrmacht on the eastern front. Radio *Freies Deutschland* was heard by many at home and at the front. A special stimulus to this was the broadcasting of names and greetings by members of the Wehrmacht who were now prisoners of war. It was especially important that people in the front line and in the homeland were aware that many thousands of German prisoners were alive. This knowledge alone saved the lives of tens of thousands who, without it, would have committed suicide in hopeless situations.

War front lines on German soil

In the autumn of 1944 East Prussia became a battlefield. In the west also the front line was already being pushed back onto German soil. It was so to speak the last but one minute before the land war covered the whole of Germany. At this point fifty prisoner-of-war German generals assembled in Osero, a country house near Moscow and Paulus's former place of detention. Walter Ulbricht spoke on behalf of the National Committee about the military situation. I had a comfortable place and was able to observe the attentive audience well. How the times had changed, I thought to myself. When had a Prussian-German general ever thought that the leading Communists would conduct the future direction of the war much more competently than all the German generals put together! This man had warned us already two years ago. 'Enemy propaganda' we called it then. But how right he had been!

Some of the generals had prepared an appeal to the people and the Wehrmacht. Several present based their agreement on personal experiences and assessments. There were several small amendments. Then General von Seydlitz was able to confirm unanimous agreement. Field Marshal Paulus was the first to sign, followed by the other forty-nine generals.

In January 1945 the Red Army launched the Vistula offensive, the last of the Second World War. A few months later the battle of Berlin came to an end and the Soviet Army hoisted a victory flag over the Reichstag. The Wehrmacht High Command surrendered unconditionally on the 8th May 1945 to the Soviet Union and its Western Allies. Hitler and his propaganda chief Goebbels committed suicide.

A few weeks before we heard of an event that appalled both me and many of my Luniovo comrades: the beautiful city of Dresden, with its irreplaceable historical buildings, crumpled into dust and ashes on the night of 13th/14th February 1945. Ten thousand people of all ages lay buried under the rubble. Anglo-American bombers had been responsible for this act of barbaric destruction. In no way was it a military necessity to turn this open city on the Elbe into a sea of flames. The war was already militarily decided. Soviet forces were approaching the city from the east. No Soviet aircraft had dropped a single bomb on the city. Swiss newspapers said that the British and Americans had wanted to prevent Dresden falling intact into the Red Army's hands. We in Luniovo came to the same conclusion. The Elbe city was an important communications junction. Apparently the Western Powers wanted to slow down the Soviet advance into the heart of Germany. The terror attack on Dresden was another link in the chain of hostile acts by the imperialist circles in England and America against their Soviet allies, who above all had already witnessed the long delays visible on the second front in the west. Here lay the kernel of a policy of the Western Powers against their Socialist allies, which in the post-war years proved to be the seeds of the 'Cold War'.

[*The Anglo-American attacks on Dresden were in fact in response to a specific request from the Soviet Government – Translator.*]

History acknowledges the National Committee

The last months of the war were for me and my comrades especially difficult to bear. My heart bled when I heard the daily reports from the front describing how the war was destroying and annihilating as it bit deeper into Germany. In Hitler's Volkssturm children and old men were being driven into the slaughter. And above all there were no generals who had even the remnants of a sense of responsibility, and even now, long past the point of no return, they ordered the Wehrmacht's senseless resistance to continue. The finale in Germany echoed what had happened to the German army on the Volga, but on a worse scale. The human victims and losses of material that this demanded exceeded my worst fears. The National Committee 'Freies Deutschland' and the League of German Officers had unfortunately been right in calling on the people and the Wehrmacht for almost two years to put an end to Hitler and the war, or there would be the worst catastrophe in German history.

In alliance with the leading worker class

But back to Luniovo in the spring of 1945. In me the knowledge ripened that a free, better Germany must be renewed from the ground up. Neither the gun-manufacturing magnates nor Hitler's generals had stood up to the test of history. Liebknecht, Thälmann, Pieck, Ulbricht and their comrades had all opposed the war. Their class, the working class, which already for decades had been responsible for the greatest creation of national wealth, must now also become the politically leading class, the ruling class in Germany. Only this way could peace in Germany find a secure home. In the 'Freies Deutschland' movement we had learnt that the leader of the workers' movement had begun honestly combining the peasantry, the managers and other workers. We too, the officers and generals of Hitler's army, had been sincerely offered a hand in this joint national movement.

The Allies' Potsdam Agreement confirmed the National Committee's thinking about the new Germany: Fascism and militarism were to be torn out by the roots, the economic and financial monopolies smashed, the whole of Germany democratically remodelled. It was not easy for me and most of my comrades to accept the eastern boundaries established by the conquerors. There were many difficult discussions about this. But I already knew the previous history and course of the war in Poland. The pincers formed by East Prussia and Silesia had twice been used by German militarism to attack Poland. Over six million Poles were destroyed and murdered in the Second World War. As bitter as it was, Germany had to acccpt the consequences of Hitler's war crimes. The security claims of Poland and the Soviet Union were justified.

Not all the generals and officers who had signed the proclamations against Hitler in the previous weeks wanted to accept the reality of German responsibility for the war. Several crumbled away in the following period; they broke away from the 'Freies Deutschland' movement and returned to the font of the incurables. A little time later I encountered many hate-filled looks from such people in Voikovo.

Even during the last days of the war a number of leading Communists, headed by Walter Ulbricht, departed to work in Germany. Throughout the summer several groups of anti-Fascists, among them soldiers and officers, were flown in from the Red Army's occupied zone so that they could take part in the building of a new Germany, but the return was not so quick for everyone. Some members of the National Committee allowed themselves to be carried away by the reproaches of the German emigrants against the Soviet Union. The effect of the whole atmosphere did not change the course of things.

The last complete session of the National Committee 'Freies Deutschland' took place on the 2nd November 1945. Erich Weinert drew up a detailed statement. After the work at the front, he praised above all the contribution of the re-education of the prisoners of war, which was especially valuable for the democratising of large sections of the German people. The basic elements of the National Committee now lived on in Germany in the block of democratic parties. In the homeland the block had taken over the immediate guidance of the political, economic and social organisations. Thus the existence of the National Committee outside Germany had become superfluous. At the conclusion of the session, Weinert suggested the disbandment of the National Committee 'Freies Deutschland'. General von Seydlitz submitted an appropriate proposal for the League of German Officers. The radio and newspaper *Freies Deutschland* also ceased their activities.

Paulus as a witness at Nuremburg
On the 18th October 1945 the opening session of the International Military Court was held in Berlin for the acceptance of witness statements against the main war criminals. This gave us plenty to talk about. I felt great satisfaction that Hitler's closest accomplices – Göring, Keitel, Jodl, Raeder, Dönitz, Rosenberg, Ribbentrop and others – should have to atone for the crimes against peace and mankind for which they were substantially to

blame. *Pravda* and *Isvestia* brought out daily reports on the course of the process, which contained so many infamous details that I as a German sometimes felt quite mortified. This I had also participated in for years, contributing my whole strength into it to support goals that were thoroughly anti-human and criminal!

Paulus had been working very intensely. I knew that this was connected with the process, but I was not a little astounded when I heard on the radio that he would appear at Nuremberg as a witness against the war criminals. In the many hours in which – bound by Hitler's order – he had decided to hold on in the cauldron on the Volga, he had let fall from time to time a bitter word about the whole war. Now, however, in his statement at Nuremberg he produced a clear condemnation of the war. Without holding back, he went through the previous history of the war since the autumn of 1940 exploring Hitler Germany's systematic preparations for a war of conquest against the Soviet Union. Here are some extracts from his interview with the Soviet main prosecutor, General Rudenko:

General Rudenko: 'Under what conditions was the armed assault conducted on the Soviet Union that had been prepared by the Hitler regime and by the Wehrmacht High Command?'

Paulus: 'The attack on the Soviet Union proceeded, as I have explained, according to a long-prepared and careful plan. The attacking troops were first established in depth in the concentration areas. They were at first, according to special instructions, ordered forwards by sectors into the starting positions and then moved off along the whole front from Rumania to East Prussia; apart from this, the Finnish War was under way at the same time. . . .

'A great deceptive undertaking organised from Norway to the French coast was planned to suggest the intention of a landing in England in June 1941, and with it distract attention from the east. But not only for the operational, but especially for the tactical surprise, all requirements were met. For example, the forbidding of all visible reconnaissance over the border before the war began. This implied on one hand that we would have to bear losses that could arise through the sacrifice of reconnaissance in the interest of surprise, but on the other hand it meant also that the enemy would not fear an attack over the border.

'All these measures show it concerned a criminal assault here . . .'

General Rudenko: 'Who among the accused was an active participant in the development of the war of attack on the Soviet Union?'

Paulus: 'Of the accused, as far as those I can see, Hitler's first military advisers. That is, the chief of the Wehrmacht High Command, Keitel, the chief of the Wehrmacht Command Office, Jodl, and Göring in his capacity as commander-in-chief of the Luftwaffe and as the head of the armaments industry . . .'

I heard that Paulus had also spent several days in Dresden. I would have loved to hear how it looked – and the other German cities – from his own personal experience. But I did not meet up with him as he had gone to new accommodation in the Soviet Union since his return. Instead of this meeting with Paulus, I experienced something quite different. In March or April 1946 I was summoned by the commandant of our camp. 'How is your family, Colonel Adam?' he asked, once I had sat down.

What sort of a question is that, I thought, when he knows that I have had no news from home. Not exactly friendly, I replied: 'How would I know, I have received no post so far.'

With a gentle smile he took hold of a file and pulled out a postcard. 'Is this perhaps addressed to you?'

I grabbed it hastily. My heart threatened to burst as I recognised my wife's handwriting. Then I had to smile. The card was addressed simply to 'Colonel Adam, Stalingrad'.

'Now you can see how diligent our post is,' said the commandant. 'Now send your correct address home. Your wife and daughter will be waiting anxiously for a sign of life from you. And my congratulations on this first news.'

He gave me a plain postcard from a stack and I left beaming. I now knew that my wife and daughter had survived the war!

Holding-on strategy in Voikovo
In the middle of May 1946 Luniovo was cleared. Already during the previous months many members and associates of the National Committee and the League of German Officers had gone back home or moved to other camps. With a group that contained among others Generals von Seydlitz, von Lenski and Dr Korfes, Majors Homann and von Frankenberg, I went to the generals' camp at Voikovo. The camp's commandant, political officer and interpreter greeted us warmly as old acquaintances. Less friendly was our reception by the German general prisoners of war. Most of them I hardly knew personally at all, and many of them I had never even heard of. But even the former generals of the 6th Army with whom I had lived for over a year in 1943/44 were afraid of talking to me. The only one to greet me as an old friend was General Wulz.

I was allocated a room already occupied by an admiral, two generals and a Labour Corps major. These gentlemen would have preferred to show me the door. Only reluctantly did they clear a space for me. Their main preoccupation was playing cards and their main conversational topics were 'the grand old times', the rank lists and their experiences in officers' messes. They had little interest in the copious library, much more in the food.

It is not easy for these groups of poorly spirited, defeated lords of the battlefield to find the right words. Egbert von Frankenberg, who experienced this time in Voikovo with me, has written in his book *Meine Entscheidung* ('*My Decision*') of his successful attempt to present some of these 'heroes' in all their stupidity, arrogance and, at the same time, political menace.

Several days after our arrival a room became available that I moved in to together with von Lenski, Dr Korfes, von Frankenberg, Homann and other comrades. I was happy not to have to listen to the brainless nonsensical reminiscing of my former roommates. At about the same time there were several moves going on within the camp. Soldiers of the support company – German, Rumanian, Italian and Hungarian – moved furniture and mattresses about. New beds and wardrobes were set up. Everything indicated that the camp was expecting new arrivals. One day it happened. The camp gate opened and in streamed some generals heavily laden with suitcases, blankets and many other things that we could barely remember. They were mainly the generals who had been captured in Kurland, but also others who until then had been accommodated in Krasnogorsk or Susdal. Many of them I knew. We watched their noisy arrival out of our windows. The camp road was overfilled in no time. Calls were exchanged between the newcomers and the 'old hands'. Then the stream gradually eased off as the new arrivals occupied their allocated rooms.

In leaving the building, I met two generals whom I knew from the War School in Dresden. Surprised, they shook my hand warmly. Had these gentlemen drawn similar consequences from their experiences as I had? But this supposition turned out to be an error. They believed that they would only meet those of a similar disposition in the generals' camp. The old ones soon briefed them. Several hours later, when I came across one of the two generals on the camp street, he turned around and went off.

In the camp there were now about 170 German, 36 Hungarian, 6 Rumanian and 3 Italian generals. They were guided by the holding-out strategies of Foertsch, Wuthmann, Specht, Hax and Marcks. Whoever strayed from the dictated line was tyrannised. In the ranks of the eternally written-off were most of those generals who, back in December, had been among the fifty who had signed the appeal together with Paulus and Seydlitz. In a kind of honorary legal proceedings conducted by the reactionary group these gentlemen had to 'confess'. They used lies and defamation to justify the steps they had taken at the time and maintained that they had signed under pressure. Once they had disassociated themselves from the League of German Officers, they were taken honourably back into the community of Hitler's most loyal officers. The whole episode left me speechless. These people were like chameleons. No wonder the soldiers of the support company made no secret of their contempt for this kind of general. But there were also some with sufficient spiritual independence not to let themselves be cowed. Among them was General Dr Altrichter.

Equally friendly, he returned my greeting without reacting to the angry looks of the others. He told me that his son, who was a year younger than my Heinz and had attended the same school in Dresden, had fallen as a young soldier. Like Paulus, Altrichter was an educated type. Among the generals he was regarded as an odd fellow, as he avoided their company, their superficial conversation and their card games. Mainly he sat alone on a remote bench in the beautiful park, reading or writing about religious matters. It was maliciously said that he wanted to found a new religious community. But as he was not brought up spiritually, he sought to set himself apart in the eyes of the others. In fact, General Altrichter rejected their narrow-minded snobbery and their military inflexibility, even if he did not join the declared anti-Fascists.

We had very close connections with the Rumanian generals. They came to our room, went out with us for walks, and always greeted us in a friendly manner. They hated Hitler and his clique, who had brought so much trouble and distress. We talked for hours in German or French about the future tasks of our people.

The three Italian generals were dedicated Fascists and stayed close to the reactionary group of German generals. The Hungarian generals held themselves back at first. They played no part with the fanatical cranks among the German generals, and seemed, despite various developments, indifferent. In the course of time we nevertheless noticed that there were some cracks in the Hungarian generals' united front. Almost all of them hated Hitler's Germany, and some had drawn similar conclusions from their experiences about the new reorganisation of their homeland.

That is something like the picture I drew in the first weeks of my second stay in Voikovo. Despite the social proscribing that the majority of Hitler's devoted henchmen sought to hang over us, we made contact with two young generals, Giese and Neumann. They also moved into our room.

The 'Foertsch Staff'
The weeks and months I spent in Voikovo from 1946 to 1947 were not useless for me. I turned my studies to many fields, including politics, science and literature, increased my knowledge of the Russian language and worked on my hobby, mathematics. I attentively read the German newspapers, which reached us somewhat late but apparently without gaps. Shortly before I had left Luniovo came the news of the unification of the two German workers' parties as the Socialist United German Party (*Sozialistischen Einheitspartei Deutschlands*). My friends and I took this event to be of great historical significance, for it was clear to us that without firm leadership by a united, purposeful workers' party, a basically renewed Germany could not be achieved. We were proud that the way of the community of all democratic and constructive forces that had been combined in the 'Freies

Deutschland' movement had been initiated, and was now established in East Germany. The daily contact with the strategies of imperialism and militarism in the Voikovo Camp was a good school for us in our later political work. The convulsive troubles of this clique to preserve its self-containment, the prevention of individuals stepping out of line, showed its weakness. News from Germany that involved critical thoughts was simply dismissed as untrue. A stubborn rejection of all new things was the general line of these gentlemen. Should one dare to dance out of line, he was brought back to common sense with the threat of a court of honour.

The leaders of the reaction were some of the former general staff officers. At their head stood General Foertsch, chief of the general staff of Army Group 'Kurland'. Not an awkward man, he knew how to tread carefully and to reveal little. Nevertheless, we discovered on various occasions that he really was a wire-puller. 'With the Americans against the Russians' was his motto. Now and then we heard from this or that general that he nevertheless looked anxious before he started even a short conversation. To the 'Foertsch Staff' belonged General Niehoff, commandant of Breslau, General Wuthmann, commandant of the German troops on Bornholm, General Hermann, a young Luftwaffe commodore, and General Marcks, chief of staff of Army Group 'Kurland'.

For a long time we had been aware that certain generals were meeting regularly at a particular place in the park. From a distance one could see them discussing and writing. By accident it happened that one day the Second-Lieutenants von Einsiedel and von Puttkamer, who had come from Luniovo with us, were witness to a spiritedly presented speech. It was hard to believe what was reported to us. The defeated generals had analysed the Eastern Campaign in their own way, drawing conclusions for the structure and arming of the German army after the conclusion of peace agreements, and they noted quite carefully what could be done better in the future.

Weeks later, at about two o'clock in the morning, I was awoken by loud voices. In the room stood a Soviet officer with two soldiers. 'Control,' he said.

There was lively activity everywhere. The windows were also lit in the building opposite mine. Awkwardly enough, baggage, beds and clothing were checked. Nothing escaped the searching eyes. Boxes full of material – mainly written pieces, letters and books – went to the headquarters. A cannonade of protests came from the generals. Soon afterwards some of the seized items were returned, but suspicious materials, including the generals' war interpretation, found their way into the files of the Soviet authorities. We heard that black-lists had also been found with our names on them. What this meant, whispered General Niehoff to me when we met in the Linden alley, is that 'you rascals will be the first we hang when we go home'.

Poor wretch, I thought. Niehoff was not only a fully hard-boiled reactionary, but also a common pig, who used filthy language and told dirty stories such as I had never heard from anyone before. With his chest full of high decorations, he strutted through the camp and trumpeted his smutty jokes loudly so that nobody could fail to hear them. Apparently he believed he could impress people that way. One day, however, he and his kind had the wind knocked out of their sails. It was the end of 1946 when the camp commandant, on the basis of a Four Power decision, had all decorations and badges of rank confiscated. This also applied to the generals' red-gold insignia, and all the silver tinsel. Without them, the uniforms really looked stained and faded. The truth of the words 'clothing makes men' could seldom have been clearer than in this example.

'Colonel Adam to the transport!'
During the course of the summer members of the support company erected a small log hut behind the kitchen building under the direction of a Soviet specialist. It consisted of three rooms that could be heated by a single stove. Once the hut was ready, the camp commandant said that we could move inside. This we naturally did, and gladly. The big room accommodated General von Seydlitz, the painter Lieutenant-Colonel Professor Kaiser and myself, while the smaller of the rooms was occupied by Generals von Lenski and Dr Korfes. In the front room lived the two prisoner-of-war soldiers who had been allocated to us. The hut became the centre of our group. But it did not remain all that long in the old form. In the spring of 1947 von Lenski was moved to Paulus at Turmilino near Moscow and General Buschenhagen moved in with us; previously he had been with Paulus, together with Vincenz Müller and Dr General Professor Dr Schreiber.

To the annoyance of the guard of generals, Buschenhagen reported how generously he had been treated by the Soviet citizens. Several times he had visited Moscow with its many places of interest. He was full of praise for the museums and galleries, the wonderful underground railway and the resilience with which the Soviet people went about overcoming the difficulties caused by the war.

Months later, on a hot day in July, I was standing at the work bench I had made for myself behind the hut, dressed only in my sports clothing, working on a wooden suitcase. A sergeant came up to me, smiling broadly, and called out: 'To the camp commandant immediately!'

'I must change my clothes. I cannot appear in front of the camp commandant like this.'

'But quickly, Comrade Colonel!'

A few minutes later I stood in front of the camp commandant.

'Good day, Comrade Colonel,' he greeted me. 'I have been tasked with informing you that you will be leaving our camp today. Pack your things in peace and say goodbye to your comrades. At 1800 hours the evening meal will be ready for you in the kitchen, then return here at 1900 hours.'

'Can you tell me where I am going?'

The camp commandant smiled: 'I cannot tell you that, but it is in a westerly direction. I wish you all the best for the future. Have a good journey!'

I had never moved through the camp so quickly. On the way I encountered General Wulz. 'I am going away, Father,' I called out to him.

'Where to?' he asked.

'In a westerly direction, more I do not know. At 1900 hours I am off to Ivanovo.'

The news of my departure spread quickly through the whole camp. Even generals who otherwise avoided our log hut were curious. My things were soon packed and I was able to say farewell to my comrades with whom I had a firm friendship. That was not easy, but we were convinced that in any case we would all see each other again in Germany and that the work we had begun here would be continued.

I was accompanied by a major and the interpreter Lebedev to Ivanovo, where we climbed into the night train for Moscow. For a long time I gazed through the compartment window and thought about Germany, my homeland. In Mecklenburg, Brandenburg, Sachsen-Anhalt, Thüringen and Saxony were stationed units of the Red Army, while in the west sat the British, French and Americans.

My wife lived with our daughter in an old house in Münzenberg, not far from Bad Nauheim in Hessen. That was in the American Occupation Zone. If anyone had asked me: where do you want to go, where would you like to work in future?, I would have replied without hesitation from earnest conviction: 'Where the new Germany is being built, there will I put my whole strength for disposal. But will my wife and daughter follow me?'

Another encounter with the Volga city

The train rolled into the Kasaner station. We were in Moscow. A Soviet lieutenant was waiting for me. After a hearty farewell from my escort, I went with the lieutenant to a car parked in front of the station. 'Where are we going?' I asked.

He smiled: 'You will see.'

Once we had left the city behind us, I recognised from previous experience that this was not the way to Krasnogorsk. Perhaps to Turmilino? I puzzled about a remembered description by General Buschenhagen. Then there must soon be an airfield on the right side of the road. In fact, there it was already. The aircraft were standing there in rows.

In the middle of a wood we came across an extended settlement of small and large wooden houses, single and double-storey, with stone-built buildings in between, shaded by trees and surrounded by gardens. This was a so-called *Datschen* town, where the houses were usually only occupied in the summer months. Behind a tall wire fence was our goal, a charming country house with a glazed-in veranda and a terrace that extended deep into the garden.

While I was being greeted by a major, my friend Arno von Lenski also arrived around the corner. From him I learnt that Paulus, Müller and Professor Dr Schreiber were not present at the moment but were expected soon. Arno von Lenski told me further that I would be making a long journey with him to the Volga.

'What will we do there? The population are not very friendly towards officers of the 6th Army.'

Lenski was holding a book with the title *The Stalingrad Battle*. 'This is a screenplay by the Soviet author Virta. The direction emphasises that in the film the German side is not falsely nor distortedly shown. I have already had a look at it. Tomorrow we will go through it together. We will be in Stalingrad for the exterior shots. The interior scenes are being filmed in Moscow.

'Indeed that is interesting. And when does it start?' I asked.

'At the latest in a week.'

A few days later we were sitting in a fast train to Stalingrad. As we approached our destination, the former battlefield extended to the left and right of the railway line. It still had not been possible to remove all the rubble. Mountains of iron and steel, smashed vehicles, burnt-out tanks and exploded gun barrels recalled the fury of the fighting here. There were lots of new buildings in Gumrak, and the airfield was in use. The city had bled from a thousand wounds, but new life was already growing.

The horrible past grew paralysingly high within me. I saw the tens of thousands of wounded, sick and half-starved troops of the German 6th Army, the piles of stacked frozen corpses that the iron-hard earth refused to accept. I recalled the terrible days and nights between hope and destruction, the last hours of the frightful finale. But that was not quite the last of it. It was quite different from five years before when I acknowledged the great blame that we Germans heaped upon ourselves when we broke through the border, killing and destroying in the Soviet land. In the face of the city on the Volga arising anew, I swore once more to use all my strength to ensure that eternal friendship would reign between the German and Soviet peoples.

In the following days we had opportunity now and then to look around the city and the neighbourhood. In the big factories in the north, especially the tractor factory, production was in full swing. The main road had been rebuilt south of the Zaritza, and on the river bank rose a white theatre. The trams were running. Cinemas, libraries, schools and hospitals had opened their doors. Everywhere ruins were being blown up, the rubble cleared away to make way for new housing blocks.

Lenski and I wanted to see a lot, and speak to people. There was an opportunity to do this during our extensive walks that we made in the afternoons with our attendant and an interpreter. We were particularly interested in the area in which the Soviet 62nd Army under General Chuikov had fought so hard and bitterly. One small incident showed that the spirit of these fighters remained alive. On the high bank of the Volga, not far from the bombed and burnt-out oil tanks, we met a man at work with a spade. He recognised us as former German officers and spoke to us. It transpired that he had been a senior officer in the big battle.

'Are you a Stalingrader?' I asked him.

'No, neither my wife nor I were born in Stalingrad. But when the war came to an end, we decided to live and work in this historical city,' said the colonel, who had eventually commanded a division, decisively.

'So, do you already live here?'

'Yes,' he said, 'over there.' He pointed at a ruin. 'That was once a house. You can see what remains of it. We lived like that often during the war. My wife and I have set up makeshift accommodation for us in there. And here we are building a new little house from the material lying around. Here, that is the ground plan.'

He drew the tracing of a rectangle, on the sides of which he had raised the ground for the walls, and continued: 'Should you come back in a few years, you will not see any more of the consequences of the war. Probably I will then be living in a modern house with many storeys.'

One time a cross-country vehicle took us to the Mamai-Kurgan, the dominating hill on which so much blood had flowed. Now, though, the ground looked ploughed over. Shell crater next to shell crater. And masses of blown-up shells, cartridge cases, machine-gun belts, bits of weapons and even human bones.

One day we stood in front of the rebuilt department store, at the place where my way into captivity had begun. A bronze tablet next to the entrance recorded that on the 31st January 1943 in the cellars of this building the headquarters staff of the German 6th Army under Field Marshal Paulus had been taken prisoner.

Part of the filming, about which von Lenski and I would advise, was to take place on the open square before the department store. Late one afternoon, in the presence of some senior Soviet officers, a German tank 'attack' took place. Tanks bearing the Balkenkreuz rolled over the rubble. Flames shot out of empty window holes in the ruins. Infantry with machine pistols and hand grenades attacked with a loud 'Hurrah!' Captured German officers and soldiers had been especially newly provided with uniforms for this purpose. Understandably, thousands of civilians could not miss watching this display when the rumour went round that Paulus himself would be taking part. The scenes must have aroused some bitter memories among these people. But there was no word of disgust about the German staff officers present.

With Paulus at Turmilino
At the end of September our filming mission came to an end. We made the return journey via Moscow to Turmilino, where we met Paulus and Vincenz Müller. They were as happy about our reunion as we were. The accounts from both sides went on all day long. Several times, accompanied by the camp commandant, I drove with Arno von Lenski to Moscow to get to know people, the city and museums.

Suddenly winter was upon us, the seventh that I had experienced in the Soviet Union. Christmas was drawing near. It always brought a certain melancholy with it. On the other hand I became involved at this time with the preparation of small gifts that were cut, painted or written; for me it was a special task. On the whole every day of captivity involved various activities: studying, reading, shovelling snow, walking, chatting. In the many weeks of captivity I had learnt that this was better borne when existence was governed by a set plan. So every day I sought to live to a kind of hourly programme. This saved much useless brooding, shortened the time and helped me above all to extend my knowledge systematically.

On the 28th March 1948 I celebrated my 55th birthday. Three days later we were visited by the head of prisoner-of-war affairs from Moscow. He invited us all to the lounge. This must mean something important!

With a grin the Soviet general began his performance. 'Actually I was coming tomorrow, the 1st April. But I had heard that this day is not quite taken seriously by the Germans. So, to avoid the suspicion of an April jest, I have come here today.'

After a few seconds he went on, turning to Paulus. 'Generals Müller and Lenski, General Dr Professor Schreiber and Colonel Adam will be released tomorrow and will soon return to Germany. You, Field Marshal, must have a little patience. We will bring other generals to you to keep you company. The vehicle that will take these gentlemen away will bring the new generals with it.'

I need not say anything about the joy that overcame the four of us. It was difficult for Paulus, but he did not lose his composure for a moment. He even congratulated us with a gentle smile.

Once the Soviet general had left, I went to my room as if in a dream. Now the yearned-for day of going home was tangibly near! For a long time I had realised that captivity offered me a unique opportunity to learn and study, and I had used it with all my might. But Germany remained the homeland to which I felt bound by innumerable threads.

Sunk in my thoughts, I went over to the window. There I saw Paulus alone out in the garden. He was walking up and down the main path as if in a dream. I hurried to him. Visibly pleased by my appearance, he said: 'It is difficult for me, Adam, having to remain alone. But it is quite right this way. It would be incomprehensible if an army commander-in-chief went back as long as so many prisoners of war are having to work on the reconstruction of the Soviet Union. Naturally it would be easier for me if you could all remain with me, but that would not be right. You are more urgently needed in Germany.'

'You can be assured, Field Marshal, that the parting from you comes hard. We will not forget you.'

'Where will you take up your work? Your family is living in the west.'

'Certainly, but I have already informed my wife that I will be remaining in the east.'

'You are right. I assume that Müller has made the same decision. But now you must go and pack, or you will not be ready for early tomorrow morning. I am going to stay in the garden.'

Returning home to the New Germany
1st April 1948. At last the vehicle arrived. The time for our farewells had come. Another firm handshake with Paulus: 'Till we meet again in Germany!' The vehicle rolled out of the gate. From Turmilino the journey went straight through Moscow and past the White Russian Station. Was this not the road to Krasnogorsk?

Yes, it was. In the camp that was so well known to us we met many of our friends from the National Committee again; they had been brought there from Susdal and Voikovo. We would all be making the journey home together. Before that we still had the opportunity to take part on a course organised by the Anti-Fascist School 27. At the centre point of the teaching plan stood questions on history, Marxist-Leninist philosophy and political economy, as well as the democratic new organisation of Germany. For me this was a worthwhile deepening and rounding off of my knowledge that I had predominantly acquired by self-study. Added to this were excursions to Moscow, to the Museum of the Revolution, to the Tretiakov Gallery, to the theatre and to Gorky Park. Unfortunately at the end of April a painful inflammation of the nerves in my left arm obliged me to give up the course and go into hospital. I was kept in for weeks. Specialists in Krasnogorsk and one of the Moscow poly-clinics tended to me. I remember with gratitude the senior lady doctor from Krasnogorsk, Magnitova, who gave her first name. She not only looked after my health carefully, she also gave me courage and confidence whenever I expressed doubts whether I would be fit enough for the journey home. 'Keep calm,' she said. 'You will not miss the transport, especially since the little grandchild is waiting for his grandpa.'

This lady doctor had done a lot of good for the German prisoners of war. She was generally revered as 'the Angel of Krasnogorsk'. She saw to it that I received special treatment from the Moscow doctors. It worked, and by the end of June I was able to be released as cured and to return to my comrades in the barracks.

During my stay in the hospital I had seen among the German newspapers that I was given to read an occasional copy of the *National Zeitung*. In a June number was the news that two new political parties had been founded in the Soviet zone: the Democratic Farmers' Party of Germany and the National-Democratic German Party. Today, writing more than fifteen years later, I can still recall the content and language of the programme explanations of the National-Democratic Party.

On the 10th September the vehicles were ready to take us to the Byelorussian station in Moscow. Happily we shook the hands of the Soviet officers and soldiers. Even Magnitova, so highly esteemed with her snow-white hair, appeared to wish us a happy return home.

The train went too slowly, it seemed to creep over the tracks. At last we reached Brest-Litovsk and after seemingly endlessly appearing days we finally crossed over the Oder bridge at Frankfurt an der Oder. We were back in Germany.

It was a newly arisen Germany that I was entering after six years of absence. And I, the former colonel and bearer of the Knight's Cross, who had once fallen on other countries with Hitler's army, had become a new person, a determined fighter for peace.

Chapter 7

For the New Germany

In Dresden

While I was still a prisoner of war the thoughts had ripened within me about starting anew at the place where I had belonged in 1939: Dresden. Often I had pictured the world-famous silhouette of the Elbe city, with Georg Bährs powerful dome, the slender bell tower of Chiaveri's court church and the needle-pointed castle tower. What could have remained of them after the bombing in February 1945? How were the Zwinger, the Opera, the Brühlsche Terrace, the Japanese Palace and all the many other architectural jewels that I loved so much?

I was close to tears when I saw the rubble. It was just like the ruined city on the Volga in 1942/43. Could I ever be happy again in this desolation? I could. Almost unnoticeably, but nevertheless decisively, new life was thrusting its way through the rubble, at first very slowly, but constantly gaining ground. The rebuilt theatre had already celebrated its opening.

Dresden was the most important place in my work for a new Germany. First of all I applied for a position in the Saxon Ministry of Education. At the same time I pressed through what I had learned through the National Committee 'Freies Deutschland' to become involved in immediate political work. I connected with the National-Democratic German Party, whose newspaper, *National Zeitung*, I had already taken note of during my captivity. In the autumn of 1949 I became chairman of the NDGP's Saxon federation. I could already demonstrate in my political work that I had become a conscientious citizen of our German Democratic Republic.

I grew in confidence, and with the confidence came ever larger tasks. As a consequence of the elections in the autumn of 1950, I became a member of the East German Parliament and Minister of Finance in the Saxon County Government.

The transition of the German Democratic Republic into the Socialist stage of its development demanded a basic reconstruction of the structure and the working system of the state organs. In the course of these changes the former division into counties went and with it also my function as minister of a county government. Then came a new, larger proof of confidence: the call to Berlin to the staff of the People's Barracked Police in August 1952, with which I was involved for one and a quarter years.

At the beginning of October 1953 my superior, Minister of the Interior Willi Stoph, said in passing: 'Paulus is coming back in a few days' time. He's going to live in Dresden. At the same time I must ask the question whether you are prepared to take over the Officers' Academy in Dresden?'

The academy for officers of the Barracked Police, and in my beloved Dresden where Paulus would be living in the future? It could not have been better. I agreed immediately.

I also remained in this function when, after the formation of the National People's Army in January 1956, the Dresden training establishment became the academy for officers of the National People's Army. A high point in the work and life of the academy was the first big parade on Marx-Engels-Platz in Berlin on International Workers' Fighting Day, the 1st May 1956. On that sunny morning I had the high honour of leading our officers and officer cadets past the highest representatives of the new Germany, hundreds of distinguished anti-Fascist resistance fighters and many foreign delegations.

Upon the conclusion of my 65th year on the 31st March 1958 I retired from active service in the National People's Army.

Farewell to Paulus
A lot of nonsense was written about Paulus's return in the West German newspapers. He arrived at the Ostbahnhof station in Berlin on the Blue Express accompanied by several enigmatic commissars. He had a mysterious task from Stalin, carrying with him a manuscript that declared the invincibility of the Soviet Union in deterring the aggressive intentions of the Western Powers. Not all of the nonsense was true. Paulus came simply as a returnee, upon whom Germany's catastrophic war had been a heavy burden. He came as a person who wanted to make things good again.

After his warm reception in the capital by the Minister of the Interior, I escorted Friedrich Paulus to Dresden on the 25th October 1953, where he occupied a house on the Weissen Hirsch. Naturally the winter battle on the Volga was our main topic of conversation. 'It has not been easy for me over the past years,' said Paulus. 'However, I believe I have drawn the right conclusions. Please read my declaration, which I issued upon leaving the Soviet Union.'

He handed me a document that I read with growing pleasure, although it contained a sober, well thought-out decision:

> As leader of the German troops in the battle of Stalingrad, so fateful for my Fatherland, I have learnt down to the roots about all the horrors of the war of conquest, not only for the Soviet people we fell upon, but also for my own soldiers. The lessons of my own

experience, as well as those learnt during the course of the whole world war, have led me to the knowledge that the fate of the German people cannot be formed from thoughts of power, but rather from a lasting friendship with the Soviet Union, as well as with all peace-loving peoples. Therefore it seems to me that thoughts of peaceful war agreements also being pursued in the west are not the only suitable means for a peaceful reconstruction of German unity and ensuring peace in Europe. Through these agreements much more dangerous would be the increasing and prolonging of the division of Germany. I am therefore convinced that the only real way to a friendly reunification of Germany and a progression to peace can only be achieved by a peace treaty on the basis of the Soviet note to the Western Powers on the German question of the 15th August of this year.

Therefore I have also decided, after returning to my homeland, to put all my strength in cooperating to achieve the honourable goal of a peaceful reunification of Germany and the friendship of the German people with the Soviet people as well as with all other peace-loving peoples.

I do not want to leave the Soviet Union without saying to the Soviet people that I once came in blind obedience as an enemy of your country, but now I am leaving it as a friend of your country.

The real causes of catastrophe
Our officers had passed to me a request for Friedrich Paulus to give a lecture at the academy on the battle on the Volga. In the course of a visit I brought him this request and added that two days had been set aside for it in May 1954. He was immediately in agreement and soon set to work on it. He prepared sketch maps from memory and on the basis of notes that we had made in the first year of our captivity after talks with generals and staff officers. At the end of April he invited me to visit him. We talked about his thoughts in broad outline. I asked him too if his lecture dealt with the reasons for the German defeat.

'Of course,' he said. 'I think something along these lines: the main reason for the German catastrophe at Stalingrad, as for the whole disastrous course of the war, lay in the fatal underestimation of the Soviet Union by the German Army High Command and the over-evaluation of its own possibilities. The German war leadership followed adventurous and rapacious aims. They thought that the Soviet state would fall apart under the blows of the German Wehrmacht. But it showed, despite the worst tests, an unprecedented steadfastness. The Soviet commanders demonstrated high military competence and the soldiers of the Soviet Army defended their homeland with amazing tenacity and bravery, as it stood unshakeably behind them and delivered them ever more and ever better weapons. That is how the Soviet High Command's plans for the Stalingrad battle could run like clockwork and lead to a basic change in the course of the Second World War.'

I could only confirm this appraisal. 'You remember how we crossed the Don in August 1944. We knew that a hard battle awaited us. However, no one believed that the Red Army would defend itself with such determination and ferocity. Where did the enemy soldiers and officers get their strength? We could find no satisfactory answer at the time. Only in captivity did the veil lift from these secrets. We got to know what Socialism and Communism meant to these people. For hundreds of years it was suppressed, deprived and trampled on. In October 1917 the hour of freedom hit them. To us much of what was happening in the east seemed incomprehensible; the Soviet people on the other hand knew what they had, why they were superior to us. They knew what they were fighting and dying for.'

'I can understand', said Paulus, 'how today in West Germany these simple truths are denied by the generals despite their own experiences. However, we must let the whole world know and finally understand that the future of the German people must be based not on might and power but rather on friendship with all peace-loving peoples, especially the Soviet Union.'

The one-time 'simple soldier' had learnt to view world events through political eyes. From the man who previously had to resolve the conflict between orders and knowledge, and obedience to senseless orders, a political person had emerged who was willing to commit his strength and knowledge to the prevention of war and the peaceful reunification of Germany. This was also detected by the officers of the high school, among whom Friedrich Paulus was neither enhanced by nor blamed for his description of the battle. He concluded his presentation with the words: 'All peace-loving people can only be horrified that today in West Germany a policy is being followed that has the same dangerous side to it as the previous history of the Second World War. The Paris and Bonn Agreements are leading the Federal Republic along the same paths that led in the Second World War to Stalingrad and then ended in a national catastrophe.'

This made a deep impression, and many were obliged to revise their former sceptical condemnation of Paulus as a man.

Fully in the spirit of his Dresden lecture, Paulus then turned to an international press conference in Berlin on the 2nd July 1954, which was conducted against the so-called 'Politics of the Strong' by Professor Albert Norden. Among other things he said: 'Since my return to Germany last year I have been impressed even more strongly that high-ranking American politicians and soldiers talk and work on the German question as if the Second World War had not even occurred, although it ended with such a frightful defeat on German soil. But what strikes and moves me much more is the fact that in West Germany in the highest governmental positions, and also in the press and on the radio, exactly the same attitude is taken and esteemed about all lessons of the past renewing a policy of strength, representing and supporting a policy of preparing for war on German soil.'

The east–west officers' meeting
Paulus was of the firm opinion that the German question must be resolved by negotiations between the Germans in the east and the west. The plans for the rearmament of West Germany and the inclusion of West German divisions in the NATO forces gave him no rest. On a Sunday morning towards the end of 1954 he told me that he had decided to make a speech to former officers of the German Democratic Republic and the Federal Republic. Numerous letters, especially from West Germany, had strongly reinforced him in his project. I was astonished how much work he had already done on it.

'I will make clear to the West German participants that the Paris Agreements on the reunification of Germany prevent and deepen the division of Germany. I want to demonstrate that a policy of strength can no longer lead to success. We former officers must assist the Germans from here and there to understand each other.'

'Do you believe that the former officers who have lived in West Germany since 1945 will go along with this argument?'

'It will not be easy for them. Certainly they will bring up the old argument of the "unpolitical" officer about whom we often heard during captivity. I will then recall how we got there. It must be clear to the officer that through his unpolitical behaviour he became the greatest political tool. He must be subjective in dealing in good faith as we did at the Volga. By blind compliance with orders we were objectively also guilty of criminal conduct. How unscrupulously did Hitler misuse our unpolitical attitude to the damage of the German people and to the shame of the German name!'

During these last words Paulus had risen from his chair and strode off across the big room. Then he stopped, standing in front of me. 'That, my dear Adam, is what especially those former officers think that let them obtain the West German military contingent from the government of the Federal Republic. One day the German people will ask them the direct question: "What did you do then for the unity and sovereignty of our Fatherland, what have you done for peace?"'

I reinforced Paulus in his thoughts. He nodded in agreement and picked up a sheet of paper. 'I want to conclude my discourse with an appeal to all the assembled comrades, including all other officers and soldiers in the east and west, to unite our Fatherland. Don't be silent those who must be involved in Germany's existence and future!'

It was an impressive experience when Friedrich Paulus spoke in Berlin on the 29th January 1955, after the sounds of the old German soldiers' song 'Ich hatt' ein Kameraden' had accompanied our remembrances of the fallen former officers from East and West Germany. Most of them thought inwardly and vowed 'Never again!' I was convinced that many West German participants also made this vow.

The 'unpolitical' soldier von Manstein

However, the number of inflexible Hitler generals who dipped their pens deep into the ink for their memoirs increased. The one that annoyed Paulus most of all was Manstein's book *Verlorene Sieg* ('*Lost Victory*'). When I was with him again in the summer of 1956, he brought it out: 'This you must read yourself. According to what it says here, Manstein is completely blameless for the destruction of the 6th Army. This man writes knowing the truth, but ascribes all the blame to me and Hitler. You yourself heard almost all the talks I had with him over the Decimetre apparatus. You know how he kept back from me the true situation at the front, and paralysed my freedom of action. And now he prints all this, the former commander-in-chief of Army Group 'Don'. He falsifies the facts to hide the real truth from our people. This man I once regarded highly. Now he lies with all the others who sail the old course away from their equal responsibility for the downfall of the 6th Army, their equal responsibility for the war and its bitter end.

'As long as I live I will try to negate this attempt to wash his hands of the business. Manstein, the Army High Command and the Wehrmacht High Command – and all of us who from the beginning approved and pursued Hitler's policies – are guilty for the misfortune. Anyone who has even a spark of honour in them must admit and tell the people the truth, so that we never again come to a Stalingrad.'

Paulus's late insights were especially valuable to our people. Spoken by a former expert on wars of conquest, today they belong to the foundation of a necessary turn-around in West German policy.

Conclusion and outlook

Unfortunately Paulus's health was getting worse. He often had to interrupt his work. His intention of writing a history of the battle on the Volga remained incomplete. On the 1st February 1957, fourteen years after the end of the great battle, he closed his eyes for ever. I had lost a good friend and comrade. Painfully I took my farewell of Friedrich Paulus, whose fate had been so closely entangled with mine for fifteen decisive years of life.

More than twenty years have now passed since that decisive battle on the Volga. Many of those who survived it are no longer with us. Those who at that time were in their prime of life are rapidly approaching the grave. And even the youngest survivors of the participants in that great winter battle are today close to fifty years old. Thus the number of living witnesses to the German tragedy on the Volga are diminishing. Thus all the more important are the written accounts and the works that contain their knowledge and experience.

I am fortunate to be able to be in Germany as the new age breaks, the age of Socialism. The way was not easy and it will not be easy in the future. But the way was and is the right one. It is the only possible consequent alternative to the way of wars of conquest that came to an end on the Volga.

Never again will a war start from German soil. No, never again may our Fatherland raise the fury of war! Germany is not to become an atomic graveyard!

All was and is to be done to establish a blooming German Fatherland with an order of society that excludes imperial arbitrariness and military demons, an order of society that with the prosperity of its people enjoys national sovereignty and dignity, social equality and the friendship of other peoples, and an order of society that is firmly grounded. That is the bequest of the dead and the survivors of the frightful battle on the Volga.

German Generals Captured at Stalingrad

Field Marshal Paulus, commander-in-chief, 6th Army
Lieutenant-General Schmidt, chief of staff, 6th Army
General Dr Professor Renoldi, Chief Medical Officer, 6th Army
Colonel-General Heitz, Commander VIIIth Corps
Colonel-General Strecker, Commander XIth Corps
General of Artillery, von Seydlitz-Kurzbach, Commander LIst Corps
General of Artillery Pfeffer, Commander IVth Corps
Lieutenant-General Schlömer, Commander XIVth Panzer Corps
Major-General Vassol, Artillery Commander, LIst Corps
Major-General Wulz, Artillery Commander, IVth Corps
Lieutenant-General Deboi, Commander 44th Infantry Division
Lieutenant-General Roske, Commander 71st Infantry Division
Lieutenant-General Rodenburg, Commander 76th Infantry Division
Lieutenant-General Sanne, Commander 100th Jäger Division
Lieutenant-General Sixt von Arnim, Commander 113th Infantry Division
Major-General Dr Korfes, Commander 295th Infantry Division
Major-General von Drebber, Commander 297th Infantry Division
Lieutenant-General Edler von Daniels, Commander 376th Infantry Division
Major-General Magnus, Commander 389th Infantry Division
Lieutenant-General Leyser, Commander 29th (Motorised) Infantry Division
Major-General Lattmann, Commander 14th Panzer Division
Major-General von Lenski, Commander 24th Panzer Division
Major-General Bratescu, Commander 1st Rumanian Cavalry Division
Major-General Dimitriu, Commander 20th Rumanian Infantry Division